Human Rights in
Islamic North Africa

# Human Rights in Islamic North Africa

*Clashes Between Constitutional Laws and Penal Codes*

E. IKE UDOGU

McFarland & Company, Inc., Publishers

*Jefferson, North Carolina*

Library of Congress Cataloguing-in-Publication Data

Names: Udogu, E. Ike, author.
Title: Human rights in Islamic North Africa : clashes between
   constitutional laws and penal codes / E. Ike Udogu.
Description: Jefferson, North Carolina : McFarland & Company, Inc.,
   Publishers, 2020. | Includes bibliographical references and index.
Identifiers: LCCN 2019055594 | ISBN 9781476680651 (paperback :
   acid free paper) ∞
   ISBN 9781476638690 (ebook)
Subjects: LCSH: Criminal law—Africa, North. | Law—Africa,
   North—Islamic influences. | Criminal law—Egypt. | Law—
   Egypt—Islamic influences.
Classification: LCC KQC978 .U36 2020 | DDC 345.61—dc23
LC record available at https://lccn.loc.gov/2019055594

British Library cataloguing data are available

ISBN (print) 978-1-4766-8065-1
ISBN (ebook) 978-1-4766-3869-0

Front cover: The white street of Medina
in Asilah, Morocco, © 2020 Lu Yang/Shutterstock

Printed in the United States of America

McFarland & Company, Inc., Publishers
   Box 611, Jefferson, North Carolina 28640
   www.mcfarlandpub.com

To human rights advocates worldwide

# Acknowledgments

I am highly indebted to the efforts and work of human rights campaigners, many of whom have placed their lives in jeopardy in the struggle to advance human rights globally and to chronicle their activities, too. They have produced poignant reports on human rights infractions that students of human rights have been able to consult in journals and books, on websites and elsewhere for their research. It is their stories and those of rights scholars that I synchronize in my discourses in each chapter of this volume. Consequently, my special thanks are extended to non-governmental organizations (e.g., Amnesty International, Human Rights Watch, etc.), governmental agencies (such as the U.S. Department of State), and international governmental organizations (as, for example, the United Nations). My thanks to human rights academics, some of whose works I cite in this volume.

I extend my special thanks to Matthew Holbrook and John W. Neal, my diligent graduate assistants, for their research support. I salute the Department of Government and Justice Studies, Appalachian State University, for its persistent support of my scholarly endeavors. To my family and children, thank you for your unwavering encouragement. Finally, my thanks to McFarland, which also published my book *Liberating Namibia: The Long Diplomatic Struggle Between the United Nations and South Africa* (2012).

# Table of Contents

# Abbreviations and Acronyms

**ACHPR**  African Charter on Human and Peoples' Rights
**AD**  Anno Domini
**BC**  Before Christ
**BCE**  Before the Common Era
**BRSC**  Benghazi Revolutionary Shura Council
**CEDAW**  Convention on the Elimination of All Forms of Discrimination Against Women
**CNCPPDH**  National Consultative Commission for the Promotion and Protection of Human Rights
**CNDDC**  National Committee for the Defense of the Rights of Unemployed
**CNDH**  National Council on Human Rights
**DSS**  State Security Department
**FGM/C**  Female Genital Mutilation/Cutting
**FLN**  National Liberation Front
**GNC**  General National Congress
**HoR**  House of Representatives
**HRW**  Human Rights Watch
**ICCPR**  International Covenant on Civil and Political Rights
**ICRC**  International Committee of the Red Cross
**ILO**  International Labor Organization
**ISIS**  Islamic State of Iraq and Syria
**LGBTI**  Lesbian, Gay, Bisexual, Transgender and Intersex
**MENA**  Middle East and North Africa
**MOI**  Ministry of Interior
**MOSS**  Ministry of Social Solidarity
**MRA**  Ministry of Religious Affairs
**NATO**  North Atlantic Treaty Organization
**NCCLHR**  National Council on Civil Liberties and Human Rights
**NCW**  National Council for Women

**NGO**  Non-Governmental Organization
**NSA**  National Security Agency
**NTC**  National Transition Council
**SNJT**  National Union of Tunisian Journalists
**TDC**  Truth and Dignity Commission
**UDHR**  Universal Declaration of Human Rights
**UN**  United Nations
**UNICEF**  United Nations Children's Fund
**UNSMIL**  United Nations Support Mission in Libya
**U.S.**  United States

# Preface

It is safe to argue that it is common for academics to write copiously in their disciplines with a view to augmenting the literature and knowledge base in their specialty. Many scholars, too, write books, articles, monographs and templates for resolving societal problems. Occasionally, they experience discomfiture when the recommendations in their studies lack efficacy. This is partly the case because political leaders do not implement the models constructed by researchers for solving political, economic and social quagmires in a nation-state because of self-interest or group interests. The preceding postulation applies to many countries in the global south. Even so, students of the developing nations are relentless in their struggle to tackle vexing societal problems that are rampant there. Accordingly, as lifelong learners, they continually challenge themselves to study, learn and write more in their fields of expertise to persuade lawmakers of the cogency and validity of their scholarship for solving issues in the developing world.

In writing this book, *Human Rights in Islamic North Africa: Clashes Between Constitutional Laws and Penal Codes*, I took to heart the foregoing suppositions. In truth, the more I write on the perplexing, challenging and conflictive politics in the developing nations, the more I am intellectually provoked with the urge to study further and to seek frameworks to resolve problems impeding the advancement of development in the region. Human rights infractions in the global south are among these quandaries. Therefore, I embarked on this project because I have a special impulse to learn about North Africa as an Africanist. My approach and discourses in this study are to point out some major human rights dilemmas and to suggest ways to mitigate these rights imbroglios in Islamic North Africa.

This volume begins with a brief introduction to the entire edifice. This is followed by five chapters, one each on Algeria, Egypt, Libya, Morocco, and Tunisia. I alphabetized these countries in my analysis in the text. The rest of the volume contains an elaborate bibliography—to make up for the contemporary nature of this study—and appendices drawn from relevant United Nations' human rights documents.

1

Having taken into consideration the historic uniqueness of North Africa, I think it is critical to provide an aide-mémoire (memory aid) with which to understand the contemporary politico-religious and socio-cultural developments that help shape the inimitable character of these states. Accordingly, in my discourses on the challenges of human rights practices facing these Islamic polities, I did not apply a uniform template, because each country is special. In other words, I did not apply "a one size fits all approach" simply because they are Islamic states. This is so because their histories are not entirely similar given the ethnic, religious and cultural compositions of these states; and, this is not to mention the impact of different European colonial influences in the area.

In each chapter of the text, I provide a lengthy excerpt from the country's constitution relating to human rights. This effort is deliberate because of the assumed "sacrosanctity" of this document and its creeds in most societies—democratic and non-democratic systems. In much of Africa, however, conflicts, which stultified the growth agenda since the continent gained home-rule from the colonial powers, have their roots in part in non-compliance with the tenets of the constitution. This is so because many—if not most—leaders on the continent seldom adhere to the precepts of their national constitution. For example, some leaders elongate their stay in power by abrogating the constitution or simply amending it at their will to further their self-interest and the interest of their immediate political cabal. However, the adherence to the principles of a constitution is crucial for promoting human rights, political stability and advancement of peaceful coexistence.

I reproduced substantial extracts from the constitutions of the countries under study also to underscore their expected supremacy over the countries' penal code. Problematically, some politicos and orthodox Islamists invoke canons in the penal code to wiggle out of respecting the human rights principles enshrined in the constitution. By doing so, political actors not only strategically nullify dogmas relating to human rights in the constitution, but also bring to the fore the clashes between theory and practice in the execution of rights principles—a concern that finds expression in this text.

Further, this work is contemporary. Accordingly, my application of current literature is common in the text, while I provide in the bibliography an elaborate list of primary and secondary sources of relevant books on this topic helpful to students of human rights. My major sources of reference are United Nations human rights instruments; U.S. Department of State annual human rights reports; Human Rights Watch; Amnesty International; and an anthology of works written by some national and international human rights scholars that I consulted to enrich my analysis in this volume. My cross-fertilization of issues and ideas drawn from the preceding human rights corpus, inter alia, provides me with different analytical perspectives on each state. In short, my exposure to the various rich sources of information as I wrote this text helped me paint each country's human rights problems somewhat differently. I produce a unique and refreshing contemporary work on human rights issues in each of these vibrant Islamic countries. In addition, my methodological approach provides the reader comparative understanding of the level of human rights contravention in these states and the reasons for the clash between theory and practice.

More importantly, my dialogues in this volume inform lawmakers regarding statutory areas in which they have confronted the challenges to human rights violations superlatively and areas that need improvement. Metaphorically, too, my analysis offers "political photosynthesis" to major actors in these nation-states. It does so by showing how policymakers may use their power derived from the constitution and international human rights instruments (the sun) to convert legislations into actionable human rights (oxygen) beneficial for the survival of the entire society. In this way, these states are likely to ameliorate the clash between theory and practice and further peaceful coexistence amongst the diverse collectivities in dynamic Islamic North Africa. The foregoing narrative is the gist of this volume, *Human Rights in Islamic North Africa: Clashes Between Constitutional Laws and Penal Codes.*

# Introduction

## *A Constitution vs. a Penal Code—The Discourse*

The character of a nation-state today reflects its history. More notably, antiquity provides an academic a significant context within which to narrate a country's story. Thus, in each chapter of this volume, I provide a short stimulating history of the state discussed in the text. Therefore, this brief introduction presents a general overview of the details of the nations studied in this book against the framework of their historicity. These histories will help expose to non-experts in North African politics the extent to which the past helps form the present political and social characteristics of Algeria, Egypt, Libya, Morocco and Tunisia. Indeed, it is the impact of ancient chronicles of these societies that gave this region its powerful and inexpungible religious complexion—Islam.

Moreover, this concise introductory chapter reviews two major contending and overarching areas of interest and issues—the constitution and the penal code. The contradictions that exist in the interpretations of both sets of laws complicate the successful implementation of human rights dogmas in the above countries of study. It is to this end that I reproduce a substantial excerpt of the constitution of each state devoted to the principles of the respect for the human rights of citizens. Problematically, tenets in the constitutions are now and again in conflict with precepts in the penal codes; this paradox produces discord between theory and practice in the enforcement of human rights in my argumentations in the text. The robust replications of human rights principles mined from the official constitutions of these Islamic states will provide readers with adequate reference sources related to human rights infringements.

These "sacrosanct" constitutions contain elaborate and well-articulated human rights laws with which to fight human rights infractions. Yet, their successful applications in these states in the struggle against human rights breaches is inadequate; this collision between constitutional dogmas, aimed at tackling rights breaches, and the inability of political actors to enforce the same rights represents a central crux in my notional dialogues in this book.

In short, the guardians of power, due partially to the canons in the penal code and cultural customs, do not always respect the legal provisions in the constitution relating to human rights. This is the case because dogmata in the penal code sometimes collide with constitutional norms on human rights. Therefore, this book shines light on human rights challenges that the custodians of the state and citizens of these societies confront despite official commitments by policymakers to enforcing human rights principles enshrined in the constitution. The effective execution of a constitution's human rights precepts is imperative for promoting good governance and political stability in a society; this is so in Islamic North African states where elements of the penal code intermittently encroach on the constitutional efficacy of rights matters.

## Constitution and Constitutionalism

Metaphorically, a constitution is the engine of a car—the state. When this engine is dysfunctional because the driver fails to follow the rules established for its maintenance, the vehicle will not function effectively. Moreover, when the motorist attempts to cut corners in attempts to run the automobile, s/he might end up spending more cash to fix the vehicle or it might die because of inadequate care. Allegorically, the foregoing theory suggests that when political actors fail to live up to the prerequisite of a constitution and its shining human rights provisions adequately, this condition can create ignitable conflict with the propensity to lead to dysfunctionality and state collapse.

Even so, the governance character and behavioral patterns of citizens in the Islamic North African countries derive their roots from antiquity and the countries' colonial experience.[1] In fact, in a more recent situation, the Ottoman Empire contributed immensely to the socio-religious nature of North African societies. Following the defeat of the Ottoman Empire in World War I, however, some Western colonial powers established themselves in the region. In this case, the main colonists were France, Britain, Spain and Italy. These colonizers and their genre of leadership influenced how the native leaders in the region drafted their constitutions and led their nations. The constitutions that the Western powers imposed on their outposts contradicted many of the Islamic laws enshrined in the Sharia laws or Islamic form of jurisprudence, for example. The conflicts regarding how to implement the Sharia laws and at the same time apply the substance of national constitutions exacerbate the dilemmas in enforcing human rights provisions in the constitutions. In any case, more on the above deliberation later. Suffice it to say, however, that despite the foregoing dialogue constitutions are critical for delineating the power and conduct of lawmakers at least on paper. Constitutions also outline how a national government and its institutions should operate in most political systems.

The objectives of a constitution are imperative for checking on potential malfeasance of officials of a regime.[2] In much of Africa—especially in Islamic North Africa—where Sharia laws sometimes compete against precepts of the constitution, the enforcement of national laws can be complex and strident. This development explains partially why many conservative political actors show less enthusiasm for the enforcement of human rights principles contained in constitutions. This is especially the case if such human rights tenets flout religious dogmas.

However, what is a constitution? Jan-Erik Lane affirms that a constitution is "a compact document that comprises a number of articles about the State, laying down rules which State activities [legislators and citizens] are supposed to follow. Whether these rules [or laws] are obeyed or implemented is another question."[3] Jack C. Plano and Milton Greenberg define a constitution as "a fundamental or 'organic' law that establishes the framework of government of a state, assigns the powers and duties of governmental agencies, and establishes the relationship between the people and their government."[4] Elsewhere, I define it as a document that outlines the manner and nature of interactions between the government and the citizens. It also establishes the institutions and structures with which to govern a polity.[5] In theory, a constitution, inter alia, outlines the following basic functions:

- A national mission statement and the core values of that government. In this way, it serves the purpose of shaping the culture and future institutions in a positive way.
- Recognition of individual rights and responsibilities.
- Establishes the proper role of government.
- Establishes the rule of law that helps promote fairness and justice.
- Promotes a system that divides power among the various organs of government and furthers a system of checks and balances.
- Outlines the major characteristic functions of elected leaders and their subordinates.
- Checks the power of government and makes it accountable to the citizens.[6]

The overall content of a constitution can be complex or simple given the history and socio-cultural specificity of the society in which this legal document operates. Thus, within this context, it might be difficult to write about a global or precise theory of constitutions. Accordingly, "what there is is a set of ideas, concepts and models drawn from various disciplines that refer to constitutions, either the constitutions of many countries in the world or to some ideal constitution."[7] In truth, constitutional theory hardly possesses core established doctrines. Among academics this dilemma makes the subject a major issue of inquiry and discourse. This is especially the case since some aspects of constitutional theory deal with the complexities of how countries, with their unique cultures, function.

There is an inconsistency flowing from the whole matter of constitutions because even though they might be indispensable for the peaceful governance of a polity, notionally speaking, they can also be problematic in their operation in many states, including in Islamic North Africa. In Islamic countries, the contradictions in their constitutional laws vis-à-vis their Sharia laws and creeds in the penal codes are confounding. Such antinomies render it difficult to implement human rights canons contained in national constitutions. Furthermore, some constitutions "lack national legitimacy" in part because they are seldom seen and understood by citizens in pastoral North Africa. Sociologically, too, most rural families in this region are more concerned about their daily survival than with human rights issues enshrined in national constitutions. Indeed, Allah's "laws and guidance in the Quran and Sharia" are what truly matter to pastoral citizens. In addition, many in these societies cannot read or write in the dominant languages, let alone comprehend some of the complex legal jargons of the constitution.[8] The elites who write the constitution do not subject it to a national referendum, to advance its legitimacy. Such a plebiscite can further the document's national—urban and rural—acceptance and support.[9] Indeed, as Donald S. Lutz poignantly notes,

> in a sense, the entire idea of a constitution rests on an assumption of human fallibility, since, if humans were angels, there would be no need to erect, direct, and limit government through a constitution....
>
> A constitution, [therefore], was viewed as a means not merely to make collective decisions in the most efficient way possible but to make the best possible decisions in pursuit of the common good under a condition of popular sovereignty....
>
> Popular sovereignty implies that all constitutional matters should be based upon some form of popular consent, which in turn implies a formal, public process.[10]

The process of promulgating the contents of a constitution in many developing societies is made difficult by the "absence" of constitutionalism. This is a situation generally made more severe by the actions of some of the guardians of power, who attempt to manipulate the legal document by using extra-juridical means. In this practice, the powerbrokers temporarily ignore the tenets of the constitutional document because provisions in it impinge upon their self-interest.[11] Moreover, in the authoritarian systems that are commonplace in much of the global south, some leaders oftentimes behave as though they have regal or "deistic" immunity regarding provisions of the national constitution.[12] Indeed, to paraphrase Robert Bolt's play *A Man for All Seasons*: "The law is not a 'light' for the [privileged in society] to see by; the law is not an instrument of any kind. The law is a causeway upon which, so long as [one] keeps to it a citizen may walk safely."[13] Apropos the foregoing references to the law, a constitution designed for a society contains laws and regulations to advance socio-political stability as long as the authorities and citizens equally abide by its precepts. What, then, is constitutionalism that students of constitutions commonly accentuate and promote, especially in the quest to further stability and good governance? Constitutionalism is

> the political doctrine that claims that political authority should be bound by institutions that restrict the exercise of power. Such institutions offer rules that bind both the persons in authority as well as the organs or bodies that exercise political power. Human rights are one central component [or appurtenance] of constitutionalism; another essential element is the separation of powers in government.[14]

Additionally, William G. Andrews notes that "constitutionalism, deriving its authority from the belief in transcendent principles of justice and rights, controls government by limiting its authority and establishing regular procedures for its operation."[15] Carl Friedrich defines constitutionalism thus: "An institutionalized system of effective regularized restraints on governmental action…. Such restraints may be extra-legal as, for example, regular and effective criticism and possible opposition by political parties, the press, or pressure groups."[16] In Islamic North Africa and much of Africa, what we have is constitutions without constitutionalism.

The kernel of this brief introductory chapter is not about the theories of constitution and constitutionalism per se even though the importance of these concepts intersects within the superstructure of this text. In fact, this chapter will shine light on how the application of two contending legal documents—the constitution and the penal code—poses problems for human rights enforcement and exacerbates the clash between theory and practice in this study.

## Penal Code and Human Rights Constraints

Germaine to the following discourses is how the penal codes of Algeria, Egypt, Libya, Morocco and Tunisia have impinged on the implementation of human rights provisions in these countries' constitutions. In brief, my explorations will show, inter alia, how lawmakers and civil society groups sometimes clash over human rights implementations and issues; indeed, it is because some laws in the penal code contravene those that call for the respect of rights in the constitution that human rights dilemmas have become combustible in some of these Islamic states. Nonetheless, my theory is that the validity of compromise between the canons of a penal code and principles of human rights in a constitution is critical when they collide; this counsel is important for the attainment of rights for all citizens.

The discussions below are concise examples to illustrate some of the constitutional provisions on human rights that contradict elements of the penal codes of Algeria, Egypt, Libya, Morocco, and Tunisia; they serve as a general introduction to, and taste of, the superstructure of this volume, *Human Rights in Islamic North Africa: Clashes Between Constitutional Laws and Penal Codes.*

## *Algeria*

Article 41 of the Algerian constitution states: "The freedom of expression, association and assembly shall be guaranteed to the citizen" (see Table I, Chapter 1).[17] Nonetheless, Human Rights Watch (HRW) reports that the government has not always lived up to this precept. The regime continues to repress peaceful assembly by preventing some public gatherings. Indeed, Article 97 of the Algerian penal code criminalizes any group that organizes without government sanction regardless of the peaceful nature of their protest. The penalty for such a violation in the public arena is up to a year in the pen. It was in view of this code that the court convicted nine labor rights campaigners for their peaceful protest to support unemployed workers.

The government frequently denies human rights activists the right to register as associations or non-governmental organizations (NGOs) and to operate freely, under Law 12–06. The state generally dubs human rights groups "troublemakers" for being too nosy. Commonly, their offense centers on attempts at exposing the regime's human rights malfeasance. For example, "the Algerian League for Human Rights ... and Youth Action Rally ... were among a number of formerly registered associations whose new applications for registration received no answer from the Ministry of Interior, leaving them in legal limbo."[18]

Similarly, although Article 41 of the constitution (see Table I, Chapter 1) sanctions freedom of expression and speech, Article 100 of the penal code nullifies this provision (of the national constitution). For instance, law enforcement agents arrested and sentenced Rachid Aouine to six months in prison. Aouine was sentenced because of violation of Article 100 of the penal code that criminalizes citizens or culprits for "inciting an unarmed gathering."[19] This action was taken by officials possibly because one of Aouine's Facebook posts had the propensity to aggravate members of the security forces and incite them to action against the government.

## Egypt

Article 75 of the constitution (see Table I, Chapter 2) states, inter alia, that all citizens have the right to form NGOs. NGOs will attain legal status upon being registered. Mikhail suggests that this article implies that "such associations and foundations shall have the right to practice their activities freely, and administrative agencies may not interfere in their affairs or dissolve them or dissolve their boards of directors or boards of trustees save by a court judgment."[20]

Despite the impressive provision of Article 75 of the constitution, Article 78 of the Egyptian penal code renders the constitutional guarantee null and void. In fact, Article 78 of the penal code states:

> 1. Whoever asks himself or a third party, or accepts or takes, even by intermediation, from a foreign country or from one operating in its interest, money or any other benefit, or a promise to get something of that, with the aim of committing an act prejudicial to a national interest of the country, shall be sentenced to temporary hard labor and to a fine of not less than one thousand pounds and not exceeding what he was given or promised to be given.
>
> 2. The penalty shall be permanent hard labor and a fine of not less than one thousand pounds and not exceeding what he has been given or promised to be given, if the offender is a public official, or a person charged with a public service, or conferred with a public representative quality, or if he commits the crime in time of war.
>
> 3. Whoever, gives, offers, or promises something of the foregoing, with the aim of committing a deed harmful to a national interest of the country, shall be punished with the same penalty.[21]

Article 78 of the 1937 Egyptian penal code was, however, amended, stating that "anyone who receives foreign funding [that could harm] the national interests will be punished by life imprisonment and a fine of no less than half a million Egyptian pounds."[22] Critiques of the foregoing amendment contend that violating the "national interests," as rationale for penalizing a citizen or group, is ambiguous and problematic. In this schema, in other words, the government reserves the right to label real or putative matters as "national interests"; this national interest question can be taken as a strategic move for stifling activities of human rights campaigners or other similar NGOs in civil society.[23] Even so, in 2012, Egyptian authorities operating within the context of Article 78 of the penal code, not Article 75 of the constitution, attacked the offices of several NGOs. Agents arrested and "convicted forty-three local and international civil society workers to one, two, or five years in prison for operating in Egypt without a license as well as receiving foreign funds."[24]

Despite the foregoing situation, Egypt has made important strides in amending the contentious Article 242 of the penal code on female genital mutilation (FGM). Indeed, many academics and citizens have sought ways to protect women from anachronistic practices that find expression in patriarchal systems of gender-based oppression.[25] Women's rights groups express concern that the controversial Article 242 of the penal code alludes to the act of FGM as a misdemeanor.[26] Debatably, this provision of the code violates Article 51 of the constitution, which states: "Dignity is a right for every person that may not be infringed upon. The state shall respect, guarantee and protect it" (see Table I, Chapter 2). Egypt made some modifications to Article 242 of the penal code, perhaps due to vocal opposition to the code by international human rights organizations and women's rights groups. In fact, in 2016, the Egyptian People's Assembly, kowtowing to international pressure, took the bold step of amending Article 242 of the penal code. The amendment calls for the criminalization of the act or performance of FGM. It should be noted, however, that whereas the state parliamentary gesture is popular in urban settings in the republic, the same might not be the case in pastoral Egypt where old habits die hard. In fact, a study undertaken by the Ministry of Health supported the preceding theory. This survey also affirmed that "96% of girls in rural communities had undergone FGM, as opposed to 85% in urban areas."[27] Little wonder, then, that Egyptian female activists do not believe in the efficacy of the modification to Article 242 of the penal code, arguing that mere preachments on the amendment are inadequate. What is important, as a rights issue, is enforcement.[28]

## Libya

Article 45 complements Article 37 of the constitution, which states: "Freedom of speech and its integrity shall not be separated." In fact, Article 45 affirms that "the state shall take necessary measures to protect and care for Libyans abroad. [It will] ensure their affiliation with their homeland, as well as follow violation of their rights and extend the jurisdiction of the Libyan judiciary pertaining to these rights" (see Table I, Chapter 4).

Despite the injunctions in Article 45, Amnesty International (AI) reports that Moad al-Hnesh, a Libyan engineer, faced incarceration for life in Libya for expressing his opinion regarding the political turmoil in the country. The Libyan regime charged him with misconduct against the state of Libya in 2011 for his activities in the United Kingdom. Furthermore, he was condemned for publishing provocative and inflammatory false information on the internal happenings and the conditions in the country.

For anti–Gaddafi Libyan revolutionaries, the coup de grâce against al-Hnesh for his actions in the U.K. was his participation in pro–Gaddafi rallies in London on June 28, 2011. His activities in London provoked the invocation of Article 178 of Libya's penal code. This article criminalizes the conduct of Libyans abroad—especially behaviors considered to be contrary to the national interest of Libya. Such crimes carry a sentence of life imprisonment. In addition, al-Hnesh, under provisions of Article 195 of the penal code, was liable to another 15 years for publicly insulting the Libyan people. It was alleged al-Hnesh had unwittingly said the anti–Gaddafi revolutionaries were rats.[29]

Tripoli's stance on this matter brings to the fore the discrepancies between the precepts of Articles 37 and 45 of the national constitution and provisions of the penal code, as for example, Articles 178 and 195, on human rights issues in the country. What this development suggests is that the constitution does not mean much against the backdrop of the interests of powerful custodians of power in Libya. Put in another way, some of the influential leaders see the constitution as a nuisance when it comes to their socio-political self-/group interests. Accordingly, one way to weaken the effect of the constitution on human rights is to intermittently invoke unique features of the penal code; in this instance, the state surreptitiously curtailed al-Hnesh's rights by the application of the principles in the penal code while ignoring his human rights enshrined in the constitution.

## Morocco

Article 19 of the Moroccan constitution states: "The man and the woman enjoy, in equality, the rights and freedoms of civil, political, economic, social, cultural and environmental character, enounced in this Title and in the other provisions of the Constitution, as well as in the international conventions and pacts duly ratified by Morocco."[30]

The impressive expression of the preceding provision of Article 19 may be a farce against the background of some principles in Morocco's penal code. For example, Article 475 of the penal code provides, inter alia, that whoever "'abducts or deceives' a minor, without using violence, threat or fraud, can escape prosecution and imprisonment if (i) the abductor marries the victim, and (ii) those persons who have a right to request annulment of the marriage do not file a complaint."[31] In short, this precept may permit rapists to avoid prosecution if they marry the victim. Little wonder, then, that human rights campaigners have not only challenged the foregoing provisions in Article 475 that led a 16-year-old girl, Amina Filali, to commit suicide for being forced to marry her rapist,[32] but also other related tenets of the penal code.

For example, Articles 486, 488, 490 and 496 of the penal code are problematic to human rights promoters who seek modification to these laws. Under Article 486, the sentence for a man who has sexual activity with a woman who did not solicit it is 10 years in prison. If the girl is a minor (under 18) or the victim is disabled or pregnant the period of incarceration is 10–20 years. Woe betide a man who has an affair with a virgin. Under such a circumstance, Article 488 provides a draconian sentence of up to 20 years in jail. Article 490 criminalizes mutual sexual relations between unmarried citizens. The sentence for such an act runs between a month and one year. Article 496 states that hiding a married woman "evading the authority [of an abusive husband or wife beater] to which she is legally subjected is due a punishment of between one and five years' imprisonment and a fine."[33] Indeed, this provision suggests that authorities can criminalize shelter homes that provide succor to battered women. This situation is a paradox in view of Article 19 of the constitution in a polity where women, socio-politically, seldom enjoy equivalent rights with men. This problem, ironically, will continue to fester if principles in the national constitution and penal code continue to lock horns on human rights issues in Morocco.

## Tunisia

Tunisia is the most liberal Islamic state in North Africa and, indeed, the entire Middle East. This acknowledgment is due in part to its progressive laws on women's rights vis-à-vis the other Islamic states in the region. Yet, the country confronts an issue as to whether the constitution is superior to the penal code or vice versa. One of the problems that arise from the fact that both legal documents operate side-by-side in the republic is that frequently lawmakers invoke provisions of the penal code to nullify human rights precepts enshrined in the national constitution when it is in their interest to do so.

For instance, Article 31 of the constitution avers: "Freedom of opinion, thought, expression, information and publication shall be guaranteed. These freedoms shall not be subject to prior censorship." Despite Article 31, Article 128 of the penal code punishes anyone "accusing, without proof, a public agent of violating the law with up to two years in prison."[34] Considering this code, conjecturally, it is illegal for a citizen to state casually that a Minister is incompetent for enacting a repugnant policy against the interest of the citizenry without proof. Put in another way, to express a nonchalant opinion without proof that a Minister has gone "bananas" for promulgating an unpopular policy can earn the citizen up to two years in detention under provisions of Article 128 of the penal code.

Such was the case of one Walid Zarrouk, an erstwhile law-enforcement agent and a member of the Union for a Republican Police. Zarrouk was sentenced to one year of incarceration for having accused the authorities of bringing trumped-up charges against citizens who criticized government agents in a television interview.[35] As if to teach Zarrouk a lesson and a priori dissuade others who might follow his footstep, he was further sentence to eight months for his quote in a daily newspaper disparaging the Minister of the Interior. Additionally, a "Tunis court sentenced him to one year in prison for Facebook posts that criticized an investigative judge and a judiciary spokesperson."[36] Unlike in the Occident, in much of Africa, where many political leaders consider themselves sacrosanct and above the law once voted into an office, an electoral irony flows from the politics and genus of governance.

In short, presidents or prime ministers see themselves as "custodians" of the constitution. Consequently, some leaders construe themselves to be immune from the law they oversee, and therefore ignore constitutional principles that run against their interests, such as term limits; in short, they often end up abusing the legal document.[37] It is probably this attitude of certain African leaders that prompted Amna Guellali in the Zarrouk case to articulate a poignant opinion. Guellali declared: "No one is safe from prosecution under Tunisia's overly broad laws criminalizing free speech. Six years after Tunisians ended Zine Abidine Ben Ali's authoritarian rule, prosecutors and courts still subject Tunisians to trials for exercising their rights to freedom of speech [as protected in Article 31 of the constitution]."[38]

In sum, I brought to light, inter alia, some of the discourses on the problems created by the complex intersection between the application of precepts in the constitution and dogmas in the penal code to human rights quagmires in Islamic North Africa. My hope is that the preceding dialogues will help readers comprehend the challenges to human rights practices in this volume. Idealistically, my postulation in this book is simple. It is that if the human rights of citizens, as expressed in national constitutions, international human rights instruments, and other relevant documents, are respected, political stability and peaceful coexistence will be furthered in Islamic North Africa.

# 1

## Algeria

### Ancient History

The history of the aboriginals in what is modern Algeria is complicated. Nevertheless, the character of the original inhabitants is like that of those who roamed around the Mediterranean coastal region before the 15th century BC. The nomadic lifestyle of the indigenous people was an outcome of the search for food, along with commerce and wars with other inhabitants of the savanna. However, one group identified as indigenous to the area was the Berbers, who may have migrated from southwestern Asia as long ago as the third millennium BC.[1]

Historically, Algeria, like much of North Africa, came under the influence of, and periodic occupation by, the Minoans (before 2000 BC) and Phoenicians (about 900 BC), who founded Carthage (around 800 BC).[2] However, it was the Carthaginians, Romans and Byzantines who were the dominant forces in the area, and who operated vis-à-vis the autochthonous Berbers before the arrival of the formidable Islamic and Arab forces in the seventh century.[3] In order to contextualize the historic development of Algeria in this chapter, I shall examine the political and social situation in the area, Arab and Islamic influence, and the French colonization of the territory.

Following the consolidation of Carthaginian authority on the coast, the influence on the aboriginal inhabitants inland increased substantially. Remarkably, Berber civilization had reached a point at which agriculture, manufacturing, trade and political organization sustained several communities. Trade relationships between Carthage and the Berber societies in the interior flourished. Moreover, Carthaginian territorial conquest and imperialism led to the enslavement and conscription into the military of some Berbers and the imposition of taxes on others. During the onset of the fourth century BC, Berbers constituted the largest troop of the Carthaginian armed force. In a mutiny, Berber warriors revolted from 241 to 238 BC. This rebellion happened in part because of their poor salaries in the aftermath of the defeat of

Carthage in the first of three Punic wars (between Rome and Carthage from 264 BC to 146 BC). These gallant mutineers succeeded in occupying a large part of Carthage's North African territory; they even organized themselves efficiently to the point that they minted their own coins that bore the name Libyan—a name invented by the Greeks to signify natives of North Africa.[4] Carthaginian suzerainty in North Africa gradually declined as an outcome of the settlers' defeat by the Romans in the Punic Wars in 146 BC.[5]

Fortuitously, the collapse of Carthaginian authority boosted the influence of Berber chiefs in the interior. Remarkably, by the second century BC, the Berbers established many quasi-independent kingdoms.[6] Even so, "the high point of Berber civilization, unequaled until the coming of the Almohads and Almoravids more than a millennium later, was reached during the reign of Masinissa in the second century B.C."[7]

The conquest of Carthage and rule by the Romans led to displacements and dislocation of the Berbers' way of life. Those Berbers who led a nomadic life were compelled to re-locate from their traditional domicile. Sedentary ethnic groups forfeited their freedom and primordial attachment to the land. There were resistance movements against Roman occupation but in many instances, they were futile. For example, in AD 238, landlords revolted without success against the emperor's fiscal regimes. Accordingly, the relationship between politically active Berbers and the Roman authority became discordant.

Let it suffice to say that cities in Roman North Africa were homes to Jews expelled from Palestine in the first and second century AD for their recalcitrance and opposition to Roman hegemony and rule. In addition, the reign of Emperor Constantine, who claimed to have conquered by the forces of his divine vision of the cross (in hoc signo vinces, in this sign conquer) imposed Christianity in the Roman Empire. This act exacerbated the Jewish exodus from Palestine to other regions of the world—not least North Africa. These Jews and other exiled Jews referred to themselves as the Jewish Diaspora (or dispersed Jews). For the record, however, some Berbers who inter-mixed with the Jewish population converted to Judaism.[8]

The Vandals, a Germanic tribe, and Byzantines from Constantinople also had their military expeditions in the region. Around 429 AD, the Vandals undertook their expedition through Spain to North Africa to take on the Romans. The Vandals in the same year conquered Carthage. The Byzantines, wanting to participate in the scramble for North Africa, went on a military blitz and destroyed the Vandal kingdom in 533 AD. Despite this success, however, the Byzantine rule was wobbly partly because of official corruption, incompetence, and lack of enthusiastic support from Constantinople regarding African affairs. As an outcome of this development, many pastoral areas returned to Berber control and rule.[9]

The history from the arrival of Islam and the Arabs in 642 to the arrival of the French in 1830 is incisive. Islam and the purveyors of this religion—the Arabs—have had a prolonged impact on the populations of North Africa. Indeed, it has been noted laconically that "the new faith, in its various forms, would penetrate nearly all segments of society, bringing with it armies, learned men, and fervent mystics, and in large part replacing tribal practices and loyalties with new social norms and political idioms."[10] It was between 642 and 669 that Arab military adventures in the Maghreb happened, resulting in the expansion of Islam in its wake. Very much as in Christianity, unique and powerful sects sprang out of this religion, including in Algeria.

However, the conversion of Berbers to the religion did not ipso facto result in their total allegiance to the Arab-dominated Caliphate. This was the case in part because the governing Arabs imposed an offensive taxation system on them. Moreover, Algerians who converted to the Islamic faith considered themselves neophytes without political influence.[11] That notwithstanding, some of the major sects that operated religiously, dynastically, and mystically in the region were Fatimids (Shia), Almoravids, Almohads, Zayanids and Marabouts.[12]

Peculiarly, the Ottoman occupation of Algeria occurred as the outcome of a collaboration between two Muslim pirates (privateers) whom the Europeans gave the famous moniker Barbarossa. They were two brothers, Aruj and Khair ad Din; they were responsible for spreading the authority of the Ottoman Empire to Algeria. Algiers became the heart of the Ottoman operation in the Maghreb, from which Tunis, Tripoli, and Tlemcen came under its control. In 1518, Algeria became theoretically an integral part of the Ottoman Empire although the indigenous leaders enjoyed a measure of autonomy.[13] Indeed, following the institution of regular Ottoman administration, governors with the title of pasha ruled for three-year terms. Turkish was the lingua franca and Arabs and Berbers, paradoxically, were excluded from government posts.[14]

In later years, however, the governance technique was refined, taking on the framework of the Ottoman Empire. In fact, Arthur Edge notes:

> Despite usurpation, military coups, and occasional mob rule, the day-to-day operation of government was remarkably orderly. In accordance with the millet system applied throughout the Ottoman Empire, each ethnic group—Turks, Arabs, Kabyles, Berbers, Jews, Europeans—was represented by a guild that exercised legal jurisdiction over its constituents.[15]

## Modern History

France's colonial adventure in Algeria followed a pattern similar to that of other colonial powers—Portugal, Britain, Belgium, Germany and others—in Africa. In the 18th and 19th centuries, it was prestigious, inter alia, to possess colonies globally. The start of the conquest of Algeria by the French happened in 1827, when the dey (or governor) of Algiers became furious at the refusal of the French government to defray an old debt incurred during the Napoleonic wars. He "struck the French consul on the shoulder with a fly-whisk during an interview."[16] In response to this act, the king of France demanded an apology for the dey's insolence toward his representative. When the dey did not express remorse for his action, the French seized on this excuse and "opportunity" to blockade the port of Algiers to teach the governor a lesson for his recalcitrance to the king's order. In 1830, French soldiers landed in Algiers and captured the city.

Between 1830 and 1847, the French confronted resistance from the interior. Abd al-Qadir, a Muslim cleric, who had earlier fought the French gallantly, led the confrontation. The French accepted al-Qadir, a clever and valiant warrior, as a leader of an Algerian nation in the hinterland. A nationalist to the core, al-Qadir disparaged France's armed struggle against his army thus: "France will march forward, and we shall retire, but France will find it necessary to retire, and we shall return. We shall weary and harry you, and our climate will do the rest."[17]

To put down the revolt against French authority by Abd al-Qadir, the French commander declared a total war. In this schema, the French army burned villages and crops, and destroyed livestock. Additionally, the French imposed fines on those who maintained unflinching support for the cleric. This tactic, called "pacification," was the coup de grâce that brought the Algerian resistance to its knees; in 1847, the emir surrendered.[18]

The story of resistance to colonization by the Kabyles who lived to the east of Algiers was striking. Despite the Kabyles' chivalry, however, they submitted themselves to French suzerainty in 1857. Even so, in 1871 they resisted a series of obnoxious fiats that made all Muslims French subjects and not citizens of the land of their birth. These offensive decrees made them inferior to French and other Europeans settlers. Furthermore, the French overseers seized more than a million acres of Muslim lands and sold off these territories to European colonizers. To exacerbate autochthonous angst, the European immigrants violated the human dignity of Algerian Muslims in this society. This occurred following France's special ordinances promulgated to treat native Algerians differently from Europeans. Indeed, Algerian Muslims were punished sometimes with "severe fines and sentences for ... insulting a European or wearing shoes in public. (It was assumed that a Muslim caught wearing shoes had stolen them.)"[19]

French colonists also usurped the arable lands, which they developed into modern agricultural projects. They integrated the agricultural system into the French economy and provided France with wine, citrus, olives and vegetables. In this schema, colons (French settlers) kept 30 percent of the fertile land and 90 percent of the farmland to themselves. Special taxes were levied on Algerian Muslims by French authorities. By contrast, the colons did not pay most taxes.[20] The French colonial policies of assimilation and mission civilisatrice (civilizing mission), and the foregoing strict genus of governance in Algeria, presented a political scenario that was ripe for rebellion against France. It was bad enough that the French forcibly occupied this land and exploited the national resources. The existing situation was offensive enough when the legitimate owners of the land—the Algerians—were asked to pay more taxes than the colons to the colonial overseers; indeed, what a paradox. In truth, it could be surmised that it was native Algerians who should have been paid substantial taxes for the occupation of their land by French settlers!

## Independence

The independence movement in Algeria followed the same trajectory as those organized by anti-colonial agitators in other parts of Africa in the first half of the 20th century, but picked up steam after World War II. Several thousand Algerians joined the French army in the war against Germany. Many soldiers experienced the political rights they had been denied while risking their lives to protect France. Additionally, clerics, teachers, and others were galvanized into action in Algeria by Arab nationalist movements for emancipation in the Middle East and elsewhere.

On May 8, 1945, marking the date on which the Allied victory over Nazi Germany happened, Muslims celebrating the outcome of the war organized a parade. At the same time, they protested vociferously for equality and human dignity in their society; this outburst led to political commotion in the city of Setif. Many French settlers died during the demonstration. In a riposte, French troops and angry mobs assailed Muslim neighborhoods, torching homes and slaughtering thousands of Muslims. From this point on, radical Muslim leaders insisted that armed struggle against French occupation of Algeria was their only path to independence. Because it was suicidal to take on the mighty occupying armed forces of France, the plan was to fight a guerrilla war. The major group that led the armed struggle for emancipation was the National Liberation Front (FLN).

After the defeat of France at the battle of Dien Bien Phu in Indochina in 1952, Paris moved to Algeria, as it were, to hold on to this colony in North Africa. Even so, Algerians were determined to fight for their freedom by whatever means possible, including, but not limited to, terrorism. Following the unrest in France in the wake of plastic bombs exploding intermittently in conspicuous locations in both France and Algeria, many French citizens became sick and tired of these terrorist acts. It was against the backdrop of the internal socio-political disarticulations and malaise in France rather than FLN military victory over French forces per se that Paris negotiated with the liberation movement for Algerian independence. The Algerians hoisted their flag of green and white on July 5, 1962, under the leadership of Ahmed Ben Bella.

In sum, it is against the background of the preceding concise ancient and modern histories of the founding of Algeria that I shall reference a classic episode—the Battle of Algiers. I do so with a view to exposing France's colonial human rights infractions in the country—a precursor to post-independence Algeria's human rights quagmire.

## The Battle of Algiers and Human Rights Infractions

In alluding to France's human rights practices in this chapter, I intend to highlight and reveal the fact that human rights quandaries in post-colonial Algeria have their antecedents partially in the sociology of what happened in the country during colonial rule. Accordingly, my hypothesis is "Algerians who were tortured and whose human rights were violated during colonization ended up infringing the rights of Algerians when they acceded to power." Put in another way, the governance techniques of post-colonial political chieftains mimicked those of their former colonial overseers. A priori, one could contend that many post-colonial Algerian leaders are committing the same "sins" as did their colonial superintendents by violating the human rights of their fellow citizens. This thesis, among other ideas, is an expressed opinion in this chapter. In attempts to further my argumentations on the matter of contemporary human rights challenges in Algeria, I shall allude to the application of wanton torture of Algerians by French forces during the Battle of Algiers. Torture, as a human rights violation, is in contravention of Article 5 of the Universal Declaration of Human Rights. In fact, Article 5 states: "No one shall be subjected to torture or to cruel, inhuman or degrading treatment or punishment."[21]

In the Battle of Algiers, also known as the battle for Algerian independence from France, torture was applied indiscriminately by security forces that infringed on Article 3 of the Geneva Conventions on war. This article, among other things, states unequivocally:

> In the case of armed conflict not of an international character occurring in the territory of one of the High Contracting Parties, each Party to the conflict shall be bound to apply, as a minimum, the following provisions:
> (1) Persons taking no active part in the hostilities, including members of armed forces who have laid down their arms and those placed 'hors de combat' by

sickness, wounds, detention, or any other cause, shall in all circumstances be treated humanely. [This should be done] without any adverse distinction founded on race, colour, religion or faith, sex, birth or wealth, or any other similar criteria. To this end, the following acts are and shall remain prohibited at any time and in any place whatsoever with respect to the above-mentioned persons:
>    (a) Violence to life and person, in particular murder of all kinds, mutilation, cruel treatment and torture.

Incontrovertibly, it might be foolhardy to assume that the culture of torture in Algeria started with the Battle of Algiers. However, torture intensified during this war partly because an attempt by Algerians to decouple from France after World War II could rob France of its colonial prestige—even wealth—among other Western powers. After all, the use of torture had its roots in the country as long ago as 1830 when France colonized Algeria. Marshal Thomas Bugeaud, the first Governor-General of Algeria, perfected torture as a contraption for subjugating Algerians to French authority. To be sure, mistreatment was a stratagem and practice commonplace within the French Empire. It was invented for intimidating France's subjects as part of its unique colonial policy of assimilation, so that they would not nurse the idea of revolting against the mother country—France. All the same, France did not enjoy a monopoly on the use of torture as a tactic for maintaining stability in its colonies. Other European powers applied torture to maintain relative peace in their colonial territories in Africa,[22] Asia, Latin America and elsewhere. Possibly, this development prompted the liberal French philosopher Alexis de Tocqueville to note in 1841 in the African case:

> War in Africa is a science. Everyone is familiar with its rules and everyone can apply those rules with almost complete certainty of success. One of the greatest services that Field Marshal Bugeaud has rendered his country is to have spread, perfected and made everyone aware of this new science.... As far as I am concerned, I came back from Africa with the pathetic notion that at present in our way of waging war we are far more barbaric than the Arabs themselves are. These days, they represent civilization [and] we do not. This way of waging war seems to me as stupid as it is cruel. It can only be found in the head of a coarse and brutal soldier.[23]

A re-run of the above policy in the Battle of Algiers, as reflected in the torture of the freedom fighters of the FLN, forms the basis of my discourses regarding France's human rights breaches in Algeria. French authorities claimed that the tactic applied by the FLN in the national liberation movement was terrorism. Subsequently, that indictment of the FLN emboldened the colonists in Algeria to use whatever means necessary to defeat the insurgents called terrorists. One of the methods employed to subdue the activists included the application of torture indiscriminately against detained FLN soldiers and sympathizers. The methods of torture included, but were not limited to, stripping of the victims, hanging them by the feet or hands, water torture, torture by electric shock, sleep deprivation and rape. The outcome of these measures in the process of interrogation was to make the culprits reveal their accomplices, leaders and other information useful for French counter-offensive to the rebellion. Nonetheless, these cruel and forbidding techniques for soliciting information from citizens are in contravention to the Geneva Conventions ratified by France in 1951.

The International Committee of the Red Cross (ICRC) complained and condemned the serious abuse of the technique of interrogation applied by the security forces. A substantial number of detainees suffered from severe burns from electric shocks applied to their highly sensitive parts.[24] Authorities ignored the "vocal protest of the ICRC to the French government about the activities of its agents and the harsh methods of interrogation." This was especially the situation in the spring of 1957 when the incidents of extreme torture increased considerably.[25] Partially prompted by the exacerbation of torment in the colony, the popular French newspaper Le Monde published findings on the methodical torture in Algeria, which pricked the conscience of the international public and unleashed a storm and volley of protests in France and elsewhere. Moreover, correspondents of this newspaper article sadly documented the hopelessness of the ICRC, which had been unsuccessful in effectively putting a stop to major cruelty and human rights infringements despite its commendable exertions over the years. A potential reason why torture was difficult to stop was that the mandate of the ICRC delegates in Algeria was tactically restricted to Article 3 of the Geneva Conventions, which limited its activities in the country. In addition, the French government only permitted visits to detention sites.[26]

In their petition to the United Nations (UN) on the human rights atrocities committed by France in Algeria, Ferhat Abbas and Mohamed Yazid pleaded with the president of the UN General Assembly, on behalf of the FLN, to end the brutalities. As a matter of profound concern, Abbas and Yazid protested the lynching, plundering, and terror committed by the French security forces in the casbah of Algiers. Their appeal or entreaty to the UN ended with a call for assistance. In this regard, the international community, through its collective influence, was to use its full force to bring pressure to bear on the French government to put a stop to the "wanton massacre" of the Algerian people.[27] The grave human rights breaches committed by French security forces were referenced repeatedly in the arguments put forward by the FLN against France's harsh colonial administrative modus operandi and became a crucial rallying cry of its propaganda war during the Battle of Algiers.[28]

In the plea to the UN Secretary-General Dag Hammarskjold in April 1959, on this human rights question, FLN delegates disparaged not only torture and military executions, but also the forced internal displacement and relocation of more than a million Algerians. Many innocent Algerians were living in crowded squalor.[29] France's many infractions of the Geneva Conventions, as for example execution of prisoners, were vehemently condemned by the Red Crescent in various Arab states. The Red Cross in other regions of the world like Hungary, East Germany, and Venezuela expressed dismay at the violation of the Geneva Conventions by the French security forces.[30]

It is enough to say, however, that my allusion to the preceding human rights breaches in Algeria is instructive and ironic in a way. France's colonial objective in Africa was, among other things, mission civilisatrice. However, France's human rights violations during the FLN's war of national liberation may be contextualized within the period and circumstance following the aftermath of the country's defeat in Vietnam (Indochina) after World War II. An angst of sorts flowing from another colony—Algeria—de-coupling from the French colonial empire may have struck a deadly blow to France's psyche and standing within the community of European colonial powers. Theoretically, this set of circumstances may have blinded French policymakers in their decision to apply torture and violate the human rights of Algerians with impunity. After all, France has frequently portrayed itself, with pride, as a country that has advanced—and still advances, at least on paper—liberté, égalité et fraternité as its revolutionary slogan to the world. In France, to be sure, despite the foregoing brief chronicle, some factions, especially left-wing groups, denounced the war and human rights contraventions during the Battle of Algiers. It is comforting that in September 2018, French President Emmanuel Macron issued an official mea culpa for France's atrocities during the war against Algerian citizens.

In truth, my above historical and political chronicles, especially with respect to human rights breaches by the French authorities in Algeria, pose salient and poignant questions central to this volume—human rights challenges in Islamic North Africa. After all, has the leadership since independence done better in Algeria than the French security forces rightly condemned for human rights infringements? Are Algerians fully enjoying their human rights under the contemporary leadership? Are there potential strategies that might advance human rights practices in Algeria? In Algeria, do human rights theories clash with practice? The foregoing queries will inform my deliberations in the following pages of this chapter.

Table I is a snapshot of human rights provisions contained in the 1996 constitution—a social contract sometimes referred to as a living document that binds governors and the governed in a society, without the legitimacy and efficacy of which a state could collapse. I have mined liberally this excerpt from the original document; the rationale for this approach is noted previously in the preface and the introduction. Moreover, my elaborate presentation of human rights laws in the Algerian constitution in this chapter, and those of other countries in other chapters, provides in one fell swoop an immediate source of reference for readers of this volume. It is important to scholars who seek to ascertain the extent to which the Algerian government and its appropriate institutions practice the tenets of the constitution relating to the human rights of compatriots. Also, it will be foolhardy for the literati in this polity to write an impressive constitution if lawmakers end up ignoring its tenets. Even so, my reference to precepts in the Algerian constitution and other international human rights instruments is challenging. It will show that it is one thing to write an inspiring constitution and sign international human rights documents, and quite another to implement their principles judiciously; thus, it will shine light on the clashes that oftentimes arise between rights doctrines articulated in the constitution and actual practice of the precepts in a republic.

## Table I: Constitution of the People's Democratic Republic of Algeria (1989 Revised in 1996)

### Chapter IV: Rights and Liberties

| Articles |
| --- |
| Art. 29—All citizens are equal before the law. No discrimination shall prevail because of birth, race, sex, opinion or any other personal or social condition or circumstance. |
| Art. 30—The Algerian nationality is defined by the law. Conditions for acquiring, keeping, loosing or forfeiture of the Algerian nationality are defined by the law. |
| Art. 31—The aim of the institutions is to ensure equality of rights and duties of all citizens, men and women, by removing the obstacles which hinder the progress of human beings and impede the effective participation of all in the political, economic, social and cultural life. |
| Art. 32—The fundamental human and citizen's rights and liberties are guaranteed. They are a common heritage of all Algerians, men and women, whose duty is to transmit it from generation to another in order to preserve it and keep it inviolable. |
| Art. 33—Individual or associative defence of the fundamental human rights and individual and collective liberties is guaranteed. |
| Art. 34—The State guarantees the inviolability of the human entity. Any form of physical or moral violence or breach of dignity is forbidden. |
| Art. 35—Infringements committed against rights and liberties and violations of physical or moral integrity of a human being are repressed by the law. |
| Art. 36—Freedom of creed and opinion is inviolable. |
| Art. 37—Freedom of trade and industry is guaranteed, it is carried out within the framework of the law. |
| Art. 38—Freedom of intellectual, artistic and scientific innovation is guaranteed to the citizen. Copyrights are protected by the law. The seizure of any publication, recording or any other means of communication and information can only be done in pursuance of a warrant. |

Art. 39—The private life and the honour of the citizen are inviolable and protected by the law. The secrecy of private correspondence and communication, in any form, is guaranteed.

Art. 40—The State guarantees home inviolability. No thorough search can be allowed unless in pursuance of the law and in compliance with the latter. The thorough search can only be in pursuance of a search warrant emanating from the competent judicial authority.

Art. 41—Freedom of expression, association and meeting are guaranteed to the citizen.

Art. 42—The right to create political parties is recognized and guaranteed. However, this right cannot be used to violate the fundamental liberties, the fundamental values and components of the national identity, the national unity, the security and integrity of the national territory, the independence of the country and the People's sovereignty as well as the democratic and republican nature of the State. In respect to the provisions of the present Constitution, the political parties cannot be founded on religious, linguistic, racial, sex, corporatist or regional basis. The political parties cannot resort to partisan propaganda on the elements mentioned in the previous paragraph. Any obedience, in any form, of the political parties to foreign interests or parties is forbidden. No political party can resort to any form of any nature of violence or constraint. Other obligations and duties are prescribed by the law.

Art. 43—The right to create associations is guaranteed. The State encourages the development of associative movement. The law defines the conditions and clauses of the creation of associations.

Art. 44—Any citizen enjoying his civil and political rights has the right to choose freely his place of dwelling and to move on the national territory. The right of entry and exit from the national territory is guaranteed.

Art. 45—Any person is presumed not guilty until his culpability is established by a regular jurisdiction with all the guarantees required by the law.

Art. 46—None is guilty unless it is in accordance with a promulgated law prior to the incriminated action.

Art. 47—None can be pursued, arrested or detained unless within the cases defined by the law and in accordance with the forms prescribed.

Art. 48—In the field of penal investigation, custody is under judiciary control and cannot exceed forty-eight (48) hours. The person held in custody has the right to be immediately in contact with his family. The extension of the period of custody can occur, exceptionally, only within the conditions established by the law. At the expiry of the period of custody, it is compulsory to proceed to a medical examination of the person detained if this latter asks for it, and in any cases, this person is informed of this right.

Art. 49—Miscarriage of justice leads to compensation by the State. The law determines the conditions and modes of compensation.

Art. 50—Any citizen fulfilling the legal conditions can elect and be elected.

Art. 51—Equal access to functions and positions in the State is guaranteed to all citizens without any other conditions except those defined by the law.

Art. 52—Private property is guaranteed. The right to inherit is guaranteed. The "Wakf" properties and the foundations are recognized; their intended purpose is protected by the law.

Art. 53—The right for education is guaranteed. Education is free within the conditions defined by the law. Fundamental education is compulsory. The State organizes the educational system. The State ensures the equal access to education and professional training.

Art. 54—All citizens have the right for the protection of their health. The State ensures the prevention and the fight of endemics and epidemics.

Art. 55—All citizens have right for work. The right for protection, security and hygiene at work is guaranteed by the law. The right to rest is guaranteed; the law defines the relevant clauses.

Art. 56—The trade union right is recognized to all citizens.

Art. 57—The right to strike is recognized; it is carried out within the framework of the law. The law may forbid or limit the strike in the field of national defence and security, or in any public service or activity of vital interest for the community.

Art. 58—The family gains protection from the State and the society.

Art. 59—The living conditions of the citizens under the age of working or those unable or can never be able to work are guaranteed.

Art. 60—Ignorance of the law is no excuse. Every person should abide by the Constitution and comply with the laws of the Republic.

Art. 61—The duty of every citizen is to protect and safeguard the independence of the country and the integrity of its national territory as well as all the symbols of the State. Treason, spying, obedience to the enemy as well as all the infringements committed against the State security are severely repressed by the law.

Art. 62—Every citizen should, loyally, fulfill his obligations towards the national community. The commitment of every citizen towards the Mother Country and the obligation to contribute to its defence are sacred and permanent duties. The State guarantees the respect of the symbols of the Revolution, the memory of the "chouhada" and the dignity of their rightful, and the "moudjahidine".

Art. 63—All the individual liberties are carried out within the respect of the rights of others recognized by the Constitution, in particular, the respect of the right for honour, intimacy and the protection of the family, the youth and childhood.

Art. 64—The citizens are equals before the taxes. Everyone should participate in financing the public expenses, in accordance with his contributory capacity. No taxes can be laid down unless in accordance with the law. No tax, contribution or duty of any nature can be laid down with a retrospective effect.

Art. 65—The law sanctions the duty of parents in the education and protection of their children as well as the duty of the children in helping and assisting their parents.

Art. 66—The duty of every citizen is to protect the public property and the interests of the national community and to respect the property of others.

| Art. 67—Any foreigner being legally on the national territory enjoys the protection of his person and his properties by the law. |
| Art. 68—None can be extradited unless in accordance and in implementation of the extradition law. |
| Art. 69—In no case, a political refugee having legally the right of asylum can be delivered or extradited. |

Source: https://www.confinder.richmond.edu/admin/docs/local_algeria.pdf

## Algeria Human Rights Report: A Brief Synopsis

A brief political history of the country is useful in the following discussion.[31] Algeria is unique politically in that it is not a kingdom or sheikdom like some of the Islamic states in the Middle East. In fact, Algeria is a republic and a multiparty state with a presidential system to boot. The citizens elect the president and head of state for a five-year term. The president has real power in that he or "she" has constitutional power to hire and sack cabinet members and the head of government—i.e. the prime minister. Very much like the British system, the Algerian electoral process has no term limits; consequently, President Abdelaziz Bouteflika has dominated the political space since 1999 by any means possible.[32] Little wonder, then, that he was easily re-elected in the election held in April 2014 and remained in power until April 2019, despite his poor health. To hold on to power ad infinitum, civilian authorities working at the behest of the government have generally maintained active control over the security forces, with which political entrepreneurs have expediently violated the human rights of opposition factions.[33]

Some of the major human rights infractions reported by the U.S. Department of State in its splendid summary report on human rights issues in Algeria for 2015 were

> restrictions on the freedom of assembly and association, lack of judicial independence and impartiality, and overuse of pretrial detention.
>
> Other human rights concerns were the excessive use of force by police, including allegations of torture; limitations on the ability of citizens to choose their government; widespread corruption accompanied by reports of limited government transparency; and societal discrimination against persons with disabilities, persons living with HIV/AIDS, and lesbian, gay, bisexual, transgender, and intersex (LGBTI) persons. Women faced violence and discrimination, and there was some reported child abuse. Additionally, the government maintained restrictions on worker rights and did not actively combat conditions of forced labor.[34]

Central to the exploration that follows are discourses on selected topics and issues pertaining to the dilemmas of enforcement of human rights in Algeria. I shall apply the U.S. Department of State's report as my template.

In my critique and discussions of human rights infringements in Algeria, I reference and draw my analytic sap from the Algerian national constitution of 1996, too. Other documents that I have consulted are the Universal Declaration on Human Rights, the International Covenant on Civil and Political Rights (ICCPR), an Amnesty International report, and Human Rights Watch reports, inter alia.

## Respect for the Integrity of the Person, Including Freedom from Arbitrary or Unlawful Deprivation of Life

On September 15, 2015, the media reported the deaths of two individuals—Benchitkh Aissa and Afari Baaouchi—in Ghardaia and Laghouat prisons, respectively. In Aissa's case, his lawyer contended that Aissa suffered from depression and prison wardens and other officials ignored him by not offering him the necessary healthcare to overcome his malady.[35] The neglect by the state's agents and agencies to provide care to Aissa and others violated Articles 34 and 54 of the Algerian constitution. Moreover, Article 3 of the Universal Declaration of Human Rights states: "Everyone has the right to life, liberty and security of person."[36] Article 6 of the International Covenant on Civil and Political Rights elaborates on the provision. It insists on the recognition of individuals' inherent rights to life. Further, it states that to advance its practice it would be incumbent on nation-states to protect this right for everyone by law and give more consideration to individuals in penitentiaries.[37] Obviously, this article does not exclude individuals in prisons from the right to life. Unfortunately, convicts are treated with disdain and deprived of their human rights in Algeria and much of the developing world.

### Torture and Other Cruel, Inhuman, or Degrading Treatment or Punishment

Article 1 of the United Nations Convention on torture defines torture

[to mean] any act by which severe pain or suffering, whether physical or mental, is intentionally inflicted on a person for such purposes as obtaining from him or a third person information or a confession, punishing him for an act he or a third person has committed or is suspected of having committed.... It does not include pain or suffering arising only from, inherent in or incidental to lawful sanctions.[38]

Despite the above provision in the UN Convention on torture, NGOs and national human rights groups and campaigners proclaim that government agents and agencies occasionally applied torture and abusive techniques to attain real and false confessions. For example, on July 9, 2015, security officers arrested Kamel Eddin Fekhar, leader of the Movement for the Autonomy of Mzab, and 24 of his supporters on 18 charges. These indictments included, among other things, threatening the state's sovereignty and national security, encouragement of murder, and an armed rally. In this case, Fekhar's lawyers released information alleging that police abused the detainee while he was in custody. His attorney declared that on July 26, 2015, the 12th day of Fekhar's hunger strike, and notwithstanding poor and deteriorating health, wardens of the jail refused to transfer him to an infirmary.[39] Furthermore, other inmates in the same penitentiary made similar claims. One of those inmates was Belkacem Khencha. Law enforcement agents detained Khencha in January 2015, for demonstrations on behalf of the unemployed in Laghouat and specifically for his protests. During his six months of incarceration, Khencha complained that prison guards beat up him and the eight protesters sentenced with him. Additionally, they did not receive medical treatment while in detention.[40] These actions by relevant state agents are not in consonance with the tenets of Chapter IV, under Rights and Liberties, of the Algerian constitution. It is noteworthy, however, that to lessen the frequency of torture perpetuated by some rogue agents in the polity, the law at least on paper calls for from 10 to 20 years' imprisonment for such cruel practices. Nevertheless, the record suggests that there is no retribution against agents charged with torture and cruelty against citizens. For that reason, national and international NGOs report that the lack of enforcement of the law against torture, and lack of retribution against such violators of human rights, create a problem of impunity in the society.[41]

## Arbitrary Arrest

The constitution, as in Article 47, and law forbid arbitrary arrest and detention of citizens; yet agents of the state frequently apply ambiguous interpretations of state laws to violate the rights of citizens. For instance, "inciting an unarmed gathering" and "insulting a government/political actor, institution, and religious dogmas" are offences against the state. The state can also detain persons considered to be provoking citizens to create public disorder or foment insurrections against the republic. Indeed, agents of the state have arrested journalists, cartoonists, and human rights activists, among others, on the above charges. Some cases in point:

> In February, a court in Oran convicted Mohamed Chergui of insulting the prophet Muhammad after Mohamed Chergui's employer, the newspaper El Djoumhouria, complained about an article he submitted based on foreign academic research about Islam. He received a three-year prison term and a fine of 200,000 Algerian dinars (approximately US$1,900) in his absence. His prison term was later reduced to a one-year suspended sentence, against which he appealed.

In March, a court in El Oued sentenced anti-corruption and [National Committee for the Defense of the Rights of Unemployed Workers] CNDDC activist Rachid Aouine to a fine of 20,000 Algerian dinars (approximately US$190) and six months' imprisonment [that was] reduced to four months on appeal.... [This episode took place] after [the court] convicted him of "incitement to an unarmed gathering."
    ... In November, a court in El Oued sentenced cartoonist Tahar Djehiche to a six-month prison term and a fine of 500,000 Algerian dinars (approximately US$4,600) for "insulting" President Bouteflika and "inciting" others to join a shale gas protest in a comment Tahar Djehiche made on his Facebook page.[42]

Amnesty International and Human Rights Watch condemned these arrests because of the infringements of the arrested individuals' rights to freedom of expression.[43] Moreover, such activities of government officials toward fellow citizens flout Articles 35 and 41 of the national constitution and Articles 9–11 of the International Covenant on Civil and Political Rights.[44]

## Political Prisoners and Detainees

Commonly, security agents of the government apply anti-terrorism laws to political opponents for intimidation purposes. The state carefully uses these laws to stifle freedom of expression and to disrupt public assembly. Sporadically, authorities invoke anti-terrorism laws farcically and spuriously to detain political activists, critics of the government and invented troublemakers. For example, in March the National Coordination of Families of Political Prisoners appealed for the release of 160 individuals that have remained in custody since the 1990s. The Prime Minister, Abdelmalek Sellal, in his denial of the existence of such persons in jail, asserted that the government held no political prisoners. He claimed that courts convicted the detainees in question of vicious crimes, making them unqualified for executive pardons under the National Charter for Peace and Reconciliation.[45] However, one problem that arises on this issue in Algeria, as in other Islamic states of North Africa, is that judges appointed by the leader or president are frequently under duress from the boss to serve at his behest.

In contemporary human rights practices in Algeria, the arbitrary interference with citizens' privacy, family, home life and correspondence are in contravention of Articles 39 and 40 of the constitution, which forbid government interference. In fact, the regime constantly conducts electronic surveillance of its citizens. This activity is common with respect to political activists, opponents, journalists, human rights groups, and real or contrived terrorists. Security officers often search homes without warrants and make surprise calls on households. To legitimize the government's interference in the privacy of fellow citizens, the government promulgated a presidential verdict on October 8, 2015, calling for the establishment of a new anti-cybercrime agency. This surveillance agency was given the task of preventing cybercrime by "whatever means" possible in the security interest of the country.[46]

Nevertheless, as noted previously, Articles 39 and 40 of the constitution repudiate the foregoing violations of human rights. Article 39 states: "The private life and the honor of the citizen are inviolable and protected by the law. The secrecy of private correspondence and communication, in any form, is guaranteed." Article 40 affirms: "The State guarantees home inviolability. No thorough search can be allowed unless in pursuance of the law and in compliance with the latter. The thorough search can only be in pursuance of a search warrant emanating from the competent judicial authority" (see Table I). Within the context of this text, the government's surveillance illustrates the clash between theory and practice in human rights discourses and observance.

The state guarantees freedom of speech and press in Article 41 of the constitution. Independent media outlets, believing that the government would protect their freedom, have criticized the state's inadequate policies. To the chagrin of the media, however, the government has harshly curtailed these rights. The government's methods of restricting press freedom involve pestering of critics, arbitrarily applying expediently invented laws, and informal pressure on publishers, editors and advertisers. Law enforcement agents and agencies have occasionally arrested, prosecuted, and imprisoned critics by applying penal code provisions strategically to nullify constitutional provisions protecting human rights (as explained in the introductory chapter of this volume).[47] Moreover, citizens are at risk if they dare to criticize the government publicly. To silence the opposition, especially political opponents, agents of the government have arrested and detained citizens who had the boldness to malign the regime. Consequently, citizens, despite the tenet of Article 41 of the constitution, have exercised caution, and still exercise carefulness, in expressing their freedom of speech.[48]

It was not ironic that on February 25, 2015, the Ministry of Communication's director of accreditation for foreign correspondence ignored provisions of the constitution, which guarantees press freedom. The ministry chafed at the activities of a correspondent of a London-based Saudi newspaper, *Asharq Al-Awsat*. The correspondent's poignant reporting from Algeria conflicted with the government's journalistic expectations. Therefore, the regime announced that it was not going to renew the paper's accreditation. On March 11, 2015, the Minister of Communication stated at a press conference that "the Algerian state has the right not to renew the accreditation of correspondents of foreign newspapers and channels who insult, defame, or make use of verbal or written violence."[49] The political paradox in such a situation is that the regime can invent charges against a newspaper and violate its right to freedom of the press if its news coverage is critical of the administration—without due process of law.

The state asserts the right to freedom of assembly, expression and association in the constitution under Article 41. Yet, the state's agents and agencies oftentimes flout these freedoms. Partially, this is the case because political actors in the system frequently apply provisions in the criminal code and extra-constitutional powers to knock down constitutional precepts on human rights. This is especially so if freedom of assembly clashes with the national interest. Take, for example, the following human rights issues in the country in 2015 and 2016 that were brought to the fore by human rights campaigners:

> The government continued to suppress peaceful protests by prohibiting all public gatherings held without prior approval. Article 97 of the penal code makes it a crime to organize or participate in an unauthorized gathering, even if it is peaceful, and imposes a penalty of up to one year in prison for demonstrating in public spaces.
>    The court [also] imposed prison sentences on at least nine labor rights activists convicted of engaging in peaceful protests in support of unemployed workers. On February 11, the First Instance Tribunal of Laghouat sentenced eight members of the National Committee for the Defense of the Rights of Unemployed Workers (Comité National pour la Défense des Droits de Chômeurs, CNDDC) to one-year prison terms, half of which it suspended, after convicting them of "unauthorized gathering."[50]
>    On January 16, police used tear gas and dispersed demonstrations in Algiers against Charlie Hebdo, the French satirical newspaper.
>    Throughout the year police dispersed unauthorized gatherings or prevented marching groups or protesters from protesting. Police typically dispersed protesters shortly after a protest began and arrested and detained organizers for a few hours. The HRW, AI, and other NGOs criticized the government's use of the law to restrict peaceful assembly.[51]

On September 23, the governor of the state/province of Bejaia issued a decree prohibiting the use of all provincial cinemas, theatres, and youth and cultural centers for purposes other than that for which they were intended. Civil society organizations decried the decision because these locations were the only free spaces available for use by associations that lacked government accreditation.[52]

As to freedom of association, Articles 41 and 42 of the constitution sanction it. Even so, the government constantly curtails the activities of associations in the society. The stringent requirements and improper implementation of the law result in basic obstacles to the development of vibrant civil society organizations that fight for their rights. Indeed, the law grants the government extensive authority in the daily activities of civil society groups. It wants civil society organizations to apply to the Ministry of Interior (MOI) for permission to function. If a group is registered, it must report to the government its activities, its sources of funding, and its personnel, including changes of its personnel. Furthermore, the law imposes an additional burden that requires civil society coalitions to obtain government preapproval before asking for and taking foreign financial support. The state will levy fines if associations are unable to present required information and documents to the regime or attempt to circumvent this law by accepting foreign cash without authorization. Additionally, it is illegal to form a political party with a religious platform, undertone and orthodoxy.[53]

By law, the MOI reserves the right to deny any grouping deemed an enemy of the state, or a menace to public order, license to operate. The ministry has sometimes used its de facto authority in defiance and contravention of Article 43 of the constitution. This precept states that "the right to create associations is guaranteed. The State encourages the development of associative movement." The MOI has sometimes used extra-constitutional powers to deny or slow down recognition of NGOs, associations, religious groups, and political parties with "antagonistic" agendas toward the state. For example, the ministry failed to give approval to operate in the country to the National Association for the Fights against Corruption. This denial happened based on a flimsy explanation that the raison d'être for the formation of the group did not conform to the law established for recognizing an association.[54] The state may have had a peculiar reason for not endorsing the group. It was, probably, because of the "sensitivity" of the manifesto of the group—fighting the endemic and perennial evil of corruption in the society.

With respect to freedom to participate in the political process, the constitution sanctions citizens' right to choose their representative freely. For instance, Article 6 states explicitly and refreshingly, too: "The people are the source of any power. The national sovereignty belongs exclusively to the people." Moreover, the constitution approves of universal and equal suffrage. However, these rights, ironically, have seldom led to a change of government through free and fair elections,[55] thus illustrating the clash between theory and practice in my contemplation in this volume. For instance, in the presidential election of April 2014 the electorate reelected President Abdelaziz Bouteflika for a fourth term. He did not campaign enthusiastically; yet, he won 81 percent of the ballots while his opponent, a previous prime minister, Ali Benflis, garnered about 12 percent of the votes.[56] Given the oddity of electoral democracy in contemporary Africa, it is safe to contend that top members of the president's party fixed this election.[57] They manipulated the outcome of the election to protect their interest despite the violation of citizens' right to free and fair elections.

## Freedom of Religion

Article 2 of the constitution states that "Islam is the religion of the State"; but Algeria is a multi-religious state—albeit with Islam the dominant religion. The constitution further forbids state institutions acting in ways that are discordant with Islam. Wittingly, the law grants, on paper, all persons the right to practice their religion so long as they do so within the spirit of public order and guidelines. Criminal act against the doctrine of Islam and, indeed, insult against the religious prophets are criminal offenses. Remarkably, the above declaration applies to any religion practicing in the country. However, attempts to convert Muslims by non–Muslims constitute a crime, although the government is relatively lukewarm in enforcing this provision of its decree.[58] This is the case probably because it violates Articles 36 and 41 of the Algerian constitution (see Table I).

Demographically, the country's population was 39.5 million in 2015. Out of this number, more than 99 percent are Sunni Muslim. The rest of the population, in terms of religious affiliation, are Christians, Jews, Ahmadi Muslims, Shia Muslims, and a community of Ibadi Muslims. The community of Christians includes "Roman Catholics, Protestant groupings such as Seventh-day Adventists, Methodists, L'Eglise Reforme (Reformed Church), Anglicans, and an estimated 1,000 to 1,500 Egyptian Coptic Christians."[59] Overall, it is estimated that the number of Christians in the country is between 20,000 and 100,000. A majority of them are foreign residents; doctrinally, it is sacrilegious for non–Muslims to convert Muslims to another religion—an offense punishable by a fine of one million dinars (approximately $11,400). The sentence is five years in prison for anyone attempting to peel off Muslims from their faith by inciting, constraining and utilizing seduction for that purpose.[60] Furthermore, "making, storing, or distributing printed documents or audio-visual materials with the intent of 'shaking the faith' of a Muslim may also be punished in this manner,"[61] which is in violation of Articles 32, 33, 36, and 41 of the constitution (see Table I above).

To further the government's respect for religious freedom, in theory at least, the Ministry of Religious Affairs (MRA) counsels whether a religious group conforms to the government's stipulated rules for a congregation. The National Commission for Non-Muslim Religious Groups, a government entity, has the legal authority to facilitate the registration procedure for all non–Muslim groups. The MRA presides over a special commission. This commission comprises the following: senior representatives of the Ministry of the National Defense, Ministry of Interior, Ministry of Foreign Affairs, the presidency, the national police, the national gendarmerie, and the National Consultative Commission for the Promotion and Protection of Human Rights (CNCPPDH). The official mandate of the CNCPPDH is to address human rights complaints. Notionally, its function is to address the concerns of individuals and groups maltreated by the MRA.[62]

Aside from daily prayers, (Friday) Islamic services may take place only in state-approved mosques—and not so for various non–Muslim religions whose members frequently met in private homes. The government can shut down any religious service in a private home, but that is in violation of Articles 39 and 40 of the constitution. For example, Article 40 affirms: "The State guarantees home inviolability." Subsequently, it is challenging for human rights dialogue that the government regulates the way and methods by which religious services are conducted. Such an intrusion into the sacredness in the way a group worships God potentially violates Article 35 of the constitution, which stipulates: Infringements committed against rights and liberties and violations of physical or moral integrity of a human being are repressed by the law" (see Table I above).

Informed by political culture, these troublesome, challenging and discriminatory laws aimed at Christians and other non–Muslims are formulated and employed by the Ministry of Religious Affairs. These human rights issues include, but are not limited to, the following (numbers added by author):

1. The family code prohibits Muslim women from marrying non–Muslim men unless the man converts to Islam. The code does not prohibit Muslim men from marrying non–Muslim women, provided the woman belongs to a religion included under the term "people of the book (i.e., Christian or Jewish)." [However, this code in part violates Article 16(1) of the Universal Declaration of Human Rights, which states: "Men and women of full age, without any limitation due to race, nationality or religion, have the right to marry and to found a family. They are entitled to equal rights as to marriage, during marriage and at its dissolution."]

2. The Ministries of Religious Affairs, Foreign Affairs, Interior, and Commerce must approve the importation of non–Islamic religious writings. Citizens and foreigners may legally import personal copies of non–Islamic religious texts.

3. The law states all structures intended for non–Muslim collective worship must be registered with the state; any modification of such structures must have prior government approval, and collective worship may take place only in structures exclusively intended and approved for that purpose.

4. Under the law, children born to a Muslim father are considered Muslims regardless of the mother's religion [in violation of Article 16(1) of the Universal Declaration of Human Rights]....

5. The constitution prohibits non–Muslims from running for the presidency. Non-Muslims may hold other public offices and work within the government.[63]

The foregoing religious injunctions problematize human rights issues and their implementations in this society. This is the case because they violate precepts in international human rights instruments. Even so the above challenges of religion should be where one of the loci of interpretation of respect for human rights respect in Algeria rests—i.e., it is where human rights need improvement. In any case, the above religious codes violate Articles 26 and 27 of the International Covenant on Civil and Political Rights. Article 26 states: "All persons are equal before the law and are entitled without any discrimination to the equal protection of the law. In this respect, the law shall prohibit any discrimination and guarantee to all persons equal and effective protection against discrimination on any ground such as race, colour, sex, language, religion, political or other opinions, national or social origin, property, birth or other status." Article 27 affirms: "In those states in which ethnic, religious or linguistic minorities exist, persons belonging to such minorities shall not be denied the right, in community with the other members of their group, to enjoy their own culture, to profess and practice their own religion, or to use their own language."[64]

It is true that minority groups of different hues, in virtually all societies around the world, suffer from one form of bigotry or another due to lack of political influence. Because of discrimination, their lives in some nation-states are constantly at risk.[65] Intra-religious prejudice based on Islamic orthodoxy is a human rights challenge in Algeria. To illustrate this issue, I shall briefly highlight in a case study the human rights contraventions against a minority religious grouping. In this regard, I mined from a Human Rights Watch article titled: "Algeria: Stop Persecuting a Religious Minority."[66]

## Ahmadiyya: A Muslim Minority Religious Sect and Human Rights

Mirza Ghulam founded the Ahmadiyya religious sect in 1889 in India. The members of the Ahmadiyya in Algeria recognize it as a Muslim community. There are approximately 2,000 in the country and ordinarily the group should not pose a threat to the dominant Sunni Muslims. Nevertheless, members of this sect have experienced bigotry and marginalization. Government agents and agencies have eyed this group with suspicion and consciously denied them the constitutional right to form associations.[67] Indeed, Minister of Religious Affairs Mohamed Aissa has referred to the presence of Ahmadis in Algeria not only as a nuisance in the society, but also as a "deliberate sectarian invasion" of the country. In response to the perceived menace to the religious health of the polity, the MRA brought a legal case against them in a peculiar bid to stop Sunnis' deviation from Muslim religious orthodoxy.[68]

For example, on November 15, 2015, a group of Ahmadis held a meeting to create a new association they called the 'Ahmed al-Khir Association (Ahmed Charity), whose raison d'être was to perform charity projects and extend succor to the poor and marginalized communities. The Ministry of Interior denied their submitted application for approval as a charity organization. The government's ostensible reasons for denying the Ahmadis' application rested on the principles of Articles 2 and 27 of Algerian Associations Law. Article 2 gives the Ministry of Interior and other agencies of the government sufficient elasticity in their decisions to refuse authorization; the Ministry of Interior may deny approval if it considers the content and aims of a group's activities to violate Algeria's "fundamental principles ... and values, public order, public morals, and the applicable laws and regulations."[69] Furthermore, Article 27 presents a list of cumbersome papers and documents that an association must provide the Ministry of Interior for evaluation. The Ministry of Interior considers the submission of these materials critical before a group can qualify for registration.[70]

There is an irony in the preceding dialogue surrounding the refusal to grant permission to Ahmadis to create a charity association. This is so against the backdrop of Article 43 of the constitution. This provision affirms: "The right to create associations is guaranteed.

The State encourages the development of associative movement." Even so, Article 43 notes that the law defines the conditions and clauses for the creation of associations. In fact, a deductive argument one could make in this instance is that juridical laws supersede the precept of the constitution; tactically, this supposition provides the government leeway to circumvent the provisions of the constitution pertaining to human rights to suit the interest of political actors and the government at will. Clearly, the antagonism of the state toward the Ahmadis had long been brewing based on the opinion of the state and its custodians. The postulation was and is that members of the group are phony Muslims whose aims, if not checked, could adulterate the doctrines of authentic Sunni Muslims in the country. Consequently, their evil machinations in the country will not happen under the watchful eyes of the state and its agents and agencies.

The strategy applied by the MOI to delegitimize the Ahmadis in the society was to demonize the group by listing the ways it didn't conform with the values and laws of Algerians. Some of these were the following: denigrating the canons of Islam; participating in unauthorized association; collecting donations without a license; and possession and distribution of documents from foreign sources that endangered national security.[71] Another strategy was to marginalize the Ahmadis by disrupting their activities in Algeria. HRW reported that to curb Ahmadis' human rights, authorities prosecuted 266 Ahmadis under one or more of the following charges:

[1] Denigrating the dogma or precepts of Islam, punishable by a prison term of three to five years and a fine of up to 100,000 Algerian dinars (US$908), under article 144 of the penal code; [2] participation in an unauthorized association, under article 46

of the Associations Law, punishable by a prison sentence of three to six months and a fine of 100,000 to 300,000 dinars; [3] collecting donations without license, under articles 1 and 8 of the decree 03–77 of 1977 regulating donations; [4] conducting worship in unauthorized places, [in violation of] articles 7, 12, and 13 of Ordinance 06–03 Establishing the Conditions and Rules for the Exercise of non–Muslim Religions; and [5] possession and distribution of documents from foreign sources threatening national security, under article 96–2 of the penal code, punishable by up to three years in prison.[72]

## Women's Rights

Germane to my discussion on women's rights in Algeria is the impressive role women played in the national liberation struggle against French colonialism. Despite their gallantry in the war, however, they continue to suffer from human rights infringements based in part on rustic traditions and theology. Indeed, as Zahia S. Salhi has noted: "Women's new status as activists during the war not only altered the division of labor between women and men, but also challenged the wider power of patriarchy, threatening to erode its power and privileges. Rejecting their restricted role as mothers, wives, and daughters in the private sphere of the household, women took on active roles in a wide public sphere. Their work was integral to the struggle for national liberation and, therefore, equally important to their own liberation."[73] Notwithstanding the positive role women played in the liberation war, it appears as if the sacrifices women made for the motherland have come to naught vis-à-vis those made by men against the backdrop of the 1984 Family Code. Little wonder, then, that Salhi in an observation on the socio-political development in Algeria lamented that women were not faring well under the dictates of the infamous Family Code, fermented and perpetrated by the barbarism of Islamic fundamentalists.[74] I will discuss the gist of the Family Code later.

It is safe to contend that the contemporary violations of the rights of women in Algeria are explainable within the context of its political, religious and cultural histories. In fact, the 1976 constitution of the FLN was unequivocal in asserting the equality of men and women in the society. It criticized the old feudal system that limited women's rights. The constitution affirmed the equality of the sexes and guaranteed their free movement within the republic. The constitution stressed that Islam was and is a liberating force that considered women and men as equals.[75] Accordingly, this legal document urged women to lead the fight to uphold the provisions in the religion that guarantee women their equality with men. To tackle women's struggle against humiliation, bigotry, injustice, et cetera requires continuous efforts—bearing in mind the feudal characteristics of the society. Despite the above inspiring phrases and encouragements, it was and is one thing to inscribe into a constitution provisions that advance women's rights in Algeria and quite another to implement them in an entrenched patriarchal and pastoral culture that is nourished by ardent reactionary religious orthodoxy. This supposition sharpens the clash between theory and practice.

Algerian women took the rousing 1976 constitutional injunctions to heart and in the 1980s decided to test the will of the state on matters of their human rights—for example, demanding that they travel unaccompanied by male relatives. In addition, enlightened female university students dealt with the problem directly by asserting their rights to partake in public demonstrations. One such protest happened at an International Women's Day celebration in which women participants, among other things, demanded the abrogation of the law impeding women's freedom of movement in the society. In response, President Chadli's regime abandoned the law against women's freedom of movement," but not without a quid pro quo—as the government decided to write a new "Family Code" to address the matter of gender roles in the republic.[76]

To the chagrin of feminists and rights activists, women's movements were not participants in the drafting of the Family Code—a paradox, indeed, since canons in the code affected their lives. Moreover, women were neither aware nor informed of their rights in the document. Thus, feminist activists rejected the Family Code in part because they had no input in producing it as noted earlier. To express their opposition to this Family Code, women's movements demonstrated against its implantation in Algiers with placards that read "No to Silence, Yes to Democracy!" and "No to the betrayal of the ideals of November 1, 1954!"[77] These women's rallies against the Family Code, however, came to naught partly because women lacked the political influence to block the code. The government promulgated the code in June 1984.

The core of the Family Code reaffirmed the traditional-cum-religious norms of the society. In lamentation after the government passed the code into law, some feminists noted in despair that this "family law ... codified the ownership of wives and children by fathers/ husbands."[78]

The Family Code and its principles, within the context of women's rights in Algeria, are problematic and challenging. This is the case because the code, among other things,

> makes it a legal duty for Algerian women to obey their husbands, and respect and serve them, their parents, and relatives (Article 39). It institutionalized polygamy and made it the right of men to take up to four wives [but not for women to take up to two men, let alone four men] (Article 8). Women cannot arrange their own marriage contracts unless represented by a matrimonial guardian (Article 11) and they have no right to apply for divorce. While a man needs only to desire a divorce to get one.... [w]omen may obtain divorce only by submitting to the practice of kho'a [i.e., a ran-

som that women must pay for their freedom] which allows women to divorce on the condition that they give up any claim to alimony (Article 54).[79]

As noted previously, the infractions of women's rights in Algeria have strong cultural and religious undertones. The scintillating fundamentalists' "poetry" quoted below supports and furthers the bias that a major—generally rural—segment of the Algerian society has against women and, a priori, their human rights:

> Housework is more suited to female biology and psychology than professional work; that rates of mortality and morbidity are higher among employed women than among women who stay at home; that employed women are less moral; and that female employment causes male unemployment....
>
> Mother, sister, wife, as your father, brother, husband, I would like your beauty to be my wealth, for I cannot live without you. I seethe with jealousy when I see you working as a secretary for a human fox, who ask for your photo before he hired you. I don't want you to be a work tool, or a scapegoat for those who seek to destroy Islamic morals.[80]

Fatima Mernissi argues, though, that "if women's rights are a problem for some modern Muslim men, it's neither because of the Koran ... nor the Islamic tradition, but simply because those rights conflict with the interests of a male elite."[81] Also, I contend elsewhere that this behavioral pattern is explainable within the context of the theory of privilege and "law of self/interest." In short, the elites, especially political elites, who are in power will not give up their privileged position in society without a fight or, in Africa, without a bloody political struggle. One of the less lethal, yet effective tools they apply to maintain their position of advantage in the struggle is the demonization of real or putative competitors for power.[82]

Setting aside the foregoing discursive discourses on the struggle of Algerian feminists for their human rights, and counter arguments by Islamic fundamentalists that the proper place for women in the society is in the home, what is the contemporary situation of women's rights in this polity? Against the backdrop of my preceding query, I shall examine very briefly some salient issues regarding women's rights in the following pages. This is the case because women's rights violations in Algeria are vast—as is the case in much of Africa and the rest of the developing world.

## Discrimination and Societal Abuses

Rape and domestic violence occur frequently in the country. These abuses happen in both spousal and non-spousal relations. The law is emphatic in its condemnation of non-spousal rape and less so in its condemnation of spousal rape. Indeed, because of the seriousness of the crime, the prison sentence for non-spousal rape is from one to five years.[83] Algerian families feel humiliated by the rape of a female relative and therefore seldom report it to law enforcement agencies for retribution. Sadly, some survivors of this crime end up in homeless shelters or charity hostels.[84]

Domestic violence against women is commonplace in the country. Even so, the requirements to prove the existence of such violence against women-beaters are difficult. In 2014, there were 7,091 cases of domestic violence. Out of this total, 5,160 reported cases were repeated physical abuse. Women's support groups reported that approximately 100 to 200 women die annually from domestic violence. Fortuitously, in a society that is relatively soft on women's issues, it is refreshing that in response to the above reports of atrocities against women, the regime acted decisively. A committee, the Council of the Nation, adopted "a law that strengthened punishments for violence against women. The law introduced sentences of one to 20 years' imprisonment for domestic violence and six months to two years' incarceration for men who withheld property or financial resources from their spouses."[85]

Prejudice toward women in the workplace and society is routine as noted earlier. As is still the case in much of the West, women in Algeria are unlikely to earn pay equal to that of their male counterparts—not to mention less likely to earn rapid promotions. Women continue to suffer from prejudice in inheritance claims vis-à-vis their male siblings. In short, they are entitled to a more limited portion than their brothers or a deceased husband's brothers. Early and forced marriages still occur in Algeria—particularly in the countryside. This is the situation despite the mandated minimum age of 19 for legal marriages. Minors cannot marry without parental consent. Despite the following stipulations, United Nations statistics in 2013 disclosed that 6 percent of women ages 20 to 49 were married before age 18.[86]

## The LGBTI Human Rights Quagmire

My discussion on the Lesbian, Gay, Bisexual, Transgender, and Intersex (LGBTI) rights quandary in Algeria is peculiar and relative. This is so in part because of the socio-cultural revolution of this lifestyle in contemporary human rights dialogues. Homosexuality is taboo in much of the developing world. It was and is still argued by some that homosexuality was never practiced in much of Africa. In Muslim societies with strict religious practices and norms, the penalty for LGBTI practices could be death. Thus, it would be suicidal to indulge in same-sex relations. Bearing the above social theories in mind, a brief probe of this peculiar phenomenon in Algeria is apposite.

The law, both common and religious, abhors and criminalizes same-sex relations by women or men. Nevertheless, the penalty for such an indulgence is relatively tolerant given the social and religious character of the state. The punishment for the practice of homosexuality could result in imprisonment from six months to three years and a fine of 1,000 to 10,000 Algerian dinars ($9.50 to $95). For homosexual acts, the prison terms range from two months to two years and fines of 500 to 2,000 dinars ($4.76 to $19). Individuals who admit membership in the LGBTI family or group confront humiliating societal and religious bigotry.[87]

Practitioners of this lifestyle, under such drastic laws, frequently remained closeted because it is common for immediate family members to disown them. In Algeria, the state promotes LBGTI individuals' ostracism by casting aspersion or vilifying them. In fact, the Minister of Religious Affairs, Mohamed Aissa, was and is critical of this way of life. He expressed his opinion poignantly on this matter thus: "Combatting individuals who promote the deviation of morality and dismantling of the family (a reference to the behavior of LGBTI individuals) was more important than the fight against Daesh [supporters of the defunct Caliphate of the Islamic State of Iraq and Syria]."[88] Further, the minister hardly ever condemns hate speech by conservative and religious extremists aimed at LBGTI communities. Because of the strong resistance of anti–LBGTI activists, membership in the LBGTI community has dwindled in Algeria.[89] The preceding development in the republic notwithstanding, it is important to respect LBGTI individuals' human rights and those of other Algerians. In this way, Algeria might be able to mitigate human rights challenges and clashes between rights theories and practices, which could further peaceful coexistence in the society.

# 2

# Egypt

## Brief History

> Egypt is the home of one of the world's first great civilizations. Around 5,000 years ago, an advanced [and unified society] developed in this land and it lasted almost 3,000 years.[1]—Robert Pateman

The history of ancient Egypt is captivating not only to Egyptologists but also to students of African history and politics. As long ago as 3200 BCE, the Egyptian civilization arguably reached a splendid apogee, marked by a development that is so different from and "outshines" its contemporary history and status. It is striking, too, that Egypt had an impressive political system at that moment in antiquity. Egypt had one of the world's first national governments, highly developed art works, an admirable writing system of hieroglyphs, and a body of literature. The society also had an enviable record of scientific knowledge, as in its 365-day calendar; it was advanced in mathematics, astronomy, and medicine. On top of that, it had a distinctive and unique form of religion.[2] Additionally, within the proximity of the modern capital, Cairo, King Mena constructed the imposing capital city of Memphis in 3200 BCE. Alexander the Great built the resplendent city named after him, Alexandria, in 332 BCE, and in the hinterland was the pious Christian monastery of St. Anthony.[3]

Indeed, Zaki N. Mahmoud provides a short list of captivating events within four periods that capture the series of political, historical, and civilizational developments in Egypt. Briefly, these phases were:

1. The ancient Egyptian civilization, which lasted about thirty-five centuries.

2. With the conquest of Egypt by Alexander the Great in the fourth century before Christ, another type of civilization began. This was the Greco-Roman period, which lasted for about ten centuries.

One can loosely call it the Christian period, as Christianity was the prevailing religion....

3. Then came the Arab conquest with its new religion of Islam (Mohammedanism) and its new language. Since about the middle of the seventh century, Egypt has been chiefly a Muslim and Arabic speaking country.

4. At the beginning of the nineteenth century, Egypt, although still Muslim and Arabic speaking, entered its fourth type of civilization. For the last one and a half centuries, it has been increasingly leaning towards the Western or science dominated culture.[4]

Historically, within the context of the preceding periods, the first era is unique in that it was the longest and marked a phase in which political, economic, social and religious development happened inside the polity's political unit. In other words, "Egyptians" were autarchic and managed their own affairs without the external invasions that were later to characterize the remarkable history of this territory. Despite ancient Egypt's development, however, it is customary for some historians to chronicle all the monarchs "from Mena, the first king, to Alexander the Great, in thirty-one dynasties; i.e. royal families."[5]

The "Golden Age" of Egyptian civilization—frequently referred to as the Age of Empire-cum-New Kingdom—lasted from about 1558 to 1080 BCE. This period some academics consider as the very height of Egyptian accomplishments in art, religion, and literature.[6] Territorially, during the reign of Ramses II (1300–1233 BCE) Egypt scored many victories in battles and extended its powers over a large part of the Middle East.[7]

However, the fall of the New Kingdom happened at about 1075 BCE. Intra-political rivalries amongst Egyptians led to the splintering of the kingdom into two factions—one group led by pharaohs and the other by priests. This split weakened the cohesiveness of the country and made the society susceptible to foreign invasions, thus serving as an example of the truth of President Abraham Lincoln's 1858 admonition that a country divided against itself [i.e. pharaohs and priests in the Egyptian case] cannot stand. This was his wise counsel when North vs. South political turmoil erupted in America. In any case, historically, Egypt slowly and progressively fell into the hands of the Assyrians,[8] Persians[9]; and Alexander the Great of Macedonia, who conquered Egypt in 332 BCE.[10]

Following the death of Alexander in 323 BCE, his general Ptolemy succeeded him, and Ptolemy's line of leadership ended with that of the brave warrior Queen Cleopatra VII.[11] Her rule began in the first century BCE. Cleopatra allied with Rome—first with Julius Caesar and later with Mark Antony, who was a co-ruler with Octavian. Cleopatra and Mark Antony in their ambition to overthrow Octavian embarked on a war in Actium, Greece, but met their Waterloo at this battle. Cleopatra and Mark Antony, in response to their defeat, took their own lives in Alexandria. Following this demise, Egypt came under the suzerainty of Rome.[12]

For approximately 300 years, Egypt served as an outpost within the vast Roman Empire that in part provided resources for sustaining Rome. Unlike the Greek rule, the Roman conquest and occupation of Egypt brought poverty to the land. As an outcome of citizens' economic misery, Rome's governance system of the territory was hated and unpopular. It was within the period of Roman rule that the leader of a new religious faith was born in Palestine. His name was Jesus Christ, and he preached the gospel of peace, love and salvation for all but mainly for the downtrodden. Egyptians were quick to embrace the religion that brought them psychological relief during the period of their economic desperation. It was remarkable that between 30 BCE and AD 10 there arrived in Egypt two major forces. These were political and religious potencies—one led by Caesar and the other by Christ. Joseph, Mary, and Jesus from Bethlehem, it is alleged, travelled through Egypt where Jesus himself performed miracles healing and consoling the people.[13] St. Mark, who visited Egypt in AD 45, was a founder of the Church; he started preaching the gospel of Christ in Alexandria and as the teaching of the Christian doctrine started to spread like wildfire, the Roman administration was confounded and sought to slow down its momentum and spread.[14] Indeed, in AD 204, Romans in Egypt received a decree that forbade them from embracing the religion.[15] Nevertheless, it was during the reign and supremacy of Emperor Constantine in 313 AD that Christianity became the official religion of the Roman Empire, and that included Egypt, too.[16]

The centrality of the preceding narrative is anchored on the thesis that the contemporary Coptic Church and its religious activities in Egypt have their antecedents in the aftermath of the birth of Christianity in the country; and that the modern Coptic Christians are a remnant of those who survived the Arabs and their Islamic conquest of Egypt in 640 AD. Accordingly, Copts, it could be argued, are the primordial and authentic descendants of Egypt.[17]

With the split of the Roman Empire around 395 BCE into Rome and Constantinople, Egypt was placed under the rule of the Eastern Roman emperors and in this case the Byzantine emperors. The Byzantine suzerainty over Egypt expired following the conquest of Egypt by the powerful Arab Islamic crusaders around 639–641 AD, as noted earlier. The Islamization of the territory ensued immediately following the victory.[18] The Arabs and their various Islamic sects competed for control of power in Egypt. Arabs' institutionalization of their language and religion in Egypt are notable until this day. The Ottomans governed Egypt from 1517, following the defeat of the Mamluks,[19] until the arrival of the French in 1798–1801 under the leadership of Napoleon Bonaparte.[20]

Anglo-French colonial rivalry for glory and wealth, inter alia, played itself out in Egypt. France's interest in Egypt was to deny Britain a shorter route to India to exploit the lucrative business in the Eastern trade. Acknowledging the French aims and strategy in Egypt, Britain mounted an opposition to France's ambition and sent its forces under the command of Lord Nelson to confront the French in Alexandria. In 1801, in an alliance with the Ottoman Turks, the British defeated Napoleon's forces—but not until after the French had introduced their culture, mechanics, engineers, architects, archeologists, academics, and others to the country.[21]

After the British and Turkish victory over France, there was confusion resulting from a power struggle in the country. In 1803, the British left Egypt, thereby relinquishing authority to the Ottomans. Nevertheless, a mutinous Albanian officer in the Turkish army named Muhammad Ali rebelled against the Ottoman leadership and seized power in 1805. He not only crowned himself Egypt's new leader, but also conferred on himself the title Khedive, or emperor. He led Egypt for 43 years and was pro–West in his foreign policy. Ali's sobriquet was "the father of modern Egypt" because of his political, economic, social, and educational development projects in the country.[22]

Ali's descendants governed Egypt until the middle of the 20th century.[23] Egypt's pro–West stance exposed it to the political vagaries of some Western powers—principally Britain and France. The country's indebtedness to these foreign countries weakened the society. In a country suffering from economic malaise, the opulent lifestyle of the ruling family in Egypt and Europe did not help matters either. British presence and power in the country grew so strong that London intervened in the nation's internal affairs to the chagrin of many Egyptian elites. The intrusions in Egypt's domestic affairs aroused anti–British sentiments and upheavals organized by political activists that culminated in British military invasion and takeover of the country in 1882.[24]

To assuage the activism of nationalists and prevent potential major anti–British revolts in the polity, Britain promised the public that its occupation was going to be short. Even so, following the Berlin Conference of 1884–85, European powers accepted British control over Egypt. It was, however, after the outbreak of World War I in 1914, that Britain fully declared Egypt its protectorate or colony. After the end of the war in 1918, Egyptian nationalists rose up to demand their freedom and one of the dramatis personae in the fight for self-rule was Saad Zaghlul. Egypt was granted limited or conditional home-rule on February 28, 1922, that allowed London to intervene militarily should the need arise.

In 1939, the outbreak of World War II necessitated the protection of Egypt from potential attack by the Axis—Germany, Japan, and Italy. At the end of the war in 1945, the Palestinian issue came to the fore. Indeed, in 1948, the United Nations partitioned Palestine into Arab and Jewish states—an arrangement that was snubbed by Arab countries. In attempts to nullify this

UN framework, Egypt joined forces with Iraq, Jordan, and Syria in a war against Israel. These countries were defeated to the dismay of Egypt—the major Arab country in this military attack against Israeli forces.[25]

Amongst Egyptian military officers, it was believed that the defeat of Egyptian forces by Israel was due in part to the lack of adequate war materiel to prosecute the battle. Thus, the king was blamed for ineffectively stocking Egypt's war arsenal. Colonel Gamal Abdel Nasser and a group of young military officers overthrew the king on July 23, 1952. This coup-d'état toppled the last monarch, King Farouk, thus ending the Albanian dynasty in Egypt.[26] This concise mosaic of historic events in Egypt provides a succinct overview of the past and politics of Egypt. It is against the preceding notable historic backdrop that I shall commence my analysis on human rights challenges in this chapter. Table I below is a comprehensive snapshot of human rights principles extracted from the 2014 constitution.

## Table I: 2014 Egyptian Constitution

### Chapter III: Public Rights, Freedoms and Duties

**Article 51: Human Dignity**—Dignity is a right for every person that may not be infringed upon. The state shall respect, guarantee and protect it.

**Article 52: Torture**—All forms of torture are a crime with no statute of limitations.

**Article 53: Equality in Public Rights and Duties**—Citizens are equal before the law, possess equal rights and public duties, and may not be discriminated against on the basis of religion, belief, sex, origin, race, color, language, disability, social class, political or geographical affiliation, or for any other reason. Discrimination and incitement to hate are crimes punishable by law. The state shall take all necessary measures to eliminate all forms of discrimination, and the law shall regulate the establishment of an independent commission for this purpose.

**Article 54: Personal Freedom**—Personal freedom is a natural right which is safeguarded and cannot be infringed upon. Except in cases of in flagrante delicto, citizens may only be apprehended, searched, arrested, or have their freedoms restricted by a causal judicial warrant necessitated by an investigation. All those whose freedoms have been restricted shall be immediately informed of the causes therefore, notified of their rights in writing, be allowed to immediately contact their family and lawyer, and be brought before the investigating authority within twenty-four hours of their freedoms having been restricted. Questioning of the person may only begin once his lawyer is present. If he has no lawyer, a lawyer will be appointed for him. Those with disabilities shall be provided all necessary aid, according to procedures stipulated in the law. Those who have their freedom restricted and others possess the right of recourse before the judiciary. Judgment must be rendered within a week from such recourse, otherwise the petitioner shall be immediately released. The law shall regulate preventive detention, its duration, causes, and which cases are eligible for compensation that the state shall discharge for preventative detention or for execution of a penalty that had been executed by virtue of a judgment that is overruled by a final judgment. In all cases, the accused may be brought to criminal trial for crimes that he may be detained for only in the presence of an authorized or appointed lawyer.

**Article 55: Due Process**—All those who are apprehended, detained or have their freedom restricted shall be treated in a way that preserves their dignity. They may not be tortured, terrorized, or coerced. They may not be physically or mentally harmed or arrested and confined in designated locations that are appropriate according to humanitarian and health standards. The state shall provide means of access for those with disabilities. Any violation of the above is a crime and the perpetrator shall be punished under the law. The accused possesses the right to remain silent. Any statement that is proven to have been given by the detainee under pressure of any of that which is stated above, or the threat of such, shall be considered null and void.

**Article 56: Supervision of Prisons**—Prison is a house for reform and rehabilitation. Prisons and detention centers shall be subject to judicial oversight. All that which violates the dignity of the person and or endangers his health is forbidden. The law shall regulate the provisions to reform and rehabilitate those who have been convicted, and to facilitate a decent life once they are released.

**Article 57: Private Life**—Private life is inviolable, safeguarded and may not be infringed upon. Telegraph, postal, and electronic correspondence, telephone calls, and other forms of communication are inviolable, their confidentiality is guaranteed, and they may only be confiscated, examined or monitored by causal judicial order, for a limited period of time, and in cases specified by the law. The state shall protect the rights of citizens to use all forms of public means of communication, which may not be arbitrarily disrupted, stopped or withheld from citizens, as regulated by the law.

**Article 58: Inviolability of Homes**—Homes are inviolable. Except in cases of danger, or if a call for help is made, they may not be entered, searched, monitored or wiretapped except by causal judicial warrant specifying the place, time and purpose thereof. All of the above is to be conducted in cases specified by the law, and in the manner prescribed. Upon entering or searching homes, those inside shall be notified and informed of the warrant issued in this regard.

**Article 59: Right to Safety**—Every person has the right to a secure life. The state shall provide security and reassurance for citizens, and all those residing within its territory.

**Article 60: Inviolability of the Human Body**—The human body is inviolable. Any assault, defilement or mutilation thereof is a crime punishable by law. Organ trafficking is forbidden, and no medical or scientific experiment may be performed thereon without the documented free consent of the subject, according to the established principles of the medical field as regulated by law.

**Article 61: Tissue and Organ Donation**—Donation of tissues and organs is a gift of life. Every human has the right to donate his body organs during his lifetime or after his death by virtue of a documented consent or will. The state commits to the establishment of a mechanism to regulate the rules for organ donation and transplant in accordance with the law.

**Article 62: Freedom of Movement**—Freedom of movement, residence and emigration is guaranteed. No citizen may be expelled from state territory or banned from returning thereto. No citizen may be banned from leaving state territory placed under house arrest or banned from residing in a certain area except by a causal judicial order for a specified period of time, and in cases specified by the law.

**Article 63: Force Migration**—All forms of arbitrary forced migration of citizens are forbidden. Violations of such are a crime without a statute of limitations.

**Article 64: Freedom of Belief**—Freedom of belief is absolute. The freedom of practicing religious rituals and establishing places of worship for the followers of revealed religions is a right organized by law.

**Article 65: Freedom of Thought**—Freedom of thought and opinion is guaranteed. All individuals have the right to express their opinion through speech, writing, imagery, or any other means of expression and publication.

**Article 66: Freedom of Research**—Freedom of scientific research is guaranteed. The state shall sponsor researchers and inventors and protect and work to apply their innovations.

**Article 67: Artistic and Literary Creation**—Freedom of artistic and literary creation is guaranteed. The state shall undertake to promote art and literature, sponsor creators and protect their creations, and provide the necessary means of encouragement to achieve this end. No lawsuits may be initiated or filed to suspend or confiscate any artistic, literary, or intellectual work, or against their creators except through the public prosecution. No punishments of custodial sanction may be imposed for crimes committed because of the public nature of the artistic, literal or intellectual product. The law shall specify the penalties for crimes related to the incitement of violence, discrimination between citizens, or impugning the honor of individuals. In such cases, the court may force the sentenced to pay punitive compensation to the party aggrieved by the crime, in addition to the original compensations due to him for the damages it caused him. All the foregoing takes place in accordance with the law.

**Article 68: Access to Information and Official Documents**—Information, data, statistics and official documents are owned by the people. Disclosure thereof from various sources is a right guaranteed by the state to all citizens. The state shall provide and make them available to citizens with transparency. The law shall organize rules for obtaining such, rules of availability and confidentiality, rules for depositing and preserving such, and lodging complaints against refusals to grant access thereto. The law shall specify penalties for withholding information or deliberately providing false information. State institutions shall deposit official documents with the National Library and Archives once they are no longer in use. They shall also protect them, secure them from loss or damage, and restore and digitize them using all modern means and instruments, as per the law.

**Article 69: Intellectual Property Rights**—The state shall protect all types of intellectual property in all fields and shall establish a specialized body to uphold the rights of Egyptians and their legal protection, as regulated by law.

**Article 70: Freedom of the Press**—Freedom of press and printing, along with paper, visual, audio and digital distribution is guaranteed. Egyptians—whether natural or legal persons, public or private—have the right to own and issue newspapers and establish visual, audio and digital media outlets. Newspapers may be issued once notification is given as regulated by law. The law shall regulate ownership and establishment procedures for visual and radio broadcast stations in addition to online newspapers.

**Article 71: Freedom of Publication**—It is prohibited to censor, confiscate, suspend or shut down Egyptian newspapers and media outlets in any way. Exception may be made for limited censorship in time of war or general mobilization. No custodial sanction shall be imposed for crimes committed by way of publication or the public nature thereof. Punishments for crimes connected with incitement to violence or discrimination amongst citizens or impugning the honor of individuals are specified by law.

**Article 72: Independence of Press Institutions**—The state shall ensure the independence of all press institutions and owned media outlets, in a way that ensures their neutrality and expressing all opinions, political and intellectual trends and social interests; and guarantees equality and equal opportunity in addressing public opinion.

**Article 73: Freedom of House**—Citizens have the right to organize public meetings, marches, demonstrations and all forms of peaceful protest, while not carrying weapons of any type, upon providing notification as regulated by law. The right to peaceful, private meetings is guaranteed, without the need for prior notification. Security forces may not attend, monitor or eavesdrop on such gatherings.

**Article 74: Freedom to Form Political Parties**—Citizens have the right to form political parties by notification as regulated by the law. No political activity may be exercised or political parties formed on the basis of religion, or discrimination based on sex, origin, sect or geographic location, nor may any activity be practiced that is hostile to democracy, secretive, or which possesses a military or quasi-military nature. Parties may only be dissolved by a judicial ruling.

**Article 75: Right to Establish Association**—Citizens have the right to form non-governmental organizations and institutions on a democratic basis, which shall acquire legal personality upon notification. They shall be allowed to engage in activities freely. Administrative agencies shall not interfere in the affairs of such organizations, dissolve them, their board of directors, or their board of trustees except by a judicial ruling. The establishment or continuation of non-governmental organizations and institutions whose structure and activities are operated and conducted in secret, or which possess a military or quasi-military character are forbidden, as regulated by law.

**Article 76: Right to Form Syndicates**—The establishment of federations and syndicates on a democratic basis is a right guaranteed by law. Such federations and syndicates will possess legal personality, be able to practice their activities freely, contribute to improving the skills of its members, defend their rights and protect their interests. The state guarantees the independence of all federations and syndicates. The boards of directors thereof may only be dissolved by a judicial ruling. Syndicates may not be established within governmental bodies.

**Article 77: Trade Unions**—The Law shall regulate the establishment and administration of professional syndicates on a democratic basis, guarantee their independence, and specify their resources and the way members are recorded and held accountable to ethical codes of moral and professional conduct. No profession may establish more than one syndicate. Receivership may not be imposed nor may administrative bodies intervene in the affairs of such syndicates, and their boards of directors may only be dissolved by a judicial ruling. All legislation pertaining to a given profession shall be submitted to the relevant syndicate for consultation.

**Article 78: Housing**—The state guarantees citizens the right to decent, safe and healthy housing, in a way that preserves human dignity and achieves social justice. The state shall draft a national housing plan that upholds environmental particularity and guarantees the contribution of personal and collaborative initiatives in its implementation. The state shall also regulate the use of state lands and provide them with basic facilities, as part of a comprehensive urban planning framework for cities and villages and a population distribution strategy. This must be done in a way that serves the public interest, improves the quality of life for citizens and preserves the rights of future generations. The state shall draft a comprehensive, national plan to address the problem of informal areas that includes providing infrastructure and facilities and improving quality of life and public health. The state shall also guarantee the provision of necessary resources to implement the plan within a specified time frame.

**Article 79: Food**—Each citizen has the right to healthy, sufficient amounts of food and clean water. The state shall provide food resources to all citizens. It also ensures food sovereignty in a sustainable manner and guarantees the protection of agricultural biological diversity and types of local plants to preserve the rights of generations.

**Article 80: Rights of the Child**—A child is considered to be anyone who has not reached 18 years of age. Children have the right to be named and possess identification papers, have access to free compulsory vaccinations, health and family care or an alternative, basic nutrition, safe shelter, religious education, and emotional and cognitive development. The state guarantees the rights of children who have disabilities, and ensures their rehabilitation and incorporation into society. The state shall care for children and protect them from all forms of violence, abuse, mistreatment and commercial and sexual exploitation. Every child is entitled to early education in a childhood center until the age of six. It is prohibited to employ children before they reach the age of having completed their primary education, and it is prohibited to employ them in jobs that expose them to risk. The state shall establish a judicial system for child victims and witnesses. No child may be held criminally responsible or detained except in accordance with the law and the time frame specified therein. Legal aid shall be provided to children, and they shall be detained in appropriate locations separate from adult detention centers. The state shall work to achieve children's best interest in all measures taken with regards to them.

**Article 81: Rights of the Disabled**—The state shall guarantee the health, economic, social, cultural, entertainment, sporting and education rights of dwarves and people with disabilities. The state shall provide work opportunities for such individuals, and allocate a percentage of these opportunities to them, in addition to equipping public utilities and their surrounding environment. The state guarantees their right to exercise political rights, and their integration with other citizens in order to achieve the principles of equality, justice and equal opportunities.

**Article 82: Youth**—The state guarantees the care of youth and young children, in addition to helping them discover their talents and developing their cultural, scientific, psychological, creative and physical abilities, encouraging them to engage in group and volunteer activity and enabling them to take part in public life.

**Article 83: The Elderly**—The state shall guarantee the health, economic, social, cultural and entertainment rights of the elderly, provide them with appropriate pensions to ensure them a decent standard of living, and empower them to participate in public life. The state shall take into account the needs of the elderly while planning public utilities. It also encourages civil society organizations to participate in caring for the elderly. All the foregoing takes place as organized by law.

**Article 84: Sports**—The state guarantees the right of everyone to practice physical sports. State institutions and society shall work to discover and sponsor gifted athletes and take necessary measures to encourage the practice of sport. The law shall regulate the affairs of sports and civil sports bodies in accordance with international standards, and how to settle sporting disputes.

**Article 85: Right to Address Public Authorities**—Each individual has the right to address public authorities in writing and in signature. No address shall be in the name of groups except for legal persons.

**Article 86: Duty to Safeguard National Security**—Preservation of national security is a duty, and the commitment of all to uphold such is a national responsibility ensured by law. Defense of the nation and protecting its land is an honor and sacred duty. Military service is mandatory according to the law.

**Article 87: Citizen Participation in Public Life**—The participation of citizens in public life is a national duty. Every citizen has the right to vote, run in elections, and express their opinion in referendums. The law shall regulate the exercise of these rights. Performance of these duties may be exempted in cases specified by the law. The state shall enter the name of every citizen in the voter registration database without request from the citizen himself, once the citizen meets voting requirements. The state shall also purge this database periodically in accordance with the law. The state guarantees the safety, neutrality and fairness of referendum and election procedures. The use of public funds, government agencies, public facilities, places of worship, business sector establishments and non-governmental organizations and institutions for political purposes and electioneering is forbidden.

**Article 88: Egyptians Living Abroad**—The state shall protect the interests of Egyptians living abroad, protect them, guarantee their rights and freedoms, enable them to perform their public duties towards the state and society, and engage them in the nation's development. The law shall regulate their participation in elections and referendums in a way consistent with their particular circumstances, without being restricted by the provisions on voting, counting of ballots and announcing of results set forth in this Constitution. This shall be done with the granting of guarantees that ensure the fairness and neutrality of the election and referendum process.

**Article 89: Slavery, Oppression, Trafficking**—Slavery and all forms of oppression and forced exploitation against humans are forbidden, as is sex trafficking and other forms of human trafficking, all of which are punishable by law.

**Article 90: Charitable Endowment**—The state shall encourage the charitable endowment system to establish and sponsor scientific, cultural, health, and social institutions and others and to ensure their independence. Its affairs shall be managed in accordance with the conditions set by the person who created the endowment. This will be regulated by law.

| |
|---|
| **Article 91: Asylum**—The state shall grant political asylum to any foreigner who has been persecuted for defending the interests of peoples, human rights, peace and justice. Extradition of political refugees is forbidden. All of the above is according to the law. |
| **Article 92: Limitation Clause**—Rights and freedoms of individual citizens may not be suspended or reduced. No law that regulates the exercise of rights and freedoms may restrict them in such a way as infringes upon their essence and foundation. |

Source: https://www.constituteproject.org/constitution/egypt_2014pdf (retrieved 8/20/17).

Few societies can be effectively administered, it is safe to contend, without a set of rules, codified or uncodified, outlining how political actors, civil servants and citizens are to conduct themselves within the society. For the most part, these written rules are important to advancing political stability and avoiding anarchy. Besides references to the institutions and structures, many constitutions contain special human rights provisions, including the Egyptian constitution. This is the case because the respect for human rights is critical in promoting peaceful coexistence within Egypt's political, ethnic and religious mosaic. Despite the impressive inclusion of human rights precepts in this constitution, however, research outputs and observations suggest that the guardians of the state and their representatives flout human rights provisions—often in pursuit of their insular interests. The extensive extract of the human rights tenets mined from the Egyptian constitution in Table I above provides an analytic tool with which to discuss, vis-à-vis other legal documents (e.g., penal code, Sharia laws, etc.), the human rights challenges in Egypt.

According to the 2015–16 Amnesty International Report on Egypt,

> The human rights situation [in Egypt] continued to deteriorate. The authorities arbitrarily restricted the rights to freedom of expression, association and peaceful assembly, enacted a draconian new anti-terrorism law, and arrested and imprisoned government critics and political opposition leaders and activists, subjecting some to enforced disappearance. The security forces used excessive force against protesters, refugees, asylum seekers and migrants. Detainees faced torture and other ill-treatment. Courts handed down hundreds of death sentences and lengthy prison sentences after grossly unfair mass trials. There was a critical lack of accountability; most human rights violations were committed with impunity. Women and members of religious minorities were subject to discrimination and inadequately protected against violence. People were arrested and tried on charges of "debauchery" for their perceived sexual orientation or gender identity. The army forcibly evicted communities from their homes along the border with Gaza. Executions were carried out following grossly unfair trials.[27]

Additionally, the U.S. Department of State 2015 human rights report is in accord with the above observations.[28] HRW accounts of 2015 enumerate the wanton violations of the rights of ordinary Egyptians, and add that Egypt's human rights crisis following the so-called Arab Spring revolution was the most serious in the annals of the nation-state's modern history.[29] It is around the foregoing human rights issues that I shall examine some pertinent human rights contraventions in Egypt.

## Respect for the Integrity of the Person and Freedom from Arbitrary or Unlawful Deprivation of Life

The flagrant violation of this provision of human rights is common in the republic. This is the case even though the constitution condemns it. There were several reports confirming the fact that arbitrary or unlawful killings happened in the process of conducting arrests, disbanding political activists, or remanding persons in custody.[30]

Human Rights Watch reports of 2014 and 2015 refer to the fact that security forces used excessive force to disband protests in early 2014 following the political instability that arose after the advent of the Arab Spring in North Africa. Indeed, HRW affirmed that "nearly 20 people, most of them Morsy [Morsi] supporters, died in clashes with police in the first three days of January. On January 25, the third anniversary of the 2011 uprising, at least 64 demonstrators died in conflicts with police in protests throughout the country."[31] The security forces responsible for the unrest in the country that led to the coup that overthrew President Mohammed Morsi were not arrested. An assumption here is that the government and its agencies are seldom enthusiastic about protecting the rights activists.[32] It is safe to contend, too, that such arbitrary and unlawful deprivation of life undertaken by proxies of the government is strategic. It is intended to discourage human rights activists from agitating for their rights in ways that threaten the political life of the government and its custodians.

Nevertheless, arbitrary or unlawful deprivation of life not only runs contrary to the spirit of the national constitution but also violates provisions on this matter in international human rights instruments. For example, Article 4 of the African Charter on Human and Peoples' Rights (ACHPR) proclaims: "Human beings are inviolable. Every human being shall be entitled to respect for his life and the integrity of his person. No one may be arbitrarily deprived of this right."[33] Article 6 of the International Covenant on Civil and Political Rights declares: "Every human being has the inherent right to life. This right shall be protected by law. No one shall be arbitrarily deprived of his [her] life."

## Torture and Other Cruel, Inhuman, or Degrading Treatment or Punishment

The international community underscores the above injunctions in several international human rights compacts and nation-states have done the same in their national constitutions. Little wonder, then, that for clarification, the United Nations Convention against Torture and Other Cruel, Inhuman or Degrading Treatment or Punishment provides a lucid definition of torture in Article 1. It states: "For the purposes of this Convention, the term 'torture' means any act by which severe pain or suffering, whether physical or mental, is intentionally inflicted on a person for such purposes as obtaining from him or a third person information or a confession."[34]

To emphasize the need to avoid torture in national politics, the Egyptian constitution deplores its application in Article 55 (see Table I). Additionally, Article 5 of the African Charter on Human and Peoples' Rights affirms: "Every individual shall have the right to the respect of the dignity inherent in a human being and to the recognition of his legal status. All forms of exploitation and degradation of man [and woman] particularly slavery, slave trade, torture, cruel, inhuman or degrading punishment and treatment shall be prohibited."[35] Article 7 of the International Covenant on Civil and Political Rights avers: "No one shall be subjected to torture or to cruel, inhuman or degrading treatment or punishment. In particular, no one shall be subjected without his [her] free consent to medical or scientific experimentation."[36] Article 5 of the Universal Declaration of Human Rights proclaims: "No one shall be subjected to torture or to cruel, inhuman or degrading treatment or punishment."[37]

Despite the inspiring condemnation of torture in the foregoing international human rights declarations—as well as in the Egyptian constitution— the use of torture to extract information from individuals persists. Indeed, the constancy of application of torture and or cruel, inhuman and degrading treatment and punishment in the politics of Egypt is peculiar. The state has allowed—may still allow—a form of torture known as "rendition." Rendition is a practice in which nations that legally or legislatively condemn the practice of torture could send a culprit to Egypt for torment. This practice happened when Egypt received captured terrorists alleged to have committed terrorist acts against the West during the epoch of the "War on Terror." Egypt tormented these radicals and did so for information gathering in return for compensation from the U.S. I will highlight some special examples of cases of arrested citizens to illustrate this dimension of rights and the challenges they present for Egypt in the following dialogue.

A 2016 Amnesty International report notes the activities of the fearsome National Security Agency (NSA) in abducting, torturing and holding many Egyptians incommunicado as a stratagem to intimidate opponents of the government and suppress peaceful dissent. In the guise of the War on Terror, NSA is known to have arrested "hundreds of students, political activists and protesters, including children as young as 14."[38] These tortured political agitators and purported enemies of the state are said to have vanished and were declared to have never existed in society at all.[39]

Human Rights Watch reports that on July 1, 2015, a special constabulary acting on tips from the MOI's National Security Agency attacked an apartment in a Cairo suburb and murdered nine Muslim Brotherhood officials. The regime said the nine belonged to a "special operation committee" and died during the exchange of gunshots.[40] HRW disputed the state's account, affirming that the deaths were extra-juridical executions, and presented an anthology of reports on this matter thus:

> At least 90 people died in local police stations and security directorates in the governorates of Cairo and Giza alone in 2014.... That number represented a 38 percent increase from the year before.[41]
> National Security officers were responsible for dozens of enforced disappearances, often targeting political activists. Human Rights Watch documented the cases of five forced disappearances ... between April 2014 and June 2015. Three of these cases resulted in death. The Egyptian human rights group Freedom for the Brave documented 164 enforced disappearances between April and June.[42]
> Between August 2015 and August 2016, the Egyptian Commission for Rights and Freedoms, an independent group, documented 912 victims of enforced disappearance.[43]

Furthermore, arbitrary arrests and detentions, enforced disappearances, torture and other ill-treatment of individuals happened with reckless abandon in 2015. In 2014 (22,000) and 2015 (11,877) alleged members of terrorist groups—many said to be sympathizers with the dreaded and vilified Muslim Brotherhood—were arrested. In addition, convicts held by the powerful state security forces and military intelligence were tortured. They were subjected to electric shocks, beating with fists, whips, and rifle butts, sexual assault, attack by dogs, and forced standing for hours on end. Security forces frequently took pleasure in flogging detainees at the time of their arrest and when transferring them between police stations and prisons. In some cases, there were reports of deaths in custody because of torture and other ill-treatment and lack of access to adequate medical care.[44]

## Prison and Detention Center Conditions

Prisons and detention centers in much of the developing world are designed for punishment purposes and not for rehabilitation, as is frequently the situation in the Occident. Retribution, it is hoped, is a necessary way of returning convicts to social righteousness. Even so, it is a fallacy or inadequate theory that punishment in these facilities will discourage prisoners from returning to crime. Consequently, conditions in these institutions in Egypt, as in much of Africa, are harsh and potentially life-threatening due in part to overcrowding, physical abuse, inadequate medical care, and poor infrastructure.[45]

Furthermore, the U.S. Department of State Bureau of Democracy, Human Rights, and Labor observed that prison cells were congested, and that convicts had inadequate access to medical care, proper sanitation, food, and potable water. Such unhealthy conditions facilitate the spread of tuberculosis and other communicable diseases. Prison temperatures were uncontrolled and the lighting system grossly inadequate. Moreover, prison guards mistreated prisoners, including juveniles in adult facilities, frequently. Custodial conditions for women were relatively better than jail situations for men. Even so, some unscrupulous prison guards violated women's human rights in the prisons. In response, several inmates demonstrated against their appalling conditions, using hunger strikes as a weapon of protest. Such was the case at Aqrab Prison in December 2015.[46] However, the state and its agencies ignored these protests in a society that despises crimes and felons. After all, most ordinary Egyptian citizens with no criminal records lack the amenities that convicts demand, and it would be imprudent to supply these services to prisoners—who are generally seen as depraved citizens in the society.

Mass arrests and application of pretrial imprisonment in 2015 made more severe the harsh conditions and congestion in prisons, resulting in deaths in prisons and detention centers. In June 2015, the National Council for Human Rights (NCHR) reported that jail populations attained 160 percent of maximum capacity and police station detention centers exploded to 300 percent of maximum capacity.[47] Health care provisions in jails were inadequate and problematic, leading to the deaths of many prisoners from conceivably curable natural causes. In this instance, relatives of some deceased convicts maintain that top prison administrators and staffs deliberately denied their loved ones in jail access to life-saving medical care. In other cases, staff members of the prisons denied appeals to transfer prisoners to the hospital sometimes on the basis that non-convicted citizens do not have such rights. In short, why, then, should convicted anti-social agitators and troublemakers be accorded rights at all?

## *Respect for Civil Liberties: Freedom of Speech and Press*

The constitution contains a corpus of articles that relate to freedom of speech and press. For example, Article 65 (freedom of thought), Article 70 (freedom of the press), Article 71 (freedom of publication), and Article 72 (independence of press institutions) are spot on with respect to civil liberties (see Table I). Egypt as a signatory to relevant international human rights instruments furthers the republic's notional commitment to media freedom. For example, Article 19 of the Universal Declaration of Human Rights avers:

"Everyone has the right to freedom of opinion and expression; this right includes freedom to hold opinions without interference and to seek, receive and impart information and ideas through any media and regardless of frontiers."[48] Article 19 of the International Covenant on Civil and Political Rights affirms reassuringly:

1. Everyone shall have the right to hold opinions without interference.

2. Everyone shall have the right to freedom of expression; this right shall include freedom to seek, receive and impart information and ideas of all kinds, regardless of frontiers, either orally, in writing or in print, in the form of art, or through any other media of his [or her] choice.

3. The exercise of the rights provided for in paragraph 2 of this article carries with it special duties and responsibilities. It may therefore be subject to certain restrictions, but these shall only be such as are provided by law and are necessary:

    a. For respect of the rights or reputations of others;
    For the protection of national security or of public order (ordre public), or of public health or morals.[49]

Nonetheless, the foregoing theories are superb on paper but in terms of their practicality in Egyptian society, they are problematic. This reality brings to the fore the clash between theory and practice in my contemplation. Accordingly, I will briefly highlight in a summary some of the conflicts between the preceding theories of rights to freedom of speech and the press, and the problems of enforcement in my subsequent discussions. This task will be done by illustrating rights violations instead of rights implementations. Indeed, Amnesty International reported that journalists working for groups critical of the government and its agents and agencies, or that have connections with opposition factions, were constantly intimidated with prosecution. Media personnel were harassed for reporting "fake news" and on other alleged politically inspired felonious acts. In such a tense scenario between state officials and the media, journalists and social and political activists faced arrests, trial and imprisonment on indictments that included provoking or participating in demonstrations and spreading "false rumors" aimed at defaming officials and damaging national morality.[50] Court judges, often appointed by the government, sent some of the journalists to long-term incarceration. In addition, citizens frequently faced prosecution for "defaming religion," especially Islam, and deprecating "public morals" when they asserted their rights to freedom of expression.[51] The state's legislative sermon is that the sacrosanctity of religion must always be borne in mind when writing on sensitive theological matters. So, such issues ought to be outside the purview and scrutiny of the press because they are explosive. In short, citizens, journalists, and human rights campaigners must avoid comments considered by the authorities as blasphemous to the religion.

To muzzle freedom of speech and the press, AI reported, on April 11, 2015, a court in Cairo sentenced 14 opposition-linked journalists to 25-year prison terms after convicting them of broadcasting false news. The court also sentenced another journalist to death for allegedly forming media committees and leading and funding a banned group.[52] On May 1, 2016, security officers stormed the Press Syndicate in Cairo and detained journalists Amr Badr and Mahmoud al-Saqqa on charges of inciting protests and publishing false rumors in violation of Article 71 (paragraph 2) of the national constitution (see Table I).

Human Rights Watch also expressed concerns that law enforcement agents incarcerated dozens of citizens for relatively mundane transgressions such as possessing flyers with anti-military catchphrases and rapping in public against the police.[53] On July 28, 2016, a Cairo Court for minor misconduct sentenced Hisham Geneina, Egypt's erstwhile top fraud overseer, for circulating false information. This ex-civil servant received a one-year suspended jail sentence. In May 2016, security forces detained four members of the Street Children satire group who had the audacity to post videos on YouTube that mocked President Abdel Fattah el-Sisi and his government's oppressive and intolerable policies. Also, a novelist, Ahmed Naji, was sentenced to a two-year jail term for what the prosecution termed "sexually explicit" content in his book titled *Using Life*. This book was deemed sacrilegious because excerpts in the novel appeared in a newspaper.[54] Paradoxically, the state's foregoing actions violate the tenets of Articles 70, 71, and 72 of the national constitution (see Table I).

In human rights dialogue, the U.S. Department of State's account on freedom of speech, expression and human rights in Egypt is comprehensive and poignant. Admittedly, citizens expressed their views on a wide range of political and social topics. However, they did so—and still do so—at their own risk—i.e., individuals and groups must know where to draw the line to avoid the wrath of the government and human rights abuses from the security forces. Commonly,

> the government investigated and prosecuted critics for alleged incitement of violence, insults to religion, or insults to public figures and institutions, such as the judiciary and the military. Individuals also faced societal and official harassment for speech viewed as sympathetic to the [much maligned] MB [Muslim Brotherhood], such as using a hand gesture showing four fingers, a reference to the 2013 security operation to disperse the sit-in at Rabaa al-Adawiya Square.[55]

Counterterrorism laws are broad in scope and they include, among other factors, "any act harming national unity or social peace." Human rights activists continue to affirm great trepidation that authorities could use the vague description and explication of what terrorism means to suffocate non-violent speech and nonviolent opposition activity. For instance, indigenous and international rights campaigners reported increased indictments under the blasphemy law, principally targeting minority Christians and atheists. It was within this context that a misdemeanor court sentenced 21-year-old student Karim El Banna to three years' detention for denigrating Islam. This conviction happened in the wake of a post on Facebook supporting a campaign titled "Professing Atheism."[56]

State agencies curtail the freedom of the press and media despite provisions in the constitution protecting such rights. To limit media freedoms, the authorities control their licensing and monitor the printing and delivery of most newspapers, including private newspapers and especially those of opposition political factions.[57] To counter information harmful to the government's interest, State Information Services embarked on an initiative called Fact Check Egypt aimed primarily at "censoring" foreign journalists.

Violence and harassment are common tactics applied by government agents and agencies for intimidating journalists and in the process violating their constitutional and civic rights to interrogate and report news items. Human rights violations include prohibiting journalists from covering the polling process, arrests, damaging journalists' equipment, and verbal assault to prevent them from uncovering embarrassing electoral malfeasance.[58]

## Rights to Peaceful Assembly and Association

The above rights—peaceful assembly and association—are sanctioned in international human rights declarations to which Egypt is a signatory. The ACHPR declares in Article 10(1): "Every individual shall have the right to free association provided that he abides by the law." Article 11 of the ACHPR also proclaims: "Every individual shall have the right to assemble freely with others. The exercise of this right shall be subject only to necessary restrictions provided for by law in particular those enacted in the interest of national security, the safety, health, ethics and rights and freedoms of others."[59] Article 20(1) of the UDHR affirms: "Everyone has the right to freedom of peaceful assembly and association," and Article 20(2) states: "No one may be compelled to belong to an association."

The ICCPR, in Articles 21 and 22, provides a comprehensive menu and explanations of rights to peaceful assembly and association accordingly:

> Article 21: The right of peaceful assembly shall be recognized. No restrictions may be placed on the exercise of this right other than those imposed in conformity with the law and which are necessary in a democratic society in the interests of national security or public safety, public order (ordre public), the protection of public health or morals or the protection of the rights and freedoms of others.

Article 22: 1. Everyone shall have the right to freedom of association with others, including the right to form and join trade unions for the protection of his [her] interests.

2. No restriction may be placed on the exercise of this right other than those which are prescribed by law and which are necessary in a democratic society in which the interests of national security or public safety, public order (ordre public), the protection of public health or morals or the protection of the rights and freedoms of others. **This article shall not prevent the imposition of lawful restrictions on members of the armed forces and of the police** [emphasis mine] in their exercise of this right.

3. Nothing in this article shall authorize States Parties to the International Labour Organisation Convention of 1948 concerning freedom of association and protection of the right to organize to take legislative measures which would prejudice, or to apply the law in such a manner as to prejudice, the guarantees provided for in that Convention.[60]

The Egyptian constitution, especially in Article 75 (see Table I), provides for the foregoing freedoms. Yet, Egypt implemented a 2013 demonstrations law that comprises an extensive list of banned actions and grants the Minister of Interior the authority to forbid or cut down on planned protests. This law was not and is not in conformity with international norms regarding freedom of assembly as stated in the preceding international human rights documents. The problem is that commonly, the government restricts those demonstrations that it deems anti-social and anti-government even when the protests are peaceful. Indeed, thousands of citizens remained in custody who were detained in 2013 and 2014 because of their partaking in protests. In short, they were deemed provocateurs for exercising their rights. Human rights activists frequently condemned such government denial of the rights to assembly or association because they are rights guaranteed in the constitution and international human rights compacts sanctioned by Egypt.[61]

Human Rights Watch has documented a series of activities that run contrary to the rights to peaceful assembly and association. In September 2014, HRW affirmed that President el-Sisi signed a revision to the penal code. The amendment to the code decrees a life sentence and a financial penalty of 500,000 Egyptian pounds (U.S. $69,900) to any individual or group that accepts foreign funding that could harm the national interests of the country. Civil society groups' operational efficacy suffered since the fiat froze their external support. This was especially the case with respect to human rights NGOs that relentlessly expose human rights violations in the country. To strengthen the policy of checking the activities of human rights NGOs, the Social Solidarity Ministry in 2014 wrote a law on associations. This regulation gives the government security agencies veto power over NGO operations and authority to monitor the sources of their funding.[62]

Subsequently, in 2016 a Cairo criminal court—an extension of the government—accepted an appeal from a panel of investigative judges to freeze the resources of three groups and the personal properties of five citizens who founded or led popular human rights groups. In addition, Parliament, in attempts to curb the vexatious activities of human rights activities in the country, quickly approved a new piece of legislation. This regulation, without public discourse or input from the civil society, was aimed at abolishing or limiting NGO human rights work in the republic. This law will place all NGOs under the supervision and veto power of a council controlled by aficionados of the General Intelligence Service and the Interior and the Defense Ministries, with the power to break up any real or imagined culpable NGOs.[63] Such a development highlights one of the numerous human rights challenges that the regime confronts and may continue to confront in Egypt.

## Freedom of Religion

Article 2 of the 2014 constitution proclaims: "Islam is the religion of the state and Arabic is its official language. The principles of Islamic Sharia are the principal source of legislation." Article 3 addresses the situation of Christian and Jewish populations in the society thus: "The principles of the laws of Egyptian Christians and Jews are the main source of laws regulating their personal status, religious affairs, and selection of spiritual leaders." In other words, Egyptian Christians and practitioners of Judaism are bona fide citizens and could practice their religious orthodoxies freely. However, Islamic jurisprudence as represented in the Sharia is the law of the land and supreme on matters of culture, state and politics. Accordingly, it would be difficult, if not impossible, for Egyptians who are non–Muslims to be elected president of the republic—a problematic issue in human rights philosophy because it smacks of prejudice.

To be sure, there are numerous non–Muslim religions groupings in Egypt. Some are not recognized and therefore marginalized in the society. Demographically,

approximately 90 percent of the population is Sunni Muslim and approximately 10 percent Christian (estimates range from 5 percent to 15 percent). Approximately 90 percent of Christians belong to the Coptic Orthodox Church.... Other Christian communities together constitute less than 2 percent of the population and include the Armenian Apostolic, Catholic (Armenian, Chaldean, Melkite, Maronite, Greek, Roman, and Syrian), Orthodox (Greek and Syrian), Anglican/Episcopalian, and Protestant Churches, which range in size from several thousand to hundreds of thousands. The Protestant community includes Presbyterians, Baptists, Brethren, Open Brethren, Seventh-day Adventists....
Shia Muslims range from 800,000 to two million.... There are also small groups of Quranists and Ahmadi Muslims....

There are many foreign resident adherents of various religious groups, including Roman Catholics, Protestants, and members of The Church of Jesus Christ of
Latter-day Saints (Mormons).[64]

Challengingly, the state confronted several political issues when President
Anwar Sadat tactically embraced Islam and Islamists as a counterbalance to
the political force and threat of the ideological left. This political maneuver
in the society fortuitously augmented human rights problems in the 1970s.[65]
The political marriage between Sadat and religion empowered Islamists in
the polity. These extremists intermittently unleashed mayhem on "unbe-
lievers" that violated the human rights of members of other religious communities. The overzealous dogmatic activities of Islamists in the country
were, and frequently are, carried out in violations of tenets in the national
constitution and international human rights declarations regarding freedom
of religion.

Specifically, Article 53 of the state's constitution, under the category of
equality in public rights and duties, shines light on the principle that no one
in the republic should be discriminated against based on religion (see Table
I). Article 8 of the African Charter on Human and Peoples' Rights avers,
"Freedom of conscience, the profession and free practice of religion shall be
guaranteed. No one may, subject to law and order, be submitted to measures
restricting the exercise of these freedoms."[66] Article 18 of the UDHR avows,
"Everyone has the right to freedom of thought, conscience and religion; this
right includes freedom to change his [her] religion or belief, and freedom,
either alone or in community with others and in public or private, to manifest
his religion or belief in teaching, practice, worship and observance."[67] Article
18 of the ICCPR on religious freedom applies, mutatis mutandis, to Article 18
of the UDHR.[68]

Article 64 (see Table I) of the constitution describes freedom of belief
as "absolute" but only provides adherents of Islam, Christianity, and Judaism
the right to practice their religion freely and to build houses of worship. The
government, in violation of Article 18 of both the UDHR and ICCPR, loathes
conversion from Islam by citizens born Muslim to any other religion and
levies serious penalties on Muslim-born citizens who dare to convert to other
religions. To add power to the preceding dogma, the constitution in Article 2
decrees Islam as the state religion and the principles of Sharia as the primary
source of legislation, as noted earlier. Parliament is responsible for passing
laws on the construction and renovation of Christian churches. This legislative power remains a real source of contention between the government and
the primordial Christian Coptic Church. This is so partly because the licen-
sure rules allow the government to deny church building permits to Copts,
for example. This procedure is problematic and irritating to Copts who have
limited or no ways to seek redress when denial of permits happens. Such

strict rules do not apply to issuance of certificates for building mosques.[69] In response to government's actions on this matter, Coptic communities frequently resort to constructing churches without a license. On occasion, the defiance by Copts over such discriminatory practice has led to conflicts between Muslims and Coptic Christians.

The government occasionally failed to respond or was tepid in its response to religious violence, especially outside of major urban areas, and this has led to disastrous consequences.[70] However, civil servants frequently participated in informal "reconciliation sessions" to tackle episodic religious violence and tension. Officials contend that such meetings barred additional riots. Nevertheless, some of these well-intended meetings have occasionally led to fallout harmful to minority parties.[71] It is worth noting, however, that government and religious institutions responded positively to President el-Sisi's call for tolerance with some efforts to limit sectarianism and violence. It is true in Egypt that, for the most part, far-right and conservative Muslim activists are culpable of prejudice against minority religious factions. Even so, the government is occasionally proactive in advancing peaceful coexistence between the sects in the republic. Such was the case when the armed forces completed the reconstruction of 26 of the 78 churches and other Christian properties incinerated by Islamist mobs. Muslim extremists have displaced their frustrations on Christians following the political demise of the Muslim Brotherhood–led régime in 2013.[72] Despite this gesture at promoting harmony between Muslims and Christians in the society, the bombing on December 11, 2016, of a church in the Cairo cathedral complex was unnerving. This church is the seat of the Coptic pope. The Egyptian regime blamed the Muslim Brotherhood for blasting the basilica. This assault on the church created problems in the country on the question of freedom of worship and intolerance toward minority religious sects.[73]

In sum, the constitution specifies Islam as the state religion and the primacy of the doctrine of Sharia as the source of legislation; also, the constitution confines the freedom to practice religious rituals to adherents of Islam, Christianity, and Judaism—the divine religions—leaving other religions and their rights to practice their faiths in limbo. Although neither the constitution nor the civil or penal codes ban efforts to proselytize Muslims, conversion from Islam to another religion is apostasy and prohibited based on the Sharia's pedagogy and instructions. Suffice it to say, however, that a 2008 ruling allowed for conversion from Islam to other religions for individuals who were not born Muslim but later converted to Islam. This process can be explained within the context of what I term the "theory of reversion." In keeping with Sharia laws, non–Muslim men must convert to Islam to marry Muslim women, although non–Muslim women need not convert to marry Muslim men—arguably a case of gender discrimination.[74] A non–Muslim woman who converts to Islam must divorce her husband if he is not Muslim and is unwilling to convert. The preceding doctrinal regulations are antithetical to the human rights principle of equivalent rights for men and women. Article 16 of the UDHR and Article 23 of the ICCPR affirm the equal rights for men and women on this matter. For example, as noted previously, Article 16 of the UDHR declares, "Men and women of full age, without any limitation due to race, nationality or religion, have the right to marry and to found a family. They are entitled to equal rights as to marriage, during marriage and at its dissolution."

According to Article 98(f) of the Egyptian penal code, exploiting religion to promote extremist thought with the aim of inciting strife, denigrating any of the divine religions, which are Islam, Christianity and Judaism, and harming national unity carry penalties ranging from six months' to five years' incarceration.[75] At the pastoral level, this law, however, is not always judiciously applied. Overall, because Egypt is an Islamic state the conflict between its religious regulations and human rights principles can be striking, and yet peculiar. For example,

> the law does not recognize the Bahai Faith or its religious laws and bans Bahai institutions and community activities....
>
> The government has the authority to appoint and monitor imams who lead prayers in licensed mosques and pays their salaries. According to law, penalties for preaching Islam without a license include a prison term of up to one year and/or a fine of up to 50,000 Egyptian pounds (EGP) ($6,390) for preaching or giving religious lessons without a license from the Ministry of Awqaf (Religious Endowments) or Al-Azhar....
>
> The government recognizes only the marriages of Christians, Jews, and Muslims. Since the state does not recognize Bahai marriage, married Bahais are denied the legal rights of married couples of other religious beliefs, including those pertaining to inheritance [and] divorce.[76]

## Government Practices and Religious Minorities: An Overview

The régime and law enforcement agencies are generally reluctant to stop, examine, or prosecute misconduct targeting members of religious minority groups. This pattern of behavior, sometimes driven by political considerations, fosters an environment of impunity, as suggested by local human rights groups and activists working in the country.[77] Authorities are frequently unsuccessful in protecting Christians targeted by kidnappers and extortionists. Problematically, evidence suggests that law enforcement officials are sometimes unenthusiastic in responding to these criminalities, especially in Upper Egypt. Even though the state sporadically prosecutes citizens for denigrating religion, some minority religious assemblies continue to face harassment from fanatic religious officials. Some aficionados, mainly those at the powerful Al-Azhar, malign the religious freedoms of Shia and Bahais, for example. Politically, the administration sometimes expediently acquiesces to anti–Semitic speeches, too.[78]

The Ministry of Social Solidarity (MOSS), the organ of the government that oversees NGOs' registration, declared on May 6, 2015 the creation of a commission whose function would be that of investigating NGOs that ostensibly practice or promote Shia religious rites. The perennial Sunni-Shia religious antagonisms, based partially on pedagogic orthodoxy of theology, possibly led to the creation of this commission. The law regulating NGOs prohibits the establishment of unions or federations for religious purposes. Parenthetically, on May 19, 2015, police raided an NGO run by Shia community leader Taher El-Hashemi. This invasion happened after security officers received information that this NGO was proselytizing for Shia Islam and broadcasting its sermons without a proper license. The police confiscated books that purportedly incited hatred against Sunni Islam and promoted Shia articles of faith. The Shia leader, El-Hashemi, was in custody briefly, but his religious freedom was abrogated. However, his release came about after he and his followers had learned a hard lesson—not to preach.[79]

For five years in a row, authorities annulled a yearly Jewish pilgrimage, which included the involvement of several Israeli citizens, to the monument of 19th-century scholar Rabbi Yaakov Abu Hassira. The annulment happened following an official court decision to prohibit forever the Abu Hassira festival in December 2014. The court defended its decision by affirming that the annual festival or jubilee was a "violation of public order and morals" and "incompatible with the solemnity and purity of religious sites."[80]

The human rights problems that many minorities confront in all societies, and in all regions of the world, can be daunting and this situation is more telling in much of the developing nations, especially those with scarce resources. Ethnicity, religion and gender are some of the elements employed by dominant groups to marginalize minorities politically, economically and socially. States sometimes apply ethnicity, religion and gender to violate minorities' human rights.[81] Therefore, it is not confounding that in Egypt,

> the government discriminated against religious minorities in public sector hiring and staff appointments to public universities…. No Christians served as presidents of the country's 17 public universities and few Christians occupied dean or vice dean positions in the public university system. Only Muslims could study at Al-Azhar University, a publicly funded institution. Additionally, the government barred non–Muslims from employment in public university training programs for Arabic language teachers because the curriculum involves study of the Quran.
>
> The total number of members of parliament was 596, of whom 568 were elected … and 28 were appointed by President Sisi. Thirty-six Christians were elected to parliament.[82]

The above excerpt demonstrates the existence of bias toward minority religious groups; it illustrates the violations of the human rights of non–Muslims to fair employment in the universities and adequate participation in government; it also brings to the limelight the incongruities that exist between theory and practice in human rights observance in the republic, borne in part by religious bigotry. Put in another way, while the constitution and international human rights conventions forbid, notionally, bigotry in almost all its forms, the practice of rights principles is problematical due to the conflicting provision of government laws and citizens' human rights. For example, Article 23(1) of the UDHR states: "Everyone has the right to work, to free choice of employment, to just and favorable conditions of work and to protection against unemployment." Article 23(2) declares: "Everyone, without any discrimination, has the right to equal pay for equal work."[83] Article 1(1) of the International Labor Organization (ILO) defines discrimination to include "any distinction, exclusion, or preference made on the basis of race, colour, sex, religion, political opinion, national extraction or social origin which has the effect of nullifying or impairing equality of opportunity or treatment in employment or occupation."[84] Article 53 of the national constitution synchronizes with the preceding ILO precept.

## Women: Discrimination and Societal Abuses

That women suffer from social, economic and political bias in virtually all societies, in all regions of the world, is a given. Accordingly, in contemporary deliberations on prejudice against women the emphasis has been on how to improve the foregoing conditions so that women will enjoy equivalent rights with men. Ironically, in international protocols, conventions, and national constitutions references to the theoretical equality of men and women are bold and inspiring. However, the actual practice of these declarations has been deficient globally; and, this antinomy is more poignant in Islamic states of the global south, where the clash between theories of human rights and practice thereof is highly conspicuous.

For instance, Article 18(3) of the ACHPR declares, "The State shall ensure the elimination of every discrimination against women and also ensure the protection of the rights of the woman and the child as stipulated in international declarations and conventions."[85] Article 3 of the ICCPR affirms: "The States Parties to the present Covenant undertake to ensure the equal right of men and women to the enjoyment of all civil and political rights set forth in the present Covenant."[86] The preamble of the UDHR proclaims, inter alia, "The peoples of the United Nations have in the Charter reaffirmed their faith in fundamental human rights, in the dignity of and worth of the human person and in the equal rights of men and women and have determined to promote social progress and better standards of life in larger freedoms."[87] Further, the UDHR avers emphatically in Article 1: "All human beings are born free and equal in dignity and rights."[88]

The Egyptian constitution, under Article 1, affirms that all citizens "are equal in rights, freedoms, and general duties without discrimination based on religion, belief, gender, origin, race, color, language, disability, social class ... or any other reason."[89] In Egypt, the foregoing principles are sound on paper; the issue, though, is enforcement; this situation again brings to the fore the inconsistency between theory and practice on human rights matters in the country. Consequently, the question is, to what extent has Egypt lived up to its constitutional and international obligations of respecting the human rights of women in the polity? In response to the preceding query, I shall highlight some major aspects of women's rights that the state has failed to uphold despite tenets in its constitution asserting these rights for women. The hope is that by doing so, the state will be encouraged to do more to observe these rights.

## Rape and Domestic Violence

Yahia Salah El Hadidi has noted in an illuminating study, "Violence against Women in Egypt: A Review of Domestic Violence and Female Genital Mutilation,"[90] that

> most married women in Egypt agree that husbands are at least sometimes justified in beating their wives. 86% of ever-married women agree that husbands are justified in beating their wives in some situations. The women are most likely to agree that a man is justified in beating his wife if she refuses sex or answers him back, though they are less likely to agree he is justified in doing so if she burns the food.[91]

In a survey published by the UN in 2013, more than 99 percent of women and girls interviewed reported that they had experienced some form of sexual pestering. There have been a handful of convictions since the introduction of a new law that makes sexual harassment a crime punishable by a minimum of one year in prison.[92] Additionally, unmarried women and girls confront violence on an alarming scale domestically and in public—not to mention sexual mob assaults and torture in state penitentiaries. Concerned about the human rights violations on this matter, Circles of Hell, a civic group, published a distressing report exposing the breaches of women's rights. This group acted partly because of weak Egyptian laws intended to stop the practices and culture of routine sexual and gender-related violence that are present in the republic.[93]

In response to this concern, the regime announced some measures to tackle the issue, including the introduction of a law criminalizing sexual harassment. To further the government's aims of solving this problem, the MOI includes an agency responsible for fighting sexual and gender-based violence. The National Council for Women (NCW), a quasi-governmental body, was set up to add more oomph to the crusade for combating violence against women and gender-based violence. This group is responsible for harnessing and coordinating the government and civil society strategies to improve the conditions of women in the society. Indeed, the NCW undertook a 5-year national strategy to fight violence against women with four bold strategic aims: **prevention, protection, intervention,** and **prosecution.**[94] The MOI appointed Brigadier General Nahed Salah, a female warrior, to tackle the incidence of violence against women. Lamentably, although some might say pragmatically, Salah's measured counsel and solution for women, in the campaign against violence toward women, was to "avoid talking or laughing loudly in public and to be cautious about how they dress to avoid street harassment [by boys and men]."[95] These rational recommendations were and are only good on paper. The execution of the fight against violence toward women lacked enthusiasm, with no follow-up.[96]

Moreover, President Abdel Fattah el-Sisi's public commitments to abolish violence against women in the republic have come to naught; his pledges are not yet translated—and may not be converted—into a consistent and sustainable strategy for eliminating violence against women.[97] In the society, overall, political actors are expediently ignoring the problem and skillfully dodging important reforms critical for efficiently mitigating violence against women.

## Discrimination

It is a fact that there exist engrained discriminatory attitudes toward women despite the state's constitutional provisions forbidding prejudice. Women in Egypt, as elsewhere in the developed and developing world, continue to face extensive societal discrimination, threats to their physical safety, and workplace prejudice. Prejudicial injustices tend to favor men but impede women's social and economic advancement. The constitution provides for equal rights for male and female citizens. Yet, in the administration of the republic women still do not effectively enjoy the same legal rights and opportunities as men; and, in the state, bigotry continues to be ubiquitous. Some aspects of the law and traditional practices endure to disadvantage women in family, social, and economic life despite attempts to change some of these cultural norms by legislation.

For example, laws affecting matrimony and personal status commonly correspond to an individual's religious affiliation. A female Muslim citizen cannot legally marry a non–Muslim man, as noted previously. Woe betides a

Muslim woman who does so; she will face weighty societal harassment and ostracism. "Khula" divorce allows a Muslim woman to obtain a divorce without her husband's consent; in this scheme, however, she will have to relinquish all her financial rights, including alimony, dowry, and other benefits. The Coptic Orthodox Church allows divorce only in exceptional circumstances that include adultery or conversion of one spouse to another religious congregation.

Women face widespread and inordinate discrimination in the labor force. Bigotry flouts national and international conventions on women's rights. For example, Article 53 of the national constitutions (see Table I) repudiates prejudice in the labor force. Article 15 of the ACHPR affirms emphatically: "Every individual shall have the right to work under equitable and satisfactory conditions, and shall receive equal pay for equal work."[98] Article 7a (1) of the International Covenant on Economic, Social and Cultural Rights calls for "fair wages and equal remuneration for work of equal value without distinction of any kind ... with equal pay for equal work."[99]

Notionally, labor laws promote the dictum of equal rates of pay for equal work for men and women in the public establishments but not the private sector. In 2014, the World Economic Forum discovered that the country's women received "78 percent of the income of their male counterparts."[100] Educated women have employment opportunities. Nevertheless, socio-cultural pressure against women pursuing a career is strong. Women's rights activists argue that religious impact, coupled with traditional and social attitudes and practices, constrains further gains for women. Apropos the foregoing assumptions is the perceived threat to some men's egos when women are highly successful in traditional societies and settings. Some, if not most, men abhor the prospect of playing the second fiddle in the household, if their spouse is intellectually and financially superior to them. This condition can be socially difficult and emotional in a country in which men see themselves as breadwinners and authoritative heads of the household.

The military controls large and important segments of the country's economy. The armed forces exclude women from high-level positions. Women are discouraged from serving as warriors. Consequently, they have limited access to high-paying jobs that are open to men. Women may serve—frequently as nurses—in the medical corps of the armed forces. The system excludes them from compulsory military service—a shared practice in much of the developing world.

## Female Genital Mutilation/Cutting (FGM/C)

By definition, female genital mutilation/cutting is a "procedure involving partial or total removal of the external female genitalia ... for non-medical reasons.... The United Nations uses the term 'female genital mutilation' to convey that this practice is a violation of human rights of girls and women [and to drum up worldwide support in the struggle to end this practice]."[101]

Historically and contextually, female genital cutting (also known euphemistically as female circumcision) is a widespread practice in approximately 28 African nation-states. Thus, Egypt is not unique in the practice of FGM/C. Further, FGM/C (like male circumcision) has been in practice for ages in many societies in North Africa (and other Middle Eastern countries).[102] In Egypt, the prevalence of FGM/C is 91.1 percent and for a nation-state with a legislation banning female circumcision, this percentage is extraordinarily high.[103]

What truly makes Egypt special—if not exceptional—on this matter is the vocal uproar against the practice in the society ignited by the power of modern mass communications technology that led to the 2008 rule outlawing FGM/C. To be sure, the Egyptian High Court had prohibited the practice in 1997.[104] However, as argued earlier, there are problems between theory and practice in the enforcement of human rights principles in the society, often because of politics and culture.

In any case, an event happened in 2007 that made the issue as combustible as it became and a catalyst for the public outcry against the practice of FGM/C. In 2007, anecdotally, a 12-year-old girl, Badour Shaker, died because of the circumcision performed on her at a clinic by a possibly quack doctor in the southern town of Maghagh. Soon after the death of Shaker, the Egyptian Ministry of Health made a declaration that it "is prohibited for any doctors, nurses, or any other person to carry out any cut of, flattening or modification of any natural part of the female reproductive system, either in government hospitals, non-government or any other places."[105] The nation's first lady and religious groups expressed concern regarding the death of Shaker. For example, the Patriarch of the Christian Coptic Church, Pope Shenouda III, publicly disclosed his opposition to FGM/C.[106] The U.S. State Department and several international agencies took actions between 2000 and 2016 to bring pressure to bear on Egypt. They encouraged the republic to desist from the practice of FGM/C.

Statistically, based on the 2014 Egypt Demographic and Health Survey (EDHS), published by the Health Ministry, "the percentage of girls between 15 and 17 years old who had undergone FGM/C decreased to 60 percent, from 74 percent in 2008. According to the same survey, 92 percent of ever-married women between 15 and 49 years old had undergone FGM/C. The survey showed that 56 percent of mothers supported FGM/C, a decrease from 75 percent in 2000."[107] It is refreshing that the Egyptian Health Ministry, the EDHS, the UN Population Fund, the United Nations Children's Fund (UNICEF), and other partners worked jointly on a project to curb FGM/C.

Following the collaboration of these major forces, the Egyptian government embarked on a new National Strategy for the Abandonment of FGM/C.[108]

It is comforting that, to do battle with the human rights dilemma of FGM/C in Egypt, Parliament enacted stringent penalties on August 31, 2016. The new amendments to the penal code dispense jail terms of five to seven years for individuals who undertake the practice of female genital mutilation and up to 15 years if the it leads to permanent disability or death.[109] Affirming the seriousness of this matter in Egypt, Rothna Begum, a Middle East women's rights researcher, suggested that the severer penalties for FGM/C in the country now exemplify the terrible and potentially deadly consequences of the unfair practice.[110] Even so, the result of this positive step in rural Egypt might prove otherwise—at least for now.

## Child Abuse and Human Rights

A popular aphorism in many societies is "children are our future"; therefore, they must be properly educated and carefully nurtured for future leadership in political, social and economic sectors in a polity. In truth, adults socialize children. The way adults socialize kids might inform how those children govern in adulthood. The preceding postulations in part inform the inclusion in most national constitutions and international human rights instruments provisions for protecting children's rights. For example, Articles 80 and 82 of the national constitution (see Table I) outline strikingly the rights of children in Egypt. Article 18(3) of the ACHPR enjoins member-states to eliminate every discrimination against women and calls for the protection of the rights of women and the child.[111] Article 24 of the ICCPR, on children's rights, declares: "Every child shall have, without any discrimination ... the right to such measures of protection as required by his [her] status as a minor, on the part of his [her] family, society and the State."[112] Article 25(2) of the UDHR avers: "Motherhood and childhood are entitled to special care and assistance. All children whether born in or out of wedlock, shall enjoy the same social protection."[113]

Bearing in mind the significant role parents, families and the state must play in the protection of the rights of children, UNICEF and the UN approved a resolution: the UN Convention on the Rights of the Child. Comprehensive references to the rights of the child are contained in this document. For instance, Article 4 of this Convention affirms compellingly:

> Governments have a responsibility to take all available measures to make sure children's rights are respected, protected and fulfilled. When countries ratify the Convention, they agree to review their laws relating to children. This involves assessing their social services, legal, health and educational systems, as well as levels of funding

for these services. Governments are then obliged to take all necessary steps to ensure that the minimum standards set by the Convention in these areas are being met. They must help families protect children's rights and create an environment where they can grow and reach their potential.... Article 41 of the Convention points out that when a country already has higher legal standards than those seen in the Convention, the higher standards always prevail.[114]

How has Egypt fared on the matter of children's rights? The constitution defines a child as an individual under the age of 18. The tenets of the constitution, as in Articles 80 and 82, inter alia, state that the government will protect minors from all forms of violence, abuse, mistreatment, and commercial and sexual exploitation. Yet, there were—and are—extensive reports of child abuse, as chronicled by Human Rights Watch. In fact, HRW logged in hundreds of cases each month, and many cases went unrecorded; for human rights observers, these circumstances expose the contradictions between theory that guarantees the rights of the child and practice in which these rights are violated in the polity.[115] Furthermore, based on UNICEF reports, at least 80 percent of children between 13 and 17 years old were unprotected from violence—physical, emotional, or sexual.[116] Lamentably, these children are some of those who will in future assume leadership positions in the country; indeed, by socialization, they might become victimizers of their children based on their experiences as minors.

Further, human rights groups, such as Amnesty International, have reported that children face maltreatment in custody, including torture, cohabiting in cells with adults, rejection of their rights to counsel, et cetera. The preceding actions are in violation of provisions in the national constitution and international human rights conventions and norms to which Egypt is a signatory. Early and forced marriage are human rights problems, especially in pastoral Egypt. By law, the legal age of marriage is 18, as noted previously; but this is only true on paper in Egypt and much of Africa. The High Commissioner for Human Rights in Geneva reported in 2014 that "23 percent of girls married before age 18; as many as 21 percent married before age 15," although the Minister of Population said 15 percent of all marriages in the country were child marriages.[117]

The law is strict on commercial sexual exploitation of children and child pornography, and rightly so to protect the human rights of children. Legislation provides for jail terms of not less than five years with a fine up to $26,000 for the violation of minors under 18. Critical to human rights dialogues on children's rights, too, is the issue of displaced children. The MOSS projects the number of street children to be 20,000; observers believe this number is rather conservative. In fact, civil society groups approximate the number to be in the millions; the rights to safe shelter and environment of these minors are in jeopardy. Many of these children are victims of violence and sexual abuse that includes forced prostitution. The MOSS offers shelters to homeless children but these are not satisfactorily run or operated. Thus, children return to the streets. It is encouraging that the Ministry of Health and Population does provide mobile health clinics, nurses and social workers to address the needs of displaced children. Religious institutions and NGOs also perform an outstanding effort by providing succor to homeless children, including meals, clothing, and literacy classes.[118] In this way, they have mitigated the human rights infractions against these children—some of whom are likely to become potential leaders in the Republic of Egypt.

# 3

## Libya

### Brief History

The ancient history of Libya has much in common with those of other countries in North Africa. The indigenous Berbers, who inhabited the territory, had no written language to inform scholars about the histories of their peoples. Consequently, the tales about the happenings in the area were those told by Greek and Roman administrators who arrived in the region, geographers and other explorers. Therefore, the information about the original people who populated the area was not firsthand. Moreover, it would suffice to say that others who might have not had any relationship to the prehistoric public wrote accounts of the autochthonous inhabitants in books.[1]

In any case, the peoples of the coastal region and the Mediterranean shoreline from as long ago as 7000 BCE shared identical cultures. They were adept at the cultivation of crops and the domestication of cattle critical for commerce and their daily survival. In the hinterland, commonly referred to as the Sahara Desert, flourished nomadic herdsmen and hunters who migrated from place to place in search of water for themselves and grasslands where they hunted animals and grazed their cattle. The savanna people wandered around in the region until harsh weather conditions in about 2000 BCE created aridity in the territory. This population might have either immigrated to modern Sudan or integrated with ethnic Berbers.[2]

The Berbers represent another group whose origin in the area is not well known. Even so, their military prowess and activities in the region were outstanding.[3] They were familiar with classical Greece and Rome, which gave the name "Libyan" to all Berbers. In terms of organization, they were characteristically clannish and tribal, very much like in the rest of ancient and modern Africa; their allegiance was to the family, tribe, and clan.[4] Indeed, the Greek philosopher, Herodotus, on his visit to North Africa, chronicled their socio-political civilization splendidly.[5]

The story of the conquest of Libya by foreign powers is similar to that of other North African countries. Sequentially, Phoenicians, Romans, Arabs, Turks and Italians conquered Libya.[6] Other forces that invaded and governed Libya were the Vandals, Byzantines and Greeks after the fall of the Roman Empire.[7] Nonetheless, before the birth of modern Libya, there were "autonomous" regions that clustered with their distinct qualities. These were Tripolitania, in the west, Cyrenaica, in the east, and Fezzan, in the southwest. Libya became what it is today following the unification of these regions. The histories of the founding of Tripolitania, Cyrenaica and Fezzan are inundating. However, for illustration, a summary will suffice.

## Tripolitania

Phoenician entrepreneurs who were natives of what is now Lebanon were active traders in the Mediterranean region. In about 1000 BCE, their commercial adventures brought them to the North African coast in search of gold, silver, ivory, apes, and peacocks. Soon after, they established several trading depots along the shorelines of the Mediterranean. In the process of trading with the indigenous Berbers in the area, the Phoenicians constructed a major settlement at Carthage. From this stronghold, Carthage extended its suzerainty over much of North Africa. Phoenicians in Carthage even established their unique genus of civilization, dubbed Punic. Their settlements and development projects across the region, among other things, brought together three cities: Oea (Tripoli), Labdah (later named Leptis Magna), and Sabratah. Tripolis became the name of the unified cities.[8]

The Romans, on a quest for lucrative business in North Africa and for power and glory, invaded Carthage in the third century BCE during the conflicts dubbed the Punic Wars (264–241, 218–201, and 149–146 BCE). The Romans triumphed in these wars and succeeded in reducing Carthage's authority in the area. Because Rome was apprehensive of possible renewal of war by the Phoenicians, it decided to destroy Carthage once and for all. Rome, with the rallying cry "Delenda est Carthago," Carthage must be destroyed, sacked Carthage in 146 BCE. Rome under the reign of Julius Caesar established Tripolitania as one of the Roman provinces.[9]

## Cyrenaica

Greeks founded the region of Cyrenaica and city of Cyrene around 630–632 BCE. Greeks were as adventurous as the Phoenicians. Consequently, after about 200 years of their occupation of Cyrenaica, they expanded their holdings by establishing four more cities. These cities were known as Barce (Al Mari), Euesperides (later Berenice, present day Benghazi), Teuchira (later

Arsinoe, present-day Tukrah), and Apolonia (later Susa, the port of Cyrene). Unique to the character of these cities was that they became autonomous— each establishing a republic of sorts and inventing their diverse and "unique democratic" institutions. These five towns collectively formed a Pentapolis. They traded with each other while maintaining their strong independence. Because they were often in fierce economic and political competition with each other, their rivalries made them reluctant to cooperate even when confronted by a common and formidable adversary.[10]

Historically, Egyptians and Carthaginians sought to conquer Pentapolis and exploit it. There was intense and violent resistance to the invasions. In 525 BCE, however, the army of Persia captured Cyrenaica. The Persians and Egyptians governed Cyrenaica intermittently for almost 200 years. It was not until 331 BCE that Alexander the Great recaptured Cyrenaica for the Greeks. Following Alexander's death in 323 BCE, his general Ptolemy took control of his African and Syrian territories while other Greek city-states and republics retained their home-rule. Because of the leaders' inability to maintain stability in the governance of their city-states, the Ptolemaic dynasties were compelled to impose constitutions on the republics. In later years, however, a federation of the Pentapolis was established. In this arrangement, a king from the Ptolemaic lineage governed the Pentapolis. Ptolemy Apion, the last Greek ruler of the Pentapolis, ceded Cyrenaica to Rome in 96 BCE because he could not defend it. Rome annexed the area around 74 BCE and united it with Crete as one of its realms.[11]

## Fezzan

The Garamentes arrived in the area called Fezzan around 1000 BCE. Fezzan was populated by people of Arab origin mixed with Berbers and Black Africans.[12] They avoided the coastal shoreline. This was probably because of the brutal struggles for territorial control between the Phoenicians and Greeks. They lived in the hinterland where they established their kingdom protected from invasion by the Sahara Desert. Their ways of life were mysterious, perhaps because of their nomadic lifestyle, and their political activities were limited. Their movements as traders depended on the existence of oases indispensable for their day-to-day existence. Moreover, from their capital, Germa, they managed the desert trade, which ran from Ghadamis to the Niger River. They also traded with Egypt and Mauritania.

The Garamentes also interacted with the Carthaginians in commerce. Carthaginians hired Garamentes to transport gold and ivory that they bartered for salt from Sudan to their Mediterranean storehouses. They were superb technicians who also built elaborate pyramids, like the Egyptians, in honor of their dead. Notwithstanding the harshness of the environment,

the Romans undertook several military expeditions to conquer the Garamentes. In the end, though, Rome struck durable commercial deals and
signed military agreements with the Garamentes toward the end of the first
century AD.[13]

## Arab Conquest and Islam

In the seventh century, following the death of the Prophet Muhammad
in 632 AD, his disciples embarked on Islamic crusades to spread the Muslim religion from Arabia to other regions of the world. During the religious
campaigns, the Byzantine domains of Egypt, Syria, and Persia were ripe for
the picking. The addition of North Africa to the military menu of areas to
be conquered happened rather swiftly. Alexandria in Egypt fell in 643 AD In
modern Libya, Cyrenaica was subdued in 644, Tripolitania fell in 646, and
Fezzan capitulated in 663 AD In the military conflict, the gallant Berbers
initially resisted the invading Arab armies, but their efforts were in vain, as
they were also conquered. Arab success and authority had spread all over
North Africa by 715 AD.[14] The Arabs' governance technique, of Libya and
their territories elsewhere, was unique. The Arabs came into North Africa
as conquerors and missionaries, not as colonists per se. Their warriors married among the indigenous populations and pursued a policy of assimilation
while teaching the Arab culture and Islamic religion.[15] Indeed, as Ronald
Bruce St. John notes, "Of all the historical phases through which Libya
passed, the seventh century arrival of the Arabs, bringing with them the
Arabic language, Islam, and a new way of life, had the most lasting effect on
contemporary Libyan society."[16]

## Ottoman Empire

The Ottoman Empire rose at about 1300 AD at the site of today's Istanbul,
Turkey. In the Ottomans' expansionist drive, soldiers invaded and captured
Libya in 1551. A special group of Turkish warriors, known as janissaries, set-
tled in Libya. Very much like the Arab conquerors before them, they married
indigenous women and integrated into the society.[17] The Turks reigned in
Libya for about three centuries.

During their occupation, they made sure that Libyans inculcated the
Turkish culture and way of life. At about 1661, Ottoman power and influence
started to wane due in part to internal rivalries, corruption, and political disarticulations. The political intrigue in Libya was exacerbated in the late 18th
century and early 19th century by France, Britain, and the United States in
pursuit of their national interests in Libya.[18]

## Italians

In 1911, Italy wanted to join, as it were, the prestigious club of Britain, France, Portugal, Germany, and other European powers that had colonies in Africa. With the declining power of the Ottoman Empire in North Africa, Italy chose to take on the Ottoman Empire in Libya. In that war of 1911, Italy defeated the Ottoman Empire.[19] It was a sweet victory recalling that, historically, Rome once conquered and occupied what is now Libya. Christian Italy, in its quest to destroy Arab culture in Libya, mimicked Germany's colonial policy in southwest Africa (Namibia) in the early 1900s when it wiped out the Herero in the so-called German-Herero War.[20] Libyans in areas occupied by the Italian forces had limited political rights. Libyans who were reluctant to obey Italian rules were murdered. In the drive to penetrate the hinterland and subdue the Bedouins, "[Italian forces] sealed Bedouin wells, destroyed herds of cattle, and put people into concentration camps. The hanging of Libyans in every city became a daily event."[21]

The 1911 to 1943 Italian colonization was relatively short but eventful. World War I happened from 1914 to 1918. During this period, Italy directed its attention to the European theatre of war thus relaxing its grip on Libya. In World War II (1939–1945), Italy de-coupled from its alliance with Britain and others and joined with Germany and Japan to form the Axis. In the war, the Axis fought against the Allied Forces—Britain, France, the Soviet Union, China, and the United States. The Axis was defeated. Libya's fate as a colony of Italy was in limbo following the Axis's capitulation. Because Libya was of strategic importance to the Allied forces, these powers competed for who should take over control of the territory, for as the aphorism goes, to the victor go the spoils of war. As a compromise, with the United Nations serving as the interlocutor between contending powers, Libya achieved its independence on December 24, 1951.[22] Subsequently, Libya became the first country in Africa to gain self-rule. It was also the first state created by the UN General Assembly. A Libyan National Assembly chose Muhammad Idris al-Sanusi as the country's first king.[23]

## Monarchy and Revolution

King Idris, who was also the chief of state in the 1951 constitution, headed the government. A prime minister and cabinet represented the executive branch of government. A Chamber of Deputies (Lower House) and Senate (Upper House) were instituted. Despite this administrative and governance architecture, the king wielded enormous powers that he, regrettably, abused from time to time in a constitutional government.[24] For example, King Idris upon acceding to power swiftly showed the style of rule he favored—absolute, which was characteristic of kings of antiquity. There was one hotly contested election in 1952, after which Idris "banned all political parties, banished most of his relatives to the desert, and deported the leader of the main opposition party."[25]

This faux pas, or false step, and the king's dependency policy that exposed the state's economy to Western exploitation, were problematic to members of the informed public and opposition forces. Further, both Britain and the United States maintained military bases in the country that threatened Libya's sovereignty. In addition, social and civil unrest in the country and an outbreak of demonstrations during the 1967 war between Israel and its Arab neighbors made the situation in the polity quite combustible. For a brief time, political commotion shook the social and political fabric of Libyan society.

Problematically, the king's parochial concern and insular interest for Cyrenaica, his political and religious base, did not endear the other regions of the state to his leadership of the constitutional federal arrangement. Added to the political and social quandaries in the country was the rampancy of corruption and administrative malfeasance in the bureaucracy. As an outcome of national malaise, a group of young military officers captured the state palace in Tripoli on September 1, 1969, while the King was in Turkey for vacation and a medical check-up. The leader of the coup d'état was Col. Muammar Gaddafi.[26] He was in power from 1969 to 2011. He lost power on October 20, 2011, due to political upheaval in the country triggered by opposition factions with military support from North Atlantic Treaty Organization (NATO) forces.

The toppling of Gaddafi, without a legitimate successor, left a power vacuum and increased political anarchy in the republic. The National Transition Council (NTC), a collection of opposition leadership councils that fought ferociously against the Gaddafi regime and took over the administration of the country after Gaddafi's demise in October 2011. Stepping into the void created by the collapse of an authoritarian system in which Gaddafi saw himself as "Libya and Libya as Gaddafi," the NTC was unable to impose law and order in a revolutionary state. Consequently, in an attempt to stabilize the nation, the NTC transferred power to a General National Congress (GNC), with Nouri Abusahman as its president.

In June 2014, the electorate went to the polls to elect a new parliament to succeed the GNC. The chosen political actors formed the Council of Representatives, which for security reasons relocated its seat of power in the famous city of Tobruk. In the interim, political instability continued to dominate the political landscape in Tripoli and elsewhere amongst powerful, competing, and rebellious gangs. In 2015 the United Nations, playing the role of a middleman, hammered out an agreement with various antagonistic blocs in the society with a view to promoting international peace and security. This mediation effort led to the formation of a unity government and the Presidency Council. Prime Minister Fayez Sarraj headed this council. Challengingly for the country, neither the political factions in Tripoli nor those in Tobruk were enthusiastic in recognizing or accepting the legitimacy of the unity government. Nevertheless, to boost the support of his administration, the Prime Minister Sarraj and some of his subordinates moved the seat of government from Tobruk to Tripoli in 2016. Given the tense political climate in Tripoli and the republic itself, he set up his administration in a fortified naval base.[27]

In summation, Table I below, posted by BBC News on October 31, 2017, chronicles some key dates in Libya's history.

## Table I

| |
|---|
| **7th century BC**—Phoenicians settle in Tripolitania in western Libya, which was hitherto populated by Berbers. |
| **4th century BC**—Greeks colonize Cyrenaica in the east of the country, which they call Libya. |
| **74 BC**—Romans conquer Libya. |
| **AD 643**—Arabs conquer Libya and spread Islam. |
| **16th century**—Libya becomes part of the Ottoman Empire, which joins the three provinces of Tripolitania, Cyrenaica and Fezzan into one regency in Tripoli. |
| **1911–12**—Italy seizes Libya from the Ottomans. Omar al-Mukhtar begins 20-year insurgency against Italian rule. |
| **1942**—Allies oust Italians from Libya, which is then divided between the French and the British. |
| **1951**—Libya becomes independent under King Idris al-Sanusi. |
| **1969**—Muammar Gaddafi, aged 27, deposes the king in a bloodless military coup. |
| **1992**—UN imposes sanctions on Libya over the bombing of a Pan Am airliner over the Scottish town of Lockerbie in December 1988. |
| **2011**—Violent protests break out in Benghazi and spread to other cities. This leads to civil war, foreign intervention and eventually the ouster and killing of Gaddafi. |
| **2016**—Following years of conflict, a new UN-backed "unity" government is installed in a naval base in Tripoli. It faces opposition from two rival governments and a host of militias. |

Source: "Libya: Country Profile," BBC News, https://www.bbc.com/news/world-africa-13754897 (retrieved 1/3/18).

Given the political issues Libya confronted from 1969 to 2011, it was and is important for the republic to construct a template likely to exculpate the country from its checkered political history laced with human rights infractions. One strategy for attaining this objective was writing a new constitution—one adequate for commanding national legitimacy. However, the process of writing the 2017 constitution was difficult. This was the case because of the political turbulence the country experienced following the overthrow of Gaddafi's regime and the emergence of antagonistic groups struggling to control the machinery and accoutrements of power. Because it was important to meet the demands of the many clashing forces and their competing interests, the 2017 constitution is elaborate. Germane, however, to the thrust of this chapter and volume itself is the segment of the constitution that addresses the human rights issues of Libyans in Chapter II: Rights and Freedoms. My central thesis is that if these well-articulated principles of human rights (see Table II) are enforced political stability will reign, and peaceful coexistence will be furthered in the state. Thus, I shall intermittently refer to the human rights principles in the constitution in my ensuing analysis.

## Table II: Constitution of Libya 2017
### CHAPTER II: RIGHTS AND FREEDOMS

| | |
|---|---|
| 7* | Male and female citizens shall be equal in and before the law. There shall be no discrimination between them and all forms of discrimination for any reason such as ethnicity, colour, language, sex, birth, political opinion, disability, origin or geographical affiliation shall be prohibited in accordance with the provisions of this constitution. |
| 31 | Every human being shall have the right to life, it shall not be permissible to surrender it and the State shall ensure its protection and take the necessary measures to ensure indemnity [blood money] of the dead when the perpetrator is unknown in accordance with the regulations of the law. |
| 32 | Every human being has the right to personal, physical, and mental safety. Material gain from a human being and his organs shall not be permissible. The State shall take the necessary measures to compensate victims of calamities for citizens and legal residents. |
| 33 | Every human being shall have the right to security and tranquility. The State shall be committed to providing security and tranquility to its citizens and to each resident in its territory. |
| 34 | The State shall be committed to protecting human dignity and preventing all types of violence, torture, inhumane, cruel and humiliating treatment as well as enforced disappearance. The statute of limitations shall not apply to their crimes. All forms of slavery, involuntary servitude, forced labour and human trafficking shall be prohibited, unless out of a necessity or to carry out a punishment according to a court ruling. |
| 35 | Private life shall enjoy its sanctity. It shall not be permissible to enter private places except for a necessity, and they shall not be searched except in the case of flagrante delicto or with a court warrant. In addition, it shall not be permissible to prejudice personal data, or monitor communications and correspondence except based on the permission of the competent judge. |
| 36 | All patterns of behavior that constitute crimes against humanity, war crimes, and genocide shall be prohibited. The statute of limitations shall not apply to them, and it shall not be permissible to pardon them in contradiction with the provisions of the Constitution. International jurisdiction of the Libyan judiciary shall apply on them. |

| 37 | Freedom of speech and its integrity shall not be separated. Expression and publication are two safe guarded rights. Necessary measures shall be taken to protect private life and prohibit incitement to hatred, violence, and racism on the basis of ethnicity, colour, language, sex, birth, political opinion, disability, origin, geographic affiliation or any other reasons. Charging with infidelity [Takfir] and imposition of opinion by force shall also be prohibited. |
|---|---|
| 38 | The State shall guarantee the freedom, plurality, and independence of the press and media. Citizens shall have the right to ownership of press and media outlets. It shall be prohibited to suspend them except by a judicial order and it shall be prohibited to disband them except by a court ruling. Precautionary imprisonment in case of journalism shall not be permissible. |
| 39 | Every citizen shall have the right to vote in referenda as well as to vote or run as a candidate in free, fair, transparent, and equitable elections in which all citizens are equal in accordance with the law. It shall be prohibited to deprive eligible citizen from them except based on a judicial ruling. |
| 40 | Every citizen shall have the right to choose his political leanings. The State shall guarantee the freedom to form political parties based on national unity, transparent financing, renunciation of violence and hate speech. Every citizen shall have the right to join or withdraw from them without discrimination. |
| 41 | The State shall guarantee the freedom to form and join civil society organizations according to the standards needed for [creating a] balance between the requirements of their independence and transparency needs. It shall not be permissible to suspend their work except by a judicial order and it shall not be permissible to disband them except by court ruling. |
| 42 | The State shall guarantee for citizens and civil society organizations the right to democratic participation in their realm of activity by submitting petitions or legislative proposals in accordance with a regulatory law issued for this purpose. |
| 43 | The State shall guarantee the right to peaceful assembly, association, and demonstration, and it shall take the necessary measures to protect property and persons. It shall not use force except at a minimum level and in the case of necessity. |
| 44 | The right to movement and residency, to move property, the freedom to exercise economic activity within the entirety of the country, freedom of travel, and the right to immigration shall be guaranteed to all citizens. A travel ban shall only be by a justified judicial order and for a period defined by the law. It shall be prohibited to deport citizens or prevented them from returning to their homeland. It shall also be prohibited to extradite [citizens] except based on international obligation of an international judicial body. |
| 45 | The State shall take the necessary measures to protect and care for Libyans abroad, ensure their affiliation with their homeland, participation in the electoral process and their contribution to development, as well as follow violation of their rights and extend the jurisdiction of the Libyan judiciary pertaining to these rights. |

| 46 | The State shall develop the necessary measures for transparency and shall ensure the freedom of receiving, sending, exchanging and perusal of information, as well as multiplicity of its sources in a manner that does not prejudice military secrets, public security secrets, the requirements of the administration of justice, the sanctity of private life and what was agreed upon with another country as secret, with the right to keep the source confidential. |
|----|----|
| 47 | The State shall guarantee to citizens the right to safe and adequate drink and food and shall develop the necessary policies to achieve water and food security. |
| 48 | Health is a right for every human being and is a duty upon the State and society. The right to live in a sound environment shall be guaranteed to all. The State shall guarantee comprehensive and quality healthcare to all citizens and shall provide preventive services to them. It shall also provide treatment services to them in all stages based on a symbiotic system. It shall ensure the fair geographic distribution of health facilities. Not providing treatment in various forms to any human being in cases of emergency or danger to life shall be prohibited. |
| 49 | The State shall be committed to supporting and caring for women, laws that ensure their protection, promoting their status in society, eliminating the negative culture and social customs that detract from their dignity, as well as prohibiting discrimination against them, and ensuring their right in public elections and giving them opportunities in all areas; it shall also take the necessary measures to support their acquired rights. |
| 50 | 1. The State shall guarantee to all citizens decent life and welfare that commensurate with its economic conditions.<br>2. Social security shall be a right for citizens, and the State shall protect the rights of its residents.<br>3. Society shall be based on social solidarity, and the State shall guarantee decent life for the needy, including the elderly, orphans, widows and divorcees, in addition to those who do not marry at an early age as well as those who have lost support.<br>4. The State shall guarantee the rights of the retirees in a manner that ensures that pensions are compatible with legal positions irrespective of the date of retirement.<br>5. The State shall be committed to providing social care and education for children of unknown parentage so as to ensure their integration in society. The law shall regulate their situations in a manner that achieves this.<br>　　At all events, the State shall devise regulations to achieve cooperation and social solidarity among citizens. |
| 51 | The State shall protect the material and intangible rights of intellectual property in all forms and in all domains, and it shall support it in accordance with what is specified by the law. |

| | |
|---|---|
| 52 | Education shall be a protected right, which the State shall be committed to promoting and providing to every citizen based on his mental and scientific capacities without discrimination; it shall be compulsory until the age of eighteen and free to citizens in all stages in public education institutions and in accordance with what the law determines for resident foreigners. The State shall support private education and ensure its compliance with its educational policies. The State shall also ensure the inviolability of educational institutions.<br><br>Educational curricula shall be based on the standards of quality in accordance with international standards and the teachings and values of the Islamic religion, parameters of Libyan identity, benefiting from human experiences, strengthening the concept of citizenship, social harmony, and peaceful coexistence, as well as teaching human rights and fundamental freedoms. |
| 53 | The State shall take the necessary measures for the independence of universities and research centers and shall guarantee their competitiveness and academic freedom in line with the general national standards. The right to affiliation shall not be restricted except by standards of scientific competence appropriate for the area of specialization.<br><br>The state is committed to encouraging and developing technical education as appropriate to the development imperatives. |
| 54 | The State shall commit to taking the necessary measures to develop scientific research and provide it with institutional frameworks. It shall ensure the rights of researchers, sponsor creativity and innovation. Priority shall be given to the different types and stages of education and to scientific research in the distribution of national income in a progressive manner that is compatible with international standards. |
| 55 | Every person, individually or collectively, shall have the right to use and learn their languages and to participate in cultural life The State shall guarantee the protection of Libyan languages and provide the necessary means to develop teaching and using them in the media. The State shall also guarantee the protection and promotion of local cultures, heritage, traditional knowledge, literature, and arts, and shall disseminate cultural services. |
| 56 | Every citizen has the right to work. The state shall work to provide safe and appropriate conditions of work. The worker has the right to choose the type of work and fairness of its terms, along with guaranteeing union rights. The state shall ensure raising the value of work and provide opportunities for job seekers. |
| 57 | Sports as a hobby or a profession shall be a right for every individual. The State shall take the necessary measures to support it, advance it and encourage investment in it, as well as provide the proper sports installations for the areas according to their needs. It shall ensure the independence of sports bodies as well as the settlement of disputes between them in accordance with international standards. |
| 58 | Private property shall be safeguarded as a right. No custodianship shall be imposed on private property except by a court ruling and in the cases that are determined by the law. Expropriation shall only happen for public interest with a fair compensation. In cases other than emergency and martial law, compensation shall be in advance. Property shall only be seized by a judicial ruling. General seizure shall be prohibited. |

| 59 | The State shall take all measures for children to fully enjoy their rights and protect them from conditions that endanger their interests, education, and growth. The state shall base its legislations and policies on the best interests of the child. |
|---|---|
| 60 | The State shall be committed to guaranteeing the health, social, educational, economic, political, sports and entertainment rights of persons with disability on equal footing with others. The State shall customize public and private facilities and surrounding environment that enable them to integrate into society in a complete and effective manner. The State shall take the necessary measures to activate the laws that guarantees that. |
| 61 | The right to litigation shall be guaranteed for all. Every person shall have the right to a fair trial before his natural judge and within a reasonable period in which all guarantees shall be provided. No legislation shall be immune from appeal and no conduct detrimental or threatening to rights and freedoms may be excluded from judicial jurisdiction. |
| 62 | Principle of Criminal Legitimacy and Assumption of Innocence Crimes shall be classified into felonies, misdemeanors, and infringements. There shall be no felony or misdemeanor except by law. Infringements shall not be punishable by custodial sentences. Punishment shall be for acts [committed] subsequent to the date on which the law entered into force. The sentence shall be personal and proportionate to the crime and its perpetrator. An accused person shall be innocent until proven guilty. |
| 63 | Every individual shall enjoy respect of human dignity, as his right, in all criminal proceedings. Competent authorities shall justify their orders that affect rights and liberties. There shall be no detention except in places designated for this purpose and for a specific legal period that is proportionate with the accusation, while making this [detention] known to the competent judicial body and the family or chosen person of the detained; his place shall be specified and he shall be given enough time and the necessary facilities to prepare his defense; he shall be informed of his right not to be forced to submit evidence against himself and his responsibility for any statements he makes, as well as to utilize an interpreter and to choose and contact an attorney. The State shall guarantee judicial assistance. |
| 64 | Every individual shall have the right to personal freedom. There shall be no deprivation of freedom except in the case of insufficient measures, procedures, or alternative penalties. The state shall be committed to rehabilitating prisoners and integrating them into society. Any person who is deprived of his freedom as a precaution or in implementation of a sentence shall be entitled to proper reparations upon an order that there is no cause for prosecution, based on the regulations of the law. |
| 65 | Any restriction of rights and liberties must be necessary, clear, defined, and proportionate to the interest to be protected and the characteristics of democratic society. Revoking guarantees provided by the law shall be prohibited. All this shall not contravene with the provisions of this Constitution. |

| 66 | All legislative and executive policies and development programs shall be based on the protection and promotion of human rights. In this regard, the State shall periodically evaluate its legislation and policies with subsequent publication of the bases and results of the evaluation in the official newspaper. |

*Article 7 is an addendum to Chapter II: Rights and Freedoms.

Source: https://www.libyaobserver.ly/news/libya-constitution---chapter-two (Retrieved 1/3/2018).

## Libya and Human Rights: General Introduction

Some basic human rights concerns in this chapter, as in the other chapters of this volume, are about torture, religion, women's rights, ethnic/racial discrimination and freedom of speech and the press. My analysis will focus on the challenges that violations of the above rights present to the society. The compelling human rights quagmires in 2015, and after, are reflections of the political chaos that arose in Libya following the abrupt overthrow of the strongman, Muammar Gaddafi, from power. This period of anarchy in the republic ushered in an era of ineffective governance, absence of the rule of law, insecurity of citizens, collapse of the institutions, and abuses of the human rights of Libyans. Members of the armed factions who committed rights violations were terrorists, criminal gangs and rivals of the government. Collectively, these groups' militant activities were associated with state failure. Because of the absence of the rule of law, it was possible for the following rights problems to foment. These are: arbitrary and unlawful killings and impunity, assassinations of politicians and human rights defenders, torture and other cruel, inhuman, or degrading treatment or punishment, and harsh and life-threatening conditions in detention and prison facilities.[28]

Additionally, the following rights abuses were observed:

[1] Lengthy pretrial detention; [2] denial of fair public trial; [3] an ineffective judicial system...; [4] arbitrary interference with privacy and home; [5] use of excessive force and other abuses in internal conflicts; [6] limits on the freedoms of speech and press, including violence against, and harassment of, journalists; [7] restrictions on freedom of religion; [8] abuses of internally displaced persons, refugees, and migrants; [9] violence and social discrimination against women and ethnic and racial minorities, including foreign workers; [10] trafficking in persons; [11] legal and social discrimination based on sexual orientation; and [12] violations of labor rights.[29]

The character of the weak and volatile Libyan state makes the preceding human rights infringements feasible, and these are some of the human rights challenges that will continue to confront the country. In short, Libya's failed state was unable to undertake measures to examine, indict, and discipline those who flouted the human rights of citizens. Regrettably, this was and is the situation whether members of the security forces or other agents and agencies of the government carried out those abuses. It is within the context of the foregoing postulations that I shall examine areas of rights infractions beginning with the use of torture by agents of the administration. I will do so, inter alia, within the overarching issues of the lack of respect for the integrity of the person and deprivation of life of Libyans.[30]

## Torture and Other Cruel, Inhuman, or Degrading Treatment or Punishment

To be sure, Article 34 (see Table II) of the constitution is impressive on the defense against torture and other cruel, inhuman, or degrading treatment or punishment of citizens. Yet, the lack of enthusiasm of the government/s of the post–Gaddafi administration for implementing these provisions of the constitution left many problems unsolved. Furthermore, Article 5 of the African Charter on Human and Peoples' Rights condemns torture[31] as does Article 7 of the International Covenant on Civil and Political Rights.[32] The historic UN Convention against Torture and Other Cruel, Inhuman or Degrading Treatment or Punishment states in Article 4(1): "Each State Party shall ensure that all acts of torture are offences under its criminal law. The same shall apply to an attempt to commit torture and to an act by any person which constitutes complicity or participation in torture." Article 4(2) affirms: "Each State Party shall make these offences punishable by appropriate penalties which take into account their grave nature."[33]

Despite the above constitutional and international human rights injunctions to live up to the foregoing commitments, torture and other cruel, inhuman or degrading treatment and punishment continue to persist in Libya. Human Rights Watch's accounts on Libya on these rights issues are revealing as well as poignant. Ironically, Libya's legitimate government was and is culpable, although it seldom admits it, for widespread arbitrary detentions and for torture under the pretext that the instability in the country warrants it in the eastern region of the state. Even so, HRW agents, in their formidable capacity as protectors of human rights globally, are diligent in exposing rights infractions committed by the authorities in detention facilities. For instance, HRW uncovered the existence of torture in al-Bayda and Benghazi custodies administered by the Libyan Army, the Ministry of Justice, and the Ministry of Interior (MOI).[34]

HRW interviews of detainees revealed that many were tortured until they "admitted" to grave crimes. Further, HRW documented other forms of human rights infringements and political malfeasance in the republic. The human rights breaches included, but were not limited to, "lack of due process, absence of medical care, denial of family visits, lack of notification of families about their detention, and poor conditions. [Sadly], the detainees included children under 18."[35] A visit to three detention centers under the supervision of the Libyan Army and the MOI Counter Terrorism Unit uncovered more rights violations. It was revealed that there were 450 "security detainees" supposedly held because of the political turbulence in the country. Many were tortured in violation of Article 34 of the constitution (see Table II). A few prisoners said agents of the state announced their confessions in the national media. This act led to their exposure to the public and molestation of their families by rogue agents of the state in violation of Article 64 (see Table II) of the constitution. Access to defense lawyers and presentation to a judge never happened.[36] This denial of rights was and is in violation of Articles 61, 63 and 64 of the constitution (see Table II). The techniques applied for obtaining confessions from inmates were diverse. They included beating with plastic pipe on their bodies or soles of their feet or with electric cable, chains, or sticks, application of electric shocks, solitary confinement, and denial of food and hygiene facilities.[37] Other methods were burns inflicted by boiling water and heated metal.[38]

In eastern Libya, too, many human rights observers chafed at the long-term random detentions, the gravity of which they claimed might constitute crime against humanity. Moreover, the United Nations Support Mission in Libya (UNSMIL) affirmed that in 2015 forces loyal to Operation Dignity abducted civilians suspected of sympathizing with the Benghazi Revolutionary Shura Council (BRSC). The kidnapping of these Libyans happened because they or their relatives participated in the fight against forces of Operation Dignity. The Ministry of Justice, the Ministry of Interior, or the Ministry of Defense held these captives under their nominal supervision. Oddly, some of the detention centers were unofficial temporary facilities that included farms, military bases and a hotel in Benghazi.[39]

The Birsis detention facility, managed by the Department of Combating Terrorism of the Ministry of Interior, gained notoriety in 2015 due to frequent information of arbitrary and incommunicado detention of individuals for prolonged periods of time including torture and other ill-treatment. Even some captured civilians appeared in televised "confessions" shown on the Libya Awalan channel declaring their engagement in fighting and murder.[40] Armed insurgents affiliated with the BRSC took part in the kidnapping of civilians based on their real or imagined political or religious membership and family connections. The fate and whereabouts of those held by the BRSC were unknown. This group included 130 detainees from the Buhdeima military prison in October 2014. Their conditions, following their detention, remained uncertain, with concerns for their lives and safety.[41]

A comprehensive report, titled "The Endless Wait: Long-Term Arbitrary Detentions and Torture in Western Libya,"[42] chronicles the long-term arbitrary detention, torture and other ill-treatment in four jails in Tripoli and Misrata. The Judicial Police run the detention camps and the Judicial Police are under the supervision of the Justice Ministry of the Tripoli-based de facto government.[43] The outcome of the political imbroglio that reached its heights in 2011 gave license to the interim government to arrest thousands of Libyans who were then detained at will without trial or being charged with a crime.[44] Such detentions contravene Articles 61 and 63 (see Table II) of the Libyan constitution. The preceding narrative depicts and presents human rights challenges in the republic.

Between September 16 and September 20, 2015, HRW agents interrogated 120 detainees in four penitentiaries, two located in Tripoli (Ain Zara and al-Baraka) and two located in Misrata (al-Jawiyyah and al-Huda). The prisoners were without attorney or judicial representation to defend them and were in custody for a long period incommunicado. In addition, they experienced torture and other ill-treatment; forced confessions; lack of due process, including lack of access to lawyers; long-term solitary confinement; and in some cases, poor detention conditions.[45] Many of the prisoners interviewed were supporters of the dethroned erstwhile leader, Muammar Gaddafi.[46]

The United Nations was concerned enough about the deteriorating human rights violations in Libya that in March 2015, the UN Human Rights Council commissioned an investigative body under Resolution 28/30. The Council's mandate was to examine the widespread human rights infractions against international humanitarian law—the laws of war and other legal norms. Rights activists anticipated that the outcome of this investigation would bring the culprits or violators of the human rights of innocent citizens to book. Regrettably, attempts to put a stop to torture and other ill-treatment of internees came to naught, partially because of political instability.[47] Further, the UNSMIL recorded allegations of torture and other ill-treatment in a few detention accommodations in western Libya. These detention centers were run by the Faruk, Sareya al-Ula, Nasr and Sila' al-Tamwiniya armed groups in al-Zawiya; the Abu Salim, Shahid Hamza, Fursan Janzur, and the Mitiga-based Quwwa al-Rad' armed groups in Tripoli; and others. It also received reports of deaths of individuals held by armed groups in al-Zawiya and Warshafana.[48]

It is critical that all conflicting parties in Libya are under obligation to adhere to international humanitarian law and the laws of war that govern political and military actors during situations of armed conflict. Generally, it is perverse not to respect international human rights conventions, because they advance international peace and security when observed. Thus, the detention of citizens must go along with due process of law that promptly informs a person or group of the reason for arrest. A qualified or competent judge should immediately oversee citizens' detention in custody based on appropriate domestic law. Plaintiffs must provide detainees the right to challenge the legality of the incarceration as stipulated in the constitution and other legal documents. Indeed, a HRW petition to Libyan authorities, on the matter of torture and ill-treatment of detained individuals during conflicts, is spot on. The entreaty suggests a method for combating human rights challenges in Libya. This appeal states:

> Warring factions in Libya are bound by Common Article 3 to the four Geneva Conventions of 1949, applicable during non-international armed conflicts, which requires protecting anyone in custody, including captured combatants and civilians, against "violence to life and person, in particular murder of all kinds, mutilation, cruel treatment and torture" and "outrages upon personal dignity, in particular humiliation and degrading treatment." No sentences may be handed down except by a "regularly constituted court" that meets international fair trial standards.[49]
>
> [Also] Common Article 3 binds all parties to the conflict to respect, as a minimum, that persons taking no direct part in hostilities as well as those placed hors de combat shall be treated humanely, without any adverse distinction.... Attacks on civilians and civilian objects are prohibited. [This includes] attacks that may be expected to cause incidental loss of civilian life.[50]

Refreshingly, Libya is a signatory to international and regional agreements that impose legal responsibilities regarding the treatment of prisoners. Article 9 of the ICCPR affirms inter alia that a qualified legal authority oversees any individual detained in custody. Article 14 of the UN Convention against Torture and Other Cruel, Inhuman or Degrading Treatment or Punishment enjoins Libya to investigate, interrogate and prosecute those culprits responsible for torture in the country. The state is to compensate anyone wrongfully victimized by such an act. Article 7 of the African Charter on Human and Peoples' Rights states that "an individual can only be detained according to the established law and that anyone detained must be brought before a competent judicial authority to be charged or released."[51]

## Freedom of Religion and Human Rights

The constitution, in theory, is clear on the issue of religion and its role in the society given the social and cultural character of Libya. Just as it is true that humans do not always follow the principles enacted in a constitution, partly because of the conflict between theory and interests, the same, arguably, is true of the practice of the canons enshrined in holy texts and individual interest/s. The struggle for who gets what, when and how often awakens the instrumentalist application of religion in many societies. Political actors invoke the sacrosanctity of religious doctrines to sabotage constitutional human rights precepts and theories; hence the clash between rights theories and practice in my contemplation. The foregoing suppositions are not lost on the motives of political elites who wrote the Libyan constitution. For example, Article 1 of the constitution states:

> Libya shall be an independent democratic state in which the people shall be the source of all powers. Its capital shall be Tripoli, **Islam shall be its religion and Islamic Sharia shall be the main source of legislation**. The State shall guarantee for non–Muslims the freedom to practice their religious rituals. Arabic shall be the official language, while the linguistic and cultural rights of the Amazigh, the Tabous, the Tuareg and other components of the Libyan society shall be guaranteed.

Within the context of the above excerpt, factions or minority groups that are non–Muslims cannot hold top executive political posts in the political system despite the declaration that Libya is a democratic state in which all citizens are entitled to equality of opportunity in the society. Such a doctrinal development unwittingly or wittingly encourages discrimination of different kinds toward fellow citizens who are not Muslims. Additionally, the political system, demographically, makes it much easier for the dominant population to dictate the political and even religious character of the polity. For example, in 2015, the headcount in Libya was approximately 6.4 million. Out of this figure, 97 percent are Sunni Muslims and three percent are Christians, Hindus, Bahais, Ahmadi Muslims, Buddhists, and Jews. Sizable members of the Amazigh ethnic minority belong to the Ibadi Muslim sect. The rest of the non–Muslim population in the country are foreigners, some of whom are members of the diplomatic corp.[52]

The Lilliputian Christian population is comprised solely of sub-Saharan African and Egyptian immigrants, sprinkled with a few U.S. and European sojourners. Roughly 50,000 are Coptic Christians. The other denominations are Roman Catholic, Anglican, and Greek and Russian Orthodox.[53] In a country of slightly over six million, these groups in no way pose a political threat to the dominant Sunni Muslims. Nevertheless, in times of political turmoil, as was the case following the 2011 revolution and collapse of the Gaddafi regime, disgruntled former agents of the government displaced their frustrations on real and putative enemies. These were antagonists responsible for upsetting the political system that served their interests. In the process of venting their anger because they were sacked from their position of privilege, these ex-officials committed human rights crimes. The breaches of the human rights of non–Muslim communities and unorthodox intra-Muslim groups are the focus of the brief analysis that follows.

The sacredness of the Sharia laws and jurisprudence in the social and political life of most Libyan citizens is never in question. The invocation and implementation of creeds in the Quran and Sharia, by the guardians of the law and conservative politicians, sometimes clash with positive constitutional human rights theories in this society, as noted earlier. Put in another way, given the post–Gaddafi anarchic polity, many Muslim extremists (internal and foreign) took it upon themselves to apply Sharia laws willy-nilly. They did so in pursuit of their grievances against Christian minorities and Muslims who failed to conform to their interpretation of accepted Islamic canons.

Lamentably, the Libyan state was unable to maintain law and order through its justice and security machineries following post–2011 revolution. Subsequently, various groups—revolutionary brigades, tribal militias, and local strongmen—established rival reigns within the region. The weak central government could not under such a circumstance respond competently to moments of violence and violation of the human rights of minority religious communities. Indeed, all that the administrators of the crippled regime could do was condemn the acts of violence, killings and violations of religious freedom. As a matter of fact, the U.S. Department of State, in view of the unstable situation, recounted:

> On February 15, a video on social media depicted the beheading of 21 men on an unidentified beach in the country. The "Tripoli Province" of Da'esh claimed responsibility for the killings and made clear the men were targeted for their religion, referring to them as "crusaders" and threatening further violence against Christians. The Egyptian government confirmed the deaths of 20 Egyptian citizens and the Ghanaian government confirmed that a Ghanaian Christian was one of those beheaded. This was followed by another video, on April 19, which showed the killing of 28 Ethiopian and Eritrean Christians by beheading and gunshot. Da'esh claimed responsibility for these killings. On October 18, a video was published depicting the killing of a Christian man from South Sudan, for which Da'esh claimed responsibility.[54]

Human rights activists may exculpate the regime and its law enforcement agencies, in this instance, for violating religious freedom. This is the case because neither the government in Bayda nor that in Tripoli was capable of effectively controlling the mosques, let alone the clerics in and outside the government's areas of administrative jurisdiction. This infraction of religious freedom contravenes Article 8 of the African Charter on Human and Peoples' Rights, which declares, "Freedom of conscience, the profession and free practice of religion shall be guaranteed. No one may, subject to law and order, be submitted to measures restricting the exercise of these freedoms." Article 18 of the International Convention on Civil and Political Rights and Article 18 of the Universal Declaration of Human Rights guarantee religious freedom. What the preceding suppositions suggest is that attempts to solve the problem of the human rights contraventions of religious minorities will not be easy despite the above protocols and constitutional safeguards. This was the circumstance in a political milieu that was and is still revolutionary and poses human rights challenges in Libya.

## Women's Rights

The discourse on women's rights in Libya is stimulating vis-à-vis the discussion on women's rights in much of the Islamic Middle East and Africa. Commonly, human rights campaigners bring to the fore the problems of discrimination against women globally, but rights activists are more energetic in the global south where bias toward women happens rampantly. This is the case, in part, because of how women's rights are visualized in contrast to the way men's rights are seen and constructed in cultural and theological contexts in the developing world. Attempts to address the anomalies that exist in the interpretations of the roles of women and men in society have been difficult due partly to the theory of cultural relativism. However, this problem has never deterred human rights academics and practitioners from proffering solutions that have been helpful to political actors in tackling women's human rights issues in all polities and in all regions of the world.

Nonetheless, powerful cultural relativists, and traditional patriarchal leaders, resist attempts by politicians to deconstruct their cultural values to promote respect for women's rights. In Libya, the clash between modernists, as represented by Muammar Gaddafi and his clique, and traditionalists whose views are steeped in Islamic values is striking. I will attempt to analytically unpack and then uncover some of the challenges to emancipating Libyan women that emerged legislatively under Gaddafi's administration.

To be sure, Libya is a signatory to international human rights conventions that emphasize the equality of women and men in a country in which traditional, cultural and theological forces are arguably anathema to the doctrine of gender equality. Overall, Libyans, especially pastoral citizens, draw their epistemology on how to govern a community, and the role of women in society, from their cultural values and theological texts. Even so, from the point of view of international human rights agreements sanctioned by Libya, the following articles on gender equality are informative. This is the case because they clash with several cultural norms and religious creeds. These are: Article 2 of the Universal Declaration of Human Rights; Article 3 of the International Covenant on Economic, Social and Cultural Rights; and Article 3 of the International Covenant on Civil and Political Rights. Superimposing on the preceding articles is Article 9 of the United Nations Convention on the Elimination of All Forms of Discrimination against Women (CEDAW). It proclaims, inter alia: "States Parties shall grant women equal rights with men ... and also equal rights in respect of their children."[55] Article 21 of Muamar Gaddafi's bold and revolutionary text, the Great Green Charter of Human Rights in the Age of the Masses, asserts, unequivocally: "The members of the Jamahiriyan society, men or women, are equal in everything which is human."[56]

## Discrimination

The epoch of Gaddafi's political reign is, sine dubio, the golden age of women's rights in Libya—at least on paper. His attempt to mitigate gender inequality amidst some of the prejudicial doctrines inherent in women's roles in the society and rights in the country's Sharia laws was impressive.[57] This is especially the case since Article 2 of the 1977 manifesto, Declaration on the Establishment of the Authority of the People states, "The Holy Koran is the constitution of the Socialist People's Libyan Arab Jamahiriya."[58]

As noted earlier, the Great Green Charter of Human Rights in the Age of the Masses proclaims the equality of men and women. It further adds that the distinction constructed or invented by society to suggest the superiority of men over women is flagrant injustice that is unjustifiable. To buttress the manifesto's principles that men and women are equal the Charter on the Rights and Duties of Women in Jamahiriya Society declares the equality of both genders in such areas as "national security duties, marriage, divorce, and child custody, the right to work, social security, and financial independence."[59] Nevertheless, family laws, which have their roots in traditional culture and values, undermine these cherished rights enshrined in the charter. It is probably this understanding that prompted crafters of the Green Charter to affirm that there are, however, biological traits that differentiate men from women. Consequently, it might be foolhardy to claim that men and women are equal (in all areas that are human),[60] thus highlighting the conflict between a positive human rights theory and practice that negates the rights theory as in the biological explication above between men and women.

Despite the declaration on gender equality in the Green Charter women, unlike Libyan men, cannot have their foreign-born spouse nationalize as Libyan. Authorities often denied children of such marriages the right to citizenship. Furthermore, in the republic, the practice of women's and men's equality is problematic in Islamic jurisprudence. For example, whereas the judicial system, in theory, allows an adult woman to pursue legal proceedings in court, she could only do so with the advisement of male siblings or relatives. In other words, only a man may take legal actions on behalf of his sister or female relative in the country. Additionally, following the interpretation of Islamic creeds, one male witness is equal to two females; thus, suggesting the superiority of men over women despite the declaration to the contrary in the Great Green Charter of Human Rights. The notion that women are not as reliable witnesses as men are in the judicial system smacks of gender prejudice.[61]

Moreover, when women and girls indulge in immoral conduct they are sent to social rehabilitation centers. When men and boys commit similar immoral delinquencies, they are not. The response is that "boys will be boys," and they are inadequately rebuked. Women housed in similar rehabilitation facilities as men receive harsher treatment. The curriculum of education for girls in these homes or treatment facilities is religious and is intended to drill into them Islamic moral codes and patterns of behavior expected of females in the nation. Although a signatory to the famous CEDAW of 1989, Libya contested the principles of Articles 2 and 16 of the CEDAW. Article 2 of the CEDAW declares: "States Parties condemn discrimination against women in all its forms, [and] agree to pursue by all appropriate means and without delay a policy of eliminating discrimination against women." Article 16(1) proclaims: "States Parties shall take all appropriate measures to eliminate discrimination against women in all matters relating to marriage and family relations and in particular shall ensure, on a basis of equality of men and women" (see appendix C).

Specifically, Libya's oppositional stance to the foregoing precepts in the CEDAW is in relation to rights and responsibilities in marriage, divorce, and parenthood. The government's position is that Articles 2 and 16 contravene Islamic values and jurisprudence on the foregoing. Further, this view is supported by Article 2 of the Great Green Charter of Human Rights that upholds the Holy Quran as the "religious" constitution of Libya; it is a situation that exposes the clash between rights theory and practice; also, it shines light on human rights challenges in the society.

If Libya is to advance women's human rights, one way to undertake this mission is to form authentic women's rights organizations. Al-Wafa and Al-Wattasimu were two groups that claim, in their own special ways, to be working toward the promotion of women's rights in the country and Africa, too.[62] However, these rights organizations were not members of civil society because they were beholden to, and worked at the behest of, the regime.[63] Consequently, their freedom to operate could be curtailed by state officials.

According to the law, women have the legal right to freedom of movement. This right is in agreement with Article 13 of the UDHR, which reads: "Everyone has the right to freedom of movement and residence within the borders of each state"; and "Everyone has the right to leave any country, including his [her] own and to return to his [her] country." Ditto Article 12 of the ACHPR and Article 12 of the ICCPR. Article 3 of the Great Green Charter of Human Rights sanctions this right for women as well. Nevertheless, in terms of practicality, many Libyan women travel mainly in the company of their male spouses or male siblings/relatives due, among other things, to the dominance of and reverence for the philosophy of patriarchy in the polity.[64]

Domestic violence by wife beaters is rampant in the country. This is so although Article 17 of Law No. 10 of 1984 forbids such an act. Indeed, this law states that male spouses must not cause physical or psychological injury to their wives. However, because Article 63 (see Table II) of the constitution requires a preponderance of evidence showing that injuries happened to prove that violence really occurred, authorities are reluctant to admit that violence against women is real in the society.

In the community, gender-based violence that happens far away from the communal center is dishonor to the family. In such a scenario, the female being victimized by a male is frequently blamed for the actions of the culprit. In short, the female victim "flaunted" herself outside the traditional supervision of a male escort. Occasionally, a judge may prosecute a grave rape of a female. Even so, ironically, rape victims may be prosecuted for indulging in the taboo of extra-marital sexual affairs if they dare to litigate the case.[65]

Economically, women fall short of males when it comes to the labor market despite their phenomenal and superior educational achievements in the republic.[66] This development in the country suggests that no matter women's higher educational attainments, their place is still in the house as homemakers. Marriage remains an obstacle to their upward mobility in the workplace. This is the case since the religious custom recommends—even demands—that husbands take care of their wives.

According to Section 31 of the Labor Law, there is no gender discrimination on wages—i.e., equal pay is given for equal work. Libya, very much like other developed and developing nations, has problems implementing the law of equal pay for men and women. Moreover, inheritance laws are in favor of men based on Islamic canons. A woman inherits half of what is due her brother/s. In this patriarchal society, both men and women display displeasure with any notion of women holding positions of power over men—a view that tenets in human rights instruments and rights advocates repudiate.[67]

Women suffer from marginalization in politics. This is the situation partially because of the conflictive nature of politics—the struggle for power. Subsequently, their representation in government is not robust. Women in Libya cannot organize and demonstrate against the government and the state itself. Their rights to participate actively in the system without encountering the wrath of the government agents and agencies cannot be guaranteed. Furthermore, the government determines when to open the political space. Socially, women's rights to take control of their bodies are limited, especially when it involves their reproductive health. Women's rights to receive abortion are limited and discussion on the subject is taboo. In fact, the rule is that a "woman who consents to or procures her own abortion … is punished with a minimum sentence of six months in prison."[68] The preceding discourse highlights the challenges to human rights in Libya.

## Racial/Ethnic Minorities and Discrimination

Articles 1, 2 and 5 of the International Convention on the Elimination of All Forms of Racial Discrimination not only expound on what racial discrimination means, but also enjoin member-states of the UN to adhere to the following protocols to eliminate racial or ethnic prejudice.

> Article 1: In this Convention, the term "racial discrimination" shall mean any distinction, exclusion, restriction or preference based on race, colour, descent, or national or ethnic origin which has the purpose or effect of nullifying or impairing the recognition, enjoyment or exercise, on an equal footing, of human rights and fundamental freedoms in the political, economic, social, cultural or any other field of public life.[69]

> Article 2(1): States Parties condemn racial discrimination and undertake to pursue by all appropriate means and without delay a policy of eliminating racial discrimination in all its forms and promoting understanding among all races, and, to this end: (a) Each State Party undertakes to engage in no act or practice of racial discrimination against persons, groups of persons or institutions and to ensure that all public authorities and public institutions, national and local, shall act in conformity with this obligation; (b) Each State Party undertakes not to sponsor, defend or support racial discrimination by any persons or organizations; (c) Each State Party shall take effective measures to review governmental, national and local policies, and to amend, rescind or nullify any laws and regulations which have the effect of creating or perpetuating racial discrimination wherever it exists.[70]

> Article 5: In compliance with the fundamental obligations laid down in article 2 of this Convention, States Parties undertake to prohibit and to eliminate racial discrimination in all its forms and to guarantee the right of everyone, without distinction as to race, colour, or national or ethnic origin, to equality before the law, notably in the enjoyment of the following rights: (a) The right to equal treatment before the tribunals and all other organs administering justice; (b) The right to security of person and protection by the State against violence or bodily harm, whether inflicted by government officials or by any individual group or institution.[71]

In Libya, Tawerghans, Tuareg, Tebu, black Libyans, Amazigh and the Mashashiya are minority ethnic groups. In the polity, agents of the regime intermittently breach their human rights.[72] For illustration, my dialogues will later center on a brief case study of the violations of the human rights of Tawerghans. My deliberations on the Tawerghans apply, mutatis mutandis, to other racial/ethnic groups. The Libyan constitution underscores the equal rights of all citizens before the law and emphasizes the right of all to enjoy equally civil and political rights, opportunities and duties of citizenship without discrimination based on religion, sect, language, wealth, sex, or tribal affiliations, inter alia. On paper, the law mandates punishment of not less than one year's incarceration for anyone guilty of bigotry based on class, group, region of origin, gender or colour.[73] Coincidentally, Article 2 of the African Charter on Human and Peoples' Rights, Article 2 of the

International Covenant on Civil and Political Rights and Article 2 of the Universal Declaration of Human Rights highlight the respect of the rights of minorities, too.

Also, despite the pleas of the above international human rights contraptions, the U.S. Department of State Country Report on Human Rights Practices in Libya for 2015 affirms that ethnic minorities confronted instances of societal racism and violence. Racial bias occurred against dark-skinned citizens, including those originally of sub-Saharan heritage. Administrative agents and agencies often differentiated between "loyal" and "foreign" populations of Tebu and Tuareg in the south and encourage deportation of minority factions associated with political opponents on the basis that they were and are not legally "Libyan." Additionally, some Tebu and Tuareg groups received inadequate services from their municipalities, depriving them of national identity proofs and thus access to work.[74]

## Tawerghans

Human Rights Watch reports that before the 2011 revolution, the Tawerghan population in Libya was approximately 42,000. This minority group received both financial and political support from Gaddafi; in return, they provided him military support to the chagrin of his political antagonists. Consequently, anti–Gaddafi forces sought revenge against these Gaddafi loyalists after the collapse of his administration.[75] Historically, Tawerghans settled in Libya as long ago as the 19th century during the period of the slave trade. They are mostly black Libyans, from sub-Saharan Africa.[76]

Civil wars, overall, create misery for ordinary citizens—not least among minorities and marginalized groups that lack the political power to avert their misfortune. Comparatively, this was the situation in the civil wars in Nigeria, Bosnia-Herzegovina, Liberia, Sri Lanka, and elsewhere. Human rights breaches are commonplace during conflicts and sometimes perpetuated by frustrated soldiers and ethnic groups who see conflicts as an opportunity to teach their imagined or true ethnic antagonists a lesson. The ethnic slaughter of Tawerghans in 2011 fits into this pattern. The onslaught on this ethnic group that happened in Tawergha is close to ethnic cleansings or genocide.

The atrocities and human rights infractions committed against Tawerghans led some observers to invoke Article 2 of the UN Genocide Convention. The United Nations enacted this convention for the prevention and punishment of the crime of genocide. This protocol draws attention to any acts committed with intent to destroy, in whole or in part, a national, ethnical, racial or religious group. The areas of concern are: (1) killing members of the group; (2) causing serious bodily or mental harm to members of the group; (3) deliberately inflicting on the group conditions of life calculated to

bring about its physical destruction in whole or in part; (4) imposing measures intended to prevent births within the group; and (5) forcibly transferring children of the group to another group.[77] Tawergha residents during the
combat between the insurgents and loyalists to the Gaddafi regime fled the
city in droves. This exodus led to the relocation of thousands in temporary
camps near Tripoli.[78]

During the Rwandan civil war, the Hutu strategy in the genocide was
to demonize and even dehumanize the Tutsis whose sobriquets were "cock-
roaches, tall trees," et cetera.[79] In contrast, in the Libyan case, revolutionaries were less derogatory. They described black Gaddafi supporters and
black-skinned inhabitants of Libya and guest workers from sub-Saharan
Africa as "mercenaries" who should be exterminated. Further, the animos-
ity toward Tawerghans has always had racist undertones; the hostility to this
group was only in "hibernation" before the 2011 civil war, when it awoke from
its slumber and erupted. This was the case despite the endorsed condemnation of racial bigotry in the constitution and the Great Green Charter of
Human Rights. Little wonder, then, that antagonism toward the Tawerghans
led to widespread carnage that included, but was not limited to, lynching
and beheadings, sometimes with the complicity of the National Transitional
Council.[80]

A Human Rights Watch account of 2016 expressed concern about the
authorities' rehabilitation scheme for displaced Tawerghans. For instance,
the local council of Misrata and allied militias persisted in stopping 40,000
inhabitants of Tawergha and residents of Tomina and Karareem from relo-
cating to their homes in what HRW dubbed a crime against humanity; this
was a collective punishment for an offence purportedly committed by some
Tawergha residents during the 2011 revolution.[81] Similarly, the United Nations
Human Rights Council observed that "members of the Tawerghan community, internally displaced since 2011, have faced particular difficulties in relation to reduced livelihoods, ethnic discrimination, and limited access to
education and health services. They have also reported arbitrary detention
and ill-treatment, especially by Misrata-based armed groups."[82] Problematically, the events described in the foregoing UN observations flout human
rights principles contained in Libya's constitution and clash with international
human rights conventions. Specifically, the acts are in violation of Article 9
of the International Covenant on Civil and Political Rights (see appendix B).

## Freedom of Speech and Press: An Overview

Virtually every nation-state enshrines provisions that call for freedom of
speech and press in its constitution. In general, the same is true with respect

to the principles of human rights. Yet, it is a given that many political actors, in many of the developing nations, see the role of the media as antagonistic if they cannot control it; political chiefs are frequently irritated when journalists and the media expose their political malfeasance in their governance techniques. Today, powerful politicians have invented and popularized the phrase "fake news" to describe uncomplimentary news attributable to their governorship. Additionally, some leaders not only enjoin the populace to treat such vital information with disdain but also declare the media to be a nuisance and national enemy.

In Libya, Articles 37 and 38 (see Table II) of the constitution provide for freedom of opinion, expression, and the press. Despite these precepts in the constitution, the government limits and sometimes denies the exercise of these rights, thus revealing the clash between positive constitutional theories and contradictory or negative practice in the society. The GNC enacted broad laws in February 2014, which criminalize acts that harm the February 17, 2011, revolution. Paradoxically, too, the House of Representatives (HoR), which became the internationally recognized government in August 2014, was unenthusiastic in promoting freedom of speech. Consequently, civil society organizations and media outlets self-censored their activities to avoid the wrath of armed groups and vigilantes who threatened and killed oppositional and rival activists.[83]

Theoretically, good governance in a polity is furthered when freedom of the press, opinion and expression predominate. To this end, I mined the impressive report on "attacks on human rights defenders, humanitarian workers, and media professionals"[84] produced by the UN Support Mission in Libya for my following analysis. I do so to shine light on the audacious undertakings of humanitarian and human rights workers critical for mitigating human rights challenges in post–Gaddafi Libya and advancing peaceful coexistence.

## Attacks on Human Rights Defenders, Humanitarian Workers and Media Professionals

In a post-war society following Gaddafi's 42-year reign in Libya, the political climate of the country was despotic. In this political scenario, the new leaders were not ready to brook criticism and opposition from opponents, because their political positions were unsteady. Armed vigilantes of different hues saw human rights defenders, concerned civil society groups and media professionals as their enemies. Thus, the regime needed to crush real or putative oppositionist forces, especially human rights activists reporting atrocities. Armed groups' harassment of civil society groups led to the curtailment of the rights to freedom of expression and association that, inexorably, resulted in self-censorship reminiscent of the period of Gaddafi's reign. In fact, little remains of the energetic media and civil society organizations that emerged immediately following the 2011 armed conflict.[85]

UNSMIL and the UN Office of the High Commissioner for Human Rights, based on their concerns over the matter of human rights infractions in Libya, published a report on March 25, 2015. This report chronicles the bodily and vocal attacks, arbitrary incarceration, closure of civil society bureaus and death threats that human rights defenders confronted in Libya.[86] For example, on March 16, 2015, armed groups stormed the Benghazi offices of the National Council on Civil Liberties and Human Rights (NCCLHR). Parenthetically, the HoR did not show enough concern about this atrocity; tactically, it did not appoint a new board of the NCCLHR to supersede the existing one at the end of 2014; this was the situation even when the law regulating the NCCLHR called for a replacement. In other words, the government did not show adequate interest in addressing the problem, possibly due to political considerations and because it was inexpedient for the regime to do.

Humanitarian workers were a constant target of vigilantes despite their efforts to provide succor to the destitute. Such was the case when members of Shaikh Taher Azzawy Charity, a benevolent organization, were abducted by radicals on their way to dispense non-food items in southwestern Libya; these captives were manhandled to teach them a lesson for meddling in the vigilantes' operations. Moreover, journalists and other media specialists across Libya were easy prey of militants, ostensibly for reporting their atrocities and human rights violations. Extremists kidnapped and tortured some reporters to intimidate and silence others who might write uncomplimentary news about their mayhem. Lamentably, on April 29, 2015, the Deputy Minister of Justice informed the UNSMIL:

> Five detained individuals "confessed" to the killing of seven journalists in two separate incidents. The victims were Barqua TV crewmembers Khaled al-Humeil, Younis al-Sal, Abdul Salam al-Kahla, Yousef al-Gamoudi, and Mohamed Jalal (an Egyptian national), who had been missing since August 2014, and two Tunisian journalists Soufiane Chourabi and Nadhir El-Ktari, missing since September 2014.[87]

Female media professionals are to act traditionally and according to religious doctrines. Failure to do so runs the risks of sexual harassment and threats for daring to report on human rights violations in the mass media. It is common for women television newscasters to receive threats on their social media pages cautioning or admonishing them to desist from working for specific TV channels. This is so especially for female anchor-persons who work for any channel that does not support Operation Dignity for women. For radical groups, it is sacrilegious to appear unveiled on TV.[88] Indeed, woe betides any woman who fails to follow the Islamic code of behavior—even when their professional duties call for adjustment to a contemporary lifestyle.

Speculatively, the human rights dilemma in Libya is likely to endure for some time to come given the country's political history. The prolonged one-man rule of the late Gaddafi, the revolution of 2011, the religious passions in the country and the clash between modernity and tradition combine to create a combustible society. This political scenario is likely to fester and impinge on human rights practices in this society for some time to come. Put in another way, the conflict between the positive human rights theories enshrined in the constitution and the reality of reactionary norms laced with theological dogmas poses major challenges to human rights observance in this polity. Even so, the contemporary discourses on human rights conundrums in Libya by academics and courageous defense of human rights by Human Rights Watch, Amnesty International and local civil society organizations are impressive. These are reassuring signs that with time, the republic will mitigate its major human rights challenges.

# 4

# Morocco

## Early History

Uniquely located geographically, Morocco is a short distance from Spain. The narrow strait of Gibraltar separates Morocco from Spain. Indeed, Morocco is closer to Europe than any other African country.[1] Yet, for many years, it escaped from being one of the European imperialist trophies. Remarkably, Morocco extended its empire into Europe—an important achievement in the history of colonization in which the narrative is fundamentally that of Arab and European conquest and occupation of Africa.

The autochthonous people of Morocco are Berbers whose influence spread across North Africa. They are Indo-Europeans who may have arrived in the region around the second century BCE. They made some contacts with oasis dwellers or savanna people. Berbers came into brief contact, too, with the Phoenicians, Carthaginians and Romans who occupied and traded in the region.[2] After the collapse of the Roman Empire, Vandals, Visigoths, and Byzantine Greeks conquered and ruled Morocco in quick succession.[3]

The immediate and extended family system formed the political, social, and cultural organization of the Berbers. Berbers lived in zones and each zone represented a clan. An alliance of clans, generally tracing their pedigree to an ancestor, composed a tribe. Because Berbers were fiercely independent, each group enjoyed its sovereignty. For mutual defense, related Berber tribes came together to form confederations. This arrangement served their interest well since war was a regular occurrence of tribal life. Their philosophy at that time is akin to a contemporary creed in international relations—nation-states don't have permanent friends, they don't have permanent enemies, they have permanent (or pragmatic) interests. Consequently, in the Berbers' interactions with invading foreign powers they switched their allegiances strategically and conveniently. For example, during the second century AD, when Christianity arrived in Morocco, Berbers accepted the religion just as they received Islam in the seventh century AD.[4] The group's interest to survive in both cases guided its decisions.

Arab conquest of Morocco followed the same path as that of other countries in North Africa. Even so, the fierce resistance of independent-minded Berbers made it difficult for the Christian missionaries and Islamic conquerors to subdue them. It was only toward the end of the seventh century that it happened. A key Arab policy in Morocco, as elsewhere in North Africa, was assimilation. The emphasis was on spreading the religion and living amongst the natives as one Muslim family.

Idris Ibn Abdillah created the first known Moroccan "state" in the late eighth century AD. He was a descendant of the Prophet Muhammad. Idris had relocated in the far west of the Islamic world to avoid the constant civil wars in the east. Because of his devoutness, wisdom, and descent from the Prophet Muhammad, Berber groups welcomed him as their political and spiritual leader. His son and heir to the throne, Idris II, founded the first capital, Fez. The king and prince calculatedly established a tradition whereby descent from the Prophet Muhammad was a significant requirement for attaining political power. This decreed custom conferred major social status in Morocco for anyone who claimed the Prophet's lineage or pedigree.[5] Following the death of Idris II internal family social and structural disarticulations created a problem of governance.[6]

As noted earlier, the Berber group considered itself independent and always guarded its interest and sovereignty jealously. Accordingly, it was striking that in the 11th and 12th centuries respectively arose two distinct Berber groups that brought real greatness to Morocco and much of Africa. These were the Almoravids and Almohads, whose genre of Islamism was highly influenced by Berber cultures and values.[7]

## Almoravids and Almohads

### Almoravids

At the beginning of the 11th century, Sanhaja chieftains who had gone to Mecca for their annual pilgrimage invited Ibn Yasin, a devout Islamic tutor, to preach to their pastoral desert tribes. Ibn Yasin's audiences were inspired by his teaching so much that they embarked on a concerted effort to revive the "authentic" faith of Islam. As an outcome of this revivalism, a strict religious brotherhood emerged at the end of the religious crusade. Buoyed by religious zeal, the Almoravid warriors went on a religious and commercial conquest. Indeed, by 1082 AD, they had "captured the whole of the Maghrib as far east as present-day Algiers, and by the end of the century they had built an empire that reached from the Senegal River in West Africa to the Ebro River in Spain."[8]

The Almoravid sultans skillfully brought political unification to all present-day Morocco and bequeathed their heirs the entire Western Sahara. Moreover, they enforced the conservative Sunni Maliki rite that became the official and dominant genus of Islam practiced in Morocco. Under the Almoravids, Morocco and Spain were for a time provisionally annexed with Muslim territories under the divine influence of the Abbasid caliphate located in Baghdad. The pragmatic acceptance of the Andalusian lifestyle and moral laxity–cum–turpitude of the Almoravids robbed them of the respect of the Sanhaja chieftains. This lack of ethics and confidence in these Berber warriors subsequently decreased the military power on which their influence rested. Ultimately, this malaise led to the downfall of the first notable Berber dynasty.[9]

## Almohads

Ibn Tumart founded the Almohads' crusade during the first half of the 12th century. He was a member of the Sunni ulama sect whose spiritual fervor following his return from pilgrimage in Mecca led him to denounce the Almoravids for their profligacy or licentiousness. Additionally, there existed a long-standing sectarian antagonism between the mountain (Almohad) tribes and the desert (Almoravid) nomads. Ibn Tumart's disciples accepted him as the sect's Mahdi. His alias was the "sinless one" sent from God to free his people. In 1121 AD, he castigated the anthropomorphism that he saw in the Berber traditional religion.[10]

Ibn Tumart was a skillful political leader who on top of his spiritual leadership gave the Almohads an efficacious formal governmental structure—the very kind that the Sanhaja Almoravids had lacked. His military acumen was impressive, too. Indeed, by 1140 the Almohad sultan had conquered most of Morocco; and in 1146, he captured Marrakech and proceeded to destroy its denizens. Ibn Tumart by this act, consequently, ended the Almoravid dynasty. Even so, Marrakech continued to serve as the capital of the new Berber dynasty, which under Sultan Yacub al Mansur in about 1184 stretched from Tripoli to Spain. This reign achieved its zenith under the leadership of Sultan Mohammed al Nasir between 1199 and 1214.[11]

The Almohads, during their campaign in Morocco, received an invitation from the taifas (principalities) of Spain to join an expedition to rout the Almoravids at Seville. This successful incursion into Spain gave the Almohad sultan ultimate religious and political authority in the region. In time, the Almohads became the first, and perhaps the last, to unite North Africa and Islamic Spain under one government.[12] Ironically, the supremacy of theology in the governance of the society gradually yielded to dynasty politics. In this schema, the struggle for political power and its rewards became the motivating factor driving the Almohad movement as blood ties (nepotism) replaced moral qualities as the qualification to hold a top post in the regime. In addition, a biased distinction between leaders drawn from the Sultan's family and tribal leaders drawn from the Almohads became apparent. Regrettably, as the empire expanded, the dynasty became more isolated from the Berber support that had propelled and sustained it.

Although the Almohads shared the crusading instincts of their Castilian opponents, the perennial battles in Spain strained their resources. Little wonder, then, that they were decisively defeated in the marathon battle of Las Navas de Tolosa in 1212 AD. Indeed, this epic battle, arguably, became a major symbol and accomplishment in the history of the Christian re-conquest of Spain. Because of this struggle and its outcome, Muslim power started to wane in Spain and this region.[13]

Two Berber empires followed the Almohads and its governance of the society. In the 16th century, however, a second Arab dynasty, the Sa'adian, ascended to power exclusively based on its members' lineage as descendants of the Prophet Muhammad.[14] Intra-family rivalries amongst heirs of the Sa'adian dynasty in the 17th century led in part its ouster by the Alaouites, a successive Arab dynasty. They also suffered from internal family squabbles and upheaval. In later centuries, internal family rivalries, societal dislocations and disgruntlement with the leadership in the polity added to the problem of management of the state. This state of discontent not only weakened policies critical for sustaining the polity but also opened it up to European invasion and occupation. Thus, it is on a concise discussion of the arrival and administration of Morocco by European powers, and resistance by nationalists to the European genus of government, that I shall focus my subsequent analysis. It should be added, however, that the issue of human dignity and rights partially informed the insurgency of Moroccan activists and autonomists during the period of colonization and the later demand for home-rule.

## European Occupation

Internal political disorder in Morocco exposed the country to European intervention, as noted previously. For example, the French during the mid-19th century from their post in Algeria dealt a heavy and mortal military blow on Morocco, which had sent forces to Algeria to assist a fellow Muslim country. In addition, toward the end of the 19th century, Morocco's economy was in serious decline and this economic woe paved the way for intervention in the internal affairs of the state by Spain and France. In fact, Morocco's inability to resuscitate the economy, in which Spain and France had invested substantially, fomented national anguish. Ominously, the economic and political discontent created a condition that made the country ripe for the picking by France and Spain—notwithstanding the competing interests of Britain, Germany, and Italy in Morocco.[15]

"He who pays the piper, names the tune" is an aphorism applicable to this phenomenon in Morocco. France and Spain dictated policies in the country since, in a way, they paid the bills. Nonetheless, this situation of dependency did not sit well with members of the informed public. Consequently, the inordinate influence of these foreign powers in Moroccan politics, society, life, and the economy exacerbated internal grievances. The complaints and protests of activists against the dominance of alien powers reached their crescendo in 1908 when Moroccans revolted against the foreign control of the country's political economy. This seemingly justifiable insurrection culminated in a backlash; it led to Spanish invasion and occupation of parts of Morocco. Sultan Abd al-Hafid, unable to reassert his authority in Morocco, capitulated in despair.[16]

Moreover, to quell the upheaval started by protesters against Spain and France, mainly, the Sultan signed the "infamous" Treaty of Fez in 1912. This pact marked the beginning of European occupation of Morocco, which became a protectorate of Spain and France simultaneously. In this plan, France became the major power in Morocco by arrogating the valuable territories—major cities and the central plains adjacent to French Algeria—to herself. Spain occupied parts of the northern coast and areas south all the way to Sidi Ifni and the arid Sahara Desert. The French Marshal, Louis Hubert Gonzalve Lyautey, was the first resident-General assigned to Morocco.[17] As was the case with the rise and fall of empires of antiquity, France and Spain experienced the same fate in Africa, too.

France's administrative system in Morocco, as was the case with those of the Germans, Portuguese, Italians and the British in Africa, met with resistance—i.e., emancipation struggles organized by nationalists. The draconian policies and leadership style of France and Spain did not find favor among the nation's autonomists; and usurpation of Moroccan lands by these powers did not help matters either. In truth, objections to the above developments galvanized political activists into action in their fight for national liberation.

## Independence

In the 1930s, national agitations against French rule in Morocco started to gather momentum. To articulate the grievances toward French colonialism and to present rousing propaganda to citizens in the society, a powerful political party was formed—the Istiglal (Freedom) Party. In the classic colonial strategy of divide-and-conquer, France attempted to pit the Arabs against the Berbers. Unfortunately for the French, they were unable to undo the glue that united these groupings in a common cause of ousting the colonialist from Morocco. When the French colonial overseers found it difficult to destroy the glue that bonded the competing ethnic factions, they opted for another subterfuge; the French appointed a new Sultan—Mohammed V.

The French made Mohammed V a Sultan when he was only 17. The assumption was that he would be so politically naïve that they could manipulate him on the throne to support French-imposed policies. To the contrary, the young and indomitable sultan made bold speeches in which he called for the rights of the Moroccan citizens and reminded the French of the country's self-governing history. Moreover, to assert his authority in the country, he bravely signed the reform manifestos requested by the nationalist cadres. On top of his support for the patriots, he was defiant when asked to sign legislation that would diminish his power. His defiance stirred Moroccan militants into action against the French colonial rule. The resistance happened in the form of rioting and violence in different parts of the country. To teach the sultan a lesson for defying Paris, the French exiled him to far-away Madagascar. He left gracefully but never abdicated his throne as the de jure sultan of Morocco. His tactical strategy not only won him praise but also boosted his popularity in the country amongst Moroccans. Indeed, the nationalist enthusiasm and revolt against French occupation reached its zenith in 1955. Confronted with the disastrous consequences of the war in Algeria, national tumult, and the heavy burden of sustaining its colonies militarily and financially, France granted Morocco self-rule in 1956.[18]

In governing a state, the significance of having a constitution or document outlining how the society is to govern itself is imperative. Undeniably, a constitution can promote peaceful coexistence if it has legitimacy or advance political instability if it lacks efficacy. Most constitutions have elaborate principles outlining the human rights of citizens. These human rights canons should induce the population of the polity to be relatively comfortable that the custodians of power will not abuse its rights; this postulation informs the reproduction of an elaborate human rights excerpt of the constitution as a point of reference in this chapter and volume.

## Table I: Constitution of Morocco 2011

19—The man and the woman enjoy, in equality, the rights and freedoms of civil, political, economic, social, cultural and environmental character, enounced in this Title and in the other provisions of the Constitution, as well as in the international conventions and pacts duly ratified by Morocco and this, with respect for the provisions of the Constitution, of the constants [constantes] of the Kingdom and of its laws.

The State works for the realization of parity between men and women.

An Authority for parity and the struggle against all forms of discrimination is created, to this effect.

20—The right to life is the first right of any human being. The law protects this right.

21—All have the right to the security of their person and of their kin, and to the protection of their assets.

The public powers assure the security of the populations and of the national territory within respect for the fundamental freedoms and rights guaranteed to all.

22—The physical or moral integrity of anyone may not be infringed, in whatever circumstance that may be, and by any party that may be, public or private.

No one may inflict on others, under whatever pretext there may be, cruel, inhuman, [or] degrading treatments or infringements of human dignity.

The practice of torture, under any of its forms and by anyone, is a crime punishable by the law.

23—No one may be arrested, detained, prosecuted or condemned outside of the cases and the forms provided by the law.

Arbitrary or secret detention and forced disappearance are crimes of the greatest gravity. They expose their authors to the most severe sanctions.

Any detained person has the right to be informed immediately, in a fashion which is comprehensible to him, of the reasons of his detention and of his rights, including that of remaining silent. He must benefit, as well, from juridical assistance and of the possibility of communication with his relations, in accordance with the law.

The presumption of innocence and the right to an equitable process are guaranteed.

Any detained person enjoys the fundamental rights and humane conditions of detention. He must benefit from programs of instruction and of reintegration.

All incitement to racism, to hatred and to violence is prohibited.

Genocide and all other crimes against humanity, the crimes of war and all the grave and systematic violations of the Rights of Man are punished by the law.

24—Any person has the right to the protection of their private life.

The domicile is inviolable. Searches may only intervene in the conditions and the forms provided by the law.

Private communications, under whatever form that may be, are secret. Only justice can authorize, under the conditions and following the forms provided by the law, the access to their content, their total or partial divulgation or their summons at the demand of whosoever.

The freedom to circulate and to establish oneself on the national territory, to leave it and to return, in accordance with the law is guaranteed to all.

25—The freedoms of thought, of opinion and of expression under all their forms are guaranteed.

The freedoms of creation, of publication and of presentation in literary and artistic maters and of scientific and technical research are guaranteed.

26—The public powers lend, by appropriate measures, their support to the development of cultural and artistic creation, and of scientific and technical research, as well as to the promotion of sports. They favor the development and the organization of these sectors in independent manner and on democratic and specific professional bases.

27—The citizens [feminine] and citizens [masculine] have the right of access to information held by the public administration, the elected institutions and the organs invested with missions of public service.

The right to information may only be limited by the law, with the objective of assuring the protection of all which concerns national defense, the internal and external security of the State, and the private life of persons, of preventing infringement to the fundamental freedoms and rights enounced in this Constitution and of protecting the sources and the domains determined with specificity by the law.

28—The freedom of the press is guaranteed and may not be limited by any form of prior censure.

All have the right to express and to disseminate freely and within the sole limits expressly provided by the law, information, ideas and opinions.

The public powers encourage the organization of the sector of the press in an independent manner and on democratic bases, as well as the determination of the juridical and ethical rules concerning it.

The law establishes the rules of organization and of control of the means of public communication. It guarantees access to these means respecting the linguistic, cultural and political pluralism of the Moroccan society.

In accordance with the provisions of Article 165 of this Constitution, the High Authority of Broadcasting sees to respect for this pluralism.

29—The freedoms of reunion, of assembly, of peaceful demonstration, of association and of syndical and political membership, are guaranteed. The law establishes the conditions of the exercise of these freedoms.

The right to strike is guaranteed. An organic law establishes the conditions and the modalities of its exercise.

30—All the citizens [feminine] and the citizens [masculine] of majority, enjoying their civil and political rights, are electors and eligible. The law provides the provisions of a nature encouraging the equal access of women and men to the elective functions.

The vote is a personal right and a national duty.

Foreigners under [Moroccan] jurisdiction enjoy the fundamental freedoms recognized to Moroccan citizens [feminine] and citizens [masculine], in accordance with the law.

Those among them who reside in Morocco can participate in local elections by virtue of the law, of the application of international conventions or of practices of reciprocity.

The conditions of extradition and of granting of the right of asylum are defined by the law.

31—The State, the public establishments and the territorial collectivities work for the mobilization of all the means available to facilitate the equal access of the citizens [feminine] and the citizens [masculine] to conditions that permit their enjoyment of the right:

- to healthcare;
- to social protection, to medical coverage and to the mutual or organized joint and several liabilities of the State;
- to a modern, accessible education of quality;
- to education concerning attachment to the Moroccan identity and to the immutable national constants;
- to professional instruction and to physical and artistic education;
- to decent housing;
- to work and to the support of the public powers in matters of searching for employment or of self-employment;
- to access to the public functions according to the merits;
- to the access to water and to a healthy environment;
- to lasting development.

32—The family, founded on the legal ties of marriage, is the basic unit of society.

The State works to guarantee, by the law, the protection of the family under the juridical, social and economic plans, in a manner to guarantee its unity, its stability and its preservation.

It assures one equal juridical protection and one equal social and moral consideration to all children, [being the] abstraction made from their familial situation.

Fundamental instruction is a right of the child and an obligation of the family and of the State.

A Consultative Council of the Family and of Childhood is created.

33—It is incumbent on the public powers to take all the appropriate measures with a view to:

- stimulate and make general the participation of youth in the social, economic, cultural and political development of the country;
- to aid the young to establish themselves in [an] active and associative life and to give assistance to them in the difficulty of scholarly, social or professional adaptation;
- to facilitate the access of the young to culture, to science, to technology, to art, to sports and to leisure, all in creation of propitious conditions for the full deployment of their creative and innovative potential in all these domains.

A Consultative Council of Youth and of Associative Action is created to this effect.

34—The public powers enact and implement the policies designed for persons and for categories of specific needs. To this effect, it sees notably

- to respond to and provide for the vulnerability of certain categories of women and of mothers, of children, and of elderly persons;
- to rehabilitate and integrate into social and civil life the physically sensory-motor and mentally handicapped and to facilitate their enjoyment of the rights and freedoms recognized to all.

35—The right to property is guaranteed.

The law can limit the extent of it and the exercise of it if the exigencies of economic and social development of the country necessitate it. Expropriation may only proceed in the cases and the forms provided by the law.

The State guarantees the freedom to contract and free competition. It works for the realization of a lasting human development, likewise to permit the consolidation of social justice and the preservation of the national natural resources and of the rights of the future generations.

The State looks to guarantee the equality of opportunities for all and one specific protection for the socially disfavored categories.

36—The infractions relative to conflicts of interest, to insider crimes and all infractions of financial order are sanctioned by the law.

The public powers are held to prevent and to reprimand, in accordance with the law, all forms of delinquency arising from the activity of the administrations and of the pubic organs, from the use of funds which they control, as well as from transfers and from the management of public markets.

Influence trafficking and trafficking in privileges, the abuse of a dominant position and of monopoly, and all the other practices contrary to the principles of free and fair competition in economic relations, are sanctioned by the law.

A National Instance of Probity, of Prevention and for the struggle against Corruption is created.

37—All the citizens [feminine] and the citizens [masculine] must respect the Constitution and conform to the law. They must exercise the rights and freedoms guaranteed by the Constitution in a spirit of responsibility and of engaged citizenship, where the exercise of the rights is made in correlation to the accomplishment of the duties.

38—All the citizens [feminine] and the citizens [masculine] contribute to the defense of the Country and of its territorial integrity against any aggression or threat.

39—All support, in proportion to their contributive faculties, the public expenditures which only the law may, in the forms provided by this Constitution, create and assess.

40—All support with solidarity and proportionally to their means, the expenses that the development of the country requires, and those resulting from calamities and from natural catastrophes.

Source: Constitution of Morocco, 2011, https://www.constituteproject.org/constitution/Morocco_2011?=en (retrieved 5/6/18).

## Human Rights: An Overview

Morocco is not a republic in that the people do not hold supreme power; rather, the ultimate authority rests with a monarch, who heads the Council of Ministers. Within the context of his power, he can sack ministers, dissolve the legislature, and even rule by decree. In short, the constitution abrogates the citizens' rights to choose or elect the head of state. This is so because the constitution places the monarchy at the helm of the political system and government. In human rights dialogues, Morocco, very much like other North African countries, confronts a variety of human rights challenges. A recount of human rights dilemmas shows:

> Security forces commit[ed] human rights abuses on multiple occasions, including torture in detention. Prison and detention conditions were [and are] substandard. The judiciary lacked [and still lacks] independence and sometimes denied defendants the right to a fair public trial. Pretrial detention frequently exceeded what the law allows.... [There are unlawful or spurious detentions of] political prisoners, many of whom authorities reportedly detained under the anti-terrorism law.... [There is curtailment of] civil liberties by infringing on freedom of speech and press, including by harassing and arresting ... print and internet journalists for reporting and commenting on issues sensitive to the government; limited freedom of assembly and association, and [some restriction of] the right to practice one's religion ... discrimination against women and girls ... [and] trafficking in persons and child labor ... particularly in the informal sector.[19]

There is a wide range of citizens' rights contraventions in Morocco. However, for illustration, the critical areas of human rights infractions I shall discuss in this chapter are torture, religious rights, women's rights, freedom of speech and press and minority rights. I have subjectively selected these issues of human rights violations for analysis in this society. I have done so partially because in national and international human rights dialogues these rights quandaries are contentious and challenging at the same time.

## Torture and Other Cruel, Inhuman, or Degrading Treatment or Punishment

The UN Convention against Torture and Other Cruel, Inhuman, or Degrading Treatment or Punishment was approved by virtually every member of the UN to illustrate the international community's resolve to mitigate this human rights quagmire. Yet, the use of torture as means to extract information from real or imagined criminals is common worldwide; it is, however, more prevalent in the developing world partly because of the prevalence of unconsolidated democracy, authoritarian leaders, political instability, corruption and weak judicial systems.

Commonly, regimes and their security agents and agencies are culpable in the act of applying torture against political opponents and activists who are demonized as enemies of the state. Morocco, like other countries in the region, is guilty in the application of torture and inhuman treatment of citizens. However, it is noteworthy that Morocco signed the UN protocol against torture that calls upon all nations to avoid torture and other means that can deny citizens their rights to fair trial. In adhering to this code of conduct victims of torture can sue the appropriate authorities and demand immediate and uncorrupted investigation of their alleged crime or offenses against the state.

It is refreshing that Morocco's penal code, at least on paper, condemns torture. The Code of Criminal Procedure affirms, "Confessions obtained through 'violence' or 'coercion' are inadmissible in court."[20] Further, the constitution in Article 22 (see Table I) states: "No one may inflict on others, under whatever pretext there may be, cruel, inhuman [or] degrading treatments." The regime, to its credit, also implemented strategies ostensibly intended to eliminate torture. For instance, in November 2014 the government approved the Optional Protocol to the UN Convention against Torture and Other Cruel, Inhuman, or Degrading Treatment or Punishment. This pact empowers the National Council on Human Rights (CNDH) to advance human rights practice in the country. CNDH does so by monitoring and acting as an investigative apparatus for deterring torture.[21] Thus, in theory and in public pronouncements, the government's stance on mitigating torture and other cruel, inhuman, or degrading treatment or punishment is impressive.

However, the actions of rogue and over-zealous regime aficionados prove otherwise as reports after reports on the application of torture in the Kingdom persist. This development exposes the conflict between the "positive" theory of human rights and the "negative" impact of non-compliance with human rights dogmas. Indeed, it might have been failed attempts made by the government to fully curb the challenge that torture presents in the polity that prompted His Majesty King Mohammed VI to denounce it. He did so while candidly admitting that there might be remote cases of its application in parts of the country.[22] AI has chronicled the methods of torture applied by the police and other security forces for obtaining information from "felons." The tactics in the polity include, but are not limited to, the following: "beatings and stress positions to asphyxiation and drowning techniques as well as psychological and sexual violence including rape threats."[23] Generally, the clash between theory and practice is evident when agents of the regime renounce torture and its accoutrements legally in public, yet apply torture and its appurtenances in practice and in secret.

Globally, it is perturbing to human rights campaigners when the human rights of a cross-section of society suffer from serious rights infractions. Additionally, when the matter of human rights infringements involves torture and other cruel, inhuman, or degrading treatment or punishment it awakens the concerns of international human rights NGOs. This trepidation explains in part why AI, whose major raison d'être is the protection of the rights of political prisoners of conscience, undertook a comprehensive investigative assignment in Morocco on this issue. Its mission was to unearth the widespread torture and the complicit nature of security agents of the Kingdom on this rights violation. AI's revealing report on the problem of torture will form the basis of my ensuing brief analysis. Shining light on this issue could provide incentives to the state, political actors, and law enforcement agents in this country to desist from applying torture against the Kingdom's law. This view is in consonance with Article 7 of the International Covenant on Civil and Political Rights[24] and Article 5 of the African Charter on Human and Peoples' Rights.[25]

Amnesty International's edifying chronicle on torture and other ill-treatment in Morocco based its observation on incidents that happened between 2010 and 2014. AI made its findings available to the public following a special mission to the country in 2013 and 2014. It based its conclusions on torture and ill-treatment of victims and on the inability of the authorities to pluck up the courage to tackle the dilemma of torture on 173 cases.[26] According to AI's account,

> Wide ranges of people are tortured. Survivors whose experience is described in this report include [but are not limited to] protesters and activists challenging poverty, inequality or the exploitation of natural resources; political and student activists with left-wing or Islamist affiliations; supporters of Sahrawi self-determination; individuals accused of terrorism offences; and people suspected of ordinary crimes.[27]

Central to the research findings is that police and security forces applied different methods (beatings, asphyxiation, stress positions, simulated drowning, and psychological and sexual violence) on arrested individuals. Law enforcement agents torture and lay blame on detained felons or other criminal factions. Clearly, this view suggests that there is contradiction between what the state splendidly affirms in the constitution as government policy against torture and ill-treatment and the practice of agents and agencies of the regime. In sort, the safeguards that exist for citizens against torture are ignored by security agents—security forces sometimes perform acts of torture to embellish their record for advancement in the agency.[28]

The state, in attempts to exculpate herself from global censure on torture and human rights infractions in the society, invited in 2013 the UN Working Group on Arbitrary Detention to visit prisons in Sale, Tangier, Tetouan, Casablanca, and Laayoune in Western Sahara. Remarkably, the UN Working Group's account on human rights violations issued in August 2014 was not favorable. The group expressed dissatisfaction with the activities of the state security force regarding how it handled problems relating to terrorism, membership in Islamist movements or supporters of self-determination for Western Sahara—a touchy issue in Moroccan politics. The UN group observed in dismay a pattern of torture and mistreatment of inmates during interrogation and in custody by police and especially by representatives of the National Surveillance Directorate.[29] Overall, human rights campaigners continue to express concern that despite evidence of torture in the society, there were and are seldom cases of authorities punishing law enforcement officers found responsible for torturing individuals or groups of citizens.

Another disquieting element of the country's human rights record is the role of the judicial system, which is weak in its adjudication of cases on torture and ill-treatment of suspects accused of criminal behavior. The courts, commonly, have a propensity for sentencing alleged victims of crimes on fabricated and coerced confessions.[30] Nevertheless, it has been noted that "compelling suspects to incriminate themselves or others, including ... the use of torture or other ill-treatment during interrogation in police custody, violates the presumption of innocence. Article 293 of Morocco's Code of Criminal Procedure (CCP), too, prohibits the use of coerced statements in proceedings"[31]; here, then, lies an enigma between the positive human rights theory in Article 293 and the negative juridical practice.

Paradoxically, the state can arrogate powers to law enforcement agents to violate citizens' rights based on Article 290 of the CCP, which states that "police interrogation reports are taken as accurate until proven otherwise."[32] On this matter, therefore, there exists obfuscation or "double jeopardy" for a victim of torture who dares to report torture incidents in the society if it is not provable or if the security force does not admit that the victim has been tortured. In short, some courts in Morocco, conniving with law enforcement agencies, incarcerate activists who report torture. In defense of the police regarding torture or degrading treatment, security forces sporadically invoke Article 264 of the penal code. This article punishes "false reporting."[33] Accordingly, Article 264 discourages aggrieved victims from exposing police malfeasance such as torture and other human rights abuses for fear of victimization. Based on the above discourse Article 264 of the penal code clashes with Article 22 of the constitution, which prohibits torture and its accoutrements.

Despite the preceding concise and conflictive analysis relating to theory and practice on the issue of torture as human rights contravention, it could be observed:

> While torture and other ill-treatment are no longer systemic in Morocco and Western Sahara, lack of accountability remains strikingly widespread. Efforts to hold those responsible for torture or other ill-treatment to account are overshadowed by continuing impunity for past abuses. The overwhelming lack of adequate investigations into allegations of torture means that even fewer prosecutions are opened, in spite of official efforts to improve accountability for torture by strengthening the prohibition on torture in national legislation.[34]

## *Religion and Human Rights*

The right to religious faith and worship are guaranteed in most constitutions and international human rights instruments, possibly to avert or at least diminish conflicts in multi-religious societies. The Moroccan constitution proclaims the Kingdom to be a sovereign Muslim country and Islam to be the religion of the nation-state. The constitution in Article 25 guarantees freedom of thought, expression and assembly (see Table I). Also, Article 18 of the International Covenant on Civil and Political Rights states: "Everyone shall have the right to freedom of thought, conscience and religion. This right shall include freedom to have or to adopt a religion or belief of his [or her] choice, and freedom, either individually or in community with others and in public or private, to manifest his religion or belief in worship, observance, practice and teaching."[35] Article 8 of the ACHPR avers: "Freedom of conscience, the profession and free practice of religion shall be guaranteed. No one may, subject to law and order, be submitted to measures restricting the exercise of these freedoms."[36] Article 18 of the UDHR affirms: "Everyone has the right to freedom of thought, conscience and religion; this right includes freedom to change his [or her] religion or belief, and freedom, either alone or in community with others and in public or private, to manifest his religion or belief in teaching, practice, worship and observance."[37]

The centrality of the discourses in the following pages is that Morocco, like other Islamic states, has not lived up to the full spirit of its constitution relating to religious freedom. In addition, Morocco's religious rights compliance is not congruent with the precepts of religious freedom noted in the preceding international human rights documents. As noted previously, Morocco is not unique in its violations of the rights of non–Muslims that are generally fomented by religious extremists. Even so, religious bigotry is not limited to Morocco and Islamic states. Indeed, in the words of Doug Bandow, "It took Christendom centuries [to tackle religious prejudice and fanaticism], but religious tolerance eventually replaced persecution. Today it's hard to find a Christian society that genuinely persecutes."[38]

Demographically, the population of Morocco in 2015 was approximately 33.3 million and about 99 percent of the population are Sunni Muslim. Less than one percent of the society are Christians, Jews and Shia Muslims. Statistically, however, there are about 2,000 to 6,000 Moroccan Christians. Some Christian leaders approximate the number to be as high as 50,000. Foreign or non–Moroccan Christians are about 30,000 Roman Catholics and 10,000 Protestants. There are several thousand Shia Muslims and roughly 350–400 Bahais. Partly because Morocco is a proclaimed Islamic state, it is estimated that about 1,000 to 3,000 Moroccan Christians worship frequently in "house" churches for fear that Muslim militants might assault them.[39] This untenable situation violates the rights of Christians to freedom of worship in the Kingdom. But the constitution and precepts in international human rights declarations, as noted previously, repudiate the precarious circumstances of Moroccan Christians to worship freely.

Morocco's religious doctrine finds expression in the Maliki-Ashari school of thought. Its dogma, among other things, "punishes anyone who 'employs enticements' to undermine the faith of a Muslim or to convert a Muslim to another religion with ... imprisonment." In theory, "voluntary conversion is not a crime under the criminal or civil codes."[40] In truth, by way of comparison, Morocco's stance on this matter synchronizes philosophically with those of Judaism and some traditional Christian sects that fear that evangelizing Christian churches could poach on their congregations and are not tolerant of such act.[41]

It is noteworthy that churches and synagogues built before independence in 1956 are legal. Some of these religious institutions stand vis-à-vis mosques and function without harassments from the state or fanatic Islamists. Churches and associations that are registered worship freely, too. It is, however, prejudicial that the government grants "special recognition" only to Sunni Maliki-Ashari Muslims and Jews as native or aboriginal Moroccan populations with freedom to practice their religion without restrictions. Other religious bodies must register to become legal before they can embark on financial transactions and even do business as private institutions.[42] In addition, Sunni Muslims and Jews receive special acknowledgment not granted native Moroccan Christians.

Although the law punishes anyone who obstructs an individual or group of individuals from worshiping or attending religious services, the actual implementation of this law is rare. In fact, the government seldom punishes culprits who flout this law for fear of possible political and social backlash from Muslim activists against the regime. For example, in 2011, in response to street protests during the Arab Spring, the king appointed a commission to draft a new constitution that would give Moroccans more freedoms. However, when the notion of religious freedom was introduced to lawmakers, the powerful ruling conservative Justice and Development Party threatened to join the street protests. The commission immediately expunged the motion from the constitution in order to prevent further instability.[43] In other words, religious fundamentalist who abhorred opening up of the space for other religions to thrive thwarted the king's objective of liberalizing religious laws to grant more freedom of worship to all Moroccans—Muslim and non–Muslim.

Notwithstanding attempts by Morocco to maintain its image as a moderate Islamic country, regrettably some of its law enforcement agents and agencies act otherwise; they are accountable for the violation of the human rights of non–Sunni Muslim groups. The Kingdom does not take proselytizing or evangelism lightly despite the lack of major threat to the dominant Sunni majority in the country. In other words, the existence of approximately one percent Christians, Bahais and Shia Muslims in the population should not pose a threat to the dominant Sunni Muslims. Even so, in 2010, the Kingdom expelled about 150 Christian foreign residents accused of evangelism. In addition, the state closed a Christian-sponsored orphanage because pupils in this institution received a Christian education.[44] To declare the state's opposition on this matter, which smacks of religious bigotry, fanatical administrative officials arrested, detained, and interrogated Moroccan Christians about their contacts with other Christians. The government as well continued to restrict the spread of Islamic materials it deemed inconsistent with the teaching of the Maliki-Ashari school of Sunni Islam and philosophy.[45] Occasionally, there have been cases of imprisonment for proselytizing.[46] However, the above actions are in violation of the Kingdom's professed tolerance to religious conversion if the process is undertaken without coercion or enticement.[47]

Ominously, in religious and human rights contexts, Moroccan followers of the Christian, Shia and Bahai faiths have expressed anxieties about government "watchdogs" surveilling their activities. This action by some officials of the government has led some worshipers to desist from worshiping in public. Moreover, representatives of foreign Christian churches sometimes discourage Moroccan Christians from attending their church. In this way, Christian evangelists are less likely to run into conflict with laws prohibiting proselytizing. Similarly, members of the Bahai faith tactically avoid declaring their religious affiliation. This is the case because some of the country's Muslims see Bahai adherents as heretical deviants from Islam and renegades from the true Islamic religion.[48]

In Islamic faith, a Muslim man is free to marry a non–Muslim woman. Woe betides Muslim women who marry non–Muslim men. This theological creed is biased against human rights principles that have no religious or nationality restrictions on the rights of adult males and females to marry. The preceding Islamic doctrine on marriage supersedes the positive human rights tenet in Article 16(1–2) of the UDHR. Article 16(1) states: "Men and women of full age, without any limitation due to race, nationality or religion, have the right to marry…. They are entitled to equal rights." Article 16(2) affirms: "Marriage shall be entered into only with the free and full consent of the intending spouses";[49] this proviso calls for no family intervention either.

The foregoing narratives referring to religious prejudice and rights infractions in the Kingdom notwithstanding, this moderate Islamic country continues with its positive and yet difficult objective of mitigating the issue of human rights in the state. Such was the case when Morocco sponsored a welcoming convocation of religious Muslim leaders, heads of state and scholars in Marrakesh. This meeting was set up to tackle the threat posed by religious extremists in the Middle East and sub-Saharan Africa. This summit produced a comprehensive document called the Marrakesh Declaration, famously referred to as the "modern update to Muhammad's Charter of Medina."[50] The declaration calls upon Muslim stakeholders, politicians, intellectuals and educational institutions to combat Islamists whose activities have had a propensity for stultifying the genial character of Islam. In addition, this declaration expressed concern over the plight of minority religious groupings and their human rights in the Muslim world. Below is a snapshot of the communique issued at the end of this stimulating conference:

WHEREAS, this conference was held under the auspices of His Majesty, King Muhammed VI of Morocco, and organized jointly by the Ministry of Endowment and Islamic Affairs in the Kingdom of Morocco and the Forum for Promoting Peace in Muslim Societies based in the United Arab Emirates;

AND NOTING the gravity of this situation afflicting Muslims as well as peoples of other faiths throughout the world, and after thorough deliberation and discussion, the convened Muslim scholars and intellectuals:

DECLARE HEREBY our firm commitment to the principles articulated in the Charter of Medina, whose provisions contained a number of the principles of constitutional contractual citizenship, such as freedom of movement, property ownership, mutual solidarity and defense, as well as principles of justice and equality before the law; and that,

The objectives of the Charter of Medina provide a suitable framework for national constitutions in countries with Muslim majorities, and the United Nations Charter and related documents, such as the Universal Declaration of Human Rights, are in harmony with the Charter of Medina, including consideration for public order… [among other factors].

URGE MUSLIM educational institutions and authorities to conduct a courageous review of educational curricula that addresses honestly and effectively any material that instigates aggression and extremism, leads to war and chaos, and results in the destruction of our shared societies;

Call upon politicians and decisionmakers to take the political and legal steps necessary to establish a constitutional contractual relationship among its citizens, and to support all formulations and initiatives that aim to fortify relations and understanding among the various religious groups in the Muslim World;

Call upon the educated, artistic, and creative members of our societies, as well as organizations of civil society, to establish a broad movement for the just treatment of religious minorities in Muslim countries and to raise awareness as to their rights, and to work together to ensure the success of these efforts.

Call upon the various religious groups bound by the same national fabric to address their mutual state of selective amnesia that blocks memories of centuries of joint and shared living on the same land; we call upon them to rebuild the past by reviving this tradition of conviviality, and restoring our shared trust that has been eroded by extremists using acts of terror and aggression;

Call upon representatives of the various religions, sects and denominations to confront all forms of religious bigotry, vilification, and denigration of what people hold sacred, as well as speech that promote hatred and bigotry; and

FINALLY, AFFIRM that it is unconscionable to employ religion for the purpose of aggression upon the rights of religious minorities in Muslim countries.[51]

## Women and Human Rights

### Discrimination

Discrimination against women in social, economic, cultural, political and religious activities is mondial. However, the bias against women in the Muslim world is relatively more poignant than in Christian societies due in part to religious canons and patriarchy. Women in both the Christian and Muslim worlds have had a history of fighting prejudice with success in some countries and resistance in others. The struggle for women's emancipation in Morocco follows the same path as those in Western (and Christian) civilizations. For example, educated and feminist groups borrowing from their experience in France and elsewhere launched a movement to exculpate themselves from the "bondage" of patriarchy and traditional culture in the 1940s. Indeed, a passionate women's organization, Sisters of Purity Association, spear-headed the procedure for women's liberation by issuing a series of demands to the guardians of the political system. Some of the bold petitions presented to the leaders were "the abolition of polygamy, full and equal political rights, and increased visibility of women in the public sphere."[52] Moreover, groups in civil society including female journalists have fought, and continue to struggle, against discrimination. Further, Moroccan academics, especially female scholars, joined others in the petition for "equality" following the attainment of self-rule from France in 1956. In dialogues on the marginalization of women in the polity, academics continue to examine and debate the issue of gender inequality. They also enquire into the theological roots of women's social, cultural, and political demotion in the Kingdom.[53]

As if to deal a fatal blow to the feminist movement seeking greater participation in the social and political life of the society, political actors and religious and patriarchal leaders promulgated the first Moudawana, also referred to as the Code of Personal Status, in 1957–58.[54] This code finds expression in the doctrine of the Maliki School of Islamic jurisprudence. Some of its principles contradict major tenets of the penal code and the national constitution. Indeed, noted Mounira M. Charrad, "Moudawana codified the subordinate status of women by delegating power over women to men as husbands and as male kin."[55] The state passed a second Moudawana (also Mudawwana) in 2004 following pressure brought to bear on the state by civil society on the issue. To be sure, the constitution of Morocco, like those of the other Islamic countries in North Africa, states emphatically that the Kingdom is an Islamic state governed by Islamic values. For simplification, I will discuss women's rights infractions in the Kingdom against the backdrop of the foregoing narratives. For this purpose, I mined the illuminating report on Gender Equality and Parity in Morocco, articulated by the CNDH, for my analysis.[56]

Before the government's enactment of the 2011 constitution, the struggle by civil society groups to address the issue of women's human rights was relentless. The "progressive" King Mohammed VI was determined to address this matter to show to the world the moderate character of Islamism in his Kingdom. Consequently, in December 2008 with a stroke of his pen, he issued an official proclamation banning prejudice against women and formally abandoned all Morocco's earlier misgivings on the CEDAW. He declared, unequivocally, "Our country has become an international actor of which the progress and daring initiatives on this matter are readily recognized."[57]

The King's pronouncement on women's rights is reflected in Article 19 of the 2011 constitution that states, among other things, "The state works for the realization of parity between men and women" (see Table I). Additionally, this precept in the constitution is in accord with Article 3 of the ICCPR that avows, "The State Parties to the present Covenant undertake to ensure the equal right of men and women to the enjoyment of all civil and political rights set forth in the present Covenant." Article 2(a–g) of the CEDAW also encapsulates the preceding principles on women's rights in the Kingdom.[58]

Commonly, human rights principles are superbly outlined in national constitutions and international human rights documents. However, the actual execution of the precepts contained in these states' documents are problematic. This is the case because individual, group and national interests frequently trump human rights preachments in a polity. The foregoing postulation is generally true in politics, and in all regions of the world. As noted earlier, I drew my source for discussing women's rights issues in Morocco in part from the CNDH 2015 report on Gender Equality and Parity in Morocco. I shall augment my following deliberations and critiques on this issue from other sources, too. Further, I will draw upon illustrations taken from international human rights instruments to back up my explorations on women's human rights violations in the Kingdom.

## Post-Constitution Legislative Reform: The Antinomy in Rights Theories and Practice

On paper, Article 19 of the constitution sanctions the equality of men and women. In addition, the Kingdom accepted Article 9(2) of the Convention on the Elimination of All Forms of Discrimination against Women. In doing so, the state grants women equal rights with men; it also endorses the equality of both genders with respect to the nationality of their children, unlike some of the Islamic states of North Africa.[59] Nevertheless, there was lack of unanimity on this question at the executive level. For instance, following the approval of the 2011 constitution, which was liberal on women's rights, and the king's endorsement of parity between men and women, the prime minister (PM) expressed his reservations on women's rights based on theological grounds. In fact, he chafed at the notion that the constitution was assailing the Islamic religion and values. The PM insisted that the Quran is against the "empowerment" of women in the manner in which women's rights are articulated in the constitution.[60] What this opposition to women's rights, especially by conservative Moroccans, suggests is that it is one thing to promulgate sound and positive national and international human rights laws, and quite another to enforce them in the state. This hypothesis is especially true in pastoral regions of the country; and this is the case if constitutional principles clash with long held traditional/cultural beliefs. In truth, constitutional principles and promises made to increase women's rights in the society have seen their gradual erosion with time and with steady opposition from the religious right and some political opportunists.[61]

Child marriage is on the rise even though the legal age is 18, which brings it up to par with that for men. Before the approval of the law that increased the marriage age for girls, females of 13–15 could be married off to men.[62] Parents arrange marriages in rural Morocco, as in much of rural Africa, and very little can be done to change this practice—at least for now. Also, it is true that pastoral folks could not care less about the national constitution, let alone international human rights conventions on women's rights. All the same, arranged marriage is in violation of Article 16(2) of the Universal Declaration of Human Rights. The UDHR declares, "Marriage shall be entered into only with the free and full consent of the intending spouses."[63]

On divorce, Article 16(1c) of the CEDAW affirms: "States Parties shall take all appropriate measures to eliminate discrimination against women in all matters relating to marriage and family relations and in particular shall ensure, on a basis of equality of men and women … the same rights and responsibilities during marriage and its dissolution."[64] Divorce happens in all societies, but it is the laws governing divorce that is critical in human rights debates. In Morocco, it is still easier for a husband to divorce his wife than for the wife to do the same. Although the 2007 Nationality Code gives men the right to pass their nationality to their foreign wives, the same is not the case for female spouses. In other words, a Moroccan man can pass his nationality to his foreign wife but not vice-versa.

The issue of inheritance is problematic in Morocco. This is so in part because of the philosophy of patriarchy and influence of religious extremists. For example, the irregular inheritance law contributes to increasing women's susceptibility to poverty. In addition, the practice of Habous and the rules governing collective land have helped deprive women of their rights to property and inheritance.[65] Theologically, inheritance matters between male and female are discriminatory. In fact, to paraphrase Surat 4:11 of the Quran, "Allah teaches you concerning your children: for the son, what is equal to the share of two daughters."[66] Besides religion, a cultural explanation in Islamic North Africa, and other African countries, flows from the concept that women will get married to men who will take care of them, and not so for men.

## Gender-Based Violence and Human Rights

Whereas revisions to the Kingdom's criminal laws aimed at reducing violence against women have been strengthened, the actual implementation of the rules in the society proves otherwise. Article 22 of the constitution states, "The physical or moral integrity of anyone may not be infringed, in whatever circumstance that may be, and by any party that may be, public or private. No one may inflict on others, under whatever pretext there may be, cruel, inhuman, [or] degrading treatments or infringements of human dignity" (see Table I). Yet, the frequency of violence (62.8 percent) against 6.2 million women at various times in the Kingdom is troublesome in human rights discourses. This phenomenon has its roots in the social acceptance of gender-based violence furthered by traditional culture and socialization.[67] Violent acts against women that are punishable in the Kingdom are unreported to law enforcement agencies. Moreover, the inefficient and from time to time corrupt practice of the legal system exacerbates the frequency of violence against women. For instance, the problems of the administration's law enforcement capacity include, but are not limited to, (1) lack of specific legislation on domestic violence; (2) non-criminalization of marital rape; (3) the law's silence on some forms of violence; and (4) the law's lack of consideration of the realities and the various aspects of gender-based violence.[68]

The U.S. Department of State account for 2015 on rape and domestic violence is revealing. The law sentences men who commit an act of rape to five to 10 years; in the case when the victim is a minor, the prison penalty runs from 10 to 20 years. As I noted previously spousal rape is not a crime. For that reason, victims seldom report the cases of sexual assaults to law enforcement. This development in the society is due in part to social stigma, which oftentimes holds the victim culpable. Further, the police are unenthusiastic about examining cases of rape and domestic violence; this is so since judges hardly ever take up domestic violence cases in court; and subsequently, women's rights suffer on this issue.[69]

Data on rape or sexual attack are difficult to come by because of lack of information and inadequate reporting. The Moroccan Woman, by the Numbers, a publication of the Bureau of Statistics in 2013, revealed that 63 percent of women reported experiencing an act of violence in the preceding year. Furthermore, some national support groups, as for example, the Democratic League for Women's Rights, estimated that women-beaters committed eight of 10 cases of violence against their wives. Official sources affirmed that the Royal Gendarmerie handled about 9,469 cases of violence against women in 2014. In 2015 alone, there were 3,055 cases of violence against women, with about 349 reported cases involving wife-beaters.[70]

Sexual harassment in the workplace is a global phenomenon and a human rights issue. It is a crime when men in a position of authority over women perpetuate such abuse. Authorities seldom effectively enforce laws against sexual harassment because men who indulge in this practice tend to be very influential both in the workplace and in the community. The judicial system allows victims of sexual harassment to sue their bosses. Even so, only a few are courageous enough to do so for fear that they could lose their job for litigating such a case. Many women worry that they might not be able to prove the charge against their perpetrator in court. The government remains active in attempts to improve the condition for women in the workplace. The state even indorsed a mandate for creating an agency, Authority for Gender Parity and Fighting All Forms of Discrimination, that would tackle the problem.[71]

The constitution provides women equal rights in civil, political, economic, cultural, and environmental affairs. Nonetheless, the law does not require equal pay for equal work. This bias not only contradicts the constitution but also the essence of the UN Convention on the Elimination of All Forms of Discrimination against Women. In addition, the partiality in enforcing equivalent pay for equal work for men and women violates Article 23(2) of the Universal Declaration of Human Rights that proclaims, "Everyone, without any discrimination, has the right to equal pay for equal work." The Kingdom has made significant strides in improving the political and economic conditions for women. However, a major issue that retards women's politico-economic advancement and parity with men in the labor force is inequality in education.[72] Inadequate education, especially in rural Morocco, promotes inequality between men and women socially and economically; poor education sharpens the level of prejudice against females because they are ignorant of their human rights. For example:

> According to the National Illiteracy Survey (Ministry of Education, 2012), the illiteracy rate is estimated at 28% (19% in urban and 42% in rural areas). Women are more affected by illiteracy (37% against 25% for men) and even more so in rural areas (55% against 31% for men). The High Commission for Planning (HCP) estimated the illiteracy rate in 2012 at 36.5% (25.3% of men and 47.6% of women).[73]

Accordingly, many problems that relate to bigotry against women are difficult to expunge from society. Religious dogma curtails a Muslim woman's rights to inherit equally with a man, as noted previously. In addition, the law allows a woman if she is the only child to receive half of the patrimony, the other half goes to relatives. Prejudicially, if the only child were to be a boy, he inherits the whole wealth. Unfortunately, the groundbreaking 2004 transformation of the Family Code did little to alter the country's inheritance laws; the 2011 constitution did not address the matter either. A yeoman's effort by the moderate CNDH to reform the country's inheritance laws to promote equality in inheritance for men and women came to naught in part because of the strong opposition to the recommendation by conservative men supported by Surrat 4:11 of the Holy Quran.[74] The foregoing discourses represent some of the challenges to human rights issues in the Kingdom.

It is refreshing, though, that despite obstacles to advancing women's human rights in some key areas in the Kingdom, women's NGOs continue with the struggle to advance social, political and economic equality in the Kingdom with some success. For instance, some of these groups have been working sturdily toward the establishment of an autonomous and resilient group to agitate for the eradication of all forms of gender discrimination. It is encouraging that the Ministry of Interior is in support of local implementation of women's rights to collective land privileges. Remarkably, the government is amenable to this reform, and in its own way is working toward its realization.[75]

On paper, the Family Code promulgated in 2004 brings the family unit under the cooperative obligation of both husband and wife. It further liberalizes the divorce law by making it available by collective agreement. Problematically, however, enactment of the Family Code, especially in pastoral Morocco, is difficult and slow. Many conformist or conservative judges remain unenthusiastic about the above provisions of the code and are reluctant to enforce them in court; thus, denying many women their human rights as enshrined in the constitution and Family Code.[76]

## Respect for Civil Liberties: Freedom of Speech and Press

Generally, the sporadic antipathy between the media and political actors is worldwide. This is the case in part because the media constantly probe the activities of corrupt state actors and their policies. Conflicts between the government and the media are more common in the developing world where transparency and accountability tend not to be the democratic norm. Appropriately, the media becomes an important watchdog. However, when the media exposes government's corruption and other malpractices that entail the infraction of citizens' human rights, journalists become the regime's and politicos' invented bête noire.

Notionally, the Kingdom's constitution and law sanction freedom of speech and press as human rights. Still, the regime criminalizes and controls freedom of expression and the social media that offend the interest of powerful groups and political actors in the country. For example, derision of Islam are disparagement of the sacrosanct monarchy are unlawful. Criticism of the government's official policy concerning territorial integrity, especially its claim to Western Sahara, is taboo to media personnel. Reproach of the above institutions and policy may result in trial under the penal code. Such prosecutions may result in fines or jail time. Government data for 2015 disclosed that 23 journalists violated the national press code. This statistic represents cases that the regime prosecuted in addition to libel charges brought against citizens. Both international and domestic human rights campaigners deplore such trials of journalists and publishers. Usually, agents of the administration apply these laws to intimidate independent human rights activists, the press and social media personnel.[77]

Contextually, the constitution in Articles 25 and 28 spells out the rights of the press and freedom of expression. Indeed, Article 25 states: "The freedoms of thought, of opinion and of expression under all their forms[,] are guaranteed." Article 28 proclaims, "Freedom of the press is guaranteed and may not be limited by any form of prior censure. All have the right to express and to disseminate freely and within the sole limits expressly provided by the law, information, ideas and opinions" (see Table I above).[78] Article 19 of the UDHR declares: "Everyone has the right to freedom of opinion and expression; this right includes freedom to hold opinions without interference and to seek, receive, and impart information and ideas through any media and regardless of frontiers."[79] Article 19(1–3b)[80] synchronizes with Article 19 of the Universal Declaration of Human Rights.

The ICCPR provisions in Article 19(3a–3b) are generally in accord with Article 28 of the Kingdom's constitution, which states, inter alia, that "government is limited only by that which the law explicitly limits." This phrase is confounding. In any case, the preceding rights precepts bring to the fore the problem of interpretation of human rights visions vis-à-vis national interests. Put differently, this regime, like other governments elsewhere, can deliberately misapply Article 19(3a–3b) to flout freedom of speech and the press if it is in its national interest to do so. I will further explain the foregoing postulations in the discussions that follow.

Take, for instance, the Press Law of 2002 that enumerates the following offenses that, if committed by media personnel, could lead to a fine or time in the penitentiary:

- Incitement to racial discrimination, hatred, or violence against a person or persons because of their race, origin, color or ethnic, or religious affiliation (article 39 bis);
- Incitement to disobedience among members of the security forces (article 40);
- Causing offense to the king, the royal princes and princesses; or causing prejudice to Islam, the monarchy, or Morocco's territorial integrity (article 41);
- Malicious publication of false news that disturbs the public order, causes panic, or disrupts discipline or morale in the army (article 42);
- Defamation of the courts, security services, state institutions or public administrations (articles 45 and 51); and
- Defamation of persons (articles 47 and 51).[81]

Human Rights Watch contends that the major deviation from the 2002 press law of the 2016 law is the elimination of prison terms for the foregoing offenses. Even so, the penal code continues to penalize many nonviolent speech offenses by citizens and journalists with prison terms.[82] The right to freedom of speech and the press continues to be violated in Morocco despite Article 28 (paragraph 2) of the constitution that supports citizens' right to free expression. All the same, the press laws and precepts in the penal code that relate to freedom of speech and the press are notable.[83] The above discussions provide a refreshing backdrop to the analysis in the following pages. It is from the account of the U.S. Department of State Bureau of Democracy, Human Rights, and Labor of 2015, that I drew my deliberations. These are case studies on freedom of speech and the press in Morocco.

Regarding freedom of speech and expression, the law forbids anyone from denigrating the institutions of the royal family, the state, or the military, among others. The state arrests and convicts any citizen who violates this tenet of the law. Such was the case when on March 23, 2015, agents of the government apprehended and detained online journalist Adil Karmouti on charges related to "public defamation, insulting employees during the exercise of their work, and libel against an organized institution." This arrest came about following the criticism of Bouchaib Amil, the head of the General Directorate of National Security and the agency itself. The state accused Bouchaib Amil of leaking videos that exposed corruption of some members of the security forces and soliciting bribes from foreign tourists and Moroccan citizens.[84]

The Kingdom curtails press and media freedoms because reporters are too noisy and are security risks. Journalists, generally, expose political and social malfeasance of law enforcement agents, to the chagrin of authorities who would like their affairs kept out of the public domain. Such conflicting interactions between journalists and state agents explain in part why the regime included in the anti-terrorism law and press code provisions that criminalize journalists and publishers who dare to violate the press code. For example, the state levies penalties on citizens and journalists on matters relating to defamation, libel, and insults to muzzle the press. One strategy to encourage self-censorship is to file trumped up charges of libel and other violations of the criminal code against specific journalists and wait for months on end to take the case to court. In this circumstance, the regime has brought politically driven investigations against the state's perennial foe—human rights activists—under Article 206 of the penal code. This provision of the code criminalizes the reception of financial and other forms of "suspicious" support from overseas to back up activities deemed capable of diminishing the Kingdom's reputation. Moreover, the anti-terrorism law and press code include provisions that permit the government to jail and impose financial penalties on journalists and publishers who allegedly connive with terrorist groups.[85]

State security officers sometimes subjected selected intrusive journalists to violence, harassment, blackmail and intimidation, applying different methods in their repertoire to suffocate unpleasant reports on government activities. In this strategy, security agents can induce journalists to self-censor, and in this way curtail their right to freedom of expression and the press. In fact, self-censorship and government restrictions on the media and human rights, among other things, remain grave obstacles to the emergence of a free, independent, and investigative press. Further, the preceding debates and concerns are human rights challenges in the Kingdom. Internet freedom remains relatively broad in the Kingdom. The government, however, can apply laws and regulations identical to those for speech and the press to the internet to violate the rights of its users.[86]

## National/Racial/Ethnic Minorities and Human Rights

Minorities in most societies, without economic and political power, are frequently at risk in the politics of who gets what, when, and how. Because they are fortuitously or intentionally marginalized in the distribution of resources they seldom enjoy the fruits of development—i.e., education, good roads, hospitals, location of industries, et cetera. In the Kingdom, some of the under-privileged regions, such as the Middle Atlas region, are the homes of a minority group—the Amazigh. The illiteracy rate of the Amazigh is approximately 80 percent. This makes it difficult for the Amazigh to compete politically, socially and economically against the majority population in power.

Furthermore, considering the group's isolation, governmental services in the Middle Atlas are negligible.

In the Kingdom, the endorsed languages are Arabic and Amazigh, while the lingua franca is Arabic—an adequate command of which is critical for economic and social mobility. Even though French and Amazigh anthologies exist in this region, they are not popular in educational establishments. The Amazigh population is small and lacks political influence in the legislature. However, it is striking that over half of Moroccans claim some Amazigh heritage. Even so, Amazigh are bothered at the steady superimposition of Arabization upon their traditions and language.

Government officials are proud to provide television access to this collectivity in three of its national dialects. These are Tarifit, Tashelhit, and Tamazight. In addition, the regime provides Amazigh language classes in the curriculum of 30 percent of schools. However, the state admits that because of lack of qualified tutors it has been difficult to increase Amazigh language education.[87]

The discrimination against Sahrawis in the Western Sahara is political and problematic given the ignitable nature of this region following the departure of colonial Spain and the annexation of the area by Morocco in its wake. Morocco claims the territory as its own. The struggle of Western Saharans to extricate themselves from Morocco based on their rights to national self-determination has been ongoing for a long time. The purpose of this brief discussion is to highlight some cases of human rights violations of the minority Sahrawis despite the sensitivity of this subject to the Moroccan government and its officials.

As noted above, the Kingdom remains adamant on its claim to Western Sahara as its province and thus part of Morocco. Consequently, the state is determined to protect the territorial integrity of the region, as an integral part of the country. To this end, Rabat applied draconian techniques, some of which violate human rights, to quell the activities of oppositional groups and individual Sahrawis fighting for autonomy. The Western Sahara situation was so challenging that the UN had to intervene to advance international peace and security in the region:

> On April 28, 2015, the United Nations Security Council voted to extend for another year the United Nations Mission for the Referendum in Western Sahara (MINURSO), the peacekeeping mission in Western Sahara. However, the Council failed once again to expand MINURSO's mandate to include a human rights monitoring and reporting mechanism.... As a result, there is no international mechanism dedicated to human rights in Western Sahara.[88]

Apropos the preceding excerpt, alleged human rights violations happened in Western Sahara against the Sahrawis. Human rights contraventions will continue to persist in the region for as long as violence is the method of the struggle for self-determination. The regimes riposte in cases of aggression has been arrests and detentions of Sahrawis. Little wonder, then, that a concerned human rights organization provides a list of discomforting human rights infringements committed in the territory.[89] This group's report alludes to more than 70 separate cases of human rights infractions. Most of the abuses relate to the right to be free from random arrest, the right to freedom of assembly and expression and the right to freedom of movement.[90]

Globally, and especially in Africa, the LGBTI community is another minority group whose human rights are frequently flouted. It is safe to disclose that the only country on the continent of Africa that embraces the LGBTI community constitutionally is the Republic of South Africa. In fact, Article 9(3) of the South African constitution states, among other things: "The state may not unfairly discriminate directly or indirectly against anyone on one or more grounds, including race, gender, sex, ... marital status ... and sexual orientation."[91]

It is the case in much of Africa that acts of violence, discrimination, and other abuses based on sexual orientation and gender identity are commonplace. Possibly, the opposition to this lifestyle in Africa explains partially why in Morocco being part of the LGBTI community is taboo. Furthermore, it explicates why the penal code criminalizes consensual same-sex sexual conduct with a maximum jail sentence of three years.[92] This provision in the penal code clashes with the positive human rights principle in Article 7 of the Universal Declaration of Human Rights. This precept affirms: "All are equal before the law and are entitled without any discrimination to equal protection of the law. All are entitled to equal protection against any discrimination in violation of this Declaration and against any incitement to such discrimination."[93]

Notwithstanding the draconian law against the LGBTI community in the society, it is noteworthy that the media and public discourses on the issue of sexuality, sexual orientation, and gender identity are increasingly more open today than in the past. Such civic discussions are likely to mitigate the negativity toward this practice in the Kingdom. That notwithstanding, the regime still deems LGBTI orientation or identity illegal as noted earlier, and the influential penal code does not outlaw hate crimes toward this group.

In the pastoral sectors of the country, sexual orientation and gender identity create a basis for societal violence and harassment due in part to traditional custom. Subsequently, LGBTI persons suffer severely from discrimination at the rural areas. It is encouraging, however, that overall, authorities appear liberal enough not to discriminate against citizens based on "sexual orientation or gender identity in employment, housing, access to education, or health care."[94]

## Conclusion: Administrative Attitude Toward International and NGO Investigations of Claimed Abuses of Human Rights

It is one thing to expose human rights breaches and quite another for governments to enforce those rights; hence academics are confronted with human rights conundrums and conflict between theory and practice in human rights scholarship. Within the context of my preceding hypothesis, however, I shall briefly conclude by examining how the Kingdom has reacted to a selection of the human rights concerns raised in this chapter. Amnesty International, Human Rights Watch, and the U.S. Department of State, inter alia, investigated and made available findings on human rights infringements in Morocco; it is enlightening that the regime's receptiveness to, and collaboration with, civil society groups and international human rights activists varied markedly. The government's cooperation depended—and still depends—on its assessment of the political ideology, motivation and even the theology of a human rights organization and the delicacy of the issue; thus, Rabat's harsh response to the human rights reports on law enforcement activities in the politically problematic Western Sahara.

For example, in May 2015,

> the release of an AI [Amnesty International] report on the continued use of abusive practices in detention facilities triggered a large-scale official media reaction sharply criticizing the report's evident "bias." On June 9, authorities expelled John Dalhuisen, AI's director for Europe and Central Asia, and Irem Arf, researcher on refugee and migrants' rights in Europe, who arrived the previous day to conduct an investigation into the treatment of sub-Saharan migrants and asylum seekers. Authorities asserted they did not have the "requisite permission necessary to conduct their research," despite previous assurances to AI that they would be able to conduct their investigation.[95]

It is worth noting that the Minister of Communications, Mustapha El Khalfi, responded to the above report in an op-ed in the *Wall Street Journal*. Here, he explained that the Kingdom based its critical reaction to AI and HRW accounts on the prejudicial reporting on human rights situations in the Western Sahara. Notwithstanding the foregoing response, however, the Kingdom works closely with important domestic human rights organizations to advance human rights causes in the country. In this regard, the CNDH has come to serve as a national social watchdog. Notably, it has in the Kingdom performed the function of monitoring and presenting relevant recommendations for alleviating torture and other forms of human rights infractions.[96]

# 5

## Tunisia

### Early History

The ancient history of native Tunisians is not well known. Nevertheless, stone tools found in the area suggest that there existed a vibrant civilization before the arrival of the Phoenicians in the 12th century BCE. Occupationally, the natives were fishermen, hunters, farmers and gatherers. Phoenician merchants from present day Lebanon took advantage of the strategic location of Tunisia in the Mediterranean vis-à-vis Europe to develop settlements along the coast. One of these cities was the famous city of Carthage established in 814 BCE; its power grew enormously, so that by the sixth century BCE, Carthage expanded to include the area of contemporary Tunisia.[1] Commercially and politically,

> Carthage was governed by a mercantile oligarchy that exercised power through a senate, composed of elder statesmen, under a constitution praised by Aristotle for providing a perfect blend of monarchy, aristocracy, and democracy. Joint executive authority was vested in two suffets (consuls), chosen annually by an electorate that was also called upon to decide on [tough] questions by referendum. The coastal countryside was closely settled with self-governing towns dependent on Carthage for foreign affairs and defense [very much like the governance structure of some societies in the Occident].[2]

The political glamour of Carthage was envied by another pugnacious power—Rome. The dominant trading influence of Carthage in the Mediterranean alerted the interest of Rome in the third century BCE. Determined to checkmate the growing power of the Carthaginians in the Mediterranean, Rome took up arms against Carthage in the historic Punic wars (264–241; 218–201; 149–146 BCE) that lasted for 118 years.[3] Rome defeated Carthage and maintained its suzerainty over the area until the Vandals (a Germanic tribe) and later the Byzantines (the Eastern Roman Empire) in the fifth century AD conquered the area.[4]

The Arab Muslim conquest of Tunisia (Ifriqyya or Ifriquiya in Arabic) happened from 670 to 698 AD. The Arabs attacked Ifriqyya under the leadership of Uqba ben Nafi from his base and city of Kairouan. Carthage, under the Byzantine Empire, fell in AD 698 to the Arabs. The Arabs' governing technique was that of establishing a political and religious unity within theological dogma drawn from the Holly Quran and its juridical text—the Sharia. Conversion of the autochthonous pragmatic Berbers to Islam was relatively smooth and based on interest and opportunism.[5] The Umayyad Rule (661–750), Abbasid rule (750–800), Aghlabid rule (800–909) and Fatimid rule (910–1044) consolidated the Islamic creed in the area.[6]

Indeed, in the long history of European and Islamic conquest of North Africa, Berbers, the indigenous ethnic group in the region, assimilated the alien religions and integrated with foreign invaders as noted previously. The Berbers, having established unity amongst their mosaic population, were able to rise within the political hierarchy and governance structure of the region under a common Islamic ideology. Such was the case under Zirid rule (1044–1148) and the powerful Almohad regime, under the leadership of Abd al Mumin, who unified the Maghrib (1160–1207). The Almohads chose a viceroy following the declining years of the empire. He was Mohamed ben Abu Hafs. He founded the long-lasting Hafsid dynasty from 1207 to 1574. During the reign of Abu Zakariya al Hafs the capital city was relocated from Kairouan to Tunis, and Ifriqyya was given the new name Tunisia.[7]

The Hafsids collaborated with the Berbers, whom they left alone to control the hinterland. Hafsids, however, controlled the coastline cities. Tunisia remained relatively peaceful until the arrival of the Ottoman Turks, who captured Tunis in 1574. Tunisia became a Turkish province and was governed by a beylerbey stationed in Algiers.[8] The Ottomans divided the Maghrib into administrative units called regencies. A governor whose title was pasha, but had no political power, headed the regency of Tunis. The bey of Tunis controlled Berber tribes in the hinterland with a military force and the Bey of Tunis, the de jure leader of Tunisia. The Turks, under the Ottoman Empire, governed the area for over 200 years.[9] This was the political organization in Tunisia until the coming of the French as a colonial power and overseer.

## *The French Protectorate*

The struggle for Africa by the Western powers seeking prestige, wealth, and the spread of Christianity, inter alia, was contentious. To ameliorate a possible clash between the contesting powers over Tunisia, it was necessary to work out an effective framework for European colonization of the country. Uniquely, Tunisia was from the 1500s to the 1800s a self-governing province of the Ottoman Empire. Its status was that of a regency in that the governors ruled as regents on the orders of the Ottoman Sultan. In other words, Tunisia was like a fiefdom. Its regents served on behalf of the Sultan as governors of the province.[10]

At a meeting held in Berlin in 1878 Britain struck a modus vivendi with France allowing Paris to do whatever it wanted in Tunisia. The quid pro quo was that France would tolerate Britain's acquisition of a leasehold of Cyprus from Turkey. It was a foregone conclusion that France, very much like the other European powers, wanted to acquire Tunisia as a bragging right. Even so, France needed plausible reasons to accomplish its ambition in the territory. Paris thought seriously about possible reasons for conquering Tunisia against the backdrop of the colonial rivalries at this important period of European colonization. In 1881, two interesting rationales for France's occupation of Tunisia were stated.

The French claimed that their intervention in Tunisia was because the bey or governor of Tunisia reneged in the payment of debts to French banks and entrepreneurs who had been giving the regime loans for many years to keep the country's economy above water.[11] A second reason was an incursion of Khumiri tribesmen into French colonial Algeria from Tunisia. Accordingly, to teach these tribesmen a lesson for their invasion of Algerian territory, France sent its warriors (36,000–40,000) to rebuff their attack.[12] The above theories aside, it was clear all along that France had been eying the territory and wanted it for its own.

This assumption was supported by the appearance of menacing French troops amassed near the capital—Tunis. The French attaché, following this siege, met the bey at the Bardo Palace with a treaty; the draft of this agreement, ostensibly, had been in the folders of the French Foreign Ministry awaiting such a propitious occasion. The pact endorsed a temporary occupation of key centers in Tunisia to stop the chaos in the territory. Tactically, this French military strategy effectively brought Tunisia under a French protectorate.[13]

In brief, the excerpt below sums up the governance structure introduced in Tunisia following French occupation:

> Under the protectorate Tunisia was governed according to a system of dual sovereignties in which the de facto sovereignty of France was superimposed on de jure sovereignty of beylicate. Tunisia remained what it had been for 300 years, the "Regency of Tunis." The pre-existing form of beylical government was maintained intact, and the established political elite continued to function within it. Although the elite readily assimilated French values, Tunisian society retained its own social standards and a tradition of higher culture that were the core of the country's sense of nationhood.[14]

## The Rise of Nationalism

Historically, the pride in French nationalism was one that led many lawmakers and French citizens to assume that its colonial subjects would wholeheartedly appreciate the French civilization and absorb it. Consequently, France pursued the policy of assimilation whereby citizens of its colonies could acquire French citizenship when they met the criteria. The French policy of mission civilisatrice in its colonies was another strategy aimed at integrating the colonized populations. Although some nationalists in French colonies or protectorates admired and even cherished French culture, they preferred independence, in which they would govern themselves, to being French citizens. Thus, the struggle for home-rule became the rallying cry of nationalists in Tunisia who wanted to remove the country from French control.

Kherredin Pasha is the father of Tunisian nationalism. He was a Mamluk from Circassia (in modern Russia). He wrote a Tunisian constitution as long ago as 1861.[15] However, in the 1890s a small Western-educated nationalist group began pressing for reforms and insisting that there was need for more Tunisians' involvement in the governance of the state. Members of this group called themselves the Young Tunisians. They promoted their propaganda in a liberal newspaper—*Le Tunisien*. Their political fervor and drive to advance the Tunisianization of the country's administrative structures and institutions led to the founding of the Destour (Constitutional) Party after World War II.[16] The intelligentsia and men of wealth and political power made up the membership of the party. In its manifesto, the Destour Party called for, among other things, a return to the Kherredin constitution of 1861 with minor changes here and there in the document. In short, the party called for a constitutional form of government that would promote equivalent rights for Tunisians and European settlers.[17]

To the French settlers in Tunisia, the declaration and demands of the Destour Party for parity with the colons was an affront to their authority. Therefore, the propaganda of the group must be suffocated. The settlers sought to carry out this objective by repression and arrest of the ringleader and his cohorts. The bey supported the call for reform. He even threatened to abdicate his position of leadership as a way of expressing his solidarity with the Destour Party. In the face of this upheaval, France stationed troops around the bey's palace. This French strategy was employed to avert a potential mass revolt against the colons. However, to mitigate the political tension in the country, the French overseers made cosmetic reforms that did not meet the petitions submitted by the nationalists. One such modification, and slap in the face, to the pro-autonomists was "an offer to grant French citizenship to Tunisians who qualified by education or service."[18] Incensed by French condescension to the party's demands, young middle-class separatists formed a new faction with a similar name, the Neo-Destour Party, in 1934. The flagbearer of the party was an astute and aggressive young French-educated lawyer—Habib Bourguiba.[19]

## Independence After World War II

The Axis (Germany, Italy, and Japan) and the Allied Forces (France, Britain, U.S., China, and Russia) fought in World War II. Germany occupied France briefly during that war. The Germans also engaged French forces in Tunisia and Tunisians fought gallantly side-by-side with the French. Following the defeat of the Axis in North Africa in 1943, France continued its control over Tunisia. Having fought with French soldiers in this war, pro-independence Tunisians expected the recompense to be sovereignty for the country. But, this demand for self-rule did not happen. France's refusal to grant autonomy to Tunisia created political angst and instability in the society. The political turmoil culminated in the sacking of the bey and attempts made to arrest the radical bête noir and nationalist Habib Bourguiba, who fled the country to Egypt in 1945.

However, experiencing a wave of political agitation for self-determination in the Arab states and Africa after World War II, the French colonialists reluctantly permitted the formation of an inclusive or bi-partite government in 1951. Tunisian nationalists and the French made up the government. The pro-autonomists felt that this concession or arrangement was inadequate and demanded the acceleration of the progress toward national sovereignty. At this point, nationalists who wanted freedom and the French whose policy was that of assimilation were on a collision course. The French reverted to repressive measures to stop the separatist agitators. In response to French oppressive policies, popular protests erupted and increased; and occasionally activists applied terrorist acts against French interests in the country in their wake.[20]

In 1954 the French became flexible on the issue of independence for Tunisia but wanted the process to be protracted. Bourguiba, who had returned to the country from exile in 1949, became the interlocutor between the Neo-Destour Party and the French representatives. France granted Tunisia independence in March 1956, with a constitutional monarchy in which the bey was head of government. However, following national legislative elections in the country, the Neo-Destour Party won the popular vote and the majority of seats in Parliament. Habib Bourguiba became the president. In 1957, Tunisia became a republic after the National Assembly wrote a new constitution that abolished the rule of the beys.[21]

All the same, this chapter is on the human rights challenges in Tunisia and debate on the conflict between theory and practice in rights enforcement. Tunisia, very much like the other countries in North Africa, is unequivocal in stating the sacrosanctity of Islam in the cultural, religious, social and political life of its citizens. The primordial attachment to Islam, and its legal canons enshrined in the Sharia, defines how citizens conduct themselves morally and socially in the polity. In 2014, Tunisia wrote a new constitution to promote peaceful coexistence in the society. It is refreshing that the constitution, very much like those of Islamic countries in the region, contains tenets on human rights. These principles explicate how to advance the rights of citizens in the republic. For example, Table I below contains an excerpt of invaluable human rights precepts of the 2014 constitution. The constitutional doctrines in Articles 21–49 form part of the major foundations on which my analysis in the subsequent discourses rests.

## Table I: Constitution of Tunisia

| | *Articles* |
|----|----|
| 21 | All citizens, male and female, have equal rights and duties, and are equal before the law without any discrimination.<br>    The state guarantees freedoms and individual and collective rights to all citizens, and provides all citizens the conditions for a dignified life. |
| 22 | The right to life is sacred and cannot be prejudiced except in exceptional cases regulated by law. |
| 23 | The state protects human dignity and physical integrity and prohibits mental and physical torture.<br>    Crimes of torture are not subject to any statute of limitations. |
| 24 | The state protects the right to privacy and the inviolability of the home, and the confidentiality of correspondence, communications, and personal information.<br>    Every citizen has the right to choose their place of residence, to free movement within the country, and the right to leave the country. |
| 25 | No citizen shall be deprived of their nationality, exiled, extradited or prevented from returning to their country. |
| 26 | The right to political asylum shall be guaranteed as prescribed by law. It is prohibited to surrender persons who have been granted political asylum. |
| 27 | A defendant shall be presumed innocent until proven guilty in a fair trial in which he/she is granted all guarantees necessary for his/her defence throughout all the phases of prosecution and trial. |
| 28 | Punishments are individual and are not to be imposed unless by virtue of a legal provision issued prior to the occurrence of the punishable act, except in the case of a provision more favourable to the defendant. |
| 29 | No person may be arrested or detained unless apprehended during the commission of a crime or on the basis of a judicial order.<br>    The detained person must be immediately informed of their rights and the charges under which they are being held. The detainee has the right to be represented by a lawyer. The periods of arrest and detention are to be defined by law. |
| 30 | Every prisoner shall have the right to humane treatment that preserves their dignity.<br>    In carrying out a punishment involving the deprivation of liberty, the state shall take into account the interests of the family and shall seek the rehabilitation and re-integration of the prisoner into society. |

| | |
|---|---|
| 31 | Freedom of opinion, thought, expression, information and publication shall be guaranteed.<br>These freedoms shall not be subject to prior censorship. |
| 32 | The state guarantees the right to information and the right of access to information and communication networks. |
| 33 | Academic freedoms and freedom of scientific research shall be guaranteed.<br>The state shall provide the necessary resources for the development of scientific and technological research. |
| 34 | The rights to election, voting, and candidacy are guaranteed, in accordance with the law. The state seeks to guarantee women's representation in elected bodies. |
| 35 | The freedom to establish political parties, unions, and associations is guaranteed.<br>In their internal charters and activities, political parties, unions and associations must respect the provisions of the Constitution, the law, financial transparency and the rejection of violence. |
| 36 | The right to join and form unions is guaranteed, including the right to strike.<br>This right does not apply to the national army.<br>The right to strike does not apply to the forces of internal security and to customs officers. |
| 37 | The right to assembly and peaceful demonstration is guaranteed. |
| 38 | Health is a right for every human being.<br>The state shall guarantee preventative health care and treatment for every citizen and provide the means necessary to ensure the safety and quality of health services.<br>The state shall ensure free health care for those without means and those with limited income. It shall guarantee the right to social assistance in accordance with the law. |
| 39 | Education shall be mandatory up to the age of sixteen years.<br>The state guarantees the right to free public education at all levels and ensures provisions of the necessary resources to achieve a high quality of education, teaching, and training. It shall also work to consolidate the Arab-Muslim identity and national belonging in the young generations, and to strengthen, promote and generalize the use of the Arabic language and to openness to foreign languages, human civilizations and diffusion of the culture of human rights. |
| 40 | Work is a right for every citizen, male and female. The state shall take the necessary measures to guarantee work on the basis of competence and fairness.<br>All citizens, male and female, shall have the right to decent working conditions and to a fair wage. |
| 41 | The right to property shall be guaranteed, and it shall not be interfered with except in accordance with circumstances and with protections established by the law.<br>Intellectual property is guaranteed. |

| 42 | The right to culture is guaranteed.<br>The freedom of creative expression is guaranteed. The state encourages cultural creativity and supports the strengthening of national culture, its diversity and renewal, in promoting the values of tolerance, rejection of violence, openness to different cultures and dialogue between civilizations.<br>The state shall protect cultural heritage and guarantees it for future generations. |
|---|---|
| 43 | The state shall promote sports and shall work to provide the facilities necessary for the exercise of physical and leisure activities. |
| 44 | The right to water shall be guaranteed.<br>The conservation and rational use of water is a duty of the state and of society. |
| 45 | The state guarantees the right to a healthy and balanced environment and the right to participate in the protection of the climate.<br>The state shall provide the necessary means to eradicate pollution of the environment. |
| 46 | The state commits to protect women's accrued rights and work to strengthen and develop those rights.<br>The state guarantees the equality of opportunities between women and men to have access to all levels of responsibility in all domains.<br>The state works to attain parity between women and men in elected Assemblies.<br>The state shall take all necessary measures in order to eradicate violence against women. |
| 47 | Children are guaranteed the rights to dignity, health, care and education from their parents and the state.<br>The state must provide all types of protection to all children without discrimination and in accordance with their best interest. |
| 48 | The state shall protect persons with disabilities from all forms of discrimination.<br>Every disabled citizen shall have the right to benefit, according to the nature of the disability, from all measures that will ensure their full integration into society, and the state shall take all necessary measures to achieve this. |
| 49 | The limitations that can be imposed on the exercise of the rights and freedoms guaranteed in this Constitution will be established by law, without compromising their essence. Any such limitations can only be put in place for reasons necessary to a civil and democratic state and with the aim of protecting the rights of others, or based on the requirements of public order, national defence, public health or public morals, and provided there is proportionality between these restrictions and the objective sought.<br>Judicial authorities ensure that rights and freedoms are protected from all violations.<br>There can be no amendment to the Constitution that undermines the human rights and freedoms guaranteed in this Constitution. |

Source: Constitution of Tunisia, 2014, https://issafrica.org/ctafrica/uploads/tunisia Constitution2014Eng.pdf (retrieved 3/13/18).

## Pre-2011 Revolution, Human Rights: Torture, Inhuman or Degrading Treatment or Punishment

The international community is very serious in its opposition to torture, inhuman or degrading treatment or punishment; indeed, the United Nations highlights its concerns on this matter in Article 4(1–2) of the convention on torture. Article 4(1) enjoins member-states of the UN thus: "Each State Party shall ensure that all acts of torture are offences under its criminal law. The same shall apply to an attempt to commit torture and to an act by any person which constitutes complicity or participation in torture." Article 4(2) bids member-state accordingly: "Each State Party shall make these offences punishable by appropriate penalties which take into account their grave nature."[22] The same charge to nation-states appears in Article 7 of the International Covenant on Civil and Political Rights.[23]

Globally, the constitution of virtually every country, due partly to the seriousness and gravity of the preceding injunctions, contains provisions that forbid the use of torture in interrogating citizens accused of crime. Little wonder, then, that Article 23 of the Tunisian constitution declares, "The state protects human dignity and physical integrity and prohibits mental and physical torture" (see Table I). Yet, in practice the vast majority of countries—not least Tunisia—do not fully adhere to the commitment not to use torture on their citizens—especially political enemies, extremists and terrorists, for example—that violates human rights.

Admittedly, it was within the context of the above postulation that the report of a UN special rapporteur on torture and other cruel, inhuman or degrading treatment or punishment reminded the republic, inter alia, of its commitments to human rights as follows:

> Tunisia is party to the main United Nations human rights treaties prohibiting torture and ill-treatment, including the International Covenant on Civil and Political Rights; the Convention against Torture and Other Cruel, Inhuman or Degrading Treatment or Punishment; the Convention on the Rights of the Child; the Convention on the Elimination of All Forms of Discrimination against Women…; [signatory to] the first Optional Protocol to the International Covenant on Civil and Political Rights and the International Convention for the Protection of All Persons from Enforced Disappearance.[24]

Before the Tunisian revolution of 2011, there was endemic practice of torture and ill-treatment of citizens on a socio-political basis. Indeed, several reports and testimonies exposed the crimes of torture and ill-treatment of oppositionist factions committed by President Zine el-Abidine Ben Ali's regime and his security forces. Ali's autocratic rule fostered a culture of torture and ill-treatment within the law enforcement agencies. Consequently, torture was practiced with reckless abandon and brazen impunity by such law enforcement agencies as the former State Security Department (DSS, also known as the "political police") and the Ministry of the Interior (its personnel and prison staff).[25]

As is the custom in many developing countries, torture and ill-treatment was and is normal in detention centers in Tunisia, especially in the Department of State Security custody. Regrettably, the DSS, under the command and auspices of the Ministry of the Interior, applied torture widely. Moreover, the enforcement of torture reached its crescendo following the enactment of the counter-terrorism legislation of December 10, 2003 (under Law No. 2003–75). The state did not spare political prisoners the wrath of torment. Indeed, military courts sentenced inmates to life in custody after torture and other forms of maltreatment under the anti-terrorism decree.

The impunity with which the agents and agencies of the Ben Ali's administration violated the human rights of fellow citizens was challenging. In any case, central to the hypothesis and argument here is that the state seldom examined issues of torture because the regime sanctioned them. In some cases, too, the Ali administration undertook the torture for self-preservation. Put in another way, it is safe to contend that members of DSS and other law enforcement agents felt that by their acts of persecution and ill-treatment of oppositionist factions, they were protecting the government's interests, and the quid pro quo for their rights breaches would be professional citation and career advancement.

In much of the developing world, the president appoints members of the bench. Judges generally serve at the behest of the president or prime minister.[26] Tunisia is not an exception to the preceding supposition. Thus, the president and his cohorts control the judiciary and magistrates sometimes decline cases on torture or rule in favor of the regime. Commonly, unprincipled judges make such decisions in favor of the government to save their job. In addition, adjudicators have a culture of admitting a confession obtained under torture and duress into evidence to boost their credentials as loyal civil servants of the state and president. Between 1999 and 2009, the judiciary subpoenaed 246 law enforcement agents for maltreatment of victims. Out of 246 introduced cases, the court made 228 final judgments. Lamentably, "only seven criminal convictions for acts of torture and ill-treatment were handed down against law-enforcement and prison officials under article 53 of the statute of the Internal Security Forces."[27] To human rights activists, the low number of imprisonments on this matter was improbable; it should have been more.

In addition, human rights abuses committed during and after the Jasmine Revolution were abnormal. Participants in demonstrations in Tunis,

Kasserine, and Bizerte complained that despite the relatively nonviolent nature of the protests law enforcement agents repeatedly violated their rights by interceding with inordinate use of force. Police officers used tear gas and live ammunition and between January 8 and 12, 2011, security forces shot 21 peaceful demonstrators in Kasserine and Tala. The death toll and injuries suffered during the events of December 2010 to January 2011 were astronomical. Indeed, 147 persons died, and another 510 individuals sustained injury. Human rights campaigners, however, put the death toll at almost 400, including detainees killed in prison.[28]

My subsequent dialogues center on human rights infractions committed after a combustible insurgency—the Jasmine Revolution. This uprising happened in December 2010 after a frustrated 26-year old fruit seller, Mohamed Bouazizi, set himself alight in front of a government building to protest the regime's bureaucratic malfeasance and corruption. This single act ignited what became the so-called Arab Spring, which some observers hoped would lead to democratic renaissance in North Africa and the Middle East. This episode not only unleashed human rights problems in Tunisia but also in the region created by conservative and reactionary forces opposed to democratic reforms.

For my deliberation and analysis on human rights conundrums in post–Jasmine Revolution Tunisia, I extracted information from the 2015 United States Department of State archives. I mined that year's report and applied it as my template for discussing the human rights transgressions in the republic. Also, I augmented my discourses with poignant reports on human rights abuses in Tunisia from sources catalogued by two ubiquitous and influential human rights NGOs—Human Rights Watch and Amnesty International.

Indeed, the 2015 U.S. Department of State chronicle on human rights practices in Tunisia declares, among other things:

> The most significant human rights problems included slow and opaque investigations into alleged security force human rights abuses, delays in prosecuting cases involving human rights abuses, and violence against journalists.
> Other human rights problems included physical abuse of prisoners in detention centers and prisons, poor prison and detention center conditions, arbitrary arrest and detention, lack of judicial independence, lax prosecutorial environment with poor transparency, corruption, infringement of gay, lesbian, bisexual, transgender, and intersex (LGBTI) rights, gender-based violence, and societal obstacles to the full economic and political participation of women.
> The ... investigations into police, security force, and detention center abuses lacked transparency, and frequently encountered long delays and procedural obstacles.[29]

The foregoing citation contains an array of issue areas in which the Tunisian government and its security forces are culpable with respect to human rights contraventions. Consequently, I winnowed the compiled list. It is around the issue of torture and some of the pertinent issues raised in the above quote that I center my brief reflections and dialogues on the challenges posed by human rights abuses in post–Jasmine Revolution Tunisia.

My concise deliberations below flow from the peculiar character of torture and other cruel, inhuman, or degrading treatment or punishment that happened following the historic Jasmine Revolution of 2011. As noted previously, the Tunisian national constitution and international human rights conventions forbid the use of torture, and other cruel, inhuman, or degrading treatment or punishment in the republic. Yet, security forces subjected several detainees to harsh physical treatments. The methods of torture applied included, but were not limited to, electric shocks.[30] Therefore, the Jasmine Revolution did not mitigate rights challenges in Tunisia; instead, the revolution exacerbated it. This development shines light on the clash between "positive" human rights creeds enshrined in the constitution and the nullification of such rights by state practices.

This problem in post-revolutionary Tunisia prompted Amnesty International in one its captions and reports to quip: "Evidence of torture and deaths in custody suggest human rights gains of the uprising are sliding into reverse gear."[31] Thus, "state repression, so much a feature of the past, was meant to be at an end; police brutality, torture and the abuse of human rights were to be consigned to [the dustbin of] history, [but have not been]."[32] Irrefutably, amelioration of human rights was not the case, in part, because old habits tend to die hard. Indeed, one victim of torture interviewed by Mariam Nasri, a Tunisian journalist, said that "torture is an epidemic in our country.... We must recognize this fact. Senior officials in the Ministry of Interior and the Ministry of Justice must take the necessary action to stop it."[33] It is refreshing that some popular local human rights lawyers are sharp in their condemnation of the practice of torture in police custodies and detention locations. Additionally, human rights NGOs continue to censure the government for its lackadaisical approach and frequently unwillingness to investigate torture indictments brought against its security officers.[34]

## Post-2011 Revolution, Respect for the Integrity of the Person: Arbitrary or Unlawful Deprivation of Life

Article 4 of the African Charter on Human and Peoples' Rights proclaims, "Human beings are inviolable. Every human being shall be entitled to respect for his life and the integrity of his [or her] person. No one may be arbitrarily deprived of this right."[35] Article 3 of the Universal Declaration of Human Rights avers, "Everyone has the right to life, liberty and security of person."[36] Article 6 of the UN International Covenant on Civil and Political

Rights declares: "Every human being has the inherent right to life. This right shall be protected by law."[37] Article 22 of the Tunisian constitution maintains, "The right to life is sacred and cannot be prejudiced except in exceptional cases regulated by law" (see Table I above).

Despite the foregoing international and constitutional rights proclamations on the inviolability of life, Tunisia's law enforcement agents have used extreme force that resulted in the death of civilians. The application of excessive force by security forces to deal fatal blows on political activists and alleged miscreants in the society is widespread—especially in police custody. The state traditionally applied a heavy-handed approach in attempts to intimidate civilians and to discourage citizens from irritating the regime and its custodians. For instance, on February 8, 2015, police shot and killed a 20-year-old man in Dhiba during a rally against the government. The demonstration was against the economic woes suffered by the masses in the polity. To the chagrin of the government, the media and civil society groups exposed such human rights infringements. In addition, journalist did report deaths of several individuals in detention.[38] Lamentably, journalists and rights campaigners sometimes experienced government reprisal for reporting such mishaps in the republic.

To be sure, the regime's human rights breaches against civilians now and then happen because police and National Guard personnel have suffered casualties from attacks by terrorist groups operating in the country. Indeed, in 2015, terrorist attacks killed 21 security force members, including five soldiers on April 7, four National Guardsmen on June 15, and twelve presidential guards on November 24.[39]

Another area of concern regarding human rights challenges in Tunisia is religion. My discourses center on how the sermons and practices of faith impact the rights of citizens—Muslims and non–Muslims alike. More importantly, my analysis will briefly allude to how the religious doctrine in the republic—especially in the countryside—problematizes the equal application of human rights principles to Muslims and non–Muslims. In my deliberation, I will examine some of the clashes between religious dogmata and constitutional-cum-international human rights tenets.

## Religion and Human Rights

The U.S. Department of State investigation and report on international religious freedom for 2015 summarizes its findings on Tunisia thus:

> The constitution declares the country's religion to be Islam but also declares the country to be a "civil state." The constitution designates the government as the "guardian of religion" and obligates the state to disseminate the values of "moderation and tolerance." It prohibits the use of mosques and houses of worship to advance political

agendas or objectives, and guarantees freedom of belief, conscience, and exercise of religious practice. Following deadly terrorist attacks in March and June, the government closed 80 mosques, which it said were built without proper authorization or whose imams it accused of preaching extremist theology, as well as 80 Islamic associations it accused of extremism. The Ministry of Religious Affairs (MRA) dismissed 20 imams it accused of preaching radical ideology or conducting inappropriate activities inside mosques.... The government continued to allow the Jewish and Christian communities to worship freely [but other religious sects—outside the Muslim, Christian and Jewish faiths—do not have the same rights].[40]

Generally, the confluence between religion and politics can be combustible if inadequately supervised. Such was the case in Iraq and Syria, which led to the birth of the Islamic State of Iraq and Syria (ISIS); an attempt to invent a Caliphate based on Islamic philosophy in the region resulted in an international conflict with disastrous human rights consequences in the territory and elsewhere. Because national and international wars have happened—and may yet occur—in the name of religion, political leaders are cautious about enforcing religious orthodoxy enshrined in constitutions. International human rights declarations and agreements sanction religious freedom and grant equivalent rights to all to worship and conduct their faith freely in attempts to avoid bias and to promote peaceful coexistence.

Accordingly, Article 18 of the UN International Covenant on Civil and Political Rights, avows: "Everyone shall have the right to freedom of thought, conscience and religion. This right shall include freedom to have or to adopt a religion ... and freedom ... [to practice and teach it]."[41] The same appeal appears in Article 8 of the African Charter on Human and Peoples' Rights,[42] Article 18 of the Universal Declaration of Human Rights[43] and Article 6 of the 2014 Tunisian constitution (see Table I). Tunisia is a signatory to these important international human rights documents; nevertheless, very much like other African countries, Tunisia has not always implemented relevant principles of religious rights enunciated in the above documents. Accordingly, the preceding allusions bring to light the debate on the clash between human rights theories and rights practices in Tunisia.

Demographically, Tunisia's population in 2015 was approximately 11 million. Roughly 99 percent is Sunni Muslim. Other minority religious congregations make up approximately one percent of the residents. Of these, Roman Catholics constitute approximately 88 percent, with the rest being Russian Orthodox, French Reformists, Anglicans, Seventh-day Adventists, Greek Orthodox, and Jehovah's Witnesses. The Jewish community, which has had a presence in Tunisia since antiquity, was approximately 1,500–2,000 in 2015.[44] It is the human rights challenges in this society—especially those of minority religious groups—that my dialogue in the following pages will tackle. I will briefly examine Muslim intra-sect human rights prejudice in the republic, too.

Politically, revolution of any hue can be messy and tends to produce unintended results. The Jasmine Revolution in Tunisia was not an exception to this postulation. After the 23 years of President Zine el-Abidine Ben Ali's authoritarian rule ended on January 14, 2011, the political space was opened to different political factions. This democratic opening brought in its wake the struggle for power by political parties. Indeed, the Ennahda Islamist party in a multi-party electoral contestation was elected at the polls. To be sure, the Ennahda party, whose membership claimed to have become "born again" democrats, renounced its Islamist tendencies before the elections.[45] Even so, in its administrative techniques, Ennahda appears to have borrowed a leaf from the playbook of the ousted despotic President Ben Ali. In short, Ennahda applied the Tunisian conservative and restrictive penal code to its governance genus. Since France granted self-rule to Tunisia, the new leaders' modus operandi has been monocratic. President Habib Bourguiba and his leadership genre is a good case in point. Put in another way, Ennahda's executive model suggests that *plus ça change, plus c'est la même chose*: the more things change, the more they (seemed to) stay the same in Tunisia.

The Ennahda party's nonchalant attitude toward religious persecutions of non–Muslims in Tunisia has its root in its strong conformist religious history, which its members cannot peel off in one fell swoop. Thus, while Tunisia is overall becoming more accepting of Christians since the Jasmine Revolution, there has been a visible upsurge of radical Islamic education. This extremist pedagogy is an outcome of the "new" democracy, which encourages freedom of speech. Some militants whose intentions are, among other things, to control politics and power promote the growth of political Islamism. In the current political dispensation, immediate and extended family members who convert to Christianity are in jeopardy. This is the case because community and security agents ostracize converts to Christianity from Islam.[46] Moreover, successful conversion to Christianity is often disheartening to Muslim families; it suggests family failure to fully indoctrinate relatives in Islamic philosophy.

Accordingly, Tunisian Christians may have to worship and practice their faith in "catacombs" for fear of persecution even though constitutionally there is no penalty for apostasy. In some cases, converted Tunisian Christians suffer from bigotry in employment and job insecurity just like the impact of racism in some developed countries. The supposition is that for Tunisians to fully enjoy the political, economic and social fruits in the society, it would be incumbent on compatriots to declare their allegiance to the national faith—Islam. In fact, this conviction originates from, or finds expression in, Article 1 of the constitution, which proclaims, inter alia, that "Tunisia is a free, independent state; its religion is Islam."[47] But the preceding obstacles challenge a Tunisian's rights to religious freedom and conversion. For instance, discrimination against Christians based on religion violates Article 18 of the ICCPR, Article 8 of the ACHPR, Article 18 of the UDHR and Article 6 of the Tunisian constitution.

Religious bigotry, as noted previously, is not directed only against Christians. Tunisians who exercise their freedom of speech by publishing articles offensive to Islam suffer from the political and social wrath of the government. Such was the case when two Tunisians were sentenced to a seven-year prison term for their publication of a work or opinion deemed offensive to Islam. Indeed, it was daring for journalist Najoua Jo to pose this poignant query in an opinion page: "In today's Tunisia, has anyone the right to be an atheist and to publicly avow it? The answer is clear: it is no."[48] The state convicted Ghazi Ben Mohamed Beji for blasphemy for having the audacity to publish a piece titled "The Illusion of Islam," which satirized the Prophet Mohamed's life.[49] Human Rights Watch reports that such anti–Islamic publications that are detrimental to public order and morality are indictable under Article 121(3) of the penal code. This proviso of the code stipulates:

> To "distribute, offer for sale, publicly display, or possess, with the intent to distribute, sell, display for the purpose of propaganda, tracts … that are liable to cause harm to the public order or public morals [is prohibited]. Any infraction of this law can bring about the immediate seizure of the offending material and imprisonment for six months to five years, and a fine of 120 to 1,200 dinars ($84 to $840).[50]

## Government Respect for Religious Freedom and Practices

According to human rights dialogues, the sentencing to custody of the two Tunisian journalists violated their freedom of expression. For instance, Human Rights Watch in its review of this matter expressed concern on the above court ruling. This was the situation because the state ruled on the basis of principles in the penal code, which oftentimes contradict precepts in the constitution. In addition, confusion in interpreting the law sometimes arises from the fact that the constitution declares that Islam is the country's official religion while simultaneously affirming that the country is a civil state.[51] Moreover, it is prejudicial in a democratic society that the constitution requires the president of the republic to be Muslim. Accordingly, in this political setting, a Tunisian Catholic or an Anglican, for that matter, cannot be president of the state.

The constitution guarantees freedom of belief, conscience, and exercise of religious practices. This is equally the circumstance in international human rights instruments—e.g., the ICCPR, UDHR and ACHPR. On paper, the constitution also proclaims the neutrality of mosques and houses of worship from partisan politics; however, this declaration of the "separation of religion and state" is illusory. In fact, I term this theory of separation of religion and state a "delusional constitutional construct." This is so because in most states where the constitution and political preachment of separation of church and state have been the norm, it has not been feasible to practice the precept. In political contestations, politicos have used religion as a strategy—some might say a mask—to garner support from voters, while violating the human rights of citizens, especially those outside their faith. To be sure, most Muslim activists insist that politics and religion are inseparable in their contemplation—regardless of constitutional principles suggesting the need for a divorce.

According to information from the Ministry of Religious Affairs, Christian and Jewish groups have fewer problems with registering as institutions of worship. Jews, however, receive preference over other non–Muslim groups in their social and educational operations in the society. This state policy smacks of bias against other religious groups that do not have the same rights. For instance, Jewish population are permitted to attend and manage their own religious schools while Christian schools, where they exist, need to follow state programs with Islamic teachings.[52] Additionally, according to the law, the state oversees Islamic prayer services; it subsidizes mosques, appoints imams and pays their salaries, too. Such state control of imams and the appurtenances of the mosques stifles and challenges Muslim clerics' rights to freedom of expression on theological and social issues.

## Government Practices

Overall, human rights enigmas in Tunisia have been overwhelming partially because of the nature of the contraventions. The gruesome terrorist aggression on March 18, 2015, at the Bardo Museum, one of the crown jewels of Tunisian heritage, was a critical blow on the state. Another terrorist attack happened on June 26 at two hotels in Sousse that resulted in the deaths of 22 and 38 individuals, respectively. Many of the victims were foreigners. Another terrorist attack happened on November 24 in Tunis. This onslaught killed 12 members of the presidential guard. ISIS claimed that it was responsible for the mayhem; it was intended to be retribution against "crusaders and apostates"[53] in the republic. These offenses and carnages committed by a non-state actor violate Article 6 of the ICCPR and Article 3 of the UDHR. For instance, Article 6 of the ICCPR declares, "Every human being has the inherent right to life…. No one shall be arbitrarily deprived of his [or her] life."

The feats of bloodbath carried out by ISIS may have been part of a warning against Tunis and its "moderate religious" orthodoxy. Consequently, as Muslim "traitors" to the true teaching of Islam, they were and are no different from infidels. Accordingly, their rights to life could be violated in what I suggested previously amounts to intra-religious bigotry (i.e., Sunni vs Shia and conformist vs non-conformist Muslims). Put in another way, human rights conundrums in Tunisia are not limited to non–Muslims. In retaliation for the acts of terrorism, the government through the prime minister's office revived the activities of a crisis unit it created in 2014 to fight terrorism. As noted previously, the crisis unit shut down 80 mosques and accused their imams of preaching radical theology antithetical to the government's instructions. In many cases, Tunis violated the rights of these imams by carrying out these measures without due process of law or requisite judicial review, as contended by civil society watchdog groups.[54]

The government remains adamant in its call for moderation and in its determination to combat threats of violent extremism arising from mosques. To demonstrate its pledge and determination to improve religious and political tolerance in the polity, the Ministry of Religious Affairs sacked 20 imams. The MRA alleged that these imams incited activities deemed harmful to the wellbeing of the state by preaching revolutionary theology from the mosques. The dismissed imams, who claimed that their rights to preach in mosques were violated, confronted the administration. The National Council of Mosques and Imams led the struggle. The Council expressed its opposition to the firing of these imams by demonstrating in front of the MRA building in condemnation of what it claimed were the ministry's "arbitrary decisions" to dismiss imams—thus violating their rights as clerics.

Petitions to reinstate Ridha Jaouadi, one of the firebrand imams, of the Lakhmi Mosque in Sfax, came to naught. The MRA refused to give in under pressure from the National Council of Mosques and Imams. Indeed, the MRA held that Jaouadi had preached jihad and organized trade union activities from inside the mosque in violation of the doctrine of "the separation of religion and state." The MRA condemned his inflammatory preachments and union actions because they could arouse oppositional forces in Tunisia capable of affecting the wellbeing of citizens by suffocating political stability in the republic. Subsequently, the MRA suspended Friday prayers at Lakhmi Mosque, and beefed up its security apparatus in the area. However, the administration later reopened the mosque for Friday prayers but under the supervision of a new imam appointed by the MRA—a right which the Tunisian state, as custodian of national mosques, claims.[55] Salafists, too, express consternation that the regime monitored their activities in the society. They express discomfiture that law enforcement agencies, which profile the group, violate their human rights. Because of Salafists' attire and long beards, they are suspected of been terrorists even though they claim to wear their beards to mimic the Prophet Muhammad.[56]

My previous dialogues briefly examined the critical role religion plays in the lives of citizens of the country in relation to human rights. The discourses illustrate the dilemmas that religion and its observance sporadically pose counter to human rights practices in the society; and they also highlight the clashes provoked by efforts undertaken by the government to mollify conflicts that arise in reconciling the contradictions between human rights theories and their implementations. In other words, the deliberations expose the collisions between well-crafted human rights theories in constitutions and international human rights instruments and the difficulties in their executions. Next, I will explore and debate concisely women's human rights enigmas in the republic. I do so against the backdrop of the real or putative perception of the citizens of the non–Muslim world of the marginalization and rights infractions of women in the social, political, economic and religious spheres in Muslim societies.

## Women and Human Rights

Historicizing the political development in Tunisia is useful for understanding why the observance of women's rights is important in the Islamic states of North Africa and other nation-states in the Muslim world. Tunisia's legal system is like that of the French code, possibly because of its colonial relations with France. The Sharia court system, popular in many Muslim-dominated countries, was abandoned in 1956, following the outcome of independence from France. Subsequently, the country adopted its own unified court system and a unique personal-status code. The modification of the code has happened several times with a view to fixing the principles that are prejudicial to women.[57] For example, women's and men's testimony carries identical weight in a court of law—a unique principle in the country's jurisprudence.[58]

Tunisia, in addition to departing from the negative "norms" on women's issues in the Islamic region, adopted the CEDAW in 1985. The republic did so with initial reservation about the following articles:

9(2) States Parties shall grant women equal rights with men with respect to the nationality of their children....

[States Parties shall ensure]

16(c) The same rights and responsibilities during marriage and at its dissolution;

16(d) The same rights and responsibilities as parents, irrespective of their marital status, in matters relating to their children; in all cases the interests of the children shall be paramount;...

16(f) The same rights and responsibilities with regard to guardianship, wardship, trusteeship and adoption of children, or similar institutions where these concepts exist in national legislation; in all cases the interests of the children shall be paramount;

16(g) The same personal rights as husband and wife, including the right to choose a family name, a profession and an occupation;

16(h) The same rights for both spouses in respect of the ownership, acquisition, management, administration, enjoyment and disposition of property, whether free of charge or for a valuable consideration.[59]

It is safe to contend that the debate on rejection of the preceding precepts in the CEDAW was contentious. Conservative political actors supported the ruling of the state on the objections to the above injunctions, while moderate and liberal politicians were in accord with the character of the CEDAW doctrines. Nevertheless, the refutation of Articles 9 and 16 of the CEDAW remained the position of the government for 26 years. Meanwhile human rights groups fought tooth and nail for their ratification. Pleasantly, in August 2011 the Tunisian Council of Ministers promulgated a draft decree that promised to withdraw all misgivings to the CEDAW.[60] Even so, in human rights discourses, it is one thing to proclaim human rights dogmas and quite another to implement the inspiring theories nationally—especially in the countryside where these rights tend to meet stiff opposition.

Remarkably, in Tunisia, the laws promoting equality between men and women in many areas of human rights concerns are superior to those in other Islamic North African states, several nations in the Middle East and much of Africa. For example:

1. As to nationality rights, the Nationality Code allows Tunisian women married to foreigners to transfer their nationality to their children.

2. Men and women have the same rules governing divorce, e.g., mutually agreed divorce or divorce based on the request of either spouse.

3. Both husband and wife have equal rights to the guardianship of their children.

4. Unique to inheritance rights is the ruling by the Supreme Court of Appeals that a non–Muslim woman married to a Muslim man does have inheritance rights based on constitutional guarantees of freedom of worship.

5. On the matter of freedom of movement, a Tunisian woman does not need the permission of her husband or father to travel or get a passport.

6. On protection of child marriage, the official age of marriage is 18 for boys and girls.

7. On polygamy, the state abolished it contrary to the Quran, which allows up to four wives if a man has the means to do so, inter alia.

As to protection of gender-based violence, the penal code forbids and criminalizes it, too. Impressively, the state proscribes rape both in marriage and outside of marriage.[61]

As to education, the statistics are compelling in Tunisia. Impressively, UNICEF asserts that in 2009 "the youth literacy rate [was] 96 percent for female youth and 98 percent for male youth. The net enrolment ratio for primary education [was] roughly equal for girls and boys (99 percent for girls and 98 percent for boys)."[62] Notwithstanding the foregoing data, the mental template or mindset that relegates women to the periphery in social, political, economic and cultural development has not been fully deconstructed. To be sure, reviews on reforms in favor of women's rights in Tunisia vis-à-vis other countries in the Middle East and North Africa (MENA) is notable. Little wonder, then, that Freedom House reports suggest that, overall, Tunisian women enjoy the maximum amount of freedom in MENA (Algeria, Bahrain, Egypt, Iraq, Jordan, Kuwait, Lebanon, Libya, Morocco, Oman, Palestine, Qatar, Saudi Arabia, Syria and Tunisia).[63] In Islamic North Africa, too, Tunisia tops Morocco, Algeria, Egypt and Libya in observing women's rights[64] as Table II below illustrates.

## Table II

| | Nondis-crimination and Access to Justice | Autonomy, Security, and Freedom of Person | Economic Rights and Equal Opportunity | Political Rights and Civic Voice | Social and Cultural Rights |
|---|---|---|---|---|---|
| Algeria | 3.0 | 2.4 | 2.8 | 3.0 | 2.9 |
| Bahrain | 2.2 | 2.3 | 2.9 | 2.1 | 2.8 |
| Egypt | 3.0 | 2.8 | 2.8 | 2.7 | 2.4 |
| Iraq | 2.7 | 2.6 | 2.8 | 2.2 | 2.1 |
| Jordan | 2.4 | 2.4 | 2.8 | 2.8 | 2.5 |
| Kuwait | 1.9 | 2.2 | 2.9 | 1.4 | 2.8 |
| Lebanon | 2.8 | 2.9 | 2.8 | 2.9 | 2.9 |
| Libya | 2.3 | 2.1 | 2.3 | 1.2 | 1.8 |
| Morocco | 3.2 | 3.2 | 3.1 | 3.0 | 3.0 |
| Oman | 2.0 | 2.1 | 2.7 | 1.2 | 2.1 |
| Palestine | 2.6 | 2.7 | 2.8 | 2.6 | 2.9 |
| Qatar | 2.0 | 2.1 | 2.8 | 1.7 | 2.5 |
| Saudi Arabia | 1.2 | 1.1 | 1.4 | 1.0 | 1.6 |
| Syria | 2.7 | 2.2 | 2.8 | 2.2 | 2.3 |
| Tunisia | 3.6 | 3.4 | 3.1 | 2.8 | 3.3 |
| UAE | 1.7 | 2.1 | 2.8 | 1.2 | 2.3 |
| Yemen | 2.4 | 2.3 | 2.3 | 2.6 | 2.1 |

Source: S. Nazir and L. Tomppert, eds. *Women's Rights in the Middle East and North Africa: Citizenship and Justice* (New York: Freedom House and Lanham, MD: Rowman & Littlefield, 2005).

Table II provides five indices, which rate 17 countries in the MENA on women's rights. These indicators are: (1) Nondiscrimination and Access to Justice; (2) Autonomy, Security, and Freedom of Person; (3) Economic Rights and Equal Opportunity; (4) Political Rights and Civic Voice; and (5) Social and Cultural Rights. Remarkably, as Table II shows, based on the above five indicators, Tunisia ranked at the top or next to it amongst all countries in the MENA.

To paraphrase James Madison, a U.S. 19th century president, "if only men [and women] were angels, there would be no need for government."[65] Accordingly, governments need to adopt a system of checks and balances and an efficacious constitution that can advance human dignity and political stability. In Tunisia, however, if political leaders and their cohorts follow justly constitutional principles, there may be relatively few cases of human rights challenges in the polity. Humans are not saints; they frequently act to protect their interests regardless of splendid human rights commandments and sermons. Therefore, it is imperative for local human rights NGOs, Human Rights Watch, Amnesty International and the U.S. Department of State to monitor the activities of the government and its security forces to guard against human rights breaches in the republic.

For instance, the U.S. Department of State reports that rape and domestic violence are common in the society even though forbidden by law. Rape, and ironically spousal rape, is a problem in a society that prohibits it. Generally, the state enforces the law against rape with up to 12 years and even life imprisonment, but that does not impede its recurrence. Regrettably, the penal code does not address the issue spousal rape possibly because it is difficult to legislate families' domestic affairs. Consequently, it is difficult to gather information on the regularity of this rights matter in the society. In fact, conversation on this human rights issue is taboo in many families. The topic can be wickedly embarrassing. Not surprisingly, human rights campaigners and critics of this phenomenon suggest that rape is a problem and that officials should continue to report it whenever and wherever it happens in the country.[66]

Violence against women is a real rights quagmire in this society just as is the case in much of MENA and on the African continent itself. Many wife beaters take solace in the fact that the act of aggression against women could be based in Sura 4:34 of the Holy Quran, which declares:

> Men are the protectors and maintainers of women, because Allah has given the one more (strength) than the other, and because they support them from their means. Therefore, the righteous women are devoutly obedient, and guard in (the husband's) absence what Allah would have them guard. As to those women on whose part ye fear disloyalty and ill-conduct, admonish them first, next, refuse to share their bed, and last beat them.[67]

While the above excerpt might give license to conservative Islamists to teach their wives a lesson for lack of obedience, the law prohibits violence against women. Inspiringly, a study conducted by the Tunisian General Labor

Union's National Commission of Working Women is revealing. It found that "32 percent of all women experienced some kind of physical violence, 28.9 percent experienced psychological violence or harassment, 15.7 percent suffered sexual violence or exploitation, and 7 percent experienced economic violence, including financial exploitation, extortion, or deprivation of money or the necessities of life."[68] Problematically, a high level of violence against women happens within marriage, possibly because it is sanction in Sura 4:34 as noted above.

In Tunisia, discrimination against women is less severe than in much of the Islamic world as noted in Table II. Societal norms challenge and impede women's economic and political rights. This prejudice toward females lies in the culture of the society despite the state's progressive policies toward women's rights. Although Tunisia's civil law draws its strength from the Napoleonic code, on occasion some judges have made decisions based on Sharia, the Islamic jurisprudence, as a basis for customary law. Frequently, this is the case on family matters such as inheritance disputes. On the issue of inheritance, the Quran in Sura 4 states, inter alia, "Allah enjoins you concerning your children: the male shall have the equal of the portion of two females." To avoid this prejudicial practice, some families execute "sales contracts" that allows parents and children to ensure that daughters and sons receive equal shares of property.[69] Notwithstanding the above anti-discriminatory provision pursued by enlightened citizens among the public, women continue to agitate for a national law that will abrogate the Islamic creed specifying that sons inherit double the amount received by daughters. Indeed, in a public demonstration organized by women in front of Parliament, they displayed their placards and chanted in unison that inheritance rights "are a right, not a favor."[70] The clergy rebuffed President Beji Caid Essebsi's positive response to the call for equal rights on this issue. In fact, Muslim clerics responded to the president's stance with powerful opposition to the inheritance equality scheme and agitation. They condemned the president's stance on this matter and those of the women protestors as an affront to Islamic dogmas.[71]

Discrimination against women in the workplace is global especially on the issue of equal pay for equal work. A platitudinous argument against equal pay for men and women in some developed, as well as developing societies, was and is that women would get married to men and their husbands will support them and their family financially. This anachronistic view in rights debate finds expression and articulation in Sura 4:34 of the Holy Quran that declares, "Men are the protectors and maintainers of women. Comparatively, for Christians, the Holy Bible in Ephesians 5:2 proclaims: "Wives, submit yourself unto your husbands, as unto the Lord,"[72] supports the preceding thesis.

The government is in favor of equal pay for equal work for both genders and has generally enforced the law especially in the public sector. Nonetheless, in the private sector as of 2015 women earned on average one-quarter less than men for similar work.[73] The constitution is somewhat ambiguous on this matter of equal pay for equal work for both sexes. This opinion in supported in Article 40 of the 2014 constitution, which states, "Work is a right for every citizen, male and female. The state shall take necessary measures to guarantee work based on competence and fairness. All citizens, male and female, shall have the right to decent working conditions and to a fair wage" (see Table I). The question in this principle is that of determining what a fair wage is for men or women. However, to address this human rights dilemma, the Universal Declaration of Human Rights proclaims in Article 23(2): "Everyone, without discrimination, has the right to equal pay for equal work."[74]

It is customary in most authoritarian societies for citizens to receive punishment for expressing views contrary or offensive to those held by the government. In some autocratic polities, too, it is politically sacrilegious to criticize decisions made by the president or prime minister. It could earn one serious flogging by security agents and even a jail-term. However, freedom of speech and press allows different publics to express views that are likely to inform lawmakers on issues of concern to a community. Such critical opinions on a policy, for instance, can provide a regime an opportunity to debate and pass laws likely to address the society's problems. It is against the backdrop of my foregoing postulations that I shall discuss freedom of speech and press as a human rights enigma in Tunisia.

## Civil Liberties: Freedom of Speech and Press

Articles 31 and 32 of the constitution approve both freedom of speech and press (see Table I). International human rights conventions also stress the importance of freedom of speech and press. In fact, the ACHPR states in Article 9(1): "Every individual shall have the right to receive information"; and in 9(2): "Every individual shall have the right to express and disseminate his [or her] opinions within the law."[75] Article 19(1) of the International Covenant on Civil and Political Rights affirms: "Everyone shall have the right to hold opinions without interference." In 19(2), the ICCPP states: "Everyone shall have the right to freedom of expression; this right shall include freedom to seek, receive and impart information and ideas of all kinds, regardless of frontiers, either orally, in writing or in print, in the form of art, or through any other media of his [or her] choice."[76] Ditto the above precepts of freedom of speech and press in Article 19 of the UDHR. Typically, the hypothesis is that freedom of speech and the press promotes robust democracy; this is the case because diverse and challenging opinions can help lawmakers understand the political mood of the country, and consequently write efficacious legislation.

Although the Tunisian government has generally respected freedom of speech and the press there are continuing limitations and challenges to these rights in the society. Online and print media often publish articles criticizing government's inadequate policies. Journalists and militants, however, continue to tread carefully by practicing self-censorship. Reporters maintain that they practice self-restriction to eschew violence from the government's security agents and agencies. Security forces, in defense of their actions, consider any reproach of their activities repugnant and will often fight back against the sources of the agency's' criticisms.[77]

That notwithstanding, civil servants are reminded that in human rights practice,

> international standards require that no special protection be provided for public officials—rather, the higher the rank of the public official, the more legitimate criticism of him/her becomes, for [notionally] with greater responsibility comes greater need for public scrutiny [since to paraphrase Lord Acton power tends to corrupt and absolute power tends to corrupt absolutely].[78]

However, Articles 125 and 128 of Tunisia's penal code punish those who insult public officials or report that a public executive has committed illegal acts without establishing the veracity of such claims. In Tunisia, as in much of the developing world, the more responsibility and power a public official acquires, the more authoritative and sacrosanct s/he thinks of herself or himself in society. Accordingly, a journalist who slights or satirizes a top civil servant for inadequacies in office is liable for punishment to teach the reporter a lesson not to repeat this action; this is the case even if it means violating the columnist's rights to freely report an administrative malfeasance. As noted previously, it appears that the rights that the state's constitution grants citizens, the nation also takes away with contrary principles enshrined in the penal code—a concern raised in the introduction to this volume. Such rights paradoxes that arise between the principles in the constitution and the dogmas in the penal code often prompt some human rights organizations to challenge government officials on their human rights commitments. This was the circumstance when Heba Morayef, Amnesty International's Middle East and North Africa Director, reiterated a compelling view on freedom of expression. Morayef opined, "The right to freedom of expression is essential in a robust and dynamic society. All people in Tunisia must be able to openly express their criticism of state institutions and public officials, including security forces, without the fear of prosecution."[79]

Problematic to human rights campaigners was the admission by the Minister of Interior, that the government monitors and wiretaps conversations of journalists in the society. This operation was undertaken with a view to interrogating reporters on possible "crimes against the state" and on issues that could cause damage to the public order or public ethics. The National Syndicate of Tunisian Journalists, however, protested against law enforcement officials for bringing pressure to bear on reporters who expose and criticize corrupt and harsh activities of state institutions.[80] Even so, the court tried in absentia Yassine Ayari for maligning the army and defaming high-ranking defense officials about corruption in the army in a blog. He was sentence to three years' imprisonment for this offense.[81]

As to press and media freedoms, the constitution protects them in Articles 31 and 32. Nevertheless, human rights campaigners express dismay on restraints enforced in the country following the struggle against terrorism. Indeed, in the state's war on terror the Justice Ministry published an official announcement on social media warning the public that it would invoke the counterterrorism act to indict reporters who publicize images of terrorist fatalities. The Independent Authority of Audiovisual Communication and the National Union of Tunisian Journalists (SNJT) condemned the Justice Ministry's threat. The SNJT went even further by proclaiming that the government's action was a "declaration of war against the freedom of the press."[82] Despite the foregoing resistance to the government's policy on monitoring the activities of reporters, the human rights of journalists to report news freely in the polity continue to suffer.

Further, to intimidate journalists and the media, security officials upheld their act of violence and threat during reporting on street protests. In addition, to buttress its contention on human rights contraventions committed by state security agents in the country, the Tunis Center for Press Freedom released statistics showing 277 assaults on journalists in 2014. In addition, Reporters without Borders announced with solemnity that 30 journalists were victims of law enforcement agents as they reported from the scene of a terrorist attack in the heart of Tunis.[83]

The political plight of minorities in many nation-states in Islamic North Africa and much of the global south can be dire.[84] This is so partly because they lack sufficient electoral power with which to pursue their interests, as most majorities do with their vote, in a democracy. Undeniably, recognition of minority rights in multi-ethnic and multilingual states is critical for promoting political stability and the mitigation of calls for secession. Addressing the explosiveness of the politicization of ethnicity in multi-ethnic states sometimes calls for constitutional remedy. Accordingly, many constitutions in both developed and developing nations with multiple nationalities appeal for safeguarding majority rule and minority rights crucial for advancing justice and fair play in a democracy. It is within the general framework of the foregoing suppositions that I will briefly examine the human rights challenges of minorities in Tunisia.

## Minorities and Human Rights

### Blacks

The dialogue that follows is on racism against blacks as a human rights challenge in Tunisia. Theologically, a discussion on racial bigotry in this "moderate" society should be inapt due in part to Islamic orthodoxy on this matter. Doctrinally, Islam forbids and denounces racism. For example, Surat al-Isra' 17:70 declares: "Allah created different races and tribes so that people would recognize each other and learn from each other, not so that the races would fight each other. Ethnic diversity is part of the divine plan, a means of enrichment." Additionally, Surat al-Hujurat 49:13 proclaims:

> In fact, Allah created different skin colors and languages as a sign of His creative power. Just as flowers come in many different [or assorted] colors, all as different divine signs in Allah's creation, so do human beings come in different colors.[85]

Despite the foregoing injunctions in the Holy Quran promoting the beauty and complementarity of racial diversity and rejection of ethnic prejudice, the political and rights practices by many in Tunisia and other Islamic countries prove otherwise. This development highlights the conflict between the "positive" theory of human rights and its application in this chapter and volume. Article 21 of the constitution guarantees freedoms and equivalent rights to all citizens, male or female [black or white] (see Table I). Moreover, Article 2 of the Universal Declaration of Human Rights, Article 2 of International Covenant on Civil and Political Rights, and Article 2 of the African Charter on Human and Peoples' Rights prohibit, among other factors, racial discrimination.[86] On the discourse relating to minorities and racism, within my theoretical construct, Article 1(1) of the International Convention on the Elimination of All Forms of Racial Discrimination states:

> In this Convention, the term "racial discrimination" shall mean any distinction, exclusion, restriction or preference based on race, colour, descent, or national or ethnic origin which has the purpose or effect of nullifying or impairing the recognition, enjoyment or exercise, on an equal footing, of human rights and fundamental freedoms in the political, economic, social, cultural or any other field of public life.

Article 2(1) states:

> States Parties condemn racial discrimination and undertake to pursue by all appropriate means and without delay a policy of eliminating racial discrimination in all its forms and promoting understanding among all races, and, to this end: (a) Each State Party undertakes to engage in no act or practice of racial discrimination against persons, groups of persons or institutions and to ensure that all public authorities and public institutions, national and local, shall act in conformity with this obligation.[87]

The question that perplexes many human rights observers on minority issues in Tunisian society is: Why should racism persist in arguably one of the most "liberal" Islamic states in North Africa and the Arab world? Indeed, racism in all its manifestations and ramifications is a human rights challenge in Tunisia. Yet, open and frank conversation on this matter is sensitive, and even taboo, in this republic as well as in many developing and developed countries. Some observers, despite the Quranic condemnation of racism, ascribe racist propensities in the polity to Tunisian history. It is ironic that

> despite being the first Arab country to abolish slavery (in 1846), this chapter of the past still weighs heavily on the Tunisian society of today influencing racially biased stereotypes and roles traditionally attributed to members of the Black minority, as well as racial profiling and racist violence. What makes the work on these issues even more imperative is the fact that there still is no law criminalizing racism and racial violence.[88]

Indeed, it is a given that racial bigotry toward black Tunisians has permeated the social fabric of a segment of the public. A poignant anecdote on racism, which is not unique to Tunisia, describes the experience of a young woman from the south, where most black Tunisians are domiciled. This woman refused to submit her photo in a job application. This was because of fear that her skin color could lead to her being denied an interview. This human rights scenario exists partly because of the peculiar character of racism in the society. Additionally, as noted earlier, honest discussions on racism by groups in the country are rare, and this makes human rights challenges in the republic daunting. However, such frank conversations, if held, can mitigate racial bias aimed at Tunisian black citizens and their human rights.[89]

Although racism in Tunisia has profound historical antecedent, as noted previously, it is remarkable that it was not until after the 2011 revolution that freedom of speech "flowered" and allowed Tunisian minorities to voice their grievances in the open. Hitherto, blacks spoke about racism amongst themselves and in murmurs, too. In kindergarten schools, fellow white pupils fortuitously tease black children as "kahlouche," meaning "little black" in Tunisian lingo. Black pupils are occasionally traumatized by this appellation. Moreover, the use of the name wasif (servant/attendant) to refer to black Tunisians is especially repugnant to many blacks. In southern Tunisia, the populations—blacks and whites—still use the words abid (slaves) and hurr (free) when referring to black and white Tunisians. Such association of "people of color" with the anachronistic status of slaves helps, inadvertently, to advance and prolong racism in a society in which blacks, demographically, make up 15 percent of the national population.[90]

It is a given that minorities of all hues, with a few exceptions, in all regions of the world, are confronted with human rights challenges.[91] However, in Tunisia, where the official politico-religious sermon is that bigotry based on race does not exist, it is difficulty to assail its concomitant negative effects on the affected population. Indeed, among the 217 legislators elected to the Tunisian constitutional assembly in 2011, Bechir Chammam, of the powerful Islamic party Ennahda, is the only black representative. In an interview on why he was and is the only black Member of Parliament, Chammam opined that his Islamic background and education allowed him to overcome some of the incidents that relate to his blackness in Tunisia. He attributed racial prejudice, and human rights violations, to cultural backwardness of some in the republic.[92]

To tackle the "ogre" of racism and its unintended consequences of bias and other forms of human rights infractions in the society, a group of black intellectuals and some members of the informed public founded an association called ADAM. In Tunisia, it was the first organization created for promoting the rights of the black population.[93] ADAM has organized forums and roundtable discussions to address the human rights challenges that blacks confront in the society. For example, capitalizing on the presence of a gathering of groups at an international World Social Forum held in Tunis, ADAM collaborated with this association in highlighting black human rights conundrums in the society. In fact, delegations from Brazil, France and America issued a special declaration at the end of the meeting. The proclamation called upon, inter alia, "the Tunisian government and the National Constituent Assembly to consider their claims, to include in the draft constitution the principle of the fight against all forms of discrimination, including racial discrimination and penalize racist statements and actions."[94] Despite blacks' supplication to the government to address their human rights dilemmas, the position of legislators appears to be that of nonchalance, possibly because they believe fervently and doctrinally that racism does not exist in Tunisia. Lawmakers may have also concluded that participants at this forum were a gang of rabble-rousers exercising their freedom of speech.

The Occident, because of its more laissez-faire socio-political characteristics, is more tolerant of the activities of the LGBTI community than the relatively conservative societies in the developing world. In Africa, the LGBTI lifestyle, in all its forms, is taboo. With a few exceptions, the existence of this community in Africa was unheard of until recently. Nevertheless, its lifestyles remain unacceptable on the continent except for in South Africa, with its liberal laws on LGBTI issues. Culturally, the ways of life of this group are frequently condemned.[95] Little wonder, then, that generally international human rights NGOs are the major protectors of LBGTI community rights in Africa and Tunisia itself. My foregoing brief suppositions provide a backdrop against which I will discuss the human rights quagmires and challenges of this marginalized minority group in Tunisia.

## LGBTI

Articles 2 and 22 of the ICCPR protect the rights of members of the LGBTI family. Articles 23 and 30 of Tunisia's 2014 constitution (see Table I) also protect their freedoms in the society. Nevertheless, government agents and agencies frequently challenge LGBTI rights, possibly because homosexuality remains illegal and its practice is punishable in the country under Article 230 of the penal code.[96] Article 230 condemns any sexual acts between two (or more) consenting adults of the same sex. The penalty, if caught, for any acts of homosexuality is a three-year prison term. Human rights groups have condemned this punishment. They contend that Article 230 of the penal code was and is anathema to Article 21 of the constitution on equality of all citizens before the law and Article 24 on personal privacy (see Table I).[97] It was inspiring to human rights campaigners that in May 2017, the government recognized that prejudice existed in the society against those with homosexual tendencies. The regime then proclaimed that "any person of any sexual orientation has full rights [and] any act of aggression committed against any person based on his [or her] sexual orientation is criminal and can be prosecuted."[98] Human Rights Minister Mehdi Ben Gharbia went a step further by asserting that male homosexuals will no longer undergo a torturous medical technique for ascertaining if a male was involved in same sex acts.[99] Suffice it to say, however, that the above well-intended responses to protect the rights of members of the LGBTI community face stiff challenges in pastoral communities.

The U.S. Department of State's 2015 account on human rights practices in Tunisia alludes to acts of violence, discrimination, and other abuses based on sexual orientation and gender identity related to LGBTI identity. Traditional opposition to LGBTI practices is very strong, especially in rural Tunisia, as noted earlier. In addition, conservative judges tend to be opposed to LGBTI rights. Considering this development, some human rights NGOs testify that law enforcement agents have sporadically applied extra-constitutional laws, for instance, to arrest and interrogate individuals about their sexual activities and orientation. In fact, LGBTI NGOs affirmed that 56 known cases of arrests under the sodomy law happened in 2015.[100] In addition, six men from Rakkada were sentence to a three-year incarceration each for similar offenses. To discourage this lifestyle, the court declared them persona-non-grata in their town for five years after the completion of their incarceration.[101]

In protest of the court's rulings, organizations advocating LGBTI rights ordered a campaign against the detention because of the infringement of these individuals' human rights. Further, pro–LGBTI national and international human rights NGOs canvassed for the release of the imprisoned men. But the president, informed by tradition, society's intolerance of same-sex relationships and politics, affirmed that the government did not intend to repeal the law on sodomy, to the chagrin of the LGBTI community.[102] More-over, in a November 28, 2015, plenary session of Parliament, Abdellatif Mekki called for the disbanding of an influential LGBTI non-governmental orga-nization called Shams. Shams's raison d'être was supporting sexual minori-ties materially, morally and psychologically.[103] In a challenge to the rights of member of the LGBTI community, Mekki insisted that Shams constituted a menace to Tunisian society, and that it promoted practices that were not only criminal but also injurious to society, if allowed to exist and develop.[104]

## Conclusion

It is impressive that the Tunisian government is amenable to national and international human rights NGOs investigating and publishing their findings on human rights abuses in the republic. The government received without ran-cor reports and recommendations from human rights observers. Nationally, an important human rights auxiliary of the government charged with the task of tackling rights challenges in the society is the High Committee for Human Rights and Fundamental Freedoms. The outcomes of its activities on solving human rights issues in Tunisia have not been entirely successful. This is so partly because of the conflicts in interpreting human rights tenets enshrined in the constitution and those in the penal code and other statutory laws.[105]

It is noteworthy, however, that after the combustible 2011 revolution, the administration established the Truth and Dignity Commission (TDC) in June 2014. The TDC is like South Africa's Truth and Reconciliation Commission. Sihem Bensedrine, a human rights campaigner, is the head of the Commit-tee.[106] The TDC's mandate is to investigate, applying legal and unjudicial meth-ods, gross human rights breaches committed by the Tunisian state since 1955.[107] It is encouraging and reassuring that at the end of the TDC's task, victims of human rights abuses will receive compensation as endorsed in its charter.

It is refreshing that after many years of ignoring racial prejudice in Tu-nisia, the government has taken a major step to mitigate racism toward black Tunisians with a statutory onslaught. This was the case in 2018 when the Tuni-sian Human Rights Minister, Mehdi Ben Gharbia, declared that the Tunisian government would promulgate an anti-discrimination law that will promote equal rights for all Tunisians—not least for black Tunisians who have contin-ually confronted human rights challenges in the republic. By this act, Tunisia will become the second country on the African continent, after South Africa, to pass such a law.[108] It is safe to suggest that the enforcement of the TDC's recommendations, and the judicious execution of the anti-discrimination legislation, are likely to improve and advance human rights practices in Tu-nisia for the near future.

# Appendix A

## Convention Against Torture and Other Cruel, Inhuman or Degrading Treatment or Punishment

Adopted and opened for signature, ratification and accession by General Assembly resolution 39/46 of 10 December 1984 entry into force 26 June 1987, in accordance with article 27 (1)

The States Parties to this Convention,

Considering that, in accordance with the principles proclaimed in the Charter of the United Nations, recognition of the equal and inalienable rights of all members of the human family is the foundation of freedom, justice and peace in the world,

Recognizing that those rights derive from the inherent dignity of the human person,

Considering the obligation of States under the Charter, in particular Article 55, to promote universal respect for, and observance of, human rights and fundamental freedoms,

Having regard to article 5 of the Universal Declaration of Human Rights and article 7 of the International Covenant on Civil and Political Rights, both of which provide that no one shall be subjected to torture or to cruel, inhuman or degrading treatment or punishment,

Having regard also to the Declaration on the Protection of All Persons from Being Subjected to Torture and Other Cruel, Inhuman or Degrading Treatment or Punishment, adopted by the General Assembly on 9 December 1975,

Desiring to make more effective the struggle against torture and other cruel, inhuman or degrading treatment or punishment throughout the world,

Have agreed as follows:

## Part I

### Article 1

1. For the purposes of this Convention, the term "torture" means any act by which severe pain or suffering, whether physical or mental, is intentionally

inflicted on a person for such purposes as obtaining from him or a third person information or a confession, punishing him for an act he or a third person has committed or is suspected of having committed, or intimidating or coercing him or a third person, or for any reason based on discrimination of any kind, when such pain or suffering is inflicted by or at the instigation of or with the consent or acquiescence of a public official or other person acting in an official capacity. It does not include pain or suffering arising only from, inherent in or incidental to lawful sanctions.

2. This article is without prejudice to any international instrument or national legislation which does or may contain provisions of wider application.

## Article 2

1. Each State Party shall take effective legislative, administrative, judicial or other measures to prevent acts of torture in any territory under its jurisdiction.
2. No exceptional circumstances whatsoever, whether a state of war or a threat of war, internal political instability or any other public emergency, may be invoked as a justification of torture.
3. An order from a superior officer or a public authority may not be invoked as a justification of torture.

## Article 3

1. No State Party shall expel, return ("refouler") or extradite a person to another State where there are substantial grounds for believing that he would be in danger of being subjected to torture.
2. For the purpose of determining whether there are such grounds, the competent authorities shall take into account all relevant considerations including, where applicable, the existence in the State concerned of a consistent pattern of gross, flagrant or mass violations of human rights.

## Article 4

1. Each State Party shall ensure that all acts of torture are offences under its criminal law. The same shall apply to an attempt to commit torture and to an act by any person which constitutes complicity or participation in torture.
2. Each State Party shall make these offences punishable by appropriate penalties which take into account their grave nature.

## Article 5

1. Each State Party shall take such measures as may be necessary to establish its jurisdiction over the offences referred to in article 4 in the following cases:
   a. When the offences are committed in any territory under its jurisdiction or on board a ship or aircraft registered in that State;
   b. When the alleged offender is a national of that State;
   c. When the victim is a national of that State if that State considers it appropriate.
2. Each State Party shall likewise take such measures as may be necessary to establish its jurisdiction over such offences in cases where the alleged offender is

present in any territory under its jurisdiction and it does not extradite him pursuant to article 8 to any of the States mentioned in paragraph I of this article.
3. This Convention does not exclude any criminal jurisdiction exercised in accordance with internal law.

## Article 6

1. Upon being satisfied, after an examination of information available to it, that the circumstances so warrant, any State Party in whose territory a person alleged to have committed any offence referred to in article 4 is present shall take him into custody or take other legal measures to ensure his presence. The custody and other legal measures shall be as provided in the law of that State but may be continued only for such time as is necessary to enable any criminal or extradition proceedings to be instituted.
2. Such State shall immediately make a preliminary inquiry into the facts.
3. Any person in custody pursuant to paragraph 1 of this article shall be assisted in communicating immediately with the nearest appropriate representative of the State of which he is a national, or, if he is a stateless person, with the representative of the State where he usually resides.
4. When a State, pursuant to this article, has taken a person into custody, it shall immediately notify the States referred to in article 5, paragraph 1, of the fact that such person is in custody and of the circumstances which warrant his detention. The State which makes the preliminary inquiry contemplated in paragraph 2 of this article shall promptly report its findings to the said States and shall indicate whether it intends to exercise jurisdiction.

## Article 7

1. The State Party in the territory under whose jurisdiction a person alleged to have committed any offence referred to in article 4 is found shall in the cases contemplated in article 5, if it does not extradite him, submit the case to its competent authorities for the purpose of prosecution.
2. These authorities shall take their decision in the same manner as in the case of any ordinary offence of a serious nature under the law of that State. In the cases referred to in article 5, paragraph 2, the standards of evidence required for prosecution and conviction shall in no way be less stringent than those which apply in the cases referred to in article 5, paragraph 1.
3. Any person regarding whom proceedings are brought in connection with any of the offences referred to in article 4 shall be guaranteed fair treatment at all stages of the proceedings.

## Article 8

1. The offences referred to in article 4 shall be deemed to be included as extraditable offences in any extradition treaty existing between States Parties. States Parties undertake to include such offences as extraditable offences in every extradition treaty to be concluded between them.
2. If a State Party which makes extradition conditional on the existence of a treaty receives a request for extradition from another State Party with which

it has no extradition treaty, it may consider this Convention as the legal basis for extradition in respect of such offences. Extradition shall be subject to the other conditions provided by the law of the requested State.

3. States Parties which do not make extradition conditional on the existence of a treaty shall recognize such offences as extraditable offences between themselves subject to the conditions provided by the law of the requested State.

4. Such offences shall be treated, for the purpose of extradition between States Parties, as if they had been committed not only in the place in which they occurred but also in the territories of the States required to establish their jurisdiction in accordance with article 5, paragraph 1.

## Article 9

1. States Parties shall afford one another the greatest measure of assistance in connection with criminal proceedings brought in respect of any of the offences referred to in article 4, including the supply of all evidence at their disposal necessary for the proceedings.

2. States Parties shall carry out their obligations under paragraph I of this article in conformity with any treaties on mutual judicial assistance that may exist between them.

## Article 10

1. Each State Party shall ensure that education and information regarding the prohibition against torture are fully included in the training of law enforcement personnel, civil or military, medical personnel, public officials and other persons who may be involved in the custody, interrogation or treatment of any individual subjected to any form of arrest, detention or imprisonment.

2. Each State Party shall include this prohibition in the rules or instructions issued in regard to the duties and functions of any such person.

## Article 11

Each State Party shall keep under systematic review interrogation rules, instructions, methods and practices as well as arrangements for the custody and treatment of persons subjected to any form of arrest, detention or imprisonment in any territory under its jurisdiction, with a view to preventing any cases of torture.

## Article 12

Each State Party shall ensure that its competent authorities proceed to a prompt and impartial investigation, wherever there is reasonable ground to believe that an act of torture has been committed in any territory under its jurisdiction.

## Article 13

Each State Party shall ensure that any individual who alleges he has been subjected to torture in any territory under its jurisdiction has the right to complain to, and to have his case promptly and impartially examined by, its competent authorities. Steps shall be taken to ensure that the complainant and witnesses are protected against all ill-treatment or intimidation as a consequence of his complaint or any evidence given.

## Article 14

1. Each State Party shall ensure in its legal system that the victim of an act of torture obtains redress and has an enforceable right to fair and adequate compensation, including the means for as full rehabilitation as possible. In the event of the death of the victim as a result of an act of torture, his dependents shall be entitled to compensation.
2. Nothing in this article shall affect any right of the victim or other persons to compensation which may exist under national law.

## Article 15

Each State Party shall ensure that any statement which is established to have been made as a result of torture shall not be invoked as evidence in any proceedings, except against a person accused of torture as evidence that the statement was made.

## Article 16

1. Each State Party shall undertake to prevent in any territory under its jurisdiction other acts of cruel, inhuman or degrading treatment or punishment which do not amount to torture as defined in article I, when such acts are committed by or at the instigation of or with the consent or acquiescence of a public official or other person acting in an official capacity. In particular, the obligations contained in articles 10, 11, 12 and 13 shall apply with the substitution for references to torture of references to other forms of cruel, inhuman or degrading treatment or punishment.
2. The provisions of this Convention are without prejudice to the provisions of any other international instrument or national law which prohibits cruel, inhuman or degrading treatment or punishment or which relates to extradition or expulsion.

## *Part II*

## Article 17

1. There shall be established a Committee against Torture (hereinafter referred to as the Committee) which shall carry out the functions hereinafter provided. The Committee shall consist of ten experts of high moral standing and recognized competence in the field of human rights, who shall serve in their personal capacity. The experts shall be elected by the States Parties, consideration being given to equitable geographical distribution and to the usefulness of the participation of some persons having legal experience.
2. The members of the Committee shall be elected by secret ballot from a list of persons nominated by States Parties. Each State Party may nominate one person from among its own nationals. States Parties shall bear in mind the usefulness of nominating persons who are also members of the Human Rights

Committee established under the International Covenant on Civil and Political Rights and who are willing to serve on the Committee against Torture.

3. Elections of the members of the Committee shall be held at biennial meetings of States Parties convened by the Secretary-General of the United Nations. At those meetings, for which two thirds of the States Parties shall constitute a quorum, the persons elected to the Committee shall be those who obtain the largest number of votes and an absolute majority of the votes of the representatives of States Parties present and voting.

4. The initial election shall be held no later than six months after the date of the entry into force of this Convention. At least four months before the date of each election, the Secretary-General of the United Nations shall address a letter to the States Parties inviting them to submit their nominations within three months. The Secretary-General shall prepare a list in alphabetical order of all persons thus nominated, indicating the States Parties which have nominated them, and shall submit it to the States Parties.

5. The members of the Committee shall be elected for a term of four years. They shall be eligible for re-election if re-nominated. However, the term of five of the members elected at the first election shall expire at the end of two years; immediately after the first election the names of these five members shall be chosen by lot by the chairman of the meeting referred to in paragraph 3 of this article.

6. If a member of the Committee dies or resigns or for any other cause can no longer perform his Committee duties, the State Party which nominated him shall appoint another expert from among its nationals to serve for the remainder of his term, subject to the approval of the majority of the States Parties. The approval shall be considered given unless half or more of the States Parties respond negatively within six weeks after having been informed by the Secretary-General of the United Nations of the proposed appointment.

7. States Parties shall be responsible for the expenses of the members of the Committee while they are in performance of Committee duties.

## Article 18

1. The Committee shall elect its officers for a term of two years. They may be re-elected.

2. The Committee shall establish its own rules of procedure, but these rules shall provide, inter alia, that:
   a. Six members shall constitute a quorum;
   b. Decisions of the Committee shall be made by a majority vote of the members present.

3. The Secretary-General of the United Nations shall provide the necessary staff and facilities for the effective performance of the functions of the Committee under this Convention.

4. The Secretary-General of the United Nations shall convene the initial meeting of the Committee. After its initial meeting, the Committee shall meet at such times as shall be provided in its rules of procedure.

5. The States Parties shall be responsible for expenses incurred in connection with the holding of meetings of the States Parties and of the Committee, including

reimbursement to the United Nations for any expenses, such as the cost of staff and facilities, incurred by the United Nations pursuant to paragraph 3 of this article.

## Article 19

1. The States Parties shall submit to the Committee, through the Secretary-General of the United Nations, reports on the measures they have taken to give effect to their undertakings under this Convention, within one year after the entry into force of the Convention for the State Party concerned. Thereafter the States Parties shall submit supplementary reports every four years on any new measures taken and such other reports as the Committee may request.
2. The Secretary-General of the United Nations shall transmit the reports to all States Parties.
3. Each report shall be considered by the Committee which may make such general comments on the report as it may consider appropriate and shall forward these to the State Party concerned. That State Party may respond with any observations it chooses to the Committee.
4. The Committee may, at its discretion, decide to include any comments made by it in accordance with paragraph 3 of this article, together with the observations thereon received from the State Party concerned, in its annual report made in accordance with article 24. If so requested by the State Party concerned, the Committee may also include a copy of the report submitted under paragraph I of this article.

## Article 20

1. If the Committee receives reliable information which appears to it to contain well-founded indications that torture is being systematically practiced in the territory of a State Party, the Committee shall invite that State Party to co-operate in the examination of the information and to this end to submit observations with regard to the information concerned.
2. Taking into account any observations which may have been submitted by the State Party concerned, as well as any other relevant information available to it, the Committee may, if it decides that this is warranted, designate one or more of its members to make a confidential inquiry and to report to the Committee urgently.
3. If an inquiry is made in accordance with paragraph 2 of this article, the Committee shall seek the co-operation of the State Party concerned. In agreement with that State Party, such an inquiry may include a visit to its territory.
4. After examining the findings of its member or members submitted in accordance with paragraph 2 of this article, the Commission shall transmit these findings to the State Party concerned together with any comments or suggestions which seem appropriate in view of the situation.
5. All the proceedings of the Committee referred to in paragraphs I to 4 of this article shall be confidential, and at all stages of the proceedings the co-operation of the State Party shall be sought. After such proceedings have been completed with regard to an inquiry made in accordance with paragraph 2, the Committee may, after consultations with the State Party concerned, decide to include a

summary account of the results of the proceedings in its annual report made in accordance with article 24.

## Article 21

1. A State Party to this Convention may at any time declare under this article that it recognizes the competence of the Committee to receive and consider communications to the effect that a State Party claims that another State Party is not fulfilling its obligations under this Convention. Such communications may be received and considered according to the procedures laid down in this article only if submitted by a State Party which has made a declaration recognizing in regard to itself the competence of the Committee. No communication shall be dealt with by the Committee under this article if it concerns a State Party which has not made such a declaration. Communications received under this article shall be dealt with in accordance with the following procedure;

   a. If a State Party considers that another State Party is not giving effect to the provisions of this Convention, it may, by written communication, bring the matter to the attention of that State Party. Within three months after the receipt of the communication the receiving State shall afford the State which sent the communication an explanation or any other statement in writing clarifying the matter, which should include, to the extent possible and pertinent, reference to domestic procedures and remedies taken, pending or available in the matter;

   b. If the matter is not adjusted to the satisfaction of both States Parties concerned within six months after the receipt by the receiving State of the initial communication, either State shall have the right to refer the matter to the Committee, by notice given to the Committee and to the other State;

   c. The Committee shall deal with a matter referred to it under this article only after it has ascertained that all domestic remedies have been invoked and exhausted in the matter, in conformity with the generally recognized principles of international law. This shall not be the rule where the application of the remedies is unreasonably prolonged or is unlikely to bring effective relief to the person who is the victim of the violation of this Convention;

   d. The Committee shall hold closed meetings when examining communications under this article; (e) Subject to the provisions of subparagraph

   e. the Committee shall make available its good offices to the States Parties concerned with a view to a friendly solution of the matter on the basis of respect for the obligations provided for in this Convention. For this purpose, the Committee may, when appropriate, set up an ad hoc conciliation commission;

   f. In any matter referred to it under this article, the Committee may call upon the States Parties concerned, referred to in subparagraph (b), to supply any relevant information;

   g. The States Parties concerned, referred to in subparagraph (b), shall have the right to be represented when the matter is being considered by the Committee and to make submissions orally and/or in writing;

   h. The Committee shall, within twelve months after the date of receipt of notice under subparagraph (b), submit a report:

    i. If a solution within the terms of subparagraph (e) is reached, the Committee shall confine its report to a brief statement of the facts and of the solution reached;

    ii. If a solution within the terms of subparagraph (e) is not reached, the Committee shall confine its report to a brief statement of the facts; the written submissions and record of the oral submissions made by the States Parties concerned shall be attached to the report.

In every matter, the report shall be communicated to the States Parties concerned.

2. The provisions of this article shall come into force when five States Parties to this Convention have made declarations under paragraph 1 of this article. Such declarations shall be deposited by the States Parties with the Secretary-General of the United Nations, who shall transmit copies thereof to the other States Parties. A declaration may be withdrawn at any time by notification to the Secretary-General. Such a withdrawal shall not prejudice the consideration of any matter which is the subject of a communication already transmitted under this article; no further communication by any State Party shall be received under this article after the notification of withdrawal of the declaration has been received by the Secretary-General, unless the State Party concerned has made a new declaration.

## Article 22

1. A State Party to this Convention may at any time declare under this article that it recognizes the competence of the Committee to receive and consider communications from or on behalf of individuals subject to its jurisdiction who claim to be victims of a violation by a State Party of the provisions of the Convention. No communication shall be received by the Committee if it concerns a State Party which has not made such a declaration.

2. The Committee shall consider inadmissible any communication under this article which is anonymous or which it considers to be an abuse of the right of submission of such communications or to be incompatible with the provisions of this Convention.

3. Subject to the provisions of paragraph 2, the Committee shall bring any communications submitted to it under this article to the attention of the State Party to this Convention which has made a declaration under paragraph I and is alleged to be violating any provisions of the Convention. Within six months, the receiving State shall submit to the Committee written explanations or statements clarifying the matter and the remedy, if any, that may have been taken by that State.

4. The Committee shall consider communications received under this article in the light of all information made available to it by or on behalf of the individual and by the State Party concerned.

5. The Committee shall not consider any communications from an individual under this article unless it has ascertained that:

    a. The same matter has not been, and is not being, examined under another procedure of international investigation or settlement;

    b. The individual has exhausted all available domestic remedies; this shall not be the rule where the application of the remedies is unreasonably prolonged or is unlikely to bring effective relief to the person who is the victim of the violation of this Convention.

6. The Committee shall hold closed meetings when examining communications under this article.

7. The Committee shall forward its views to the State Party concerned and to the individual.

8. The provisions of this article shall come into force when five States Parties to this Convention have made declarations under paragraph 1 of this article. Such declarations shall be deposited by the States Parties with the Secretary-General of the United Nations, who shall transmit copies thereof to the other States Parties. A declaration may be withdrawn at any time by notification to the Secretary-General. Such a withdrawal shall not prejudice the consideration of any matter which is the subject of a communication already transmitted under this article; no further communication by or on behalf of an individual shall be received under this article after the notification of withdrawal of the declaration has been received by the Secretary-General, unless the State Party has made a new declaration.

## Article 23

The members of the Committee and of the ad hoc conciliation commissions which may be appointed under article 21, paragraph I (e), shall be entitled to the facilities, privileges and immunities of experts on mission for the United Nations as laid down in the relevant sections of the Convention on the Privileges and Immunities of the United Nations.

## Article 24

The Committee shall submit an annual report on its activities under this Convention to the States Parties and to the General Assembly of the United Nations.

## Part III

## Article 25

1. This Convention is open for signature by all States. 2. This Convention is subject to ratification. Instruments of ratification shall be deposited with the Secretary-General of the United Nations.

## Article 26

This Convention is open to accession by all States. Accession shall be effected by the deposit of an instrument of accession with the Secretary-General of the United Nations.

## Article 27

1. This Convention shall enter into force on the thirtieth day after the date of the deposit with the Secretary-General of the United Nations of the twentieth instrument of ratification or accession.

2. For each State ratifying this Convention or acceding to it after the deposit of the twentieth instrument of ratification or accession, the Convention shall enter into force on the thirtieth day after the date of the deposit of its own instrument of ratification or accession.

## Article 28

1. Each State may, at the time of signature or ratification of this Convention or accession thereto, declare that it does not recognize the competence of the Committee provided for in article 20.
2. Any State Party having made a reservation in accordance with paragraph I of this article may, at any time, withdraw this reservation by notification to the Secretary-General of the United Nations.

## Article 29

1. Any State Party to this Convention may propose an amendment and file it with the Secretary-General of the United Nations. The Secretary-General shall thereupon communicate the proposed amendment to the States Parties with a request that they notify him whether they favour a conference of States Parties for the purpose of considering and voting upon the proposal. In the event that within four months from the date of such communication at least one third of the States Parties favours such a conference, the Secretary-General shall convene the conference under the auspices of the United Nations. Any amendment adopted by a majority of the States Parties present and voting at the conference shall be submitted by the Secretary-General to all the States Parties for acceptance.
2. An amendment adopted in accordance with paragraph I of this article shall enter into force when two thirds of the States Parties to this Convention have notified the Secretary-General of the United Nations that they have accepted it in accordance with their respective constitutional processes.
3. When amendments enter into force, they shall be binding on those States Parties which have accepted them, other States Parties still being bound by the provisions of this Convention and any earlier amendments which they have accepted.

## Article 30

1. Any dispute between two or more States Parties concerning the interpretation or application of this Convention which cannot be settled through negotiation shall, at the request of one of them, be submitted to arbitration. If within six months from the date of the request for arbitration the Parties are unable to agree on the organization of the arbitration, any one of those Parties may refer the dispute to the International Court of Justice by request in conformity with the Statute of the Court.
2. Each State may, at the time of signature or ratification of this Convention or accession thereto, declare that it does not consider itself bound by paragraph I of this article. The other States Parties shall not be bound by paragraph I of this article with respect to any State Party having made such a reservation.

3. Any State Party having made a reservation in accordance with paragraph 2 of this article may at any time withdraw this reservation by notification to the Secretary-General of the United Nations.

## Article 31

1. A State Party may denounce this Convention by written notification to the Secretary-General of the United Nations. Denunciation becomes effective one year after the date of receipt of the notification by the Secretary-General.
2. Such a denunciation shall not have the effect of releasing the State Party from its obligations under this Convention in regard to any act or omission which occurs prior to the date at which the denunciation becomes effective, nor shall denunciation prejudice in any way the continued consideration of any matter which is already under consideration by the Committee prior to the date at which the denunciation becomes effective.
3. Following the date at which the denunciation of a State Party becomes effective, the Committee shall not commence consideration of any new matter regarding that State.

## Article 32

The Secretary-General of the United Nations shall inform all States Members of the United Nations and all States which have signed this Convention or acceded to it of the following:
   a. Signatures, ratifications and accessions under articles 25 and 26;
   b. The date of entry into force of this Convention under article 27 and the date of the entry into force of any amendments under article 29;
   c. Denunciations under article 31.

## Article 33

1. This Convention, of which the Arabic, Chinese, English, French, Russian and Spanish texts are equally authentic, shall be deposited with the Secretary-General of the United Nations.
2. The Secretary-General of the United Nations shall transmit certified copies of this Convention to all States.

# Appendix B

## International Covenant on Civil and Political Rights

Adopted and opened for signature, ratification and accession by
General Assembly resolution 2200A (XXI) of 16 December 1966
entry into force 23 March 1976, in accordance with Article 49

## Preamble

The States Parties to the present Covenant,

Considering that, in accordance with the principles proclaimed in the Charter of the United Nations, recognition of the inherent dignity and of the equal and inalienable rights of all members of the human family is the foundation of freedom, justice and peace in the world,

Recognizing that these rights derive from the inherent dignity of the human person,

Recognizing that, in accordance with the Universal Declaration of Human Rights, the ideal of free human beings enjoying civil and political freedom and freedom from fear and want can only be achieved if conditions are created whereby everyone may enjoy his civil and political rights, as well as his economic, social and cultural rights,

Considering the obligation of States under the Charter of the United Nations to promote universal respect for, and observance of, human rights and freedoms,

Realizing that the individual, having duties to other individuals and to the community to which he belongs, is under a responsibility to strive for the promotion and observance of the rights recognized in the present Covenant,

Agree upon the following articles:

## Part I

### Article 1

1. All peoples have the right of self-determination. By virtue of that right they freely determine their political status and freely pursue their economic, social and cultural development.

2. All peoples may, for their own ends, freely dispose of their natural wealth and resources without prejudice to any obligations arising out of international economic co-operation, based upon the principle of mutual benefit, and international law. In no case may a people be deprived of its own means of subsistence.
3. The States Parties to the present Covenant, including those having responsibility for the administration of Non-Self-Governing and Trust Territories, shall promote the realization of the right of self-determination, and shall respect that right, in conformity with the provisions of the Charter of the United Nations.

## Part II

### Article 2

1. Each State Party to the present Covenant undertakes to respect and to ensure to all individuals within its territory and subject to its jurisdiction the rights recognized in the present Covenant, without distinction of any kind, such as race, colour, sex, language, religion, political or other opinion, national or social origin, property, birth or other status.
2. Where not already provided for by existing legislative or other measures, each State Party to the present Covenant undertakes to take the necessary steps, in accordance with its constitutional processes and with the provisions of the present Covenant, to adopt such laws or other measures as may be necessary to give effect to the rights recognized in the present Covenant.
3. Each State Party to the present Covenant undertakes:
   a. To ensure that any person whose rights or freedoms as herein recognized are violated shall have an effective remedy, notwithstanding that the violation has been committed by persons acting in an official capacity;
   b. To ensure that any person claiming such a remedy shall have his right thereto determined by competent judicial, administrative or legislative authorities, or by any other competent authority provided for by the legal system of the State, and to develop the possibilities of judicial remedy;
   c. To ensure that the competent authorities shall enforce such remedies when granted.

### Article 3

The States Parties to the present Covenant undertake to ensure the equal right of men and women to the enjoyment of all civil and political rights set forth in the present Covenant.

### Article 4

1. In time of public emergency which threatens the life of the nation and the existence of which is officially proclaimed, the States Parties to the present Covenant may take measures derogating from their obligations under the present Covenant to the extent strictly required by the exigencies of the situation, provided that such measures are not inconsistent with their other obligations under international law and do not involve discrimination solely on the ground of race, colour, sex, language, religion or social origin.

2. No derogation from articles 6, 7, 8 (paragraphs I and 2), 11, 15, 16 and 18 may be made under this provision.
3. Any State Party to the present Covenant availing itself of the right of derogation shall immediately inform the other States Parties to the present Covenant, through the intermediary of the Secretary-General of the United Nations, of the provisions from which it has derogated and of the reasons by which it was actuated. A further communication shall be made, through the same intermediary, on the date on which it terminates such derogation.

## Article 5

1. Nothing in the present Covenant may be interpreted as implying for any State, group or person any right to engage in any activity or perform any act aimed at the destruction of any of the rights and freedoms recognized herein or at their limitation to a greater extent than is provided for in the present Covenant.
2. There shall be no restriction upon or derogation from any of the fundamental human rights recognized or existing in any State Party to the present Covenant pursuant to law, conventions, regulations or custom on the pretext that the present Covenant does not recognize such rights or that it recognizes them to a lesser extent.

## Part III

## Article 6

1. Every human being has the inherent right to life. This right shall be protected by law. No one shall be arbitrarily deprived of his life.
2. In countries which have not abolished the death penalty, sentence of death may be imposed only for the most serious crimes in accordance with the law in force at the time of the commission of the crime and not contrary to the provisions of the present Covenant and to the Convention on the Prevention and Punishment of the Crime of Genocide. This penalty can only be carried out pursuant to a final judgement rendered by a competent court.
3. When deprivation of life constitutes the crime of genocide, it is understood that nothing in this article shall authorize any State Party to the present Covenant to derogate in any way from any obligation assumed under the provisions of the Convention on the Prevention and Punishment of the Crime of Genocide.
4. Anyone sentenced to death shall have the right to seek pardon or commutation of the sentence. Amnesty, pardon or commutation of the sentence of death may be granted in all cases.
5. Sentence of death shall not be imposed for crimes committed by persons below eighteen years of age and shall not be carried out on pregnant women.
6. Nothing in this article shall be invoked to delay or to prevent the abolition of capital punishment by any State Party to the present Covenant.

## Article 7

No one shall be subjected to torture or to cruel, inhuman or degrading treatment or punishment. In particular, no one shall be subjected without his free consent to medical or scientific experimentation.

## Article 8

1. No one shall be held in slavery; slavery and the slave-trade in all their forms shall be prohibited.
2. No one shall be held in servitude.
3.
   a. No one shall be required to perform forced or compulsory labour;
   b. Paragraph 3 (a) shall not be held to preclude, in countries where imprisonment with hard labour may be imposed as a punishment for a crime, the performance of hard labour in pursuance of a sentence to such punishment by a competent court;
   c. For the purpose of this paragraph the term "forced or compulsory labour" shall not include:
      i. Any work or service, not referred to in subparagraph (b), normally required of a person who is under detention in consequence of a lawful order of a court, or of a person during conditional release from such detention;
      ii. Any service of a military character and, in countries where conscientious objection is recognized, any national service required by law of conscientious objectors;
      iii. Any service exacted in cases of emergency or calamity threatening the life or well-being of the community;
      iv. Any work or service which forms part of normal civil obligations.

## Article 9

1. Everyone has the right to liberty and security of person. No one shall be subjected to arbitrary arrest or detention. No one shall be deprived of his liberty except on such grounds and in accordance with such procedure as are established by law.
2. Anyone who is arrested shall be informed, at the time of arrest, of the reasons for his arrest and shall be promptly informed of any charges against him.
3. Anyone arrested or detained on a criminal charge shall be brought promptly before a judge or other officer authorized by law to exercise judicial power and shall be entitled to trial within a reasonable time or to release. It shall not be the general rule that persons awaiting trial shall be detained in custody, but release may be subject to guarantees to appear for trial, at any other stage of the judicial proceedings, and, should occasion arise, for execution of the judgement.
4. Anyone who is deprived of his liberty by arrest or detention shall be entitled to take proceedings before a court, in order that that court may decide without delay on the lawfulness of his detention and order his release if the detention is not lawful.
5. Anyone who has been the victim of unlawful arrest or detention shall have an enforceable right to compensation.

## Article 10

1. All persons deprived of their liberty shall be treated with humanity and with respect for the inherent dignity of the human person.
2.

    a. Accused persons shall, save in exceptional circumstances, be segregated from convicted persons and shall be subject to separate treatment appropriate to their status as un-convicted persons;

    b. Accused juvenile persons shall be separated from adults and brought as speedily as possible for adjudication.

3. The penitentiary system shall comprise treatment of prisoners the essential aim of which shall be their reformation and social rehabilitation. Juvenile offenders shall be segregated from adults and be accorded treatment appropriate to their age and legal status.

## Article 11

No one shall be imprisoned merely on the ground of inability to fulfil a contractual obligation.

## Article 12

1. Everyone lawfully within the territory of a State shall, within that territory, have the right to liberty of movement and freedom to choose his residence.
2. Everyone shall be free to leave any country, including his own.
3. The above-mentioned rights shall not be subject to any restrictions except those which are provided by law, are necessary to protect national security, public order (ordre public), public health or morals or the rights and freedoms of others and are consistent with the other rights recognized in the present Covenant.
4. No one shall be arbitrarily deprived of the right to enter his own country.

## Article 13

An alien lawfully in the territory of a State Party to the present Covenant may be expelled therefrom only in pursuance of a decision reached in accordance with law and shall, except where compelling reasons of national security otherwise require, be allowed to submit the reasons against his expulsion and to have his case reviewed by, and be represented for the purpose before, the competent authority or a person or persons especially designated by the competent authority.

## Article 14

1. All persons shall be equal before the courts and tribunals. In the determination of any criminal charge against him, or of his rights and obligations in a suit at law, everyone shall be entitled to a fair and public hearing by a competent, independent and impartial tribunal established by law. The press and the public may be excluded from all or part of a trial for reasons of morals, public order (ordre public) or national security in a democratic society, or when the interest of the private lives of the parties so requires, or to the extent strictly necessary in the opinion of the court in special circumstances where publicity would prejudice the interests of justice; but any judgement rendered in a criminal case or in a suit at law shall be made public except where the interest of juvenile persons otherwise requires or the proceedings concern matrimonial disputes or the guardianship of children.

2. Everyone charged with a criminal offence shall have the right to be presumed innocent until proved guilty according to law.
3. In the determination of any criminal charge against him, everyone shall be entitled to the following minimum guarantees, in full equality:
   a. To be informed promptly and in detail in a language which he understands of the nature and cause of the charge against him;
   b. To have adequate time and facilities for the preparation of his defence and to communicate with counsel of his own choosing;
   c. To be tried without undue delay;
   d. be tried in his presence, and to defend himself in person or through legal assistance of his own choosing; to be informed, if he does not have legal assistance, of this right; and to have legal assistance assigned to him, in any case where the interests of justice so require, and without payment by him in any such case if he does not have sufficient means to pay for it;
   e. To examine, or have examined, the witnesses against him and to obtain the attendance and examination of witnesses on his behalf under the same conditions as witnesses against him;
   f. To have the free assistance of an interpreter if he cannot understand or speak the language used in court;
   g. Not to be compelled to testify against himself or to confess guilt.
4. In the case of juvenile persons, the procedure shall be such as will take account of their age and the desirability of promoting their rehabilitation.
5. Everyone convicted of a crime shall have the right to his conviction and sentence being reviewed by a higher tribunal according to law.
6. When a person has by a final decision been convicted of a criminal offence and when subsequently his conviction has been reversed or he has been pardoned on the ground that a new or newly discovered fact shows conclusively that there has been a miscarriage of justice, the person who has suffered punishment as a result of such conviction shall be compensated according to law, unless it is proved that the non-disclosure of the unknown fact in time is wholly or partly attributable to him.
7. No one shall be liable to be tried or punished again for an offence for which he has already been finally convicted or acquitted in accordance with the law and penal procedure of each country.

## Article 15

1. No one shall be held guilty of any criminal offence on account of any act or omission which did not constitute a criminal offence, under national or international law, at the time when it was committed. Nor shall a heavier penalty be imposed than the one that was applicable at the time when the criminal offence was committed. If, subsequent to the commission of the offence, provision is made by law for the imposition of the lighter penalty, the offender shall benefit thereby.
2. Nothing in this article shall prejudice the trial and punishment of any person for any act or omission which, at the time when it was committed, was criminal according to the general principles of law recognized by the community of nations.

## Article 16

Everyone shall have the right to recognition everywhere as a person before the law.

## Article 17

1. No one shall be subjected to arbitrary or unlawful interference with his privacy, family, home or correspondence, nor to unlawful attacks on his honour and reputation.
2. Everyone has the right to the protection of the law against such interference or attacks.

## Article 18

1. Everyone shall have the right to freedom of thought, conscience and religion. This right shall include freedom to have or to adopt a religion or belief of his choice, and freedom, either individually or in community with others and in public or private, to manifest his religion or belief in worship, observance, practice and teaching.
2. No one shall be subject to coercion which would impair his freedom to have or to adopt a religion or belief of his choice.
3. Freedom to manifest one's religion or beliefs may be subject only to such limitations as are prescribed by law and are necessary to protect public safety, order, health, or morals or the fundamental rights and freedoms of others.
4. The States Parties to the present Covenant undertake to have respect for the liberty of parents and, when applicable, legal guardians to ensure the religious and moral education of their children in conformity with their own convictions.

## Article 19

1. Everyone shall have the right to hold opinions without interference.
2. Everyone shall have the right to freedom of expression; this right shall include freedom to seek, receive and impart information and ideas of all kinds, regardless of frontiers, either orally, in writing or in print, in the form of art, or through any other media of his choice.
3. The exercise of the rights provided for in paragraph 2 of this article carries with it special duties and responsibilities. It may therefore be subject to certain restrictions, but these shall only be such as are provided by law and are necessary:
   a. For respect of the rights or reputations of others;
   b. For the protection of national security or of public order (ordre public), or of public health or morals.

## Article 20

1. Any propaganda for war shall be prohibited by law.
2. Any advocacy of national, racial or religious hatred that constitutes incitement to discrimination, hostility or violence shall be prohibited by law.

## Article 21

The right of peaceful assembly shall be recognized. No restrictions may be placed on the exercise of this right other than those imposed in conformity with the law and which are necessary in a democratic society in the interests of national security or public safety, public order (ordre public), the protection of public health or morals or the protection of the rights and freedoms of others.

## Article 22

1. Everyone shall have the right to freedom of association with others, including the right to form and join trade unions for the protection of his interests.
2. No restrictions may be placed on the exercise of this right other than those which are prescribed by law and which are necessary in a democratic society in the interests of national security or public safety, public order (ordre public), the protection of public health or morals or the protection of the rights and freedoms of others. This article shall not prevent the imposition of lawful restrictions on members of the armed forces and of the police in their exercise of this right.
3. Nothing in this article shall authorize States Parties to the International Labour Organization Convention of 1948 concerning Freedom of Association and Protection of the Right to Organize to take legislative measures which would prejudice, or to apply the law in such a manner as to prejudice, the guarantees provided for in that Convention.

## Article 23

1. The family is the natural and fundamental group unit of society and is entitled to protection by society and the State.
2. The right of men and women of marriageable age to marry and to found a family shall be recognized.
3. No marriage shall be entered into without the free and full consent of the intending spouses.
4. States Parties to the present Covenant shall take appropriate steps to ensure equality of rights and responsibilities of spouses as to marriage, during marriage and at its dissolution. In the case of dissolution, provision shall be made for the necessary protection of any children.

## Article 24

1. Every child shall have, without any discrimination as to race, colour, sex, language, religion, national or social origin, property or birth, the right to such measures of protection as are required by his status as a minor, on the part of his family, society and the State.
2. Every child shall be registered immediately after birth and shall have a name.
3. Every child has the right to acquire a nationality.

## Article 25

Every citizen shall have the right and the opportunity, without any of the distinctions mentioned in article 2 and without unreasonable restrictions:

a. To take part in the conduct of public affairs, directly or through freely chosen representatives;
b. To vote and to be elected at genuine periodic elections which shall be by universal and equal suffrage and shall be held by secret ballot, guaranteeing the free expression of the will of the electors;
c. To have access, on general terms of equality, to public service in his country.

## Article 26

All persons are equal before the law and are entitled without any discrimination to the equal protection of the law. In this respect, the law shall prohibit any discrimination and guarantee to all persons equal and effective protection against discrimination on any ground such as race, colour, sex, language, religion, political or other opinion, national or social origin, property, birth or other status.

## Article 27

In those States in which ethnic, religious or linguistic minorities exist, persons belonging to such minorities shall not be denied the right, in community with the other members of their group, to enjoy their own culture, to profess and practice their own religion, or to use their own language.

## Part IV

## Article 28

1. There shall be established a Human Rights Committee (hereafter referred to in the present Covenant as the Committee). It shall consist of eighteen members and shall carry out the functions hereinafter provided.
2. The Committee shall be composed of nationals of the States Parties to the present Covenant who shall be persons of high moral character and recognized competence in the field of human rights, consideration being given to the usefulness of the participation of some persons having legal experience.
3. The members of the Committee shall be elected and shall serve in their personal capacity.

## Article 29

1. The members of the Committee shall be elected by secret ballot from a list of persons possessing the qualifications prescribed in article 28 and nominated for the purpose by the States Parties to the present Covenant.
2. Each State Party to the present Covenant may nominate not more than two persons. These persons shall be nationals of the nominating State.
3. A person shall be eligible for re-nomination.

## Article 30

1. The initial election shall be held no later than six months after the date of the entry into force of the present Covenant.
2. At least four months before the date of each election to the Committee, other

than an election to fill a vacancy declared in accordance with article 34, the Secretary-General of the United Nations shall address a written invitation to the States Parties to the present Covenant to submit their nominations for membership of the Committee within three months.

3. The Secretary-General of the United Nations shall prepare a list in alphabetical order of all the persons thus nominated, with an indication of the States Parties which have nominated them and shall submit it to the States Parties to the present Covenant no later than one month before the date of each election.

4. Elections of the members of the Committee shall be held at a meeting of the States Parties to the present Covenant convened by the Secretary General of the United Nations at the Headquarters of the United Nations. At that meeting, for which two thirds of the States Parties to the present Covenant shall constitute a quorum, the persons elected to the Committee shall be those nominees who obtain the largest number of votes and an absolute majority of the votes of the representatives of States Parties present and voting.

## Article 31

1. The Committee may not include more than one national of the same State.
2. In the election of the Committee, consideration shall be given to equitable geographical distribution of membership and to the representation of the different forms of civilization and of the principal legal systems.

## Article 32

1. The members of the Committee shall be elected for a term of four years. They shall be eligible for re-election if re-nominated. However, the terms of nine of the members elected at the first election shall expire at the end of two years; immediately after the first election, the names of these nine members shall be chosen by lot by the Chairman of the meeting referred to in article 30, paragraph 4.
2. Elections at the expiry of office shall be held in accordance with the preceding articles of this part of the present Covenant.

## Article 33

1. If, in the unanimous opinion of the other members, a member of the Committee has ceased to carry out his functions for any cause other than absence of a temporary character, the Chairman of the Committee shall notify the Secretary-General of the United Nations, who shall then declare the seat of that member to be vacant.
2. In the event of the death or the resignation of a member of the Committee, the Chairman shall immediately notify the Secretary-General of the United Nations, who shall declare the seat vacant from the date of death or the date on which the resignation takes effect.

## Article 34

1. When a vacancy is declared in accordance with article 33 and if the term of office of the member to be replaced does not expire within six months of the

declaration of the vacancy, the Secretary-General of the United Nations shall notify each of the States Parties to the present Covenant, which may within two months submit nominations in accordance with article 29 for the purpose of filling the vacancy.

2. The Secretary-General of the United Nations shall prepare a list in alphabetical order of the persons thus nominated and shall submit it to the States Parties to the present Covenant. The election to fill the vacancy shall then take place in accordance with the relevant provisions of this part of the present Covenant.

3. A member of the Committee elected to fill a vacancy declared in accordance with article 33 shall hold office for the remainder of the term of the member who vacated the seat on the Committee under the provisions of that article.

## Article 35

The members of the Committee shall, with the approval of the General Assembly of the United Nations, receive emoluments from United Nations resources on such terms and conditions as the General Assembly may decide, having regard to the importance of the Committee's responsibilities.

## Article 36

The Secretary-General of the United Nations shall provide the necessary staff and facilities for the effective performance of the functions of the Committee under the present Covenant.

## Article 37

1. The Secretary-General of the United Nations shall convene the initial meeting of the Committee at the Headquarters of the United Nations.

2. After its initial meeting, the Committee shall meet at such times as shall be provided in its rules of procedure.

3. The Committee shall normally meet at the Headquarters of the United Nations or at the United Nations Office at Geneva.

## Article 38

Every member of the Committee shall, before taking up his duties, make a solemn declaration in open committee that he will perform his functions impartially and conscientiously.

## Article 39

1. The Committee shall elect its officers for a term of two years. They may be re-elected.

2. The Committee shall establish its own rules of procedure, but these rules shall provide, inter alia, that:
   a. Twelve members shall constitute a quorum;
   b. Decisions of the Committee shall be made by a majority vote of the members present.

## Article 40

1. The States Parties to the present Covenant undertake to submit reports on the measures they have adopted which give effect to the rights recognized herein and on the progress made in the enjoyment of those rights:
   a. Within one year of the entry into force of the present Covenant for the States Parties concerned;
   b. Thereafter whenever the Committee so requests.
2. All reports shall be submitted to the Secretary-General of the United Nations, who shall transmit them to the Committee for consideration. Reports shall indicate the factors and difficulties, if any, affecting the implementation of the present Covenant.
3. The Secretary-General of the United Nations may, after consultation with the Committee, transmit to the specialized agencies concerned copies of such parts of the reports as may fall within their field of competence.
4. The Committee shall study the reports submitted by the States Parties to the present Covenant. It shall transmit its reports, and such general comments as it may consider appropriate, to the States Parties. The Committee may also transmit to the Economic and Social Council these comments along with the copies of the reports it has received from States Parties to the present Covenant.
5. The States Parties to the present Covenant may submit to the Committee observations on any comments that may be made in accordance with paragraph 4 of this article.

## Article 41

1. A State Party to the present Covenant may at any time declare under this article that it recognizes the competence of the Committee to receive and consider communications to the effect that a State Party claims that another State Party is not fulfilling its obligations under the present Covenant. Communications under this article may be received and considered only if submitted by a State Party which has made a declaration recognizing in regard to itself the competence of the Committee. No communication shall be received by the Committee if it concerns a State Party which has not made such a declaration. Communications received under this article shall be dealt with in accordance with the following procedure:
   a. If a State Party to the present Covenant considers that another State Party is not giving effect to the provisions of the present Covenant, it may, by written communication, bring the matter to the attention of that State Party. Within three months after the receipt of the communication the receiving State shall afford the State which sent the communication an explanation, or any other statement in writing clarifying the matter which should include, to the extent possible and pertinent, reference to domestic procedures and remedies taken, pending, or available in the matter;
   b. If the matter is not adjusted to the satisfaction of both States Parties concerned within six months after the receipt by the receiving State of the initial communication, either State shall have the right to refer the

matter to the Committee, by notice given to the Committee and to the other State;

c. The Committee shall deal with a matter referred to it only after it has ascertained that all available domestic remedies have been invoked and exhausted in the matter, in conformity with the generally recognized principles of international law. This shall not be the rule where the application of the remedies is unreasonably prolonged;

d. The Committee shall hold closed meetings when examining communications under this article;

e. Subject to the provisions of subparagraph (c), the Committee shall make available its good offices to the States Parties concerned with a view to a friendly solution of the matter on the basis of respect for human rights and fundamental freedoms as recognized in the present Covenant;

f. In any matter referred to it, the Committee may call upon the States Parties concerned, referred to in subparagraph (b), to supply any relevant information;

g. The States Parties concerned, referred to in subparagraph (b), shall have the right to be represented when the matter is being considered in the Committee and to make submissions orally and/or in writing;

h. The Committee shall, within twelve months after the date of receipt of notice under subparagraph (b), submit a report:

 i. If a solution within the terms of subparagraph (e) is reached, the Committee shall confine its report to a brief statement of the facts and of the solution reached;

 ii. If a solution within the terms of subparagraph (e) is not reached, the Committee shall confine its report to a brief statement of the facts; the written submissions and record of the oral submissions made by the States Parties concerned shall be attached to the report. In every matter, the report shall be communicated to the States Parties concerned.

2. The provisions of this article shall come into force when ten States Parties to the present Covenant have made declarations under paragraph I of this article. Such declarations shall be deposited by the States Parties with the Secretary-General of the United Nations, who shall transmit copies thereof to the other States Parties. A declaration may be withdrawn at any time by notification to the Secretary-General. Such a withdrawal shall not prejudice the consideration of any matter which is the subject of a communication already transmitted under this article; no further communication by any State Party shall be received after the notification of withdrawal of the declaration has been received by the Secretary-General, unless the State Party concerned has made a new declaration.

## Article 42

1.

a. If a matter referred to the Committee in accordance with article 41 is not resolved to the satisfaction of the States Parties concerned, the Committee may, with the prior consent of the States Parties concerned, appoint an ad hoc Conciliation Commission (hereinafter referred to as the Commission).

The good offices of the Commission shall be made available to the States Parties concerned with a view to an amicable solution of the matter on the basis of respect for the present Covenant;

   b. The Commission shall consist of five persons acceptable to the States Parties concerned. If the States Parties concerned fail to reach agreement within three months on all or part of the composition of the Commission, the members of the Commission concerning whom no agreement has been reached shall be elected by secret ballot by a two-thirds majority vote of the Committee from among its members.

2. The members of the Commission shall serve in their personal capacity. They shall not be nationals of the States Parties concerned, or of a State not Party to the present Covenant, or of a State Party which has not made a declaration under article 41.

3. The Commission shall elect its own Chairman and adopt its own rules of procedure.

4. The meetings of the Commission shall normally be held at the Headquarters of the United Nations or at the United Nations Office at Geneva. However, they may be held at such other convenient places as the Commission may determine in consultation with the Secretary-General of the United Nations and the States Parties concerned.

5. The secretariat provided in accordance with article 36 shall also service the commissions appointed under this article.

6. The information received and collated by the Committee shall be made available to the Commission and the Commission may call upon the States Parties concerned to supply any other relevant information.

7. When the Commission has fully considered the matter, but in any event not later than twelve months after having been seized of the matter, it shall submit to the Chairman of the Committee a report for communication to the States Parties concerned:

   a. If the Commission is unable to complete its consideration of the matter within twelve months, it shall confine its report to a brief statement of the status of its consideration of the matter;

   b. If an amicable solution to the matter based on respect for human rights as recognized in the present Covenant is reached, the Commission shall confine its report to a brief statement of the facts and of the solution reached;

   c. If a solution within the terms of subparagraph (b) is not reached, the Commission's report shall embody its findings on all questions of fact relevant to the issues between the States Parties concerned, and its views on the possibilities of an amicable solution of the matter. This report shall also contain the written submissions and a record of the oral submissions made by the States Parties concerned;

   d. If the Commission's report is submitted under subparagraph (c), the States Parties concerned shall, within three months of the receipt of the report, notify the Chairman of the Committee whether or not they accept the contents of the report of the Commission.

8. The provisions of this article are without prejudice to the responsibilities of the Committee under article 41.

9. The States Parties concerned shall share equally all the expenses of the members of the Commission in accordance with estimates to be provided by the Secretary-General of the United Nations.

10. The Secretary-General of the United Nations shall be empowered to pay the expenses of the members of the Commission, if necessary, before reimbursement by the States Parties concerned, in accordance with paragraph 9 of this article.

## Article 43

The members of the Committee, and of the ad hoc conciliation commissions which may be appointed under article 42, shall be entitled to the facilities, privileges and immunities of experts on mission for the United Nations as laid down in the relevant sections of the Convention on the Privileges and Immunities of the United Nations.

## Article 44

The provisions for the implementation of the present Covenant shall apply without prejudice to the procedures prescribed in the field of human rights by or under the constituent instruments and the conventions of the United Nations and of the specialized agencies and shall not prevent the States Parties to the present Covenant from having recourse to other procedures for settling a dispute in accordance with general or special international agreements in force between them.

## Article 45

The Committee shall submit to the General Assembly of the United Nations, through the Economic and Social Council, an annual report on its activities.

## Part V

## Article 46

Nothing in the present Covenant shall be interpreted as impairing the provisions of the Charter of the United Nations and of the constitutions of the specialized agencies which define the respective responsibilities of the various organs of the United Nations and of the specialized agencies in regard to the matters dealt with in the present Covenant.

## Article 47

Nothing in the present Covenant shall be interpreted as impairing the inherent right of all peoples to enjoy and utilize fully and freely their natural wealth and resources.

## Part VI

## Article 48

1. The present Covenant is open for signature by any State Member of the United Nations or member of any of its specialized agencies, by any State Party to

the Statute of the International Court of Justice, and by any other State which has been invited by the General Assembly of the United Nations to become a Party to the present Covenant.

2. The present Covenant is subject to ratification. Instruments of ratification shall be deposited with the Secretary-General of the United Nations.

3. The present Covenant shall be open to accession by any State referred to in paragraph 1 of this article.

4. Accession shall be affected by the deposit of an instrument of accession with the Secretary-General of the United Nations.

5. The Secretary-General of the United Nations shall inform all States which have signed this Covenant or acceded to it of the deposit of each instrument of ratification or accession.

## Article 49

1. The present Covenant shall enter into force three months after the date of the deposit with the Secretary-General of the United Nations of the thirty-fifth instrument of ratification or instrument of accession.

2. For each State ratifying the present Covenant or acceding to it after the deposit of the thirty-fifth instrument of ratification or instrument of accession, the present Covenant shall enter into force three months after the date of the deposit of its own instrument of ratification or instrument of accession.

## Article 50

The provisions of the present Covenant shall extend to all parts of federal States without any limitations or exceptions.

## Article 51

1. Any State Party to the present Covenant may propose an amendment and file it with the Secretary-General of the United Nations. The Secretary-General of the United Nations shall thereupon communicate any proposed amendments to the States Parties to the present Covenant with a request that they notify him whether they favour a conference of States Parties for the purpose of considering and voting upon the proposals. In the event that at least one third of the States Parties favours such a conference, the Secretary-General shall convene the conference under the auspices of the United Nations. Any amendment adopted by a majority of the States Parties present and voting at the conference shall be submitted to the General Assembly of the United Nations for approval.

2. Amendments shall come into force when they have been approved by the General Assembly of the United Nations and accepted by a two-thirds majority of the States Parties to the present Covenant in accordance with their respective constitutional processes.

3. When amendments come into force, they shall be binding on those States Parties which have accepted them, other States Parties still being bound by the provisions of the present Covenant and any earlier amendment which they have accepted.

## Article 52

1. Irrespective of the notifications made under article 48, paragraph 5, the Secretary-General of the United Nations shall inform all States referred to in paragraph I of the same article of the following particulars:
   a. Signatures, ratifications and accessions under article 48;
   b. The date of the entry into force of the present Covenant under article 49 and the date of the entry into force of any amendments under article 51.

## Article 53

1. The present Covenant, of which the Chinese, English, French, Russian and Spanish texts are equally authentic, shall be deposited in the archives of the United Nations.
2. The Secretary-General of the United Nations shall transmit certified copies of the present Covenant to all States referred to in article 48.

# Appendix C

*Convention on the Elimination
of All Forms of Discrimination
Against Women*

Full text of the Convention in English

## Introduction

On 18 December 1979, the Convention on the Elimination of All Forms of Discrimination against Women was adopted by the United Nations General Assembly. It entered into force as an international treaty on 3 September 1981 after the twentieth country had ratified it. By the tenth anniversary of the Convention in 1989, almost one hundred nations have agreed to be bound by its provisions.

The Convention was the culmination of more than thirty years of work by the United Nations Commission on the Status of Women, a body established in 1946 to monitor the situation of women and to promote women's rights. The Commission's work has been instrumental in bringing to light all the areas in which women are denied equality with men. These efforts for the advancement of women have resulted in several declarations and conventions, of which the Convention on the Elimination of All Forms of Discrimination against Women is the central and most comprehensive document.

Among the international human rights treaties, the Convention takes an important place in bringing the female half of humanity into the focus of human rights concerns. The spirit of the Convention is rooted in the goals of the United Nations: to reaffirm faith in fundamental human rights, in the dignity, and worth of the human person, in the equal rights of men and women. The present document spells out the meaning of equality and how it can be achieved. In so doing, the Convention establishes not only an international bill of rights for women, but also an agenda for action by countries to guarantee the enjoyment of those rights.

In its preamble, the Convention explicitly acknowledges that "extensive discrimination against women continues to exist" and emphasizes that such discrimination "violates the principles of equality of rights and respect for human dignity." As defined in article 1, discrimination is understood as "any distinction, exclusion or restriction made on the basis of sex ... in the political, economic, social, cultural, civil or any other field." The Convention gives positive affirmation to the principle of equality by requiring States parties to take "all appropriate measures, including legislation, to ensure the full development and advancement of women, for the purpose of guaranteeing them the exercise and enjoyment of human rights and fundamental freedoms on a basis of equality with men" (article 3).

The agenda for equality is specified in fourteen subsequent articles. In its approach, the Convention covers three dimensions of the situation of women. Civil rights and the legal status of women are dealt with in great detail. In addition, and unlike other human rights treaties, the Convention is also concerned with the dimension of human reproduction as well as with the impact of cultural factors on gender relations.

The legal status of women receives the broadest attention. Concern over the basic rights of political participation has not diminished since the adoption of the Convention on the Political Rights of Women in 1952. Its provisions, therefore, are restated in article 7 of the present document, whereby women are guaranteed the rights to vote, to hold public office and to exercise public functions. This includes equal rights for women to represent their countries at the international level (article 8). The Convention on the Nationality of Married Women - adopted in 1957—is integrated under article 9 providing for the statehood of women, irrespective of their marital status. The Convention, thereby, draws attention to the fact that often women's legal status has been linked to marriage, making them dependent on their husband's nationality rather than individuals in their own right. Articles 10, 11 and 13, respectively, affirm women's rights to non-discrimination in education, employment and economic and social activities. These demands are given special emphasis with regard to the situation of rural women, whose particular struggles and vital economic contributions, as noted in article 14, warrant more attention in policy planning. Article 15 asserts the full equality of women in civil and business matters, demanding that all instruments directed at restricting women's legal capacity "shall be deemed null and void." Finally, in article 16, the Convention returns to the issue of marriage and family relations, asserting the equal rights and obligations of women and men with regard to choice of spouse, parenthood, personal rights and command over property.

Aside from civil rights issues, the Convention also devotes major attention to a most vital concern of women, namely their reproductive rights. The preamble sets the tone by stating that "the role of women in procreation should not be a basis for discrimination." The link between discrimination and women's reproductive role is a matter of recurrent concern in the Convention. For example, it advocates, in article 5, "a proper understanding of maternity as a social function", demanding fully shared responsibility for child-rearing by both sexes. Accordingly, provisions for maternity protection and child-care are proclaimed as essential rights and are incorporated into all areas of the Convention, whether dealing with employment, family law, health care or education. Society's obligation extends to offering social services, especially child-care facilities, that allow individuals to combine family responsibilities with work and participation in public life. Special measures for maternity protection are recommended and "shall not be considered discriminatory" (article 4). "The Convention also affirms women's right to reproductive choice. Notably, it is the only human rights treaty to mention family planning. States parties are obliged to include advice on family planning in the education process (article 1 .h) and to develop family codes that guarantee women's rights "to decide freely and responsibly on the number and spacing of their children and to have access to the information, education and means to enable them to exercise these rights" (article 16.e).

The third general thrust of the Convention aims at enlarging our understanding of the concept of human rights, as it gives formal recognition to the influence of culture and tradition on restricting women's enjoyment of their fundamental rights. These forces take shape in stereotypes, customs and norms which give rise to the multitude of legal, political and economic constraints on the advancement of women. Noting this interrelationship, the preamble of the Convention stresses "that a change in the traditional role of men as well as the role of women in society and in the family is needed to achieve full equality of men and women." States parties are therefore obliged to work towards the modification of social and cultural patterns of individual conduct in order to eliminate "prejudices and customary and all other practices which are based on the idea of the inferiority or the superiority of either of the sexes or on stereotyped roles for men and women" (article 5). And Article 1.c mandates the revision of textbooks, school programmes and teaching methods with a view to eliminating stereotyped concepts in the field of education. Finally, cultural patterns which define the public realm as a man's world and the domestic sphere as women's domain are strongly targeted in all of the Convention's provisions that affirm the equal responsibilities of both sexes in family life and their equal rights with regard to education and employment. Altogether, the Convention provides a comprehensive framework for challenging the various forces that have created and sustained discrimination based upon sex.

The implementation of the Convention is monitored by the Committee on the Elimination of Discrimination against Women (CEDAW). The Committee's mandate and the administration of the treaty are defined in the Articles 17 to 30 of the Convention. The Committee is composed of 23 experts nominated by their Governments and elected by the States parties as individuals "of high moral standing and competence in the field covered by the Convention."

At least every four years, the States parties are expected to submit a national report to the Committee, indicating the measures they have adopted to give effect to the provisions of the Convention. During its annual session, the Committee members discuss these reports with the Government representatives and explore with them areas for further action by the specific country. The Committee also makes general recommendations to the States parties on matters concerning the elimination of discrimination against women.

The full text of the Convention is set out herein.

## Convention on the Elimination of All Forms of Discrimination Against Women

The States Parties to the present Convention,

Noting that the Charter of the United Nations reaffirms faith in fundamental human rights, in the dignity and worth of the human person and in the equal rights of men and women,

Noting that the Universal Declaration of Human Rights affirms the principle of the inadmissibility of discrimination and proclaims that all human beings are born free and equal in dignity and rights and that everyone is entitled to all the rights and freedoms set forth therein, without distinction of any kind, including distinction based on sex,

Noting that the States Parties to the International Covenants on Human Rights have the obligation to ensure the equal rights of men and women to enjoy all economic, social, cultural, civil and political rights,

Considering the international conventions concluded under the auspices of the United Nations and the specialized agencies promoting equality of rights of men and women,

Noting also the resolutions, declarations and recommendations adopted by the United Nations and the specialized agencies promoting equality of rights of men and women,

Concerned, however, that despite these various instruments extensive discrimination against women continues to exist,

Recalling that discrimination against women violates the principles of equality of rights and respect for human dignity, is an obstacle to the participation of women, on equal terms with men, in the political, social, economic and cultural life of their countries, hampers the growth of the prosperity of society and the family and makes more difficult the full development of the potentialities of women in the service of their countries and of humanity,

Concerned that in situations of poverty women have the least access to food, health, education, training and opportunities for employment and other needs,

Convinced that the establishment of the new international economic order based on equity and justice will contribute significantly towards the promotion of equality between men and women,

Emphasizing that the eradication of apartheid, all forms of racism, racial discrimination, colonialism, neo-colonialism, aggression, foreign occupation and domination and interference in the internal affairs of States is essential to the full enjoyment of the rights of men and women,

Affirming that the strengthening of international peace and security, the relaxation of international tension, mutual co-operation among all States irrespective of their social and economic systems, general and complete disarmament, in particular nuclear disarmament under strict and effective international control, the affirmation of the principles of justice, equality and mutual benefit in relations among countries and the realization of the right of peoples under alien and colonial domination and foreign occupation to self-determination and independence, as well as respect for national sovereignty and territorial integrity, will promote social progress and development and as a consequence will contribute to the attainment of full equality between men and women,

Convinced that the full and complete development of a country, the welfare of the world and the cause of peace require the maximum participation of women on equal terms with men in all fields,

Bearing in mind the great contribution of women to the welfare of the family and to the development of society, so far not fully recognized, the social significance of maternity and the role of both parents in the family and in the upbringing of children, and aware that the role of women in procreation should not be a basis for discrimination but that the upbringing of children requires a sharing of responsibility between men and women and society as a whole,

Aware that a change in the traditional role of men as well as the role of women in society and in the family is needed to achieve full equality between men and women,

Determined to implement the principles set forth in the Declaration on the Elimination of Discrimination against Women and, for that purpose, to adopt the measures required for the elimination of such discrimination in all its forms and manifestations,

Have agreed on the following:

## Part I

### Article I

For the purposes of the present Convention, the term "discrimination against women" shall mean any distinction, exclusion or restriction made on the basis of sex which has the effect or purpose of impairing or nullifying the recognition, enjoyment or exercise by women, irrespective of their marital status, on a basis of equality of men and women, of human rights and fundamental freedoms in the political, economic, social, cultural, civil or any other field.

### Article 2

States Parties condemn discrimination against women in all its forms, agree to pursue by all appropriate means and without delay a policy of eliminating discrimination against women and, to this end, undertake:

a. To embody the principle of the equality of men and women in their national constitutions or other appropriate legislation if not yet incorporated therein and to ensure, through law and other appropriate means, the practical realization of this principle;

b. To adopt appropriate legislative and other measures, including sanctions where appropriate, prohibiting all discrimination against women;

c. To establish legal protection of the rights of women on an equal basis with men and to ensure through competent national tribunals and other public institutions the effective protection of women against any act of discrimination;

d. To refrain from engaging in any act or practice of discrimination against women and to ensure that public authorities and institutions shall act in conformity with this obligation;

e. To take all appropriate measures to eliminate discrimination against women by any person, organization or enterprise;

f. To take all appropriate measures, including legislation, to modify or abolish existing laws, regulations, customs and practices which constitute discrimination against women;

g. To repeal all national penal provisions which constitute discrimination against women.

### Article 3

States Parties shall take in all fields, in particular in the political, social, economic and cultural fields, all appropriate measures, including legislation, to ensure the full development and advancement of women, for the purpose of guaranteeing them the exercise and enjoyment of human rights and fundamental freedoms on a basis of equality with men.

## Article 4

1. Adoption by States Parties of temporary special measures aimed at accelerating de facto equality between men and women shall not be considered discrimination as defined in the present Convention but shall in no way entail as a consequence the maintenance of unequal or separate standards; these measures shall be discontinued when the objectives of equality of opportunity and treatment have been achieved.
2. Adoption by States Parties of special measures, including those measures contained in the present Convention, aimed at protecting maternity shall not be considered discriminatory.

## Article 5

States Parties shall take all appropriate measures:
a. To modify the social and cultural patterns of conduct of men and women, with a view to achieving the elimination of prejudices and customary and all other practices which are based on the idea of the inferiority or the superiority of either of the sexes or on stereotyped roles for men and women;
b. To ensure that family education includes a proper understanding of maternity as a social function and the recognition of the common responsibility of men and women in the upbringing and development of their children, it being understood that the interest of the children is the primordial consideration in all cases.

## Article 6

States Parties shall take all appropriate measures, including legislation, to suppress all forms of traffic in women and exploitation of prostitution of women.

## Part II

## Article 7

States Parties shall take all appropriate measures to eliminate discrimination against women in the political and public life of the country and, in particular, shall ensure to women, on equal terms with men, the right:
a. To vote in all elections and public referenda and to be eligible for election to all publicly elected bodies;
b. To participate in the formulation of government policy and the implementation thereof and to hold public office and perform all public functions at all levels of government;
c. To participate in non-governmental organizations and associations concerned with the public and political life of the country.

## Article 8

States Parties shall take all appropriate measures to ensure to women, on equal terms with men and without any discrimination, the opportunity to represent their Governments at the international level and to participate in the work of international organizations.

## Article 9

1. States Parties shall grant women equal rights with men to acquire, change or retain their nationality. They shall ensure in particular that neither marriage to an alien nor change of nationality by the husband during marriage shall automatically change the nationality of the wife, render her stateless or force upon her the nationality of the husband.
2. States Parties shall grant women equal rights with men with respect to the nationality of their children.

## Part III

## Article 10

States Parties shall take all appropriate measures to eliminate discrimination against women in order to ensure to them equal rights with men in the field of education and in particular to ensure, on a basis of equality of men and women:

a. The same conditions for career and vocational guidance, for access to studies and for the achievement of diplomas in educational establishments of all categories in rural as well as in urban areas; this equality shall be ensured in pre-school, general, technical, professional and higher technical education, as well as in all types of vocational training;
b. Access to the same curricula, the same examinations, teaching staff with qualifications of the same standard and school premises and equipment of the same quality;
c. The elimination of any stereotyped concept of the roles of men and women at all levels and in all forms of education by encouraging coeducation and other types of education which will help to achieve this aim and, in particular, by the revision of textbooks and school programmes and the adaptation of teaching methods;
d. The same opportunities to benefit from scholarships and other study grants;
e. The same opportunities for access to programmes of continuing education, including adult and functional literacy programmes, particularly those aimed at reducing, at the earliest possible time, any gap in education existing between men and women;
f. The reduction of female student drop-out rates and the organization of programmes for girls and women who have left school prematurely;
g. The same Opportunities to participate actively in sports and physical education;
h. Access to specific educational information to help to ensure the health and well-being of families, including information and advice on family planning.

## *Article 11*

1. States Parties shall take all appropriate measures to eliminate discrimination against women in the field of employment in order to ensure, on a basis of equality of men and women, the same rights, in particular:
   a. The right to work as an inalienable right of all human beings;
   b. The right to the same employment opportunities, including the application of the same criteria for selection in matters of employment;
   c. The right to free choice of profession and employment, the right to promotion, job security and all benefits and conditions of service and the right to receive vocational training and retraining, including apprenticeships, advanced vocational training and recurrent training;
   d. The right to equal remuneration, including benefits, and to equal treatment in respect of work of equal value, as well as equality of treatment in the evaluation of the quality of work;
   e. The right to social security, particularly in cases of retirement, unemployment, sickness, invalidity and old age and other incapacity to work, as well as the right to paid leave;
   f. The right to protection of health and to safety in working conditions, including the safeguarding of the function of reproduction.
2. In order to prevent discrimination against women on the grounds of marriage or maternity and to ensure their effective right to work, States Parties shall take appropriate measures:
   a. To prohibit, subject to the imposition of sanctions, dismissal on the grounds of pregnancy or of maternity leave and discrimination in dismissals on the basis of marital status;
   b. To introduce maternity leave with pay or with comparable social benefits without loss of former employment, seniority or social allowances;
   c. To encourage the provision of the necessary supporting social services to enable parents to combine family obligations with work responsibilities and participation in public life, in particular through promoting the establishment and development of a network of child-care facilities;
   d. To provide special protection to women during pregnancy in types of work proved to be harmful to them.
3. Protective legislation relating to matters covered in this article shall be reviewed periodically in the light of scientific and technological knowledge and shall be revised, repealed or extended as necessary.

## *Article 12*

1. States Parties shall take all appropriate measures to eliminate discrimination against women in the field of health care in order to ensure, on a basis of equality of men and women, access to health care services, including those related to family planning.
2. Notwithstanding the provisions of paragraph I of this article, States Parties shall ensure to women appropriate services in connection with pregnancy, confinement and the post-natal period, granting free services where necessary, as well as adequate nutrition during pregnancy and lactation.

## *Article 13*

States Parties shall take all appropriate measures to eliminate discrimination against women in other areas of economic and social life in order to ensure, on a basis of equality of men and women, the same rights, in particular:

a. The right to family benefits;
b. The right to bank loans, mortgages and other forms of financial credit;
c. The right to participate in recreational activities, sports and all aspects of cultural life.

## *Article 14*

1. States Parties shall take into account the particular problems faced by rural women and the significant roles which rural women play in the economic survival of their families, including their work in the non-monetized sectors of the economy, and shall take all appropriate measures to ensure the application of the provisions of the present Convention to women in rural areas.

2. States Parties shall take all appropriate measures to eliminate discrimination against women in rural areas in order to ensure, on a basis of equality of men and women, that they participate in and benefit from rural development and, in particular, shall ensure to such women the right:

a. To participate in the elaboration and implementation of development planning at all levels;
b. To have access to adequate health care facilities, including information, counselling and services in family planning;
c. To benefit directly from social security programmes;
d. To obtain all types of training and education, formal and non-formal, including that relating to functional literacy, as well as, inter alia, the benefit of all community and extension services, in order to increase their technical proficiency;
e. organize self-help groups and co-operatives in order to obtain equal access to economic opportunities through employment or self-employment;
f. To participate in all community activities;
g. To have access to agricultural credit and loans, marketing facilities, appropriate technology and equal treatment in land and agrarian reform as well as in land resettlement schemes;
h. To enjoy adequate living conditions, particularly in relation to housing, sanitation, electricity and water supply, transport and communications.

## *Part IV*

## *Article 15*

1. States Parties shall accord to women equality with men before the law.
2. States Parties shall accord to women, in civil matters, a legal capacity identical to that of men and the same opportunities to exercise that capacity. In particular, they shall give women equal rights to conclude contracts and to administer property and shall treat them equally in all stages of procedure in courts and tribunals.

3. States Parties agree that all contracts and all other private instruments of any kind with a legal effect which is directed at restricting the legal capacity of women shall be deemed null and void.
4. States Parties shall accord to men and women the same rights with regard to the law relating to the movement of persons and the freedom to choose their residence and domicile.

## *Article 16*

1. States Parties shall take all appropriate measures to eliminate discrimination against women in all matters relating to marriage and family relations and in particular shall ensure, on a basis of equality of men and women:
   a. The same right to enter into marriage;
   b. The same right freely to choose a spouse and to enter into marriage only with their free and full consent;
   c. The same rights and responsibilities during marriage and at its dissolution;
   d. The same rights and responsibilities as parents, irrespective of their marital status, in matters relating to their children; in all cases the interests of the children shall be paramount;
   e. The same rights to decide freely and responsibly on the number and spacing of their children and to have access to the information, education and means to enable them to exercise these rights;
   f. The same rights and responsibilities with regard to guardianship, wardship, trusteeship and adoption of children, or similar institutions where these concepts exist in national legislation; in all cases the interests of the children shall be paramount;
   g. The same personal rights as husband and wife, including the right to choose a family name, a profession and an occupation;
   h. The same rights for both spouses in respect of the ownership, acquisition, management, administration, enjoyment and disposition of property, whether free of charge or for a valuable consideration.
2. The betrothal and the marriage of a child shall have no legal effect, and all necessary action, including legislation, shall be taken to specify a minimum age for marriage and to make the registration of marriages in an official registry compulsory.

## *Part V*

## *Article 17*

1. For the purpose of considering the progress made in the implementation of the present Convention, there shall be established a *Committee on the Elimination of Discrimination against Women* (hereinafter referred to as the Committee) consisting, at the time of entry into force of the Convention, of eighteen and, after ratification of or accession to the Convention by the thirty-fifth State Party, of twenty-three experts of high moral standing and competence in the field covered by the Convention. The experts shall be elected by States Parties from among their nationals and shall serve in their personal capacity, consider-

ation being given to equitable geographical distribution and to the representation of the different forms of civilization as well as the principal legal systems.

2. The members of the Committee shall be elected by secret ballot from a list of persons nominated by States Parties. Each State Party may nominate one person from among its own nationals.

3. The initial election shall be held six months after the date of the entry into force of the present Convention. At least three months before the date of each election the Secretary-General of the United Nations shall address a letter to the States Parties inviting them to submit their nominations within two months. The Secretary-General shall prepare a list in alphabetical order of all persons thus nominated, indicating the States Parties which have nominated them, and shall submit it to the States Parties.

4. Elections of the members of the Committee shall be held at a meeting of States Parties convened by the Secretary-General at United Nations Headquarters. At that meeting, for which two thirds of the States Parties shall constitute a quorum, the persons elected to the Committee shall be those nominees who obtain the largest number of votes and an absolute majority of the votes of the representatives of States Parties present and voting.

5. The members of the Committee shall be elected for a term of four years. However, the terms of nine of the members elected at the first election shall expire at the end of two years; immediately after the first election the names of these nine members shall be chosen by lot by the Chairman of the Committee.

6. The election of the five additional members of the Committee shall be held in accordance with the provisions of paragraphs 2, 3 and 4 of this article, following the thirty-fifth ratification or accession. The terms of two of the additional members elected on this occasion shall expire at the end of two years, the names of these two members having been chosen by lot by the Chairman of the Committee.

7. For the filling of casual vacancies, the State Party whose expert has ceased to function as a member of the Committee shall appoint another expert from among its nationals, subject to the approval of the Committee.

8. The members of the Committee shall, with the approval of the General Assembly, receive emoluments from United Nations resources on such terms and conditions as the Assembly may decide, having regard to the importance of the Committee's responsibilities.

9. The Secretary-General of the United Nations shall provide the necessary staff and facilities for the effective performance of the functions of the Committee under the present Convention.

## *Article 18*

1. States Parties undertake to submit to the Secretary-General of the United Nations, for consideration by the Committee, a report on the legislative, judicial, administrative or other measures which they have adopted to give effect to the provisions of the present Convention and on the progress made in this respect:

   a. Within one year after the entry into force for the State concerned;

   b. Thereafter at least every four years and further whenever the Committee so requests.

2. Reports may indicate factors and difficulties affecting the degree of fulfilment of obligations under the present Convention.

## Article 19

1. The Committee shall adopt its own rules of procedure.
2. The Committee shall elect its officers for a term of two years.

## Article 20

1. The Committee shall normally meet for a period of not more than two weeks annually in order to consider the reports submitted in accordance with article 18 of the present Convention.
2. The meetings of the Committee shall normally be held at United Nations Headquarters or at any other convenient place as determined by the Committee. (*amendment, status of ratification*)

## Article 21

1. The Committee shall, through the Economic and Social Council, report annually to the General Assembly of the United Nations on its activities and may make suggestions and general recommendations based on the examination of reports and information received from the States Parties. Such suggestions and general recommendations shall be included in the report of the Committee together with comments, if any, from States Parties.
2. The Secretary-General of the United Nations shall transmit the reports of the Committee to the Commission on the Status of Women for its information.

## Article 22

The specialized agencies shall be entitled to be represented at the consideration of the implementation of such provisions of the present Convention as fall within the scope of their activities. The Committee may invite the specialized agencies to submit reports on the implementation of the Convention in areas falling within the scope of their activities.

## Part VI

## Article 23

Nothing in the present Convention shall affect any provisions that are more conducive to the achievement of equality between men and women which may be contained:

a. In the legislation of a State Party; or
b. In any other international convention, treaty or agreement in force for that State.

## Article 24

States Parties undertake to adopt all necessary measures at the national level aimed at achieving the full realization of the rights recognized in the present Convention.

### Article 25

1. The present Convention shall be open for signature by all States.
2. The Secretary-General of the United Nations is designated as the depositary of the present Convention.
3. The present Convention is subject to ratification. Instruments of ratification shall be deposited with the Secretary-General of the United Nations.
4. The present Convention shall be open to accession by all States. Accession shall be affected by the deposit of an instrument of accession with the Secretary-General of the United Nations.

### Article 26

1. A request for the revision of the present Convention may be made at any time by any State Party by means of a notification in writing addressed to the Secretary-General of the United Nations.
2. The General Assembly of the United Nations shall decide upon the steps, if any, to be taken in respect of such a request.

### Article 27

1. The present Convention shall enter into force on the thirtieth day after the date of deposit with the Secretary-General of the United Nations of the twentieth instrument of ratification or accession.
2. For each State ratifying the present Convention or acceding to it after the deposit of the twentieth instrument of ratification or accession, the Convention shall enter into force on the thirtieth day after the date of the deposit of its own instrument of ratification or accession.

### Article 28

1. The Secretary-General of the United Nations shall receive and circulate to all States the text of reservations made by States at the time of ratification or accession.
2. A reservation incompatible with the object and purpose of the present Convention shall not be permitted.
3. Reservations may be withdrawn at any time by notification to this effect addressed to the Secretary-General of the United Nations, who shall then inform all States thereof. Such notification shall take effect on the date on which it is received.

### Article 29

1. Any dispute between two or more States Parties concerning the interpretation or application of the present Convention which is not settled by negotiation shall, at the request of one of them, be submitted to arbitration. If within six months from the date of the request for arbitration the parties are unable to agree on the organization of the arbitration, any one of those parties may refer the dispute to the International Court of Justice by request in conformity with the Statute of the Court.

2. Each State Party may at the time of signature or ratification of the present Convention or accession thereto declare that it does not consider itself bound by paragraph I of this article. The other States Parties shall not be bound by that paragraph with respect to any State Party which has made such a reservation.
3. Any State Party which has made a reservation in accordance with paragraph 2 of this article may at any time withdraw that reservation by notification to the Secretary-General of the United Nations.

## *Article 30*

The present Convention, the Arabic, Chinese, English, French, Russian and Spanish texts of which are equally authentic, shall be deposited with the Secretary-General of the United Nations.

IN WITNESS WHEREOF the undersigned, duly authorized, have signed the present Convention.

https://www.ohchr.org/en/professionalinterest/pages/cedaw.aspx

# Chapter Notes

## Introduction

1. E. Ike Udogu, "Democracy in Africa: Fiction or Fact in the 21st Century," Global Awareness Society International 25th Annual Conference, Budapest, Hungary, May 2016, pp. 2–4.

2. E. Ike Udogu, "National Constitutions and Human Rights Issues in Africa," *African and Asian Studies*, 2, no. 2 (2003), p. 103.

3. Jan-Erik Lane, *Constitutions and Political Theory* (Manchester, England: University of Manchester Press, 1996), p.

4. Jack C. Plano and Milton Greenberg, *The American Political Dictionary* (Holt, NY: Rinehart and Winston Publishers, 1985), p. 33.

5. E. Ike Udogu, ed., *Democracy and Democratization: Toward the 21st Century* (Leiden, Netherlands: E. J. Brill Publishers, 1997), p. 2.

6. "The United States Constitution: The Function of the Constitution," https://home.ubalt.edu/shapiro/rights_course/chapter1text.htm (retrieved 5/3/18).

7. Lane, *Constitutions and Political Theory*, p. 1.

8. Udogu, "National Constitutions and Human Rights Issues in Africa," p. 104.

9. Udogu, "National Constitutions and Human Rights Issues in Africa," p. 104; see also Julius O. Ihonvbere, *Toward a New Constitutionalism in Africa* (London: Center for Democracy and Development, 2000).

10. Donald S. Lutz, "Toward a Theory of Constitutional Amendment," *American Political Science Review*, 88, no. 2 (1994), pp. 355–357.

11. Udogu, "National Constitutions and Human Rights Issues in Africa," p. 104.

12. Udogu, "National Constitutions and Human Rights Issues in Africa," p. 104.

13. Robert Bolt, *A Man for All Seasons: A Play in Two Parts* (New York: Random House, Inc., 1990), pp. 152–153.

14. Lane, *Constitutions and Political Theory*, p. 2.

15. William G. Andrews, ed., *Constitutions and Constitutionalism* (Princeton, NJ: D. VanNostrand, Inc., 1963), p. 26.

16. See Paul Sigmund, "Carl Friedrich's Contribution to the Theory of Constitutionalism—Comparative Government," in J. Ronald Pennock and John W. Chapman, eds., *Constitutionalism* (New York: New York University Press, 1979), p. 34; E. Ike Udogu, "Military Politics and Constitutional Discourse: Towards Nigeria's Forthcoming Republics," *Makerere Political Science Review*, 1, no. 1 (1997), pp. 5–6.

17. See Constitution of Algeria (1996), http://www.amazighworld.org/countries/Algeria/documents/constitution/eng/const.php (retrieved 5/4/18).

18. Human Rights Watch, *World Report 2016: Algeria—Events of 2015* (New York: Human Rights Watch, 2016), pp. 1–2, https://www.hrw.org/world-report/2016/country-chapters/algeria (retrieved 5/4/18).

19. Human Rights Watch, *World Report 2016: Algeria—Events of 2015*, pp. 2–3.

20. Amira Mikhail, "Open Democracy—Free Thinking for the World: The Obligation of Civil Society in Egypt," p. 2, https://www.opendemocracy.net/north-Africa-west-asia/amira-mikail/obligation-of-civil-society-in-egypt (retrieved 5/6/18); see also Table I, Chapter 2.

21. Egypt: Penal Code [Egypt]. No. 58 of 1937, August 1937, pp. 24–26, available at http://www.refworld.org/docid/3f827fc44.htlm (retrieved 5/6/18).

22. Mikhail, "Open Democracy—Free

Thinking for the World: The Obligation of Civil Society in Egypt," p. 4.

23. Mikhail, "Open Democracy—Free Thinking for the World: The Obligation of Civil Society in Egypt," p. 4.

24. Mikhail, "Open Democracy—Free Thinking for the World: The Obligation of Civil Society in Egypt," p. 2.

25. Stanlie M. James, "Transgressing Fundamental Boundaries: The Struggle or Women's Human Rights," *Africa Today*, 39, no. 4 (4th Quarter 1992), p. 39.

26. See George Sadek, "Egypt: New Law Enhancing the Penalties for FGM Approved by Parliament," *Global Legal Monitor*, Library of Congress, September 14, 2016, p. 1, https://www.loc.gov/law/foreign-news/article/egypt-new-law-enhancing-the-penalties-for-fgm-approved-by-parliament/ (retrieved 5/6/18).

27. Sadek, "Egypt: New Law Enhancing the Penalties for FGM Approved by Parliament," pp. 1–2.

28. Sadek, "Egypt: New Law Enhancing the Penalties for FGM Approved by Parliament," p. 2.

29. Damien McElroy, "Libyan Student Faces Life in Prison for Protests in London," *Telegraph*, September 10, 2013, pp. 1–2. https://www.telegraph.co.uk/news/worldnews/africaandindianocean/libya/10300381/Libyan-Student-faces-life-in-prison-for-protests-in-London.html (retrieved 5/7/18).

30. See Constitution of Morocco, 2011, https://www.constituteproject.org/constitution/Morocco_2011?=en (retrieved 5/6/18).

31. "Morocco: Human Rights Violations Under Article 475," *Human Rights Warrior*, January 17, 2014, pp. 2–7, https://humanrightswarrior.com/tag/moroccan-penal-code/ (retrieved 5/7/18).

32. Elizabeth Flock, "Morocco Outraged over Suicide of Amina Filali, Who Was Forced to Marry Her Rapist," *Washington Post*, March 15, 2012, https://www.washingtonpost.com/blogs/blogpost/post/morocco-outraged-over-suicide-of-amina-filali-who-was-forced-to-marry-her-rapist/2012/03/15/gIQApTq4DS_blog.html (retrieved 10/16/18).

33. Amnesty International, "Bias in Penal Code Puts Women and Girls in Danger in Morocco," March 1, 2013, https://www.amnesty.org/en/latest/news/2013/03/bias-in-penal-code-puts-women-and-girls-in-danger-in-morocco/ (retrieved 5/7/18).

34. Human Rights Watch, "Tunisia: Jailed for 'Defamation,'" March 21, 2017, p. 2, https://www.hrw.org/news/2017/03/21/tunisia-jailed-defamation (retrieved 5/8/18).

35. Human Rights Watch, "Tunisia: Jailed for 'Defamation,'" p. 1.

36. Human Rights Watch, "Tunisia: Jailed for 'Defamation,'" p. 2.

37. E. Ike Udogu, *Leadership and the Problem of Electoral Democracy in Africa: Case Studies and Theoretical Solutions* (Newcastle upon Tyne, UK: Cambridge Scholars Publishing, 2016), p. 4.

38. Human Rights Watch, "Tunisia: Jailed for 'Defamation,'" p. 2.

## *Chapter 1*

1. Falaq Kagda, *Cultures of the World: Algeria* (Tarrytown, NY: Marshall Cavendish Corporation, 1997), p. 21; Arthur Wayne Edge, *Global Studies: Africa*, 11th ed. (Dubuque, IA: McGraw-Hill/Dushkin, 2006), p. 107.

2. Helen C. Metz, *Algeria: A Country Study* (Washington DC: Federal Research Division, 1993), p. 7.

3. Metz, *Algeria: A Country Study*, pp. 3, 7–20; Kagda, *Cultures of the World: Algeria*, p. 24.

4. Metz, *Algeria: A Country Study*, p. 7; Kagda, *Cultures of the World: Algeria*, p. 22.

5. Kagda, Cultures of the World: Algeria, p. 22.

6. Kagda, Cultures of the World: Algeria, p. 23.

7. Metz, *Algeria: A Country Study*, p. 7.

8. Metz, *Algeria: A Country Study*, p. 11.

9. Metz, *Algeria: A Country Study*, pp. 10–11; Kagda, *Cultures of the World: Algeria*, p. 24.

10. Metz, *Algeria: A Country Study*, p. 11.

11. Metz, *Algeria: A Country Study*, p. 12.

12. Metz, *Algeria: A Country Study*, pp. 13–17; Kagda, *Cultures of the World: Algeria*, pp. 27–29.

13. Kagda, *Cultures of the World: Algeria*, p. 28.

14. Metz, *Algeria: A Country Study*, p. 19.

15. Metz, *Algeria: A Country Study*, p. 20.

16. Edge, *Global Studies: Africa*, p. 108.

17. Harold D. Nelson, *Algeria: A Country Study* (Washington, DC.: American University, Foreign Area Studies, 1979), p. 31; also cited in Edge, *Global Studies: Africa*, p. 108.

18. Marnia Lazreg, *The Emergence of Classes in Algeria* (Boulder, CO: Westview Press, 1976), p. 53; Phillip C. Naylor, *France and Algeria: A History of Decolonization and Transformation* (Gainesville, FL: University of Florida Press, 2000), p. 6; Benjamin Stora, *Algeria 1830-2000: A Short History*, translated by Jane Marie Todd (Ithaca, NY: Cornell University Press, 2001), p. 5.

19. Edge, *Global Studies: Africa*, p. 108.

20. Edge, *Global Studies: Africa*, p. 108.

21. The Universal Declaration of Human Rights, United Nations General Assembly, Resolution 217A, December 10, 1948, www.un.org/en/universal-declaration-human-rights (retrieved 2/20/17).

22. E. Ike Udogu, *Liberating Namibia: The Long Diplomatic Struggle between the United Nations and South Africa* (Jefferson, NC: McFarland, 2012), pp. 22-30.

23. Cited in "Torture during the Algerian War of Independence," Wikipedia, https://en.wikipedia.org/wiki/Torture_during_the_Algerian_War_of_Independence (retrieved 3/14/17).

24. Fabian Klose, *Human Rights in the Shadow of Colonial Violence: The Wars of Independence in Kenya and Algeria*, translated by Dona Geyer (Philadelphia, PA: University of Pennsylvania Press, 2013), p. 136.

25. Klose, *Human Rights in the Shadow of Colonial Violence: The Wars of Independence in Kenya and Algeria*, p. 136.

26. Klose, *Human Rights in the Shadow of Colonial Violence: The Wars of Independence in Kenya and Algeria*, pp. 136-137.

27. Klose, *Human Rights in the Shadow of Colonial Violence: The Wars of Independence in Kenya and Algeria*, p. 212.

28. Klose, *Human Right in the Shadow of Colonial Violence: The Wars of Independence in Kenya and Algeria*, p. 212.

29. Klose, *Human Rights in the Shadow of Colonial Violence: The Wars of Independence in Kenya and Algeria*, p. 212.

30. Klose, *Human Rights in the Shadow of Colonial Violence: The Wars of Independence in Kenya and Algeria*, p. 213. On this matter, see also the communique of the GDR to the ICRC, August 15, 1960; Hungarian Red Cross to the ICRC, September 19, 1960; Lebanese Red Cross to the ICRC, October 4, 1960; Venezuelan Red Cross to the ICRC, October 11, 1960; and Iraqi Red Crescent to the ICRC, October 16, 1960, all in ACICR, B AG 202 008-013.

31. U.S. Department of State, Bureau of Democracy, Human Rights and Labor, *Country Reports on Human Rights Practices—Algeria*, https://www.state.gov/documents/organization/253129.pdf (retrieved 4/10/17).

32. E. Ike Udogu, *Leadership and the Problem of Electoral Democracy in Africa: Case Studies and Theoretical Solutions* (Newcastle upon Tyne, UK: Cambridge Scholars Publishing, 2016).

33. Udogu, *Leadership and the Problem of Electoral Democracy in Africa: Case Studies and Theoretical Solutions*, pp. 9, 83–92.

34. U.S. Department of State, Bureau of Democracy, Human Rights and Labor, p. 1.

35. U.S. Department of State, Bureau of Democracy, Human Rights and Labor, p. 2.

36. Universal Declaration of Human Rights.

37. International Covenant on Civil and Political Rights, United Nations General Assembly Resolution 2200A, December 16, 1966, United Nations Office of the High Commissioner for Human Rights website, www.ohchr.org/EN/ProfessionalInterest/Pages/CCPR.aspx (retrieved 6/20/17).

38. Convention against Torture and Other Cruel, Inhuman or Degrading Treatment or Punishment, General Assembly Resolution 39/46, December 10, 1984, United Nations Office of the High Commissioner for Human Rights website, www.ohchr.org/EN/ProfessionalInterest/Pages/CAT.aspx (retrieved 6/20/17).

39. U.S. Department of State, Bureau of Democracy, Human Rights and Labor, p. 3.

40. U.S. Department of State, Bureau of Democracy, Human Rights and Labor, p. 3.

41. U.S. Department of State, Bureau of Democracy, Human Rights and Labor, p. 3.

42. Amnesty International, *Annual Report 2015/2016—Algeria*, https://www.amnesty.org/en/latest/Research/2016/02/annual-report-201516 (retrieved 6/22/17); see also U.S. Department of State, Bureau of Democracy, Human Rights and Labor, p. 12.

43. Amnesty International, *Annual Report 2015/2016—Algeria*. See also Human Rights Watch, *World Report 2016: Algeria—Events of 2015*; *United States Department of State-Bureau of Democracy, Human Rights and Labor*, p. 8.

44. International Covenant on Civil and Political Rights.

45. U.S. Department of State, Bureau of Democracy, Human Rights and Labor, p. 11.

46. U.S. Department of State, Bureau of Democracy, Human Rights and Labor, pp. 11–12, 16.

47. Human Rights Watch, *World Report 2016: Algeria—Events of 2015*, p. 3; U.S. Department of State, Bureau of Democracy and Labor, p. 12.

48. U.S. Department of State, Bureau of Democracy and Labor, pp. 12–14.

49. U.S. Department of State, Bureau of Democracy and Labor, p. 15.

50. Human Rights Watch, *World Report 2016: Algeria—Events of 2015*, pp. 1–2.

51. U.S. Department of State, Bureau of Democracy and Labor, p. 18.

52. U.S. Department of State, Bureau of Democracy and Labor, p. 18.

53. U.S. Department of State, Bureau of Democracy and Labor, p. 19.

54. U.S. Department of State, Bureau of Democracy and Labor, pp. 19–20.

55. U.S. Department of State, Bureau of Democracy and Labor, p. 23.

56. U.S. Department of State, Bureau of Democracy and Labor, p. 24.

57. E. Ike Udogu, ed., *Nigeria in the Twenty-first Century: Strategies for Political Stability and Peaceful Existence* (Trenton, NJ: Africa World Press, 2005), pp. 234–235; Udogu, *Leadership and the Problem of Electoral Democracy in Africa: Case Studies and Theoretical Solutions*, p. 9.

58. U.S. Department of State, Bureau of Democracy, Human Rights, and Labor, *Algeria 2015 International Religious Freedom Report*, p. 1, https://2009-2017.state.gov/documents/organization/236471.pdf (retrieved 6/24/17).

59. U.S. Department of State, Bureau of Democracy, Human Rights, and Labor, *Algeria 2015 International Religious Freedom Report*, p. 2.

60. U.S. Department of State, Bureau of Democracy, Human Rights, and Labor, *Algeria 2015 International Religious Freedom Report*, pp. 2–3.

61. U.S. Department of State, Bureau of Democracy, Human Rights, and Labor, *Algeria 2015 International Religious Freedom Report*, p. 3.

62. U.S. Department of State, Bureau of Democracy, Human Rights, and Labor, *Algeria 2015 International Religious Freedom Report*, p. 4.

63. U.S. Department of State, Bureau of Democracy, Human Rights, and Labor, *Algeria 2015 International Religious Freedom Report*, pp. 5–6; see also Universal Declaration of Human Rights.

64. See International Covenant on Civil and Political Rights.

65. E. Ike Udogu and Sambuddha Ghatak, eds., *Human Rights Dilemmas in the Developing World: The Case of Marginalized Populations at Risk* (Lanham, MD: Lexington Books, 2017), pp. xix–xxvi.

66. Human Rights Watch, "Algeria: Stop Persecuting a Religious Minority—286 Prosecutions of Ahmadis," September 4, 2017, https://www.hrw.org/news/2017/09/04/algeria-stop-persecuting-religious-minority.

67. Human Rights Watch, "Algeria: Stop Persecuting a Religious Minority—286 Prosecutions of Ahmadis."

68. Human Rights Watch, "Algeria: Stop Persecuting a Religious Minority—286 Prosecutions of Ahmadis."

69. Human Rights Watch, "Algeria: Stop Persecuting a Religious Minority—286 Prosecutions of Ahmadis."

70. Human Rights Watch, "Algeria: Stop Persecuting a Religious Minority—286 Prosecutions of Ahmadis."

71. Human Rights Watch, "Algeria: Stop Persecuting a Religious Minority—286 Prosecutions of Ahmadis."

72. Human Rights Watch, "Algeria: Stop Persecuting a Religious Minority—286 Prosecutions of Ahmadis."

73. Zahia Smail Salhi, "Algerian Women, Citizenship, and the 'Family Code,'" *Gender and Development*, 11, no. 3 (November 2003), p. 27.

74. Salhi, "Algerian Women, Citizenship, and the 'Family Code,'" p. 27; see also W. Woodhull, *Transfiguration of the Maghreb* (Minneapolis, MN: University of Minneapolis Press, 1993), p. 10; B. Shaaban, *Both Right and Left Handed: Arab Women Talk about Their Lives* (London: Women's Press, 1998), p. 199.

75. Salhi, "Algerian Women, Citizenship, and the 'Family Code,'" p. 28.

76. K. Messaoudi and E. Schemla, *Unbowed: An Algerian Woman Confronts Islamic Fundamentalism* (Philadelphia, PA: University of Pennsylvania Press, 1998), p. 49.

77. Salhi, "Algerian Women, Citizenship, and the Family Code,'" p. 30.

78. S. Joseph, ed., *Gender and Citizenship in the Middle East* (Syracuse, NY: Syracuse University Press, 2000), p. 21.

79. Messaoudi and Schemla, *Unbowed: An Algerian Woman Confronts Islamic Fundamentalism*, p. 53; Salhi, "Algerian Women, Citizenship, and the Family Code,'" p. 30.

80. Messaoudi and Schemla, *Unbowed: An Algerian Woman Confronts Islamic Fundamentalism*, pp. 87–92; see also Salhi, "Algerian Woman, Citizenship, and the Family Code,'" pp. 33–34.

81. Fatima Mernissi, *Women and Islam: An Historical and Theological Enquiry* (Oxford: Blackwell, 1991), p. ix; see also Elham Manea, *The Arab State and Women's Rights: The Trap of Authoritarian Governance* (New York: Routledge, 2011), p. 29; Joelle Entelis, "International Human Rights: Islam's Friend or Foe? Algeria as an Example of the Compatibility of International Human Rights Regarding Women's Equality and Islamic Law," *Fordham International Law Journal*, 20, iss. 4 (1996), pp. 1251–1305.

82. See Pita O. Agbese and E. Ike Udogu, "Taming of the Shrew: Civil-Military Politics in the Fourth Republic," in Udogu, *Nigeria in the Twenty-First Century: Strategies for Political Stability and Peaceful Coexistence*, pp. 25–26.

83. U.S. Department of State, Bureau of Democracy, Human Rights and Labor, p. 29.

84. Salhi, "Algerian Women, Citizenship, and the 'Family Code,'" p. 34.

85. U.S. Department of State, Bureau of Democracy, Human Rights and Labor, pp. 29–30.

86. U.S. Department of State, Bureau of Democracy, Human Rights and Labor, pp. 29–30.

87. U.S. Department of State, Bureau of Democracy, Human Rights and Labor, p. 36.

88. U.S. Department of State, Bureau of Democracy, Human Rights and Labor, p. 36.

89. U.S. Department of State, Bureau of Democracy, Human Rights and Labor, p. 36.

## Chapter 2

1. Robert Pateman, *Cultures of the World* (New York: Cavendish Square Publishing, 2015), p. 23.

2. Zaki N. Mahmoud, *The Land and People of Egypt* (Philadelphia, PA: J. B. Lippincott Company, 1959), pp. 20, 29–30; Pateman, *Cultures of the World*, p. 24; Helen Chapin Metz, *Egypt: A Country Study* (Washington DC: Federal Research Division, 1991), pp. 5–9.

3. Mahmoud, *The Land and People of Egypt*, p. 21.

4. Mahmoud, *The Land and People of Egypt*, p. 22.

5. Mahmoud, *The Land and People of Egypt*, pp. 22–23.

6. Pateman, *Cultures of the World*, pp. 26, 28.

7. P. H. Newby, *Warrior Pharaohs: The Rise and Fall of the Egyptian Empire* (London: Faber and Faber, 1980), pp. 16–17, 143–152, 155–158; Arthur Wayne Edge, *Global Studies: Africa*, 11th ed. (Dubuque, IA: McGraw-Hill/Dushkin Company, 2006), p. 115; Pateman, *Cultures of the World*, pp. 28–29.

8. Barbara Waterson, *The Egyptians* (Oxford: Blackwell, 1997), pp. 5, 177; R. Hamilton, *Ancient Egypt: Kingdom of the Pharaohs* (Bath, UK: Paragon Publishers, 2013), pp. 195–196, 215; Rosalie David, *Handbook to Life in Ancient Egypt* (New York: Facts on File, 1998), pp. 13, 39, 319–320; Newby, *Warrior Pharaohs: The Rise and Fall of the Egyptian Empire*, pp. 81, 114, 160–162.

9. David, *Handbook to Life in Ancient Egypt*, pp. 13–14, 41, 226; Hamilton, *Ancient Egypt: Kingdom of the Pharaohs*, pp. 197–198, 199–200, 220; Watterson, *The Egyptians*, pp. 5, 179–182, 231.

10. Jason Thompson, *A History of Egypt: From Earliest Times to the Present* (Cairo: American University of Cairo Press, 2008), pp. 97–98; Newby, *Warrior Pharaohs: The Rise and Fall of the Egyptian Empire*, pp. 63, 72, 98, 206; Watterson, *The Egyptians*, p. 5; Hamilton, *Ancient Egypt: Kingdom of the Pharaohs*, pp. 199–200, 220, 235; David, *Handbook to Life in Ancient Egypt*, pp. 3, 14, 42, 129, 130, 194.

11. Watterson, *The Egyptians*, pp. 206–208, 226; David, *Handbook to Life in Ancient Egypt*, pp. 3, 15, 44, 46, 53; Hamilton, *Ancient Egypt: Kingdom of the Pharaohs*, pp. 204, 224, 225; Mahmoud, *The Land and People of Egypt*, p. 33.

12. Thompson, *A History of Egypt: From Earliest Times to the Present*, pp. 123–143; Metz, *Egypt: A Country Study*, pp. 13–18; Pateman, *Cultures of the World*, pp. 29–30.

13. Mahmoud, *The Land and People of Egypt*, p. 33; David, *Handbook to Life in Ancient Egypt*, pp. 128, 132–134; Watterson, *The Egyptians*, pp. 5, 240–242; Hamilton, *Ancient Egypt: Kingdom of the Pharaohs*, pp. 204, 229, 231; Pateman, *Cultures of the World*, p. 30.

14. Mahmoud, *The Land and People of Egypt*, p. 34.

15. Watterson, *The Egyptians*, pp. 226–253; Mahmoud, *The Land and People of Egypt*, p. 35; David, *Handbook to Life in Ancient Egypt*, pp. 46–47.

16. Watterson, *The Egyptians*, pp. 228–229.

17. David, *Handbook of Life in Ancient Egypt*, pp. 194–195; Mahmoud, *The Land and People of Egypt*, p. 38; Watterson, *The Egyptians*, pp. 5, 228.

18. P. J. Vatikiotis, *The Modern History of Egypt* (New York: Frederick A. Praeger, 1969), pp. 13–32; Metz, *Egypt: A Country Study*, pp. 15–18; Watterson, *The Egyptians*, pp. 6, 232, 255, 272; Pateman, *Cultures of the World*, p. 30.

19. Mahmoud, *The Land and People of Egypt*, p. 58.

20. Pateman, *Cultures of the World*, pp. 31–32; Edge, *Global Studies: Africa*, pp. 116–117; Metz, *Egypt: A Country Study*, pp. 26–28; Thompson, *A History of Egypt: From Earliest Times to the Present*, pp. 217–223, 298–299.

21. Mahmoud, *The Land and People of Egypt*, pp. 65–66; Pateman, *Cultures of the World*, p. 31; Edge, *Global Studies: Africa*, p. 117.

22. Pateman, *Cultures of the World*, p. 31; Mahmoud, *The Land and People of Egypt*, pp. 66–84; Edge, *Global Studies: Africa*, p. 117; Metz, *Egypt: A Country Study*, pp. 28–31.

23. Pateman, *Cultures of the World*, pp. 31, 32.

24. Mahmoud, *The Land and People of Egypt*, p. 75; Pateman, *Cultures of the World*, p. 33.

25. Edge, *Global Studies: Africa*, p. 118; Pateman, *Cultures of the World*, p. 33; Mahmoud, *The Land and People of Egypt*, p. 76.

26. Mahmoud, *The Land and People of Egypt*, pp. 77–78; Edge, *Global Studies: Africa*, p. 118; Pateman, *Cultures of the World*, p. 33; Metz, *Egypt: A Country Study*, pp. 50, 56.

27. Amnesty International, *Annual Report 2015/2016—Egypt*, p. 1, https://www.refworld.org/docid/56do5b5d6.htlm (retrieved 8/20/17).

28. U.S. Department of State, Bureau of Democracy and Labor, *Country Reports on Human Rights Practices for 2015: Egypt*, p. 1, https://2009-2017.state.gov/j/drl/rls/hrrpt/humanrightsreport/index.htm?year=2015&dlid=252921#wrapper.

29. Human Rights Watch, *World Report 2015: Egypt—Events of 2014*, https://www.hrw.org/world-report/2015/country-chapters/egypt (retrieved 8/20/17).

30. U.S. Department of State, Bureau of Democracy and Labor, *Country Reports on Human Rights Practices for 2015: Egypt*, p. 2.

31. Human Rights Watch, *World Report 2015: Egypt—Events of 2014*, p. 1.

32. Human Rights Watch, *World Report 2015: Egypt—Events of 2014*, pp. 1–2.

33. African [Banjul] Charter on Human and Peoples' Rights, adopted June 27, 1981, OAU Doc. CAB/LEG/67/3 rev. 5, 21 I.L.M (1982), entered into force October 21, 1986, p. 3.

34. Convention Against Torture and Other Cruel, Inhuman or Degrading Treatment or Punishment, General Assembly Resolution 39/46, December 10, 1984, United Nations Office of the High Commissioner for Human Rights website, www.ohchr.org/EN/ProfessionalInterest/Pages/CAT.aspx (retrieved 9/15/17).

35. African [Banjul] Charter on Human and Peoples' Rights, p. 3.

36. International Covenant on Civil and Political Rights, United Nations General Assembly Resolution 2200A, December 16, 1966, United Nations Office of the High Commissioner for Human Rights website, www.ohchr.org/EN/ProfessionalInterest/Pages/CCPR.aspx (retrieved 6/20/17).

37. United Nations General Assembly, Resolution 217A, December 10, 1948, The Universal Declaration of Human Rights, www.un.org/en/universal-declaration-human-rights (retrieved 2/20/17).

38. Amnesty International, "Egypt: Hundreds Disappeared and Tortured amid Wave of Brutal Repression," p. 2, https://www.amnesty.org/en/latest/news/2016/07/egypt-hundreds-disappeared-and-tortured-amid-wave-of-brutal-repression/ (retrieved 9/25/17).

39. Amnesty International, "Egypt: Hundreds Disappeared and Tortured amid Wave of Brutal Repression," p. 2; U.S. Department of State, Bureau of Democracy and Labor, *Country Reports on Human Rights Practices for 2015: Egypt*, p. 5.

40. Human Rights Watch, *World Report 2016: Egypt—Events of 2015*, p. 2, https://www.hrw.org/world-report/2016/country-chapters/egypt (Retrieved 10/27/17).

41. Human Rights Watch, *World Report 2015: Egypt—Events of 2014*, p. 4.

42. Human Rights Watch, *World Report 2016: Egypt—Events of 2015*, p. 2.

43. Human Rights Watch, *World Report 2017: Egypt—Events of 2016*, p. 2, https://www.hrw.org/world-report/2017/country-chapters/egypt (retrieved 11/15/17).

44. Amnesty International, *Annual Report 2015/2016—Egypt*, p. 4; see "Egypt: Spate of Detainee Deaths Points to Rampant Abuse at Cairo's Mattareya Police Station," March 4, 2015; see also Amnesty International, *Annual Report 2016/2017—Egypt*, pp. 3–4. https://www.amnesty.org/en/countries/middle-east-and-north-africa/egypt/report (retrieved 12/5/17); U.S. Department of State, Bureau of Democracy and Labor, *Country Reports on Human Rights Practices for 2015: Egypt*, p. 6.

45. U.S. Department of State, Bureau of Democracy and Labor, *Country Reports on Human Rights Practices for 2015: Egypt*, p. 7.

46. U.S. Department of State, Bureau of Democracy and Labor, *Country Reports on Human Rights Practices for 2015: Egypt*, p. 7.

47. U.S. Department of State, Bureau of Democracy and Labor, *Country Reports on Human Rights Practices for 2015: Egypt*, p. 7

48. Universal Declaration of Human Rights.

49. International Covenant on Civil and Political Rights, pp. 4–5.

50. Amnesty International, *Annual Report 2016/2017—Egypt*, p. 2.

51. Amnesty International, *Annual Report 2015/2016—Egypt*, p. 3.

52. Amnesty International, *Annual Report 2015/2016—Egypt*, p. 3.

53. Human Rights Watch, *World Report 2015: Egypt—Events of 2014*, p. 5.

54. Human Rights Watch, *World Report 2017: Egypt—Events of 2016*, p. 5.

55. U.S. Department of State, Bureau of Democracy and Labor, *Country Reports on Human Rights Practices for 2015: Egypt*, p. 17.

56. U.S. Department of State, Bureau of Democracy and Labor, *Country Reports on Human Rights Practices for 2015: Egypt*, p. 17.

57. U.S. Department of State, Bureau of Democracy and Labor, *Country Reports on Human Rights Practices for 2015: Egypt*, p. 18.

58. U.S. Department of State, Bureau of Democracy and Labor, *Country Reports on Human Rights Practices for 2015: Egypt*, pp. 18–19; E. Ike Udogu, *Leadership and the Problem of Electoral Democracy in Africa: Case Studies and Theoretical Solutions* (Newcastle upon Tyne, UK: Cambridge Scholars Publishing), pp. 47–70.

59. African [Banjul] Charter on Human and Peoples' Rights, p. 4.

60. International Covenant on Civil and Political Rights, p. 5.

61. U.S. Department of State, Bureau of Democracy and Labor, *Country Reports on Human Rights Practices for 2015: Egypt*, pp. 23–25.

62. Human Rights Watch, *World Report 2015: Egypt—Events of 2014*, pp. 5–7.

63. Human Rights Watch, *World Report 2017: Egypt—Events of 2016*, pp. 3–4; Amnesty International, *Annual Report 2015/2016—Egypt*, p. 3; Amnesty International, *Annual Report 2016/2017—Egypt*, pp. 2–3.

64. U.S. Department of State, Bureau of Democracy, Human Rights, and Labor, *Egypt 2015 International Religious Freedom Report*, pp. 2–3, https://www.state.gov/document/organization/256475.pdf (retrieved 12/20/17).

65. Jason Brownlee, "Violence against Copts in Egypt" (Washington, DC: Carnegie Endowment for International Peace, November 14, 2013), p. 6, https://www.carnegieendowment.org/2013/11/14/violence-against-copts-in-egypt-pub-53606 (retrieved 12/20/17).

66. African [Banjul] Charter on Human and Peoples' Rights, p. 4.

67. Universal Declaration of Human Rights.

68. International Covenant on Civil and Political Rights, p. 4.

69. Brownlee, "Violence against Copts in Egypt," pp. 8–12.

70. Human Rights Watch, "Egypt: New Church Law Discriminates against Christians," September 15, 2016, https://www.hrw.org/news/2016/09/15/egypt-new-church-law-discriminates-against-christians (retrieved 12/24/17).

71. U.S. Department of State, Bureau of Democracy, Human Rights, and Labor, *Egypt 2015 International Religious Freedom Report*, pp. 1, 7.

72. U.S. Department of State, Bureau of Democracy, Human Rights, and Labor, *Egypt 2015 International Religious Freedom Report*, pp. 19–23.

73. Mona Eltahawy, "Egypt's Cruelty to Christians," *New York Times*, December 22, 2016, https://www.nytimes-com/2016/12/22/

opinion/egypts-cruelty-to-christians.html (retrieved 12/24/17).

74. U.S. Department of State, Bureau of Democracy, Human Rights, and Labor, *Egypt 2015 International Religious Freedom Report*, p. 6.

75. U.S. Department of State, Bureau of Democracy, Human Rights, and Labor, *Egypt 2015 International Religious Freedom Report*, p. 4.

76. U.S. Department of State, Bureau of Democracy, Human Rights, and Labor, *Egypt 2015 International Religious Freedom Report*, pp. 4, 6.

77. See Human Rights Watch, *World Report 2015: Egypt—Events of 2014*, p. 7; Human Rights Watch, *World Report 2016: Egypt—Events of 2015*, p. 5; *Human Rights* Human Rights Watch, *World Report 2017: Egypt—Events of 2016*, pp. 5–6; Amnesty International, *Annual Report 2015/2016—Egypt*, p. 5; Amnesty International, *Annual Report 2016/2017—Egypt*, p. 5.

78. U.S. Department of State, Bureau of Democracy, Human Rights, and Labor, *Egypt 2015 International Religious Freedom Report*, pp. 5, 7.

79. U.S. Department of State, Bureau of Democracy, Human Rights, and Labor, *Egypt 2015 International Religious Freedom Report*, p. 13.

80. U.S. Department of State, Bureau of Democracy, Human Rights, and Labor, *Egypt 2015 International Religious Freedom Report*, p. 14.

81. E. Ike Udogu and Sambuddha Ghatak, eds., *Human Rights Dilemmas in the Developing World: The Case of Marginalized Populations at Risk* (Lanham, MD: Lexington Books, 2017), pp. xxi–xxvi.

82. U.S. Department of State, Bureau of Democracy, Human Rights, and Labor, *Egypt 2015 International Religious Freedom Report*, p. 16.

83. Universal Declaration of Human Rights.

84. ILO Convention Prohibiting Discrimination in Employment, January 1, 1970, Equal Rights Trust website, https://www.equalrightstrust.org/content/ilo-convention-prohibiting-discrimination-employment (retrieved 12/26/17).

85. African [Banjul] Charter on Human and Peoples' Rights, p. 6.

86. International Covenant on Civil and Political Rights, p. 1.

87. Universal Declaration of Human Rights, p. 1.

88. Universal Declaration of Human Rights, p. 1.

89. U.S. Department of State, Bureau of Democracy and Labor, *Country Reports on Human Rights Practices for 2015: Egypt*, p. 37.

90. Yahia Salah El Hadidi, "Violence against Women in Egypt: A Review of Domestic Violence and Female Genital Mutilation" (Cairo: Population and Family Planning Sector, Ministry of Health & Population), pp. 103–205.

91. Hadidi, "Violence against Women in Egypt: A Review of Domestic Violence and Female Genital Mutilation," p. 103.

92. U.S. Department of State, Bureau of Democracy and Labor, *Country Reports on Human Rights Practices for 2015: Egypt*, p. 39.

93. Amnesty International, "Circles of Hell: Domestic, Public and State Violence against Women in Egypt," January 20, 2015, p. 1, https://www.amnestyusa.org/reports/circles-of-hell-domestic-public-and-state-violence-against-women-in-egypt/ (retrieved 12/28/17). For a detailed report, see https://www.amnestyusa.org/wp-content/uploads/2017/04/mde_120042015.pdf (retrieved 6/30/18).

94. U.S. Department of State, Bureau of Democracy and Labor, *Country Reports on Human Rights Practices for 2015: Egypt*, pp. 37–38.

95. Human Rights Watch, *World Report 2017: Egypt—Events of 2016*, p. 6.

96. Human Rights Watch, *World Report 2017: Egypt—Events of 2016*, p. 6.

97. Amnesty International, "Circles of Hell, Domestic, Public and State Violence against Women in Egypt," p. 1.

98. African [Banjul] Charter on Human and Peoples' Rights, p. 5.

99. International Covenant on Economic, Social and Cultural Rights, United Nations General Assembly Resolution 2200A, December 16, 1966, United Nations Office of the High Commissioner for Human Rights website, https://www.ohchr.org/en/professionalinterest/pages/cescr.aspx.

100. U.S. Department of State, Bureau of Democracy and Labor, *Country Reports on Human Rights Practices for 2015: Egypt*, p. 41.

101. S. Castello, "Female Genital Mutila-

tion/Cutting: Risk Management and Strategies for Social Workers and Health Care Professionals," *Risk Management and Health Care Policy*, 8 (2015), pp. 225–233.

102. Aisha N. Davis, "Female Genital Cutting: The Pressures of Culture, International Attention, and Domestic Law on the Role of African Women," Columbia Law School website, 2012, p. 3, http://blogs.law.columbia.edu/gslonline/files/2012/01/Davis-Female-Genital-Cutting.pdf.

103. Davis, "Female Genital Cutting: The Pressure of Culture, International Attention, and Domestic Law on the Role of African Women," p. 21.

104. K. Dalal, S. Lawoko, and B. Jansson, "Women's Attitudes towards Discontinuation of Remale Genital Mutilation in Egypt," *Journal of Inquiry & Violence Research*, 2, no. 1 (2010), p. 42.

105. Davis, "Female Genital Cutting: The Pressure of Culture, International Attention, and Domestic Law on the Role of African Women," p. 21.

106. G. Molleman and L. France, "The Struggle for Abandonment of Female Genital Mutilation/Cutting (FGM/C) in Egypt," *Global Health Promotion*, 16, no. 1 (2009), p. 59.

107. U.S. Department of State, Bureau of Democracy and Labor, *Country Reports on Human Rights Practices for 2015: Egypt*, p. 38.

108. U.S. Department of State, Bureau of Democracy and Labor, *Country Reports on Human Rights Practices for 2015: Egypt*, p. 38.

109. Human Rights Watch, "Egypt: New Penalties for Female Genital Mutilation—Further Reform Needed to Protect Girls," p. 1, https://www.hrw.org/news/2016/09/09/egypt-new-penalties-female-genital-mutilation (retrieved 12/31/17).

110. Human Rights Watch, "Egypt: New Penalties for Female Genital Mutilation—Further Reform Needed to Protect Girls," p. 1.

111. African [Banjul] Charter on Human and Peoples' Rights, p. 6.

112. International Covenant on Civil and Political Rights, p. 5.

113. Universal Declaration of Human Rights.

114. United Nations Children's Fund (UNICEF), "Fact Sheet: A Summary of the Rights under the Convention on the Rights of the Child," p. 1 (also reproduced in appendices), https://www.unicef.org/cre/files/Rights_Overview.pdf (retrieved 1/2/18).

115. Human Rights Watch, "Child Abuse in Egypt Requires Immediate Action," p. 1, https://sputniknews.com/middleast/201503041019042009/ (retrieved 1/5/18); U.S. Department of State, Bureau of Democracy and Labor, *Country Reports on Human Rights Practices for 2015: Egypt*, p. 42.

116. U.S. Department of State, Bureau of Democracy and Labor, *Country Reports on Human Rights Practices for 2015: Egypt*, p. 42.

117. Cited in U.S. Department of State, Bureau of Democracy and Labor, *Country Reports on Human Rights Practices for 2015: Egypt*, p. 42

118. U.S. Department of State, Bureau of Democracy and Labor, *Country Reports on Human Rights Practices for 2015: Egypt*, p. 43.

## *Chapter 3*

1. Helen C. Metz, *Libya: A Country Study*, 4th ed. (Washington DC: Federal Research Division, 1989), p. 4; Ronald Bruce St. John, *Libya: From Colony to Revolution* (Oxford: One World Publication, 2011), pp. 2–3.

2. St. John, *Libya: From Colony to Revolution*, p. 3.

3. St. John, *Libya: From Colony to Revolution*, p. 3.

4. Metz, *Libya: A Country Study*, pp. 4–5.

5. Mahmoud, *The Land of the People of Egypt*, p. 22–23.

6. Peter Malcolm et al., *Cultures of the World: Libya*, 3rd ed. (New York: Cavendish Square Publishing, 2016), p. 25.

7. Charles H. Cutter, *The World Today Series: Africa 2003*, 38th ed. (Harpers Ferry, WV: Stryker-Post Publications, 2003), p. 288; Malcolm et al., *Cultures of the World: Libya*, p. 25.

8. Metz, *Libya: A Country Study*, p. 5; St. John, *Libya: From Colony to Revolution*, p. 4; Cutter, *The World Today Series: Africa 2003*, p. 288.

9. Metz, *Libya: A Country Study*, p. 5; St. John, *Libya: From Colony to Revolution*, pp. 4–5.

10. Metz, *Libya: A Country Study*, pp.

6–7; St. John, *Libya: From Colony to Revolution*, pp. 6–13.

11. Metz, *Libya: A Country Study*, pp. 6–7; St. John, *Libya: From Colony to Revolution*, pp. 12–13; Malcolm et al., *Cultures of the World: Libya*, p. 27.

12. Metz, *Libya: A Country Study*, pp. 7–8.

13. Metz, *Libya: A Country Study*, pp. 7–8.

14. St. John, *Libya: From Colony to Revolution*, pp. 18–19; Metz, *Libya: A Country Study*, pp. 10–11; Malcolm et al., *Cultures of the World: Libya*, p. 28.

15. Metz, *Libya: A Country Study*, p. 12.

16. St. John, *Libya: From Colony to Revolution*, p. 19.

17. Malcolm et al., *Cultures of the World: Libya*, pp. 28–29; St. John, *Libya: From Colony to Revolution*, pp. 29–33.

18. St. John, *Libya: From Colony to Revolution*, pp. 34–35, 42–47.

19. Dirk Vandewalle, *A History of Modern Libya*, 2nd ed. (New York: Cambridge University Press, 2006), pp. 24–42; St. John, *Libya: From Colony to Revolution*, p. 57.

20. John H. Wellington, *South West Africa and Its Human Issues* (Oxford: Oxford University Press, 1967), pp. 204–224; Horst Drechsler, *The Struggle of the Herrero and Nama against German Imperialism, 1884–1915* (London: Zed Press, 1980), p. 143; E. Ike Udogu, *Liberating Namibia: The Long Diplomatic Struggle between the United Nations and South Africa* (Jefferson, NC: McFarland, 2012), pp. 24–25.

21. Malcolm et al., *Cultures of the World*, pp. 29–30.

22. Vandewalle, *A History of Modern Libya*, p. 39.

23. St. John, *Libya: From Colony to Revolution*, pp. 84–85; Metz, *Libya: A Country Study*, pp. 33–34, 37–39; Malcolm et al., *Cultures of the World: Libya*, p. 30.

24. Metz, *Libya: A Country Study*, pp. 37–38.

25. Malcolm et al., *Cultures of the World: Libya*, p. 30; Metz, *Libya: A Country Study*, p. 38.

26. Metz, *Libya: A Country Study*, pp. 41–42; Vandewalle, *A History of Modern Libya*, 78–79; Ahmida, *Forgotten Voices: Power and Agency in Colonial and Postcolonial Libya*, p. 78; Arthur Wayne Edge, *Global Studies: Africa*, 11th ed. (Dubuque, IA: McGraw-Hill/Dushkin, 2006), p. 129.

27. "Libya: Country Profile," *BBC News*, https://www.bbc.com/news/world-africa-13754897 (retrieved 1/3/18).

28. U.S. Department of State, Bureau of Democracy and Labor, *Country Reports on Human Rights Practices for 2015: Libya*, pp. 1–2, https://www.state.gov/documents/organization/253149.pdf (retrieved 1/15/18).

29. U.S. Department of State, Bureau of Democracy and Labor, *Country Reports on Human Rights Practices for 2015: Libya*, p. 2.

30. U.S. Department of State, Bureau of Democracy and Labor, *Country Reports on Human Rights Practices for 2015: Libya*, pp. 2–4.

31. African [Banjul] Charter on Human and Peoples' Rights, adopted June 27, 1981, OAU Doc. CAB/LEG/67/3 rev. 5, 21 I.L.M (1982), entered into force October 21, 1986, p. 3.

32. International Covenant on Civil and Political Rights, United Nations General Assembly Resolution 2200A, December 16, 1966, United Nations Office of the High Commissioner for Human Rights website, www.ohchr.org/EN/ProfessionalInterest/Pages/CCPR.aspx (retrieved 6/20/17).

33. Convention against Torture and Other Cruel, Inhuman or Degrading Treatment or Punishment, General Assembly Resolution 39/46, December 10, 1984, United Nations, Human Rights: Office of the High Commissioner website, www.ohchr.org/EN/ProfessionalInterest/Pages/CAT.aspx (retrieved 1/15/18).

34. Human Rights Watch, "Libya: Widespread Torture in Detention—Government Should End Arbitrary Detentions, Ill-Treatment in Eastern Libya," p. 1, https://www.hrw.org/news/2015/06/17/libya-widespread-torture-detention (retrieved 1/17/18).

35. Human Rights Watch, "Libya: Widespread Torture in Detention—Government Should End Arbitrary Detentions, Ill-Treatment in Eastern Libya," pp. 1–2.

36. Human Rights Watch, "Libya: Widespread Torture in Detention—Government Should End Arbitrary Detentions, Ill-Treatment in Eastern Libya," p. 3.

37. Human Rights Watch, "Libya: Widespread Torture in Detention—Government Should End Arbitrary Detentions, Ill-Treatment in Eastern Libya," p. 3.

38. U.S. Department of State, Bureau of Democracy and Labor, *Country Reports*

*on Human Rights Practices for 2015: Libya,* p. 5.

39. United Nations Support Mission in Libya (UNSMIL), *Report on the Human Rights Situation in Libya* (Geneva, Switzerland: Office of the United Nations High Commissioner for Human Rights, 2015), p. 19.

40. UNSMIL, *Report on the Human Rights Situation in Libya,* p. 19.

41. UNSMIL, *Report on the Human Rights Situation in Libya,* pp. 20–21.

42. Human Rights Watch, "The Endless Wait: Long-term Arbitrary Detentions and Torture in Western Libya," December 2, 2015, pp. 9–20, https://www.hrw.org/report/2015/12/02/endless-wait/long-term-arbitrary-detentions-and-torture-western-libya (retrieved 1/17/18).

43. Human Rights Watch, "Libya: Long-Term Arbitrary Detentions: Widespread Arbitrary Detention May Constitute Crimes against Humanity," p. 2, https://www.hrw.org/news/2015/12/02/libya-long-term-arbitrary-detentions (retrieved 1/17/18); Human Rights Watch, "The Endless Wait: Long-Term Arbitrary Detentions and Torture in Western Libya," pp. 9–13.

44. Human Rights Watch, "Libya: Widespread Torture in Detention"; "Libya: Long-Term Arbitrary Detentions: Widespread Arbitrary Detention May Constitute Crimes Against Humanity," pp. 2–4; U.S. Department of State, Bureau of Democracy and Labor, *Country Reports on Human Rights Practices for 2015: Libya,* p. 8.

45. Human Rights Watch, "Libya: Widespread Torture in Detention"; "Libya: Long-Term Arbitrary Detentions: Widespread Arbitrary Detention May Constitute Crimes against Humanity," pp. 5–6; U.S. Department of State, Bureau of Democracy and Labor, *Country Reports on Human Rights Practices for 2015: Libya,* pp. 9–14.

46. Human Rights Watch, "Libya: Widespread Torture in Detention"; "Libya: Long-Term Arbitrary Detentions: Widespread Arbitrary Detention May Constitute Crimes against Humanity," p. 6.

47. Human Rights Watch, "Libya: Widespread Torture in Detention"; "Libya: Long-Term Arbitrary Detentions: Widespread Arbitrary Detention May Constitute Crimes against Humanity," pp. 7–8.

48. UNSMIL, *Report on the Human Rights Situation in Libya,* pp. 17–19.

49. Human Rights Watch, "Libya: Widespread Torture in Detention—Government Should End Arbitrary Detentions, Ill-Treatment in Eastern Libya," p. 12.

50. UNSMIL, *Report on the Human Rights Situation in Libya,* pp. 5–7; International Court of Justice, "Case Concerning Military and Paramilitary Activities in and against Nicaragua (Nicaragua V. United States of America)," *I. C. J Reports,* 1986, p. 14.

51. Human Rights Watch, "Libya: Widespread Torture in Detention—Government Should End Arbitrary Detentions, Ill-Treatment in Eastern Libya," pp. 13–14.

52. U.S. Department of State, Bureau of Democracy, Human Rights, and Labor, *Libya 2015 International Religious Freedom Report,* p. 1, https://2009-2017.state.gov/j/drl/rls/irf/religiousfreedom/index.htm?year=2015&dlid=256279.

53. U.S. Department of State, Bureau of Democracy, Human Rights, and Labor, *Libya 2015 International Religious Freedom Report,* p. 2.

54. U.S. Department of State, Bureau of Democracy, Human Rights, and Labor, *Libya 2015 International Religious Freedom Report,* p. 5.

55. Convention on the Elimination of all Forms of Discrimination against Women, United Nations General Assembly Resolution 34/180, December 18, 1979, United Nations Office of the High Commissioner for Human Rights website, https://www.ohchr.org/en/professionalinterest/pages/cedaw.aspx.

56. See "The Great Green Charter of Human Rights in the Jamahiriya Era," June 12, 1988, https://www.ilo.org/dyn/natlex/docs/SERIAL/57641/65910/.../LBY57641.PDF (retrieved 1/26/2018).

57. Alison Pargeter, "Women's Rights in the Middle East and North Africa—Libya" in Sanja Kelly and Julia Breslin, eds., *Women's Rights in the Middle East and North Africa: Progress amid Resistance* (New York: Freedom House; Lanham, MD: Rowman & Littlefield, 2010); Alison Pargeter, "Women's Rights in the Middle East and North Africa—Libya, 2005," (New York: Freedom House, 2005), p. 3, http://www.refworld.org/docid/47387b6dc.html (retrieved 1/27/18).

58. Declaration on the Establishment of the Authority of the People, March 2, 1977, https://www.ilo.org/dyn/travail/docs/1528/CONSTITUTION.pdf (retrieved 1/26/18).

59. UN Development Programme (UNDP), *Promotion of Opportunities for Women's Eco-*

*nomic Empowerment* (New York: UNDP, September 2007), http://www.undp-libya.org/gender/POWER.pdf (retrieved 1/27/18); Pargeter, "Women's Rights in the Middle East and North Africa—Libya," (2010), p. 4.

60. Pargeter, "Women's Rights in the Middle East and North Africa—Libya," (2010), p. 4.

61. Pargeter, "Women's Rights in the Middle East and North Africa—Libya," (2010), pp. 5–6.

62. Global Hand, "Al Wafa Association for Human Services," http://www.globalhand.org/data/organization.2006-01-04.8236084563/, (retrieved 1/28/18).

63. Pargeter, "Women's Rights in the Middle East and North Africa—Libya," (2010), p. 4.

64. Pargeter, "Women's Rights in the Middle East and North Africa—Libya," (2010), p. 9.

65. Human Rights Watch, "EU-Libya Relations: Human Rights Conditions Required," memorandum, January 3, 2008, https://www.hrw.org/news/2008/01/03/eu-libya-relations.

66. Pargeter, "Women's Rights in the Middle East and North Africa—Libya," (2010), p. 16.

67. Pargeter, "Women's Rights in the Middle East and North Africa—Libya," (2010), pp. 15–17.

68. Pargeter, "Women's Rights in the Middle East and North Africa—Libya," (2010), pp. 19–23.

69. International Convention on the Elimination of All Forms of Racial Discrimination, United Nations General Assembly Resolution 2106 (XX), December 21, 1965 (Geneva, Switzerland: Office of the High Commissioner, 1966), https://www.ohchr.org/EN/ProfessionalInterest/Pages/CERD.aspx (retrieved 2/1/18).

70. International Convention on the Elimination of All Forms of Racial Discrimination, Article 2 (1–2).

71. International Convention on the Elimination of All Forms of Racial Discrimination, Article 5 (a-e).

72. U.K. Home Office, *Country Information and Guidance Libya: Ethnic Minority Groups* (June 2016), p. 4, https://www.gov.uk/government/uploads/attachment_data/file/566171/libya__ethnic_minority=groups.pdf (retrieved 2/2/18).

73. U.K. Home Office, *Country Informa-tion and Guidance Libya: Ethnic Minority Groups*, pp. 8–9.

74. U.S. Department of State, Bureau of Democracy and Labor, *Country Reports on Human Rights Practices for 2015: Libya*, p. 28; U.K. Home Office, *Country Information and Guidance Libya: Ethnic Minority Groups*, p. 9.

75. Fred Abrahams, "Why Have We Forgotten about Libya?" Human Rights Watch, March 25, 2013, https://www.hrw.org/news/2013/03/25/why-have-we-forgotten-about-libya (retrieved 2/2/18).

76. Human Rights Investigations, "Ethnic Cleansing, Genocide and the Tawergha," p. 2, https://humanrightsinvestigations.org/2011/09/26/libya-ethnic-cleansing-tawargha-genocide (retrieved 2/2/18).

77. Human Rights Investigations, "Ethnic Cleansing, Genocide and the Tawergha," p. 1.

78. Human Rights Investigations, "Ethnic Cleansing, Genocide and the Tawergha," p. 2.

79. Don Cheadle, Sophie Okonedo, Nick Nolte, *Hotel Rwanda*, DVD (2005).

80. Human Rights Investigations, "Ethnic Cleansing, Genocide and the Tawergha," p. 3; U.K. Home Office, *Country Information and Guidance Libya: Ethnic Minority Groups*, pp. 10–11.

81. Human Rights Watch, *World Report 2016: Libya—Events of 2015* (New York: Human Rights Watch, 2016) , https://www.hrw.org/world-report/2016/country-chapters/libya (retrieved 2/3/18).

82. UN Human Rights Council, "Investigation by the Office of the United Nations High Commissioner for Human Rights on Libya: Detailed Findings," February 15, 2016, A/HRC/31/CRP.3, http://www.refworld.org/docid/56d00d0f4.html (retrieved 2/3/18).

83. U.S. Department of State, Bureau of Democracy and Labor, *Country Reports on Human Rights Practices for 2015: Libya*, p. 14.

84. UNSMIL, *Report on the Human Rights Situation in Libya*, pp. 25–27.

85. UNSMIL, *Report on the Human Rights Situation in Libya*, p. 25.

86. UNSMIL, *Report on the Human Rights Situation in Libya*, p. 25.

87. UNSMIL, *Report on the Human Rights Situation in Libya*, pp. 26–27.

88. UNSMIL, *Report on the Human Rights Situation in Libya*, p. 27.

## Chapter 4

1. Moshe Gershovich, *French Military Rule in Morocco: Colonialism and Its Consequences* (London: Frank Cass, 2000), p. 40.

2. Pat Seward, Orin Hargraves, and Ruth Bjorklund, *Cultures of the World: Morocco* (New York: Cavendish Square Publishing, 2016), p. 22; Harold D. Nelson, *Morocco: A Country Study*, 3rd ed. (Washington, DC: Government Printing Office [GPO], 1985), p. 4.

3. Charles H. Cutter, *The World Today Series: Africa 2003*, 38th ed. (Harpers Ferry, WV: Stryker-Post Publications, 2003), p. 300; Nelson, *Morocco: A Country Study*, p. 8.

4. Nelson, *Morocco: A Country Study*, pp. 8–9.

5. Arthur Wayne Edge, *Global Studies: Africa*, 11th ed. (Dubuque, IA: McGraw-Hill/Dushkin, 2006), p. 136.

6. Edge, *Global Studies: Africa*, p. 136.

7. Nelson, *Morocco: A Country Study*, pp. 15–23; Edge, *Global Studies: Africa*, p. 136.

8. Nelson, *Morocco: A Country Study*, pp. 15–19; see also Edge, *Global Studies: Africa*, p. 136; Seward, Hargraves, and Bjorklund, *Cultures of the World: Morocco*, p. 24.

9. Nelson, *Morocco: A Country Study*, pp. 18–19; Edge, *Global Studies: Africa*, p. 136; Seward, Hargraves, and Bjorklund, *Cultures of the World: Morocco*, p. 24.

10. Nelson, *Morocco: A Country Study*, p. 19.

11. Nelson, *Morocco: A Country Study*, p. 20.

12. Edge, *Global Studies: Africa*, p. 136.

13. Nelson, *Morocco: A Country Study*, p. 20.

14. Seward, Hargraves, and Bjorklund, *Cultures of the World: Morocco*, p. 24; Nelson, *Morocco: A Country Study*, pp. 23–27; Gershovich, *French Military Rule in Morocco: Colonialism and Its Consequences*, p. 41.

15. Douglas Porch, *The Conquest of Morocco: The Bizarre History of France's Last Great Colonial Adventure, the Long Struggle to Subdue a Medieval Kingdom by Intrigue and Force of Arms, 1903–1914* (New York: Alfred A. Knopf, Inc., 1982), p. 9; Cutter, *The World Today Series: Africa 2003*, p. 301; Gershovich, *French Military Rule in Morocco: Colonialism and Its Consequences*, pp. 49–57; Seward, Hargraves, and Bjorklund, *Cultures of the World: Morocco*, pp. 26–28; Nelson, *Morocco: A Country Study*, pp. 44–52.

16. Seward, Hargraves, and Bjorklund, *Cultures of the World: Morocco*, p. 27; Nelson, *Morocco: A Country Study*, p. 43–44.

17. Nelson, *Morocco: A Country Study*, pp. 45–49.

18. Seward, Hargraves, and Bjorklund, *Cultures of the World: Morocco*, p. 28; Cutter, *The World Today Series: Africa 2003*, p. 301; Edge, *Global Studies: Africa*, p. 137.

19. U.S. Department of State, Bureau of Democracy and Labor, *Country Reports on Human Rights Practices for 2015: Morocco*, p. 1, https://2009-2017.state.gov/j/drl/rls/hrrpt/humanrightsreport//index.htm - wrapper.

20. Amnesty International, "Morocco/Western Sahara: Torture Allegations Cast Shadow over Trial," July 17, 2017, p. 2, https://www.amnesty.org/en/latest/news/2017/07/moroccowestern-saharatorture-allegations-cast-shadow-over-trial/ (retrieved 2/9/18).

21. U.S. Department of State, Bureau of Democracy and Labor, *Country Reports on Human Rights Practices for 2015: Morocco*, pp. 2–3.

22. Amnesty International, *Shadow of Impunity: Torture in Morocco and Western Sahara* (London: Amnesty International, 2015), p. 6; Aida Alami, "Torture Still Widely Used in Morocco, Amnesty International Says," *New York Times*, May 19, 2015, https://www.nytimes.com/2015/05/20/world/africa/torture-still-widely-used-in-morocco-amnesty-international-says.html (retrieved 2/9/18).

23. Amnesty International, *Shadow of Impunity: Torture in Morocco and Western Sahara*, p. 7.

24. International Covenant on Civil and Political Rights, United Nations General Assembly Resolution 2200A, December 16, 1966, United Nations Office of the High Commissioner for Human Rights website, www.ohchr.org/EN/ProfessionalInterest/Pages/CCPR.aspx (retrieved 2/10/18).

25. African [Banjul] Charter on Human and Peoples' Rights, adopted June 27, 1981, OAU Doc. CAB/LEG/67/3 rev. 5, 21 I.L.M (1982), entered into force October 21, 1986, p. 3.

26. Amnesty International, *Shadow of Impunity: Torture in Morocco and Western Sahara*, pp. 16–86.

27. Amnesty International, *Shadow of Impunity: Torture in Morocco and Western Sahara*, p. 7.

28. U.S. Department of State, Bureau of Democracy and Labor, *Country Reports on Human Rights Practices for 2015: Morocco*, p. 3; Amnesty International, *Shadow of Impunity: Torture in Morocco and Western Sahara*, p. 8.

29. U.S. Department of State, Bureau of Democracy and Labor, *Country Reports on Human Rights Practices for 2015: Morocco*, p. 3.

30. Juan E. Mendez, *Addendum, Mission to Morocco: Report of the Special Rapporteur on Torture and Other Cruel, Inhuman or Degrading Treatment or Punishment*, UN Doc. A/HRC/22/53/Add. 2 (2013), par. 23.

31. Amnesty International, *RE: Morocco/Western Sahara—List of Issues* (London: Amnesty International Secretariat, 2015), p. 3; see also Human Rights Committee, Concluding Observations on Morocco, CCPR/CO/82/MAR, December 2004, par. 16.

32. Amnesty International, *RE: Morocco/Western Sahara—List of Issues*, p. 3.

33. Amnesty International, "Morocco: Dozens Arrested over Mass Protests in RIF Report Torture in Custody," p. 2.

34. Amnesty International, *Shadow of Impunity: Torture in Morocco and Western Sahara*, p. 77.

35. International Covenant on Civil and Political Rights, p. 4.

36. African [Banjul] Charter on Human and Peoples' Rights, p. 7.

37. United Nations General Assembly, Resolution 217A, December 10, 1948, The Universal Declaration of Human Rights, www.un.org/en/universal-declaration-human-rights (retrieved 2/20/17).

38. Doug Bandow, "Morocco: The Limits of Islamic Religious Tolerance" (Washington, DC: Cato Institute, July 8, 2010) p. 1, https://www.cato.org/publications/commentary/morocco-limits-islamic-religious-tolerance (retrieved 2/15/18).

39. U.S. Department of State, Bureau of Democracy, Human Rights, and Labor, *Morocco 2015 International Religious Freedom Report*, p. 2, https://2009-2017.state.gov/j/drl/rls/irf/religiousfreedom/index.htm - wrapper.

40. U.S. Department of State, Bureau of Democracy, Human Rights, and Labor, *Morocco 2015 International Religious Freedom Report*, p. 3.

41. Bandow, "Morocco: The Limits of Islamic Religious Tolerance," p. 2.

42. U.S. Department of State, Bureau of Democracy, Human Rights, and Labor, *Morocco 2015 International Religious Freedom Report*, p. 4.

43. Kacie Graves, "Christians in Morocco: A Crisis of Faith—Forced to Worship in Secret, Moroccan Christians Struggle to Practice Their Religion," *U.S. News & World Report*, September 30, 2015, p. 3, https://www.usnews.com/news/articles/2015/09/30/christians-in-morocco-a-crisis-faith (retrieved 2/16/18).

44. Graves, "Christians in Morocco: A Crisis of Faith—Forced to Worship in Secret, Moroccan Christians Struggle to Practice Their Religion," p. 3; Bandow, "Morocco: The Limits of Islamic Religious Tolerance," pp. 3–5.

45. U.S. Department of State, Bureau of Democracy, Human Rights, and Labor, *Morocco 2015 International Religious Freedom Report*, p. 5.

46. Bandow, "Morocco: The Limits of Islamic Religious Tolerance," p. 3.

47. U.S. Department of State, Bureau of Democracy, Human Rights, and Labor, *Morocco 2015 International Religious Freedom Report*, p. 6.

48. U.S. Department of State, Bureau of Democracy, Human Rights, and Labor, *Morocco 2015 International Religious Freedom Report*, pp. 7–10.

49. Universal Declaration of Human Rights.

50. Morgan Lee, "Morocco Declaration: Muslim Nations Should Protect Christians from Persecution," *Christianity Today*, January 27, 2016, pp. 1, 3, https://www.christianitytoday.com/news/2016/january/marrakesh-declaration-muslim-nations-christian-persecution.html (retrieved 2/16/18).

51. Lee, "Morocco Declaration: Muslim Nations Should Protect Christians from Persecution," pp. 1–3.

52. Fatima Sadiqi, "Morocco," in Sanja Kelly and Julia Breslin, eds., *Women's Rights in the Middle East and North Africa: Progress amid Resistance* (New York: Freedom House; Lanham, MD: Rowman & Littlefield, 2010), p. 1, https://freedomhouse.org/sites/default/files/inline_images/morocco/.pdf (retrieved 2/20/18).

53. Sadiqi, "Morocco," p. 1.

54. Mounira M. Charrad, *Family Law Reforms in the Arab World: Tunisia and*

*Morocco* (Report of the United Nations Department of Economics and Social Affairs, Division for Social Policy and Development, Expert Group Meeting, New York, May 15–17, 2012), p. 7.

55. Charrad, *Family Law Reforms in the Arab World: Tunisia and Morocco*, p. 7; Mounira M. Charrad, *States and Women's Rights: The Making of Postcolonial Tunisia, Algeria and Morocco* (Berkeley: University of California Press, 2001), p. 28.

56. *Gender Equality and Parity in Morocco: Preserving and Implementing the Aims and Objectives of the Constitution* (Morocco: National Human Rights Council, July 2015), pp. 1–12, https://www.cndh.ma/sites/default/files/cndh_-_r.e_-_web_parite_egalite_uk_-.pdf (retrieved 2/ 21/18).

57. Women's UN Report Network (WUNRN), *Morocco—Human Rights—Women's Rights—Gender Equality Report—Rights of Religious Minorities*, February 8, 2016, p. 2, https://wunrn.com/2016/02/morocco-human-rights-womens-rights-gender-equality-report-rights-of-religious-minorities (retrieved 2/21/18).

58. Convention on the Elimination of all Forms of Discrimination against Women, United Nations General Assembly Resolution 34/180, December 18, 1979, United Nations Office of the High Commissioner for Human Rights website, p. 2, https://www.ohchr.org/en/professionalinterest/pages/cedaw.aspx.

59. Convention on the Elimination of All Forms of Discrimination against Women, p. 3; *Gender Equality and Parity in Morocco: Preserving and Implementing the Aims and Objectives of the Constitution*, p. 1.

60. WUNRN, *Morocco—Human Rights—Women's Rights—Gender Equality Report—Rights of Religious Minorities*, p. 4.

61. *Gender Equality and Parity in Morocco: Preserving and Implementing the Aims and Objectives of the Constitution*, p. 1.

62. Charrad, *Family Law Reforms in the Arab World: Tunisia and Morocco*, p. 7; *Gender Equality and Parity in Morocco: Preserving and Implementing the Aims and Objectives of the Constitution*, p. 2.

63. Universal Declaration of Human Rights, p. 4.

64. Convention on the Elimination of All Forms of Discrimination against Women, p. 6.

65. *Gender Equality and Parity in Morocco: Preserving and Implementing the Aims and Objectives of the Constitution*, p. 2.

66. *The Qur'an*, translated by M. A. S. Abdel Haleem (New York: Oxford University Press, 2004), p. 51.

67. Sadiqi, "Morocco," pp. 11–12.

68. *Gender Equality and Parity in Morocco: Preserving and Implementing the Aims and Objectives of the Constitution*, p. 4.

69. U.S. Department of State, Bureau of Democracy and Labor, *Country Reports on Human Rights Practices for 2015: Morocco*, p. 26.

70. U.S. Department of State, Bureau of Democracy and Labor, *Country Reports on Human Rights Practices for 2015: Morocco*, p. 26.

71. U.S. Department of State, Bureau of Democracy and Labor, *Country Reports on Human Rights Practices for 2015: Morocco*, pp. 28, 30.

72. *Gender Equality and Parity in Morocco: Preserving and Implementing the Aims and Objectives of the Constitution*, pp. 6–7.

73. *Gender Equality and Parity in Morocco: Preserving and Implementing the Aims and Objectives of the Constitution*, pp. 5–6.

74. U.S. Department of State, Bureau of Democracy and Labor, *Country Reports on Human Rights Practices for 2015: Morocco*, p. 29.

75. U.S. Department of State, Bureau of Democracy and Labor, *Country Reports on Human Rights Practices for 2015: Morocco*, p. 29.

76. U.S. Department of State, Bureau of Democracy and Labor, *Country Reports on Human Rights Practices for 2015: Morocco*, pp. 29–30.

77. U.S. Department of State, Bureau of Democracy and Labor, *Country Reports on Human Rights Practices for 2015: Morocco*, pp. 13–14.

78. Human Rights Watch, "The Red Lines Stay Red: Morocco's Reforms of Its Speech Laws—Background: The Press Law and the Penal Code," May 4, 2017, p. 8, https://www.hrw.org/report/2017/05/04/red-lines-stay-red/moroccos-reforms-its-speech-laws (retrieved 2/27/18).

79. Universal Declaration of Human Rights, p. 5.

80. International Covenant on Civil and Political Rights, p. 5.

81. Human Rights Watch, "The Red Lines Stay Red: Morocco's Reforms of Its Speech Laws—Background: The Press Law and the Penal Code," p. 9.

82. Human Rights Watch, "The Red Lines Stay Red: Morocco's Reforms of Its Speech Laws—Background: The Press Law and the Penal Code," p. 9.

83. Human Rights Watch, "The Red Lines Stay Red: Morocco's Reforms of Its Speech Laws," pp. 1–26.

84. U.S. Department of State, Bureau of Democracy and Labor, *Country Reports on Human Rights Practices for 2015: Morocco,* p. 14.

85. U.S. Department of State, Bureau of Democracy and Labor, *Country Reports on Human Rights Practices for 2015: Morocco,* p. 14.

86. U.S. Department of State, Bureau of Democracy and Labor, *Country Reports on Human Rights Practices for 2015: Morocco,* pp. 15–16.

87. U.S. Department of State, Bureau of Democracy and Labor, *Country Reports on Human Rights Practices for 2015: Morocco,* pp. 32–33.

88. Robert F. Kennedy Human Rights, "Western Sahara: Human Rights Violations Reported between January 1, 2015 and June 30, 2015," July 1, 2015, p. 1, https://rfkhumanrights.org/news/western-sahara-human-rights-violations-reported-between-january-1-2015-and-june-30-2015 (retrieved 2/28/18).

89. Robert F. Kennedy Human Rights, "Western Sahara: Human Rights Violations Reported between January 1, 2015 and June 30, 2015," pp. 1–16.

90. Robert F. Kennedy Human Rights, "Western Sahara: Human Rights Violations Reported between January 1, 2015 and June 30, 2015," pp. 1–2.

91. E. Ike Udogu, *Examining Human Rights Issues and the Democracy Project in Sub-Saharan Africa: A Theoretical Critique and Prospects for Progress in the Millennium* (Lanham, MD: Lexington Books, 2014), p. 32.

92. U.S. Department of State, Bureau of Democracy and Labor, *Country Reports on Human Rights Practices for 2015: Morocco,* p. 33.

93. Universal Declaration of Human Rights, p. 3.

94. U.S. Department of State, Bureau of Democracy and Labor, *Country Reports on Human Rights Practices for 2015: Morocco,* p. 33.

95. U.S. Department of State, Bureau of Democracy and Labor, *Country Reports on Human Rights Practices for 2015: Morocco,* p. 24.

96. U.S. Department of State, Bureau of Democracy and Labor, *Country Reports on Human Rights Practices for 2015: Morocco,* pp. 24–26.

## *Chapter 5*

1. Rosalind Varghese Brown, *Cultures of the World: Tunisia* (New York: Marshall Cavendish, 1993), p. 23; Richard Miles, *Carthage Must Be Destroyed: The Rise and Fall of an Ancient Civilization* (New York: Viking, 2010) pp. 59–95; Serge Lancel, *Carthage: A History* (Oxford: Blackwell, 1995), pp. 35–45; Andrew Borowiec, *Modern Tunisia: A Democratic Apprenticeship* (Westport, CT: Praeger Publishers, 1998), pp. 11–13; Arthur Wayne Edge, *Global Studies: Africa,* 11th ed. (Dubuque, IA: McGraw-Hill/Dushkin, 2006), p.142; Gerhard Herm, *The Phoenicians: The Purple Empire of the Ancient World* (New York: William Morrow and Company, Inc., 1975), pp. 181–195; 196–214; John Anthony, *Tunisia: A Personal View of a Timeless Land* (New York: Charles Scribner's Sons, 1961), pp. 68–79.

2. Robert Rinehart, "Historical Setting," in Harold D. Nelson, ed., *Tunisia: A Country Study,* 5th ed. (Washington, DC: Government Printing Office [GPO], 1988), p. 5.

3. Brown, *Cultures of the World: Tunisia,* pp. 23–25; Rinehart, "Historical Setting," pp. 6, 8; Herm, *The Phoenicians: The Purple Empire of the Ancient World,* pp. 236–245.

4. Brown, *Cultures of the World: Tunisia,* pp. 23, 26–27; Rinehart, "Historical Setting," p. 11.

5. Rinehart, "Historical Setting," pp. 12–14.

6. Brown, *Cultures of the World: Tunisia,* pp. 28–31.

7. Rinehart, "Historical Setting," p. 21; Brown, *Cultures of the World: Tunisia,* p. 32.

8. Brown, *Cultures of the World: Tunisia,* p. 33.

9. Rinehart, "Historical Setting," pp. 21–30; Brown, *Cultures of the World: Tunisia.*

10. Edge, *Global Studies: Africa*, p. 143.

11. Edge, *Global Studies: Africa*, p. 143.

12. Rinehart, "Historical Setting," p. 31; Brown, *Cultures of the World: Tunisia*, p. 36.

13. Rinehart, "Historical Setting," p. 31.

14. Rinehart, "Historical Setting," p. 32.

15. Brown, *Cultures of the World: Tunisia*, p. 36.

16. Kenneth J. Perkins, *A History of Modern Tunisia* (New York: Cambridge University Press, 2004), pp. 79–89.

17. Rinehart, "Historical Setting," p. 39; Brown, *Cultures of the World: Tunisia*, p. 38.

18. Rinehart, "Historical Setting," p. 41.

19. Rinehart, "Historical Setting," pp. 48–50; Borowiec, *Modern Tunisia: A Democratic Apprenticeship*, pp. 20–22.

20. Brown, *Cultures of the World: Tunisia*, p. 39.

21. Rinehart, "Historical Settings," pp. 48–52; Brown, *Cultures of the World: Tunisia*, pp. 38–39; Edge, *Global Studies: Africa*, p. 143; Charles H. Cutter, *The World Today Series: Africa 2003*, 38th ed. (Harpers Ferry, WV: Stryker-Post Publications, 2003), p. 309.

22. Convention against Torture and Other Cruel, Inhuman or Degrading Treatment or Punishment, General Assembly Resolution 39/46, December 10, 1984, United Nations Office of the High Commissioner for Human Rights website, www.ohchr.org/EN/ProfessionalInterest/Pages/CAT.aspx (retrieved 3/6/18).

23. International Covenant on Civil and Political Rights, United Nations General Assembly Resolution 2200A, December 16, 1966, United Nations Office of the High Commissioner for Human Rights website, www.ohchr.org/EN/ProfessionalInterest/Pages/CCPR.aspx (retrieved 3/6/18).

24. Juan E. Mendez, *Report of the Special Rapporteur on Torture and Other Cruel, Inhuman or Degrading Treatment or Punishment: Tunisia*, United Nations General Assembly: Human Rights Council, nineteenth session, agenda item 3, UN Doc. A/HRC/19/61/Add.1, p. 5; see also "Tunisia Country Visit," Anti-Torture Initiative, May 15–22, 2011 (2012 Report in English), http://antitorture.org/tunisia-country-visit/ (retrieved 3/6/18).

25. Mendez, *Report of the Special Rapporteur on Torture and Other Cruel, Inhuman or Degrading Treatment or Punishment: Tunisia*, p. 7.

26. E. Ike Udogu, *Leadership and the Problem of Electoral Democracy in Africa: Case Studies and Theoretical Solutions* (Newcastle-upon-Tyne, UK: Cambridge Scholars Publishing, 2016), pp. 9, 88.

27. Mendez, *Report of the Special Rapporteur on Torture and Other Cruel, Inhuman or Degrading Treatment or Punishment: Tunisia*, pp. 7–8.

28. Mendez, *Report of the Special Rapporteur on Torture and Other Cruel, Inhuman or Degrading Treatment or Punishment: Tunisia*, pp. 9–10.

29. U.S. Department of State, Bureau of Democracy and Labor, *Country Reports on Human Rights Practices for 2015: Tunisia*, https://www.ecoi.net/en/document/1069032.html (retrieved 3/6/18).

30. Amnesty International, "Tunisia: Evidence of Torture and Deaths in Custody Suggest Human Rights Gains of the Uprising Are Sliding into Reverse Gear," January 13, 2016, p. 2, https://www.amnestyusa.org/press-releases/evidence-of-torture-and-deaths-in-custody-in-tunisia-suggest-human-rights-gains-of-the-uprising-are-sliding-into-reverse-gear/ (retrieved 3/7/18).

31. Amnesty International, "Tunisia: Evidence of Torture and Deaths in Custody Suggest Human Rights Gains of the Uprising Are Sliding into Reverse Gear."

32. "Torture in Tunisia: We Investigate Allegations That Despite Its New Democratic Institutions, Police Torture Continues in Tunisia," *Al Jazeera*, September 2, 2015, p. 1. https://www.aljazeera.com/programmes/peopleandpower/2015/09/torture-tunisia-150902130506308.html (Retrieved 3/7/18).

33. "Torture in Tunisia: We Investigate Allegations That Despite Its New Democratic Institutions, Police Torture Continues in Tunisia," pp. 2–3.

34. U.S. Department of State, Bureau of Democracy and Labor, *Country Reports on Human Rights Practices for 2015: Tunisia*, p. 3

35. African [Banjul] Charter on Human and Peoples' Rights, adopted June 27, 1981 (OAU Doc. CAB/LEG/67/3 rev. 5, 21 I.L.M 58 (1982), entered into force October 21, 1986), p. 3.

36. United Nations General Assembly, Resolution 217A, December 10, 1948, The Universal Declaration of Human Rights, www.un.org/en/universal-declaration-human-rights (retrieved 2/20/17), p. 3.

37. International Covenant on Civil and Political Rights.

38. U.S. Department of State, Bureau of Democracy and Labor, *Country Reports on Human Rights Practices for 2015: Tunisia*, pp. 1–2.

39. U.S. Department of State, Bureau of Democracy and Labor, *Country Reports on Human Rights Practices for 2015: Tunisia*, p. 2.

40. U.S. Department of State, Bureau of Democracy, Human Rights, and Labor, *Tunisia 2015 International Religious Freedom Report*, p. 1, https://www.ecoi.net/en/document/1158907.htlm (retrieved 3/7/18).

41. International Covenant on Civil and Political Rights.

42. African [Banjul] Charter on Human and Peoples' Rights, p. 4.

43. Universal Declaration of Human Rights, p. 5.

44. U.S. Department of State, Bureau of Democracy, Human Rights, and Labor, *Tunisia 2015 International Religious Freedom Report*, p. 2.

45. Larbi Sadiki, "Why Is Tunisia's Ennahda Ditching Political Islam?" *Al Jazeera*, May 24, 2016, https://www.aljazeera.com/news/2016/05/tunisia-ennahda-ditching-political-Islam-160524094550153.html (retrieved 3/13/18).

46. Alessandra Bocchi, "How Religiously Free Is the Arab World's Most Democratic Country?" *New Arab*, August 29, 2017, https://www.alaraby.co.uk/english/indepth/2017/8/29/lifting-the-veil-religious-freedom-in-tunisia (retrieved 3/13/18); see also "Christians in Tunisia: Cause for Concern," Qantara.de, pp. 1–3, http://www.en.qantara.de/content/christians-in-tunisia-cause-for-concern (retrieved 3/13/18).

47. Constitution of Tunisia, 2014, https://issafrica.org/ctafrica/uploads/tunisiaConstitution2014Eng.pdf (retrieved 3/13/18).

48. Anna Mahjar-Barducci, "Tunisia's Religious Persecution," Gatestone Institute website, April 20, 2012, p. 2, https://www.gatestoneinstitute.org/3025/tunisia-religious-persecution (retrieved 3/13/18).

49. Mahjar-Barducci, "Tunisia's Religious Persecution," p. 2.

50. Human Rights Watch, "Tunisia's Repressive Laws: The Reform Agenda," 2011, https://www.hrw.org/sites/default/files/reports/tunisia1111webwcover.pdf (retrieved

3/13/18); see also Mahjar-Barducci, "Tunisia's Religious Persecution," p. 2.

51. U.S. Department of State, Bureau of Democracy, Human Rights, and Labor, *Tunisia 2015 International Religious Freedom Report*, p. 2.

52. Bocchi, "How Religiously Free Is the Arab World's Most Democratic Country?" pp. 5–6.

53. Greg Botelho and Jethro Mullen, "ISIS Apparently Claims Responsibility for Tunisia Museum Attack; 9 Arrested," CNN, March 19, 2015.

54. U.S. Department of State, Bureau of Democracy, Human Rights, and Labor, *Tunisia 2015 International Religious Freedom Report*, p. 5.

55. U.S. Department of State, Bureau of Democracy, Human Rights, and Labor, *Tunisia 2015 International Religious Freedom Report*, p. 5.

56. U.S. Department of State, Bureau of Democracy, Human Rights, and Labor, *Tunisia 2015 International Religious Freedom Report*, pp. 5–6.

57. United Nations Children's Fund (UNICEF), "Tunisia: MENA Gender Equality Profile Status of Girls and Women in the Middle East and North Africa," 2011, p. 1, https://www.unicef.org/gender/files/Tunisia-Gender-equlity-profile-2011.pdf (retrieved 3/17/18); Mounira M. Charrad, *Family Law Reforms in the Arab World: Tunisia and Morocco* (Report of the United Nations Department of Economics and Social Affairs, Division for Social Policy and Development, Expert Group Meeting, New York, May 15–17, 2012), pp. 1–6.

58. Freedom House, "Women's Rights in the Middle East and North Africa 2010 Report," https://www.freedomhouse.org (retrieved 3/17/18).

59. Convention on the Elimination of all Forms of Discrimination against Women, United Nations General Assembly Resolution 34/180, December 18, 1979, United Nations Office of the High Commissioner for Human Rights website, pp. 3, 6–7, 9, https://www.ohchr.org/Documents/ProfessionalInterest/cedaw.pdf (retrieved 2/17/18); UNICEF, "Tunisia: MENA Gender Equality Profile Status of Girls and Women in the Middle East and North Africa," p. 1.

60. UNICEF, "Tunisia: MENA Gender Equality Profile Status of Girls and Women in the Middle East and North Africa," p. 1.

61. UNICEF, "Tunisia: MENA Gender Equality Profile Status of Girls and Women in the Middle East and North Africa," pp. 1–2.

62. UNICEF, "Tunisia: MENA Gender Equality Profile Status of Girls and Women in the Middle East and North Africa," p. 3.

63. Sanja Kelly and Julia Breslin, eds., *Women's Rights in the Middle East and North Africa: Progress amid Resistance* (New York: Freedom House; Lanham, MD: Rowman & Littlefield, 2010), p. 4; Charrad, *Family Law Reforms in the Arab World: Tunisia and Morocco*, p. 2.

64. Charrad, *Family Law Reforms in the Arab World: Tunisia and Morocco*, p. 2.

65. James Madison, https://www.brainyquote.com/quotes/james_madison_105473 (retrieved 3/17/18).

66. U.S. Department of State, Bureau of Democracy and Labor, *Country Reports on Human Rights Practices for 2015: Tunisia*, p. 16.

67. *The Holy Quran*, Sura 4:34.

68. U.S. Department of State, Bureau of Democracy and Labor, *Country Reports on Human Rights Practices for 2015: Tunisia*, p. 16.

69. U.S. Department of State, Bureau of Democracy and Labor, *Country Reports on Human Rights Practices for 2015: Tunisia*, pp. 17–18.

70. "Tunisia Women March for Same Inheritance Rights as Men," *Yahoo! News*, March 10, 2018, p. 2, https://www.yahoo.com/news/tunisia-women-march-same-inheritance-rights-men-191154831.html (retrieved 3/20/18).

71. "Tunisia Women March for Same Inheritance Rights as Men," p. 2

72. The Gideons International, *King James Bible* (The Gideons International; National Publishing Company, 1978), p. 1219; see also https://www.kingjamesbibleonline.org/Bible-verses-About-Husband-And-Wife/ (retrieved 3/21/18).

73. U.S. Department of State, Bureau of Democracy and Labor, *Country Reports on Human Rights Practices for 2015: Tunisia*, p. 18.

74. Universal Declaration of Human Rights, p. 6.

75. African [Banjul] Charter on Human and Peoples' Rights, p. 4.

76. International Covenant on Civil and Political Rights.

77. U.S. Department of State, Bureau of Democracy and Labor, *Country Reports on Human Rights Practices for 2015: Tunisia*, pp. 9–10.

78. Cairo Institute for Human Rights Studies, "Freedom of Expression in Egypt and Tunisia," May 2015, p. 1, https://www.cihrs.org/wp-content/uploads/2013/05/Freedom-of-Expression-in-Egypt-and-Tunisia.pdf (retrieved 2/22/18).

79. Amnesty International, "Tunisia: Attack on Freedom of Expression Must End," February 2, 2018, p. 1, https://www.amnesty.org/en/latest/news/2018/02/tunisia-attack-on-freedom-of-expression-must-end/.

80. Amnesty International, "Tunisia: Attack on Freedom of Expression Must End," pp. 1–2.

81. Eric Reidy, "Questioning Freedom of Speech in Tunisia,"Al Jazeera, January 30, 2015, pp. 1–4. https://www.aljazeera.com/news/2015/01/questioning-freedom-speech-tunisia-150126104509780.html (retrieved 3/23/18); U.S. Department of State, Bureau of Democracy and Labor, *Country Reports on Human Rights Practices for 2015: Tunisia*, p. 10.

82. U.S. Department of State, Bureau of Democracy and Labor, *Country Reports on Human Rights Practices for 2015: Tunisia*, p. 10.

83. U.S. Department of State, Bureau of Democracy and Labor, *Country Reports on Human Rights Practices for 2015: Tunisia*, p. 10.

84. E. Ike Udogu and Sambuddha Ghatak, eds., *Human Rights Dilemmas in the Developing World: The Case of Marginalized Populations at Risk* (Lanham, MD: Lexington Books, 2017).

85. Abu Amina Elias, "Faith in Allah: Islam Is against Racism and Prejudice," pp. 1–2, https://abuaminaelias.com/Islam-is-against-racism-and-bigotry/ (retrieved 4/5/18).

86. Universal Declaration of Human Rights, p. 2; International Covenant on Civil and Political Rights; African [Banjul] Charter on Human and Peoples' Rights, p. 2.

87. International Convention on the Elimination of All Forms of Racial Discrimination, United Nations General Assembly Resolution 2106 (XX), December 21, 1965 (Geneva, Switzerland: Office of the High Commissioner, 1966), https://www.ohchr.org/EN/ProfessionalInterest/Pages/CERD.aspx (retrieved 2/1/18).

88. Magdalena Mach, "Racism in Tunisia—Debate within the Tunisian Left" (Rosa Luxemburg Stiftung, North African Office, May 13, 2017), p. 2, https://www.rosaluxna.org/news/racism-in-tunisia-debate-within-the-tunisian-left-13-may-2017/ (retrieved 4/6/18).

89. Mach, "Racism in Tunisia—Debate within the Tunisian Left," p. 3; see Conor McCormick-Cavanagh, "Tunisia's Dark History of Racial Discrimination," New Arab, June 10, 2016, https://www.alaraby.co.uk/english/comment/2016/6/10/tunisia-dark-history-of-racial-discrimination (retrieved 4/7/18).

90. Eileen Byrne, "Black Citizens Say Racism Is Still an Issue in the New Tunisia," National (UAE), February 18, 2014, pp. 2–4, https://www.thenational.ae/world/black-citizens-say-racism-is-still-an-issue-in-the-new-tunisia-1.256661 (retrieved 4/5/18).

91. Udogu and Ghatak, Human Rights Dilemmas in the Developing World: The Case of Marginalized Populations at Risk.

92. Byrne, "Black Citizens Say Racism Is Still an Issue in the New Tunisia," p. 5.

93. Tunisia: The Black Revolution, "In a Country That Launched the Arab Spring, Black People Organize Themselves to Defend Their Rights," p. 3, https://tahriricn.wordpress.com/2013/05/12/Tunisia-the-black-revolution (retrieved 5/5/18).

94. Tunisia: The Black Revolution, In a Country That Launched the Arab Spring, Black People Organize Themselves to Defend Their Rights," p. 5.

95. E. Ike Udogu, Examining Human Rights Issues and the Democracy Project in Sub-Saharan Africa: A Theoretical Critique and Prospects for Progress in the Millennium (Lanham, MD: Lexington Books, 2014), p. 42.

96. Human Rights Watch, "Tunisia: Men Prosecuted for Homosexuality," March 29, 2016, pp. 1–14, https://www.hrw.org/news/2016/03/29/tunisia-men-prosecuted-homosexuality (retrieved 4/5/18).

97. "Women's and Minority Rights in Tunisia: How Progressive Is the Country Really?" European Forum for Democracy and Solidarity, March 14, 2018, p. 4, https://www.europeanforum.net/headlines/womens-and-minority-rights-in-tunisia-how-progressive-is-the-country-really (retrieved 4/6/18).

98. "Women's and Minority Rights in Tunisia: How Progressive Is the Country Really?" p. 4.

99. "Women's and Minority Rights in Tunisia: How Progressive Is the Country Really?" p. 4.

100. U.S. Department of State, Bureau of Democracy and Labor, Country Reports on Human Rights Practices for 2015: Tunisia, p. 20.

101. U.S. Department of State, Bureau of Democracy and Labor, Country Reports on Human Rights Practices for 2015: Tunisia, pp. 20–21.

102. U.S. Department of State, Bureau of Democracy and Labor, Country Reports on Human Rights Practices for 2015: Tunisia, p. 21.

103. Human Rights Watch, "Tunisia: LGBT Group Suspended—Dangerous Precedent for Freedom of Association," January 16, 2016, p. 2, https://www.hrw.org/news/2016/01/16/tunisia-lgbt-group-suspended (retrieved 5/7/18); see U.S. Department of State, Bureau of Democracy and Labor, Country Reports on Human Rights Practices for 2015: Tunisia, p. 21.

104. U.S. Department of State, Bureau of Democracy and Labor, Country Reports on Human Rights Practices for 2015: Tunisia, p. 21.

105. U.S. Department of State, Bureau of Democracy and Labor, Country Reports on Human Rights Practices for 2015: Tunisia, p. 15.

106. Azadeh Moaveni, "Grasping for Truth and Dignity in Tunisia," New Yorker, December 29, 2016, p. 4, https://www.newyorker.com/news/news-desk/grasping-for-truth-and-dignity-in-tunisia (retrieved 4/7/18).

107. UN Office of the High Commissioner for Human Rights, "Taking on the Past: The Tunisian Truth and Dignity Commission," June 9, 2014, https://www.ohchr.org/EN/NewsEvents/Pages/TakingOnThePast.aspx (retrieved 5/7/18).

108. Lamine Ghanmi, "Tunisia to Become Second African Country to Legally Prohibit Racial Discrimination," Arab Weekly, April 8, 2018, pp. 1–4, https://thearabweekly.com/tunisia-become-second-african-country-legally-prohibit-racial-discrimination (retrieved 9/27/19).

# Bibliography

Abun-Nasr, Jamil M. *A History of the Maghrib*, 2nd Edition (Cambridge: Cambridge University Press, 1975).

Abun-Nasr, Jamil M. *A History of the Maghrib in the Islamic Period*, 3rd Edition (Cambridge: Cambridge University Press, 1987).

Achebe, Chinua and Richard Dicker. *Waiting for Accountability: Human Rights and the Transition to Democracy* (New York: Human Rights Watch, 1992).

Ackerly, B. A. *Universal Human Rights in a World of Difference* (Cambridge: Cambridge University Press, 2008).

Adam, B. *The Rise of a Gay and Lesbian Movement* (New York: Twayne Publishers, 1995).

Adams, C. C. *Islam and Modernism in Egypt*, Reprint (New York: Russell & Russell, 1968).

Adcock, F. E. "Delenda est Carthago," *Cambridge Historical Journal*, 8 (1946): 117–128.

*African* [Banjul] *Charter on Human and Peoples' Rights* (Addis Ababa, Ethiopia: OAU General Secretariat Division of Press and Information, 1982).

Afshari, Reza. "On Historiography of Human Rights: Reflections on Paul Gordon Lauren's *The Evolution of International Human Rights: Visions Seen*," *Human Rights Quarterly*, 29, no. 1 (February 2007): 1–67.

Ahmed, Leila. *Women and Gender in Islam: Historical Roots of a Modern Debate* (New Haven, CT: Yale University Press, 1992).

Ahmida, Ali Abdullatif. *The Making of Modern Libya: State Formation, Colonization and Resistance, 1830-1932*, 2nd Edition (Albany, NY: State University of New York Press, 2011).

Aidoo, Akwesi. "Africa: Democracy without Human Rights?" *Human Rights Quarterly*, 15 (1993): 703–715.

Al-Sayyid-Marsot, Afaf Lutfi. *Short History of Modern Egypt* (Cambridge: Cambridge University Press, 1985).

Aldred, Cyril. *The Egyptians*, 3rd Edition. Revised by Aidan Dodson (New York and London: Thames & Hudson, 1998).

Aldrich, Robert. *Greater France: A History of French Overseas Expansion* (New York: St. Martin's Press, 1996).

Alexander, Martin S., and J. F. V. Keiger. "France and the Algerian War, 1954–62: Strategy, Operations and Diplomacy," *Journal of Strategic Studies*, 25, no. 2 (June 2002): 1–32.

Alexander, Nathan. "Libya: The Continuous Revolution," *Middle Eastern Studies*, 17, no. 2 (April 1981): 210–227.

Alston, Philip. "Revitalizing United Nations Work on Human Rights Development," *Melbourne University Law Review*, 18 (1991): 216–257.

Alston, Philip. "The UN's Human Rights Record: From San Francisco to Vienna and Beyond," *Human Rights Quarterly*, 16 (1994): 375–390.

Alston, Phillip, ed. *The United Nations and Human Rights: A Critical Evaluation* (Oxford: Clarendon Press, 1992).

Alston, Philip, and James Crawford, eds. *The Future of UN Human Rights Treaty Monitoring* (Cambridge: Cambridge University Press, 2000).

Ambrose, Brendalyn P. *Democratization and the Protection of Human Rights in Africa: Problems and Prospects* (Westport, CN: Greenwood Publishing Group, 1995).
Amin, Galal. *Whatever Happened to the Egyptians?* (Cairo: American University of Cairo Press, 1995).
Amin, Qasim. *The Liberation of Women and the New Women: Two Documents in the History of Egyptian Feminism* (Cairo: American University Press, 2000).
Amiri, Linda. *La Bataille de France: La guerre d'Algérie en métropole* (Paris, 1981).
Amnesty International. *Violations of Human Rights in Libyan Arab Jamahiriya* (New York, 1984).
*Amnesty International Report* (London: 1986).
Amrouche, Fadhma A. M. *My Life Story: The Autobiography of a Berber Woman*, Translated by Dorothy S. Blair. (New Brunswick, NJ: Rutgers University Press, 1989).
Anderson, Lisa. "Rogue Libya's Long Road," *Middle Eastern Report*, no. 241 (Winter 2006): 42–47.
Anderson, Lisa. *The State and Social Transformation in Tunisia and Libya, 1830–1980* (Princeton, NJ: Princeton University Press, 1986).
Andrew, Christopher, and A.S. Kanya-Forstner. *France Overseas: The Climax of French Imperial Expansion 1914–1924* (Stanford, CA: Stanford University Press, 1981).
Anthony, John. *Tunisia: A Personal View of a Timeless Land* (New York: Charles Scribner's Sons, 1961).
Arab Commission for Human Rights. http://www.achr.nu/wiaen.htm
Arab Organization for Human Rights. http://www.law.emory.edu/ihr/mideast.html
Arat, Zehra F. *Democracy and Human Rights in Developing Countries* (Boulder, CO: Lynne Rienner, 1991).
Armbrust, Walter. *Mass Culture and Modernism in Egypt* (Cambridge: Cambridge University Press, 1996).
Asante, Molefi K., *Culture and Customs of Egypt* (Westport, CT: Greenwood Press, 2002).
Asante, S. K. B. "Nation-Building and Human Rights in Emergent Nations," *Cornell International Law Journal*, 2 (Spring 1969): 72–107
Ashford, Douglas E. *Political Change in Morocco* (Princeton, NJ: Princeton University Press, 1961).
Askew, William C. *Europe and Italy's Acquisition of Libya, 1911–1912* (Durham, NC: Duke University Press, 1942).
Aziz, N. "The Human Rights Debate in an Era of Globalization," *Bulletin of Concerned Asian Scholars* (October/December 1995): 9–16.
Baah, Richard A. *The African Human Rights System: Origin and Evolution* (New York: Palgrave Macmillan Press, 2010).
Baah, Richard A. *Human Rights in Africa: The Conflict of Implementation* (Lanham: MD: University Press of America, 2000).
Badawi El-Sheikh, Ibrahim. "The African Commission on Human and Peoples' Rights: Prospects and Problems," *Netherlands Quarterly*, 7 (1992): 120–134
Badran, Margot. *Feminists, Islam, and the Nation: Gender and the Making of Modern Egypt* (Princeton, NJ: Princeton University Press, 1995).
Badrawi, Malak. *Political Violence in Egypt, 1910–1924* (Richmond, UK: Curzon, 2000).
Bagnall, Roger S., and Domenic W. Rathbone, eds. *Egypt from Alexander to the Early Christians* (Los Angeles: J. Paul Getty Museum, 2004).
Baker, Alison. *Voices of Resistance: Oral Histories of Moroccan Women* (Albany, NY: University of New York Press, 1998).
Baker, R. W. *Egypt's Uncertain Revolution under Nasser and Sadat* (Cambridge, MA: Harvard University Press, 1978).
Baldinetti, Anna, ed. *Modern and Contemporary Libya: Sources and Historiographies* (Rome: Istituto Italiano Per L'Africa e L'Oriente, 2003).
Baron, Beth. *Egypt as a Woman: Nationalism, Gender, and Politics* (Berkeley: University of California Press, 2005).
Baron, Beth. *The Women's Awakening in Egypt: Culture, Society, and the Press* (New Haven, CT: Yale University Press, 1994).

Bates, Oric. *The Eastern Libyans: An Essay* (London: Frank Cass, 1970).

Baughan, Brian. *Human Rights in Africa* (Broomall, PA: Mason Crest Publishers, 2013).

Baxi, U. *The Future of Human Rights* (Oxford: Oxford University Press, 2002).

Baxter, Richard R. "Human Rights in War," *Bulletin of the American Academy of Arts and Sciences*, 31, no. 2 (November 1977): 4–13.

Bayefsky, Anne F. "Making the Human Rights Treaties Work." In Louis Henkin and John Lawson Hargrove, eds. *Human Rights: An Agenda for the Next Century* (Washington, DC: American Society of International Law, 1993): 229–295.

Beattie, Kirk J. *Egyptian Politics during Sadat's Presidency* (New York: Saint Martin's Press, 2000).

Beaumont, Roger. "Small Wars: Definitions and Dimensions," *Annals of the American Academy of Political and Social Science*, 541 (September 1995): 20–35.

Bedjaoui, Mohammed. *"La révolution algérienne et le droit international humanitaire,"* *L'Humanitaire Maghreb*, 5, no. 5 (June 2003): 24–25.

Beetham, D. *Democracy and Human Rights* (Cambridge: Polity Press, 1999).

Begum, Rotha. "Egypt's Historic Conviction for FGM," Human Rights Watch website, January 26, 2015, https://www.hrw.org/news/2015/01/26/dispatches-egypts-historic-conviction-fgm.

Behnke, Roy H., Jr. *The Herders of Cyrenaica: Ecology, Economy, and Kinship among the Bedouin of Eastern Libya*. Illinois Series in Anthropology, no. 12 (Urbana, IL: University of Illinois Press, 1980).

Behrens-Abouseif, Doris. *Egypt's Adjustment to Ottoman Rule: Institutions, Waqf and Architecture in Cairo (16th and 17th Centuries)* (Leiden, Netherlands: E. J. Brill, 1994).

Belden, Fields A. *Rethinking Human Rights for the New Millennium* (New York: Palgrave Macmillan, 2003).

Bello, Emmanuel G. "Human Rights: The Rule of Law in Africa," *International and Comparative Law*, 30 (July 1981): 628–637.

Ben Halim, Mustafa Ahmed. *Libya: The Years of Hope* (Longdon: AAS Publishers, 1998).

Ben Mlih, Abdellah. *Structures politiques du Maroc colonial* (Paris: Harmattan, 1990).

Benedek, Wolfgang. "The African Charter and Commission on Human Rights and Peoples' Rights: How to Make It More Effective," *Netherland Quarterly of Human Rights*, 11, no. 1 (1993): 25–40.

Bernard, Augustin. *L'évolution du nomadisme en Algérie* (Algiers: A. Jourdan, 1906).

Berque, Jacques. *French North Africa: The Maghrib between Two World Wars*. Translated by Jean Stewart. (New York and Washington: Frederick A. Praeger, 1967).

Betts, Raymond F. *Assimilation and Association in French Colonial Theory 1890–1914* (New York and London: Columbia University Press, 1961).

Bianchi, Robert, ed. *Cleopatra's Egypt: The Age of the Ptolemies* (New York: Brooklyn Museum, 1988).

Bidwell, Robin. *Morocco under Colonial Rule: French Administration of Tribal Areas 1912–1956* (London: Frank Cass, 1973).

Bierbrier, Morris L. *Historical Dictionary of Ancient Egypt* (Lanham, MD: Scarecrow Press, 1999).

Blau, J., D. L. Brunsma, A. Moncada, and C. Zimmer, eds. *The Leading Rogue State: The U.S. and Human Rights* (Boulder, CO: Paradigm Publishers, 2008).

Blunsum, Terrence. *Libya: The Country and Its People* (London: Queen Anne Press, 1968).

Blunt, Wilfrid Scawen. *Secret History of the English Occupation of Egypt* (London: Fifield, 1907).

Bohn, Dorothy. *Egypt* (London: Thomas & Hudson, 1989).

Bondzie-Simpson, E. "A Critique of the African Charter on Human and Peoples' Rights," *Harvard Law Journal*, 31 (1988): 407–430.

Borowiec, Andrew. *Tunisia: A Democratic Apprenticeship* (Westport, CT: Praeger, 1998).

Botman, Selma. *Egypt from Independence to Revolution, 1919–1952* (Syracuse, NY: Syracuse University Press, 1991).

Boutros-Ghali, Boutros. *Egypt's Road to Jerusalem: A Diplomat's Story of the Struggle for Peace in the Middle East* (New York: Random House, 1997).

Bowman, Alan K. *Egypt after the Pharaohs, 332 BC–AD 642 2nd Edition* (Berkeley: University of California Press, 1996).

Brand, L. A. *Women, the State, and Political Liberalization: The Middle Eastern and North African Experiences* (New York: Columbia University Press, 1998).

Brems, E. "Enemies or Allies? Feminism and Cultural Relativism as Dissident Voices in Human Rights Discourse," *Human Rights Quarterly*, 19, no. 1 (1997): 136–164.

Brett, Michael. "The UN and Libya," *Journal of African History*, 13, no. 1 (1972): 168–170.

Brett, Michael, and Elizabeth Fentress. *The Berbers* (Oxford: Blackwell, 1996).

Brier, Bob, and Hoyt Hobbs. *Daily Life of the Ancient Egyptians* (Westport, CT and London: Greenwood Press, 1999).

Brooks, Geraldine. *Nine Parts of Desire: The Hidden World of Islamic Women* (New York: Anchor Books, 1995).

Brown, Kenneth L. *People of Salé: Tradition and Change in a Moroccan City 1830–1930* (Cambridge, MA: Harvard University Press, 1976).

Brown, L. Carl. *The Tunisia of Ahmad Bey, 1837–1855* (Princeton, NJ: Princeton University Press, 1974).

Brownlie, I., and G. Godwin-Gill, eds. *Basic Documents on Human Rights 5th Edition* (Oxford: Oxford University Press, 2006).

Brysk, A., ed. *Globalization and Human Rights* (Berkeley, CA: University of California Press, 2002).

Bunch, C. "Women's Rights as Human Rights," *Human Rights Quarterly*, 12 (1990): 486–498.

Bunson, Margaret. *Encyclopedia of Ancient Egypt*, Revised Edition (New York: Facts on File, 2002).

Burgat, François, and William Dowell. *The Islamic Movement in North Africa* (Austin, TX: Center for Middle Eastern Studies at the University of Texas, 1993).

Burke, Edmund, III. "Pan-Islam and Moroccan Resistance to French Colonial Penetration, 1900–1912," *Journal of African History*, 13, no. 1 (1972): 97–118

Burke, Edmund, III. *Prelude to Protectorate in Morocco: Precolonial Protest and Resistance, 1860–1912* (Chicago: University of Chicago Press, 1976).

Burke, Roland. *Decolonization and the Evolution of International Human Rights* (Philadelphia, PA: University of Pennsylvania Press, 2010).

Burr, J. Millard, and Robert O. Collins. *Africa's Thirty Years' War: Chad, Libya, and the Sudan, 1963–1993* (Boulder, CO: Westview Press, 1999).

Butler, Albert Joshua. *The Arab Conquest of Egypt and the Last Thirty Years of Roman Dominion*, 2nd Edition (Oxford: Clarendon Press, 1978).

Butler, Alfred. *The Arab Invasion of Egypt* (Brooklyn, NY: A and B Books, 1922).

Cachia, Anthony J. *Libya under the Second Ottoman Occupation (1835–1911)* (Tripoli: Government Press, 1945).

Cannuyer, Christian. *Coptic Egypt: The Christians of the Nile* (New York: Harry N. Abrams, 2001).

Carter, B. L. *The Copts in Egyptian Politics* (London: Croom Helm, 1986).

Castello, S. "Female Genital Mutilation/Cutting: Risk Management and Strategies for Social Workers and Health Care Professionals," *Risk Management and Health Care Policy*, 8 (2015): 225–233.

Chamari, A. C. *La Femme et la Loi en Tunisie* (Casablanca, Morocco: The United Nations University and Edition le Fennec, 1991).

Charles-Picard, Gilbert. *La Civilisation de l'Afrique romaine* (Paris: Plom, 1959).

Charrad, M. M. "Becoming a Citizen: Lineage versus Individual in Morocco and Tunisia," in S. Joseph, ed., *Gender and Citizenship in the Middle East* (Syracuse, NY: Syracuse University Press, 2000): 70–87.

Charrad, M. M. "Contexts, Concepts and Contentions: Gender Legislation in the Middle East," *Hawwa: Journal of Women in the Middle East and the Islamic World*, 5, no. 1 (2007): 55–72.

Charrad, M. M. "Cultural Diversity within Islam: Veils and Laws in Tunisia." in H. L. Bodman and N. Tohidi, ed. *Women in Muslim Societies: Diversity within Unity* (Boulder, CO: Lynne Rienner, 1998), 63–79.

Charrad, M. M. *Family Law Reforms in the Arab World: Tunisia and Morocco.* United Nations Department of Economic and Social Affairs (UNDESA), Division of Social Policy and Development Expert Group Meeting, New York, May 15–17, 2014.

Charrad, M. M. "Gender in the Middle East: Islam, States, Agency," *Annual Review of Sociology*, 37 (2011): 417–437.

Charrad, M. M. *States and Women's Rights: The Making of Postcolonial Tunisia, Algeria and Morocco* (Berkeley, CA: University of California Press, 2001).

Chase, Anthony T. *Routledge Handbook on Human Rights and the Middle East and North Africa* (Oxford: Taylor & Francis Publishers, 2017).

Chauveau, Michel. *Egypt in the Age of Cleopatra*. Translated by David Lorton. (Ithaca, NY: Cornell University Press, 2000).

Cheah, P. "Posit(ion)ing Human Rights," *Public Culture*, 9 (1997): 233–266.

Christelow, Allan. *Muslim Law Courts and the French Colonial State in Algeria* (Princeton, NJ: Princeton University Press, 1985).

Ciment, James. *Algeria: The Fundamentalist Challenge* (New York: Facts on File, 1997).

Clarke, Bryan C. *Berber Village: The Story of the Oxford University Expedition to the High Atlas Mountains of Morocco* (London: Longmans, 1959).

Clayton, Anthony. *France, Soldiers and Africa* (London: Brassey's Defense Publishers, 1988).

Cmiel, Kenneth. "The Recent History of Human Rights," *American Historical Review*, 109, no. 1 (February 2004): 117–135.

Cohen, J. "Minimalism about Human Rights: The Most We Can Hope For?" *Journal of Political Philosophy*, 12 (2004): 190–213.

Cole, Joshua. "Intimate Acts and Unspeakable Relations: Remembering Torture and the War for Algerian Independence," in Alec G. Hargreaves, ed., *Memory, Empire and Postcolonialism: Legacies of French Colonialism* (Lanham, MD: Lexington Books, 2005), 125–141.

Conklin, Alice L. "Colonialism and Human Rights: A Contradiction in Terms? The Cases of France and West Africa, 1895–1914," *American Historical Review*, 103, no. 2 (April 1998): 419–442.

Cook, R., ed. *Human Rights of Women: National and International Perspectives* (Philadelphia, PA: University of Pennsylvania Press, 1994).

Cook, Weston F. *The Hundred Years War for Morocco: Gunpowder and the Military Revolution in the Early Modern Muslim World* (Boulder, CO: Westview Press, 1993).

Cooke, James J. "Insubordination in the French Colonial Army: Lyautey, a Case Study, 1903–1912," *Proceedings of the Second Annual Meeting of the French Colonial Historical Society*, 2 (1977): 87–95.

Cooke, James J. *New French Imperialism 1880–1910: The Third Republic and Colonial Expansion* (Hamdem, CT: Archon, 1973).

Copeland, Paul W. *The Land and People of Libya* (Philadelphia: Lippincott, 1967).

Cranston, M. *What Are Human Rights?* (London: Bodley Head, 1973).

Crecelius, Daniel, ed. *Eighteenth Century Egypt: The Arabic Manuscript Sources* (Claremont, CA: Regina Books, 1990).

Dalal, K., S. Lawoko, and B. Janson. "Women's Attitudes towards Discontinuation of Female Genital Mutilation in Egypt." *Journal of Inquiry & Violence Research*, 2, no. 1 (2010): 41–47.

Daly, Martin W., ed. *Modern Egypt from 1517 to the End of the Twentieth Century* (New York: Cambridge University Press, 1999).

Daniels, Charles. *Garamantes of Southern Libya* (Stoughton, WI: Oleander Press, 1972).

Darwin, John. *Britain, Egypt, and the Middle East* (New York: St. Martin's, 1981).

Daughty, Robert A. *The Seeds of Disaster: The Development of French Army Doctrine 1919–1939* (Hamden, CT: Archon, 1985).

Davies, W. V. *Egypt* (London: British Museum Press, 1998).

Davis, Aisha N. "Female Genital Cutting: The Pressure of Culture, International Attention, and Domestic Law on the Role of African Women," Columbia Law School website, 2012, http://blogs.law.columbia.edu/gslonline/files/2012/01/Davis-Female-Genital-Cutting.pdf

Davis, Susan S. *Patience and Power: Women's Lives in a Moroccan Village* (Cambridge, MA: Schenkman, 1983).

Dershowitz, A. *Rights from Wrongs: A Secular Theory of the Origins of Human Rights* (New York: Basic Books, 2004).

Detrick, Sharon. *A Commentary on the United Nations Convention on the Rights of the Child* (The Hague, Holland: Martinus Nijhoff, 1999).

Dicker, Richard. "Monitoring Human Rights in Africa," *Journal of Modern African Studies*, 29 (1991): 505–510.

Dickson, H. R. P. *The Arab of the Desert* (New York: HarperCollins Publishers, 1983).

Diehl, Charles. *L'Afrique byzantine: Histoire de la domination byzantine en Afrique 533–709*. 2 Vols. Reprint (Philadelphia: Burt Franklin, 1968).

Dinstein, Yoram. "Collective Human Rights of Peoples and Minorities," *International and Comparative Law Quarterly*, 25, no. 1 (January 1976): 102–120.

Dlamini, C. R. M. "Towards a Regional Protection of Human Rights in Africa: The African Charter on Human and Peoples' Rights," *Comparative and International Law Journal of Southern Africa*, Vol. 24 (1991): 189–203.

Donnelly, J. *The Concept of Human Rights* (New York: St. Martin's Press, 1985).

Donnelly, J. *International Human Rights* (Boulder, CO: Westview Press, 1993).

Douzinas, C. *The End of Human Rights* (Oxford: Hart Publishing, 2000).

Dunn, Rose E. *Resistance in the Desert: Moroccan Responses to French Imperialism 1881–1912* (Madison: University of Wisconsin Press, 1977).

Dunne, T. and N. Wheeler, eds. *Human Rights in Global Politics* (Cambridge: Cambridge University Press, 1999).

Dupree, Louis. "The Arabs of Modern Libya," *Muslim World*, 48, no. 2 (April 1958): 113–124.

Ebiasah, John K. "Protecting the Human Rights of Political Detainees: The Contradictions and Paradoxes in the African Experience," *Harvard Law Journal* 22, no. 3 (1979): 249–281.

Eckert, Andreas. "African Nationalists and Human Rights, 1940s-1970s." In Stefan-Ludwig Hoffman, ed. *Human Rights in the Twentieth Century* (Cambridge: Cambridge University Press, 2011).

El-Kikhia, Mansour O. *Libya's Qaddafi: The Politics of Contradiction* (Gainesville, FL: University Press of Florida, 1997).

El-Nahel, Galal H. *The Judicial Administration of Ottoman Egypt in the Seventeenth Century* (Minneapolis: Bibliotheca Islamica, 1979).

Elsaidi, M. H. "Human Rights and Islamic Law: A Legal Analysis Challenging the Husband's Authority to Punish 'Rebellious' Wives," *Muslim World Journal of Human Rights*, 7, iss. 2 (2011): 221–235.

Empereur, Jean-Yves. *Alexandria Rediscovered* (New York: George Braziller, 1998).

Entelis, John P. *Algeria: The Revolution Institutionalized* (Boulder, CO: Westview, 1986).

Entelis, John P. *Comparative Politics of North Africa: Algeria, Morocco, and Tunisia* (Syracuse, NY: Syracuse University Press, 1980).

Entelis, John P., ed. *Islam, Democracy, and the State in North Africa* (Bloomington, IN: Indiana University Press, 1997).

Entelis, John P., and Phillip C. Naylor, eds. *State and Society in Algeria* (Boulder, CO: Westview, 1992).

Esposito, John L., and Natana J. De Long-Bas. *Women in Muslim Family Law*, Second Edition (Syracuse, NY: Syracuse University Press, 2001).

Evans, M., and R. Murray, eds. *The African Charter on Human and Peoples' Rights: The System in Practice, 1986–2000* (Cambridge: Cambridge University Press, 2002).

Evans-Pritchard, E. E. *The Sanusi of Cyrenaica* (London: Oxford at Clarendon Press, 1949).

Evans-Pritchard, E. E. *The Sanusi of Cyrenaica* (Oxford: Clarendon Press, 1973).

Eze, Osita C. "The Organization of African Unity and Human Rights: 25 Years After," *Nigerian Journal of International Affairs*, 14 (1988): 154–188.

Fagan, Brian. *Egypt of the Pharaohs* (Washington, DC: National Geographic, 2001).

Felice, William. *Taking Rights Seriously: The Importance of Collective Human Rights* (Albany, NY: SUNY Press, 1996).

Ferneat, Elizabeth W. *In Search of Islamic Feminism: One Woman's Global Journey* (New York: Doubleday, 1998).

Findlay, Anne M., A. Findlay, and R. I. Lawless. *Morocco* (Santa Barbara, CA: ABC-CLIO, 1995).

Fitzpatrick, Joan. *Human Rights in Crisis: The International System for Protecting Rights during States of Emergency* (Philadelphia, PA: University of Pennsylvania Press, 1994).

Flower, Raymond. *Napoleon to Nasser: The Story of Modern Egypt* (London: London Editions, 1976).

Franck, Thomas M. *Human Rights in Third World Perspective* (Dobbs Ferry, NY: Oceana Publications, 1982).

Freeman, M. "Are There Collective Human Rights?" *Political Studies*, 43 (1995): 25–40.

Gadant, Monique. *Le nationalism algérien et les femmes* (Paris: Harmattan, 1995).

Galeotti, A. E. "Relativism, Universalism, and Applied Ethics: The Case of Female Circumcision," *Constellations*, 14, no. 1 (2007): 91–111.

Gardiner, A. H. *Egypt of the Pharaohs* (Oxford: Oxford University Press, 1974).

Gearty, C. *Can Human Rights Survive?* (Cambridge: Cambridge University Press, 2006).

Geertz, Clifford. *Islam Observed: Religious Developments in Morocco and Indonesia* (Chicago: University of Chicago Press, 1971).

Geertz, Clifford, Hildred Geertz, and Lawrence Rosen. *Meaning and Order in Moroccan Society: Three Essays in Cultural Analysis* (Cambridge: Cambridge University Press, 1979).

Gellner, Ernest, and Charles Micaud. *Arabs and Berbers: From Tribe to Nation in North Africa* (London: Duckworth, 1973).

Gellner, Ernest, and Jean-Claude Vatin et al. *Islam et politique au Maghreb* (Paris: Éditions du Centre National de la Recherche Scientifique, 1981).

Gershoni, Israel, and James P. Jankowski. *Commemorating the Nation: Collective Memory, Public Commemorating, and National identity in Twentieth-Century Egypt* (Chicago: Middle East Documentation Center, 2004).

Gershoni, Israel, and James P. Jankowski. *Redefining the Egypt Nation, 1930–1945* (Cambridge: Cambridge University Press, 1995).

Gershovich, Moshe. "French Control over the Moroccan Countryside: The Transformation of the Goums, 1934–1942," *The Mahgreb Review*, 22, no. 1–2 (1997): 124-137.

Gershovich, Moshe. *French Military Rule in Morocco: Colonialism and Its Consequences* (London: Frank Cass, 2000).

Gillies, David, and Clarence Dias. *Human Rights, Democracy and Development* (Geneva: UN Center for Human Rights, 1992).

Glendon, M. A. *A World Made New: Eleanor Roosevelt and the Universal Declaration of Human Rights* (New York: Random House, 2001).

Goldschmidt, Arthur. *Modern Egypt: The Formation of a Nation State*, 2nd Edition (Boulder, CO: Westview Press, 2004).

Goldschmidt, Arthur, Amy J. Johnson, and Barak Salmoni, eds. *Re-Envisioning Egypt, 1919–1952* (Cairo: American University in Cairo Press, 2005).

Goldschmidt, Arthur, and Robert C. Johnson. *Historical Dictionary of Egypt*, 3rd Edition (Lanham, MD: Westview Press, 2004).

Goodchild, Richard G. "Byzantines, Berbers and Arabs in 7th Century Libya," *Antiquity*, no. 41 (1967): 115–124.

Goodhart, Michael, ed. *Human Rights & Practice* (New York: Oxford University Press, 2009).

Gordon, David C. *Women of Algeria: An Essay on Change* (Cambridge, MA: Harvard University Press, 1968).

Gould, St. John. *Morocco* (New York: Routledge, 2002).

Grear, A. "A Tale of the Land, the Insider, the Outsider and Human Rights," *Legal Studies*, 23, no. 1 (2003): 32–65.

Gregg, Benjamin. *Human Rights as Social Construction* (Cambridge: Cambridge University Press, 2012).

Grimal, Nicolas. *A History of Ancient Egypt* (New York: Barnes & Noble, 1997).

Guillaume, André. *Les Berbères marocains et la pacification de l'Atlas Central, 1912–1933* (Paris: Julliard, 1946).

Halstead, John. *Rebirth of a Nation: The Origins and Rise of Moroccan Nationalism 1912–1944* (Cambridge, MA: Harvard University Press, 1967).

Hammoudi, Abdellah. *Master and Disciple: The Cultural Foundations of Moroccan Authoritarianism* (Chicago: Chicago University Press, 1997).

Handloff, Robert E., ed. *Mauritania: A Country Study*, 2nd Edition (Washington, DC: U.S. Government Printing Office [GPO], 1990).

Hanna, Nelly, ed. *The State and Its Servants: Administration in Egypt from Ottoman Times to the Present* (Cairo: American University in Cairo Press, 1995).

Harden, Donald B. *The Phoenicians* (New York: Praeger, 1962).

Harik, Iliya F. *Economic Policy Reform in Egypt* (Gainesville, FL: University Press of Florida, 1997).

Harris, Lillian Craig. *Libya: Qadhafi's Revolution and the Modern State* (Boulder, CO: Westview Press, 1986).

Harris, Walter B. *France, Spain and the Rif* (London: Arnold, 1927).

Hayden, P., ed. *The Philosophy of Human Rights* (St. Paul, MN: Paragon House, 2001).

Hejaiej, Monia. *Behind Closed Doors: Women's Oral Narratives in Tunis* (New Brunswick, NJ: Rutgers University Press, 1996).

Henkin, Louis. *The Rights of Man Today* (Boulder, CO: Westview Press, 1978).

Herman, D. *Rights of Passage: Struggles for Lesbian and Gay Equality* (Toronto: University of Toronto Press, 1994).

Herold, J. Christopher. *Bonaparte in Egypt* (New York: Harper & Row, 1962).

Hicks, Neil, and George Black, eds. *Islam and Justice: Debating the Future of Human Rights in the Middle East and North Africa* (New York: Lawyers Committee for Human Rights, 1997).

Hinchman, L. "The Origin of Human Rights: A Hegelian Perspective," *Western Political Quarterly*, 37, no. 1 (1984): 7–31.

Hoffmann, Stefan-Ludwig. "Introduction: Genealogies of Human Rights." In Stefan-Ludwig Hoffmann, ed. *Human Rights in the Twentieth Century* (Cambridge: Cambridge University Press, 2011), 1–26.

Hoisington, William A., Jr. *The Casablanca Connection: French Colonial Policy 1936–1943* (Chapel Hill and London, University of North California Press, 1984).

Hoisington, William A., Jr, *Lyautey and the French Conquest of Morocco* (London: St. Martin's Press, 1995).

Hölbl, Günther. *A History of the Ptolemaic Empire*. Translated by Tina Saavedia. (London: Routledge, 2001).

Horne, Alistair. *A Savage War of Peace: Algeria, 1954–1962* (New York: NYRB Classics, 1987).

House, Jim, and Neil MacMaster. *Paris 1961: Algerians, State Terror, and Memory* (Oxford: Oxford University Press, 2006).

Howard, Rhoda. "The Dilemma of Human Rights in Sub-Saharan Africa," *International Journal*, 35, no. 4 (Autumn 1980): 724–747.

Howard, Rhoda, and Jack Donnelly. "Human Dignity, Human Rights and Political Regimes," *American Political Science Review*, 80 (1986): 801–817.

Humphrey, John P. *Human Rights and the United Nations: A Great Adventure* (New York: Transnational Publisher Inc., 1984).

Hunt, Lynn. *Inventing Human Rights: A History* (London: W. W. Norton & Company, 2008).

Hunter, F. Robert. *Egypt under the Khedives, 1805–1879* (Pittsburgh: University of Pittsburgh Press, 1984).

Ibhawoh, Bonny. "Between Culture and Constitution: Evaluating the Cultural Legitimacy of Human Rights in the African State," *Human Rights Quarterly*, 22, no. 3 (2002): 838–860.

Ibhawoh, Bonny. *Human Rights in Africa* (Cambridge: Cambridge University Press, 2018).

Ibhawoh, Bonny. *Imperialism and Human Rights: Colonial Discourse of Rights and Liberties in African History* (Albany, NY: SUNY Press, 2007).

Ibhawoh, Bonny. "Restraining Universalism: Africanist Perspectives on Cultural Relativism in Human Rights Discourse." In Paul T. Zeleza and Philip McConnaughay, eds. *Human Rights, the Rule of Law, and Development in Africa* (Philadelphia, PA: University of Pennsylvania Press, 2004).

Irwin, Robert. *The Middle East in the Middle Ages: The Early Mamluk Sultanate, 1250–1382* (Carbondale, IL: Southern Illinois University Press, 1997).

Ishay, Micheline R. *The History of Human Rights* (Berkeley, CA: University of California Press, 2004).

Ishay, Micheline R., ed. *The Human Rights Reader* (New York: Routledge, 1997)

Jankowski, James. *Egypt: A Short History* (Oxford: OneWorld Publications, 2000).

Jentleson, Bruce W., and Christopher A. Whytock. "Who 'Won' Libya? The Force-Diplomacy

Debate and Its Implications for Theory and Policy," *International Security*, 30, no. 3 (Winter 2006): 47–86.

Joffé, George, ed. *North Africa: Nation, State, and Region* (London: Routledge, 1993).

Joseph, Suad, ed. *Gender and Citizenship in the Middle East* (Syracuse, NY: Syracuse University Press, 2000).

Joseph, Suad, and Susan Slyomovics, eds. *Women and Power in the Middle East* (Philadelphia, PA: University of Pennsylvania Press, 2001).

Joyce, James Avery. *Human Rights: International Documents* (Dobbs Ferry, NY: Oceana Publications, 1982).

Julien, Charles-Andre. *L'Afrique du Nord en marche: Naionalismes Musulmans et souveraineté française* (Paris: Julliard, 1952).

Julien, Charles-André. *Histoire de l'Algérie contemporaine: La conquête et les débuts de la colonization (1827–1871)* (Paris: Presses Universitaires de France, 1964).

Jureidini, Paul A. *Case Studies in Insurgency and Revolutionary Warfare: Algeria, 1954–1962* (Washington, DC: American University Special Operations Office, 1963).

Kagda, Falaq. *Cultures of the World: Algeria* (Tarrytown, NY: Marshall Cavendish Corporation, 1997).

Kalu, Awa U. and Yemi Osinbajo, eds. *Perspectives on Human Rights* (Lagos, Nigeria: Federal Ministry of Justice, 1992).

Kandiyoti, Deniz, ed. *Women, Islam and the State* (London: Macmillan Press, 1991).

Keddie, Nikki R. *Women in the Middle East: Past and Present* (Princeton, NJ: Princeton University Press, 2006).

Kedourie, Elie, and Sylvia G. Haim. *Modern Egypt: Studies in Politics and Society* (London: Frank Cass, 1980).

Keler, H. "Cultural Rights or Human Rights: The Case of Female Genital Mutilation," *Sex Roles*, 51, no. 5 (2004): 339–348.

Kelly, Sanja, and Julia Breslin, eds. *Women's Rights in the Middle East and North Africa: Progress amid Resistance* (New York: Freedom House; Lanham, MD: Rowman & Littlefield, 2010).

Kemp, Barry J. *Ancient Egypt: Anatomy of a Civilization*, 2nd Edition (London: Routledge, 2006).

Kennedy, Hugh. *The Historiography of Islamic Egypt, c. 950–1800* (Leiden, Netherlands: Brill, 2001).

Kerr, Joanna, ed. *Ours by Right: Women's Rights as Human Rights* (London: Zed Books, 1993).

Khadduri, Majid. *Modern Libya: A Study in Political Development* (Baltimore: Johns Hopkins University Press, 1963).

Khoury, Philip. *Syria and the French Mandate: The Politics of Arab Nationalism 1920–1945.* Translated by Ralph Manheim. (Princeton, NJ: Princeton University Press, 1977).

Klose, Fabian. "'Source of Embarrassment.' Human Rights, State of Emergency, and the Wars of Decolonization." In Stefan-Ludwig Hoffmann, ed. *Human Rights in the Twentieth Century* (Cambridge: Cambridge University Press, 2011), 237–257.

Knauss, Peter R. *The Persistence of Patriarchy: Class, Gender and Ideology in Twentieth-Century Algeria* (New York: Praeger, 1987).

Korey, W. *NGOs and the Universal Declaration of Human Rights: A Curious Grapevine* (New York: Palgrave Macmillan Press, 1998).

Kunig, Philip. "The Protection of Human Rights by International Law in Africa," *German Yearbook of International Law*, 25 (1982): 138–168.

Lacoste, Camille, and Yves Lacoste, eds. *L'Etat du Maghreb* (Tunis: Cérès Productions, 1991).

Lancel, Serge. *Carthage: A History.* Translated by Antonia Nevil. (Oxford: Blackwell, 1995).

Lane-Poole, Stanley. *A History of Egypt in the Middle Ages*, Reprint (London: Methuen, 1901; and New York: Haskell House, 1969).

Laqueur, Walter, and Barry Rubin, eds. *The Human Rights Reader* (New York: Meridan Press, 1979).

Lauren, P. *The Evolution of International Human Rights* (Philadelphia, PA: University of Pennsylvania Press, 1998).

Lauterpacht, Hersch. *International Law and Human Rights* (New York: F. A. Praeger, 1968).

Lawless, Richard I. *Algeria* (Santa Barbara, CA: ABC-CLIO, 1995).

Layachi, Azzedine. *State, Society and Democracy in Morocco: The Limits of Associative Life* (Washington, DC: Center for Contemporary Arab Studies at Georgetown University, 1998).

Lazreg, Marnia. *Torture and the Twilight of Empire: From Algiers to Baghdad* (Princeton, NJ: Princeton University Press, 2008).

Le Gall, Michel, and Kenneth Perkins, eds. *The Maghrib in Question: Essays in History and Historiography* (Austin, TX: The University of Texas Press, 1997).

Leca, Jean, and Jean-Claude Vatin. *L'Algérie politique, institutions et régime* (Paris: Presses de la Fondation Nationale des Sciences Politiques, 1975).

Lerner, Natan. *Group Rights and Discrimination in International Law* (Dordrecht, Netherlands: Martinus Nijhoff, 1991).

Lev, Yaacov. *Saladin in Egypt* (Leiden, Netherlands: Brill, 1999).

Lillich, Richard B., and Frank C. Newman. *International Human Rights: Problems of Law and Policy* (Boston: Little Brown, 1979).

Livezey, Lionel W. *Non-Governmental Organization and the Idea of Human Rights* (Princeton, NJ: Center for International Studies, 1988).

Long, David E., and Bernard Reich. *The Government and Politics of the Middle East and North Africa*, 4th Edition (Boulder, CO: Westview, 2002).

Lorcin, Patricia M. E. *Imperial Identities: Stereotyping, Prejudice, and Race in Colonial Algeria* (London: Tauris, 1995).

Luard, Evan, ed. *International Protection of Human Rights* (New York: Praeger, 1967).

MacMaster, Neil. *Colonial Migrants and Racism: Algerians in France, 1900–62* (New York: St. Martin's, 1997).

MacMaster, Neil. "The Torture Controversy (1998–2002): Toward a 'New History' of the Algerian War," *Modern and Contemporary France*, 10, no. 4 (2002): 449–459.

Magnarella, Paul J., ed. *Middle East and North Africa: Governance, Democratization, Human Rights* (Oxford: Taylor & Francis Publishers, 2017).

Magnarella, Paul J. "Preventing Interethnic Conflict and Promoting Human Rights through More Effective Legal, Political, and Aid Structures: Focus on Africa," *Georgia Journal of International and Comparative Law*, 23 (1993): 327–345.

Maher, Vanessa. *Women and Property in Morocco: Their Changing Relation to the Process of Social Stratification in the Middle Atlas* (London: Cambridge University Press, 1974).

Mahmud, Sakah Saidu. "The State and Human Rights in Africa in the 1990s: Perspectives and Prospects," *Human Rights Quarterly*, 15 (1993): 485–498.

Mahoney, K. E., and P. Mahoney. *Human Rights in the Twenty-First Century: A Global Challenge* (London: Nijholt, 1993).

Majed, Ziad, ed. *Building Democracy in Egypt: Women's Political Participation, Political Party Life and Democratic Elections* (Stockholm, Sweden: International Institute for Democracy and Electoral Assistance, 2005).

Malek, Jaromir, ed. *Egypt: Ancient Culture, Modern Land* (Norman, OK: University of Oklahoma Press, 1993).

Manela, Erez. *The Wilsonian Moment: Self-Determination and the International Order of Anti-colonial Nationalism* (Oxford: Oxford University Press, 2007).

Mansfield, Peter. *The British in Egypt* (New York: Holt, Rinehart & Winston, 1971).

Maran, Rita. *Torture: The Role of Ideology in the French-Algerian War* (New York: Praeger, 1989).

Marks, Stephen. "Principles and Norms of Human Rights Applicable in Emergency Situations: Underdevelopment, Catastrophes and Armed Conflict." In Karel Vasak, ed. *The International Dimension of Human Rights* (Paris: UNESCO, 1982): 175–212

Martínez, Luis. *The Libyan Paradox* (New York: Columbia University Press, 2007).

Marzouki, Ilhem. *Le movement des femmes en Tunisie au XXème siècle: Féminisme et politique* (Tunis: Cérès Productions, 1993).

Mayer, Ann Elizabeth. "Developments in the Law of Marriage and Divorce in Libya," *Journal of African Law*, 22 (1978): 30–49.

Mayer, Ann Elizabeth. *Islam and Human Rights: Tradition and Politics* (Boulder, CO: Westview Press, 1991).

Mazower, Mark. "The Strange Triumph of Human Rights, 1933–1950," *Historical Journal*, 47, no. 2 (June 2004): 379–398.

McDermott, Anthony. *Egypt after Nasser* (London: Croom Helm, 1987).

Mernissi, Fatima. *Beyond the Veil: Male-Female Dynamics in a Modern Muslim Society*, Revised Edition (Bloomington, IN: Indiana University Press, 1964).

Mernissi, Fatima. *Women and Islam: An Historical and Theological Enquiry* (Oxford: Blackwell, 1991).

Merry, S. *Human Rights and Gender Violence: Translating International Law into Local Justice* (Chicago: University of Chicago Press, 2005).

Mertus, J. J. *The United Nations and Human Rights* (London: Routledge, 2005).

Messaoudi, K., and E. Schemla. *Unbowed: An Algerian Woman Confronts Islamic Fundamentalism* (Philadelphia, PA: University of Pennsylvania Press, 1998).

Metz, Helen Chapin, ed. *Algeria: A Country Study*, 5th Edition (Washington, DC: US GPO, 1991).

Metz, Helen Chapin, ed. *Egypt: A Country Study*, 4th Edition (Washington, DC: US GPO, 1989).

Metz, Helen Chapin, ed. *Libya: A Country Study*, 4th Edition (Washington, DC: US GPO, 1989).

Miles, Richard. *Carthage Must Be Destroyed: The Rise and Fall of an Ancient Civilization* (New York: Viking, 2010).

Mitchell, Anthony. *Colonizing Egypt* (Berkeley and Los Angeles, CA: University of California Press, 1991).

Mitchell, Neil J. *Agents of Atrocity: Leaders, Followers, and the Violation of Human Rights in Civil War* (New York: Palgrave Macmillan, 2004).

Moghadam, V. M. "Tunisia." In S. Nazir and L. Tomppert, eds. *Women's Rights in the Middle East and North Africa: Citizenship and Justice* (New York: Freedom House and Lanham, MD: Rowman and Littlefield, 2005).

Mojekwu, Chris C. "International Human Rights: The African Perspective." In Jack L. Nelson and Vera M. Green, eds. *International Human Rights: Contemporary Issues* (Standfordville, NY: Human Rights Group, 1980).

Molleman, G., and L. France. "The Struggle for Abandonment of Female Genital Mutilation/Cutting (FGM/C) in Egypt," *Global Health Promotion*, 16, No. 1 (2009): 57–60.

Monshipouri, M. "Human Rights Conditions in the Third World: Historical Realities and Prospects in the 1990s," *Journal of Third World Studies*, 9, no. 1 (Spring 1992): 80–116.

Montagne, Robert. *The Berbers: Their Social and Political Organization*. Originally published as *La vie sociale et la vie politique des Berbères*, 1931. Translated by David Seddon. (London: Frank Cass, 1973).

Montagne, Robert. *Révolution au Maroc* (Paris: Éditions France-Empire, 1973).

Moore, Clement Henry. *Tunisia since Independence: The Dynamics of One-Party Government* (Berkeley and Los Angeles, CA: University of California Press, 1965).

Morkot, Robert G. *The Egyptians: An Introduction* (London: Routledge, 2005).

Morsink, Johannes. *The Universal Declaration of Human Rights: Origins, Drafting, and Intent* (Philadelphia, PA: University of Pennsylvania Press, 1999).

Moscati, Sabatino. *The World of the Phoenicians* (London: Weidenfeld and Nicolson, 1968).

Motala, Ziyad. "Human Rights in Africa: A Cultural, Ideological and Legal Examination," *Hasting International and Comparative Law Review*, 12 (1989): 373–410.

Moulay Rchid, Abderrazak. *La femme et la loi au Maroc* (Casablanca: Le Fennec, 1991).

Mower, A. Glenn, Jr. "Human Rights in Black Africa: A Double Standard?" *Human Rights Journal*, 9, no. 1 (1976): 39–70.

Moyn, Samuel. *The Last Utopia: Human Rights in History* (Cambridge, MA: Belknap Press, 2010).

Mugwanya, George W. *Human Rights in Africa: Enhancing Human Rights through the African Regional Rights System* (Leiden, Netherlands: Brill Academic Publishers, Inc., 2003).

Murphy, Emma C. *Economic and Political Change in Tunisia: From Bourguiba to Ben Ali* (New York: St. Martin's Press, 1999).

Mutua, Makau. *Human Rights: A Political & Cultural Critique* (Philadelphia, PA: University of Pennsylvania Press, 2002).

Mutua, Makau. *Human Rights Standards: Hegemony, Law, and Politics* (Albany, NY: State University of New York Press, 2016).Naim, Abd Allah. *Islamic Family Law in a Changing World: A Global Resource Book* (London: Zed Books, 2002).

An-Na'im, Abdullahi Ahmed, ed. *Toward an Islamic Reformation: Civil Liberties, Human Rights, and International Law* (Syracuse, NY: Syracuse University Press, 1990).

Nasser, Gamal Abdel. *The Philosophy of Revolution* (Cairo: Egyptian State Printing Office, 1955).

Naylor, Phillip Chiviges, and Alf Andrew Heggoy. *Historical Dictionary of Algeria*, 2nd Edition (Lanham, MD: Scarecrow Press, 1994).

Nazir, S. "Challenging Inequality." In S. Nazir and L. Tomppert, eds. *Women's Rights in the Middle East and North Africa: Citizenship and Justice* (New York: Freedom House and Lanham, MD: Rowman & Littlefield Publishers, Inc., 2005).

Nelson, Harold D., ed. *Morocco: A Country Study*, 3rd Edition (Washington, DC: US GPO, 1985).

Nelson, Harold D., ed. *Tunisia: A Country Study*, 5th Edition (Washington, DC: US GPO, 1988).

Newberg, Paula R., ed. *The Politics of Human Rights* (New York: New York University Press, 1980).

Nickel, James W. *Making Sense of Human Rights*, 2nd edition (Malden, MA: Blackwell, 2007).

Nwankwo, Clement. "The OAU and Human Rights," *Journal of Democracy*, 4 (1992): 50–54.

Obeidi, Amal. *Political Culture in Libya* (Richmond, UK: Curzon, 2001).

O'Byrne, Darren J. *Human Rights: An Introduction* (Harlow, UK: Pearson Education Limited, 2003).

Ojo, Olusola, and Amadu Sesay. "The OAU and Human Rights: Prospects for the 1980s and Beyond," *Human Rights Quarterly*, 8 (1986): 89–103.

On, Stephen. "Kant and Nietzsche on Human Rights: A Theoretical Approach," *Scandinavian Journal of Development Alternatives and Area Studies*, 19, no. 2–3 (June and September 2000): 197–207.

Park, Thomas K. *Historical Dictionary of Morocco* (Lanham, MD: Scarecrow Press, 1996).

Pazzanita, Anthony G. *Historical Dictionary of Mauritania* (Lanham, MD: Scarecrow Press, 1996).

Pelt, Andrian. *Libyan Independence and the United Nations: A Case of Planned Decolonization* (New Haven: Yale University Press for the Carnegie Endowment for International Peace, 1970).

Perkins, Kenneth J. *Historical Dictionary of Tunisia* (Lanham, MD: Scarecrow Press, 1997).

Perkins, Kenneth J. *A History of Modern Tunisia* (New York: Cambridge University Press, 2004).

Perry, Glenn E. *The History of Egypt* (Westport, CT: Greenwood Press, 2004).

Perry, M. *The Idea of Human Rights* (New York: Oxford University Press, 1988).

Peters, Julie, and Andrea Wolper, eds. *Women's Rights, Human Rights: International Feminist Perspectives* (New York: Routeledge, 1995).

Peterson, Gregory D. *French Experience in Algeria, 1954-1962: Blueprint for the U.S. Operations in Iraq* (Fort Leavenworth, KS: U.S. Army School for Advanced Military Studies, 2004).

Petry, Carl F., ed. *The Cambridge History of Egypt*, Vol. 1: *Islamic Egypt 640-1517* (Cambridge: Cambridge University Press, 1998).

Phillip, Thomas, and Ulrich Harmann, eds. *The Mamluks in Egyptian Politics and Society* (Cambridge: Cambridge University Press, 1998).

Pierre, Andrew J., and William B. Quandt, *The Algerian Crisis: Policy Options for the West* (Washington, DC: Carnegie Endowment for International Peace, 1996).

Poe, Steven C., and C. Neal Tate. "Repression of Human Rights to Personal Integrity in the 1980s: A Global Analysis," *American Political Science Review*, 80 (December 1994): 853–872.

Pogge, T. "The International Significance of Human Rights," *Journal of Ethics*, 4 (2000): 45–69.

Pogge, T. *World Poverty and Human Rights* (Cambridge: Polity Press, 2002).

Prochaska, David. *Making Algeria French: Colonialism in Bône, 1870-1920* (Cambridge: Cambridge University Press, 1990).

Prost, Antoine. "The Algerian War in French Collective Memory." In Jay Winter and Emmanuel Sivan, eds. *War and Remembrance in the Twentieth Century* (Cambridge: Cambridge University Press, 1999), 161–176.

Quandt, William B. *Between Ballots and Bullets: Algeria's Transition from Authoritarianism* (Washington, DC: Brookings Institution Press, 1998).

Quandt, William B. *Revolution and Political Leadership: Algeria 1954–1968* (Cambridge, MA: M.I.T. Press, 1969).

Ramcharan, B. G. "Human Rights in Africa: Whither Now?" *University of Ghana Law Journal*, 12 (1975): 88–105.

Ramcharan, B. G. "Strategies for International Protection of Human Rights in the 1990s," *Human Rights Quarterly*, 13 (1991): 155–169.

Reid, Donald Malcolm. *Cairo University and the Making of Modern Egypt* (Cambridge: Cambridge University Press, 1990).

Rembe, Nasila Selasini. *The System of Protection of Human Rights under the African Charter on Human and Peoples' Rights: Problems and Prospects* (Roma, Lesotho: Institute of Southern African Studies, National University of Lesotho, 1991).

Rice, Michael. *Egypt's Making: The Origins of Ancient Egypt 5000–2000 BC*, 2nd Edition (London and New York: Routledge, 1997).

Richmond, John C. B. *Egypt, 1798–1952: Her Advance toward a Modern Identity* (New York: Columbia University Press, 1977).

Risse, T., S. Ropp, and K. Sikkink, eds. *The Power of Human Rights: International Norms and Domestic Change* (Cambridge: Cambridge University Press, 1999).

Roald, A. S. *Women in Islam: The Western Experience* (London: Routledge, 2001).

Roberts, Stephen H. *The History of French Colonial Policy 1870–1925*, 2nd Edition (London: Frank Cass, 1963).

Roumani, Maurice. *The Jews of Libya: Coexistence, Persecution, Resettlement* (Portland, OR: Sussex Academic Press, 2008).

Rouner, Leroy, ed. *Human Rights and the World's Religions* (Notre Dame, IN: University of Notre Dame Press, 1988).

Rudebeck, Lars. *Party and People: A Study of Political Change in Tunisia* (Stockholm: Almqvist and Wiksell, 1967).

Ruedy, John. *Modern Algeria: The Origins and Development of a Nation* (Bloomington, IN: Indiana University Press, 1992).

Rugh, Andreas B. *Family in Contemporary Egypt* (Cairo: American University in Cairo Press, 1985).

Saadi, Nouredine. *La femme et la loi en Algérie* (Casablanca: Le Fennec, 1991).

Sabki, Hisham M. *The United Nations and the Pacific Settlement of Disputes: A Case Study of Libya* (New York: International Publications Service, 1973).

Said, Abdul Aziz, ed. *Human Rights and World Order* (New York: Praeger, 1978).

Sainsbury, Diane. *Gender, Equality, and Welfare States* (Cambridge: Cambridge University Press, 1996).

St. John, Ronald Bruce. *Historical Dictionary of Libya* (Lanham, MD: Scarecrow Press, 2006).

Salem, Norma. *Habib Bourguiba, Islam and the Creation of Tunisia* (London: Croom Helm, 1984).

Salhi, Zahia Smail. "Algerian Women, Citizenship, and the 'Family Code,'" *Gender and Development*, 11, no. 3 (November 2003): 27–35.

Scham, Alan. *Lyautey in Morocco: Protectorate Administration 1912–1925* (Berkeley, CA: University of California Press, 1970).

Schölch, Alexander. *Egypt for the Egyptians! The Socio-Political Crisis in Egypt, 1878–1882* (London: Ithaca Press, 1981).

Schwelb, Egon. *Human Rights and the International Community: The Roots and Growth of the Universal Declaration of Human Rights, 1948–1963* (Chicago, IL: Quadrangle Books, 1964).

Segré, Claudio G. *Fourth Shore: The Italian Colonization of Libya* (Chicago: University of Chicago Press, 1974).

Shaaban, B. *Both Right and Left Handed: Arab Women Talk About Their Lives* (London: Women's Press, 1998).

Sharabi, Hisham. *Neopatriarchy: A Theory of Distorted Change in Arab Society* (Oxford: Oxford University Press, 1988).

Shaw, Ian. *Exploring Ancient Egypt* (Oxford: Oxford University Press, 2003).

Shaw, Stanford J., and Ezel Kural Shaw. *History of the Ottoman Empire and Modern Turkey.* 2 Vols. (London: Cambridge University Press, 1976–1977).

Shivji, Isa G. *The Concept of Human Rights in Africa* (London and Dakar, Senegal: Council for the Development of Economic and Social Research in Africa-CODESRIA, 1989).

Silverman, David P., ed. *Ancient Egypt* (Oxford: Oxford University Press, 2003).

Simons, Geoff. *Libya: The Struggle for Survival* (New York: St. Martin's Press, 1993).

Singer, Barnett. "Lyautey: An Interpretation of the Man and French Imperialism," *Journal of Contemporary History*, 26, no. 1 (1991): 131–157.

Slama, Bice. *L'Insurrection de 1894 en Tunisie* (Tunis: Maison Tunisienne de l'Edition, 1967).

Smith, R., and C. van den Anker, eds. *The Essentials of Human Rights* (London: Hodder Arnold, 2005).

Soren, David, Aicha Ben Abed Ben Khader, and Heidi Slim. *Carthage: Uncovering the Mysteries and Splendor of Ancient Tunisia* (New York: Simon & Schuster, 1990).

Spencer, Jeffrey, ed. *Aspects of Early Egypt* (London: British Museum Press, 1996).

Stammers, Neil. "A Critique of Social Approaches to Human Rights," *Human Rights Quarterly*, 17, no. 3 (1995): 488–508

Stammers, Neil. *Human Rights and Social Movements* (London: Pluto Press, 2009).

Stammers, Neil. "Social Movements and the Social Construction of Human Rights," *Human Rights Quarterly*, 21, no. 4 (1999): 980–1008.

Steiner, H., and P. Alston, eds. *International Human Rights in Context* (Oxford: Oxford University Press, 2000).

Stone, Martin. *Agony of Algeria* (New York: Columbia University Press, 1997).

Stratton, Lisa C. "The Right to Have Rights: Gender Discrimination in Nationality Laws," *Minnesota Law Review*, 77 (1992): 197–239.

Sullivan, Denis J. *Islam in Contemporary Egypt: Civil Society vs. the State* (Boulder, CO: Lynne Rienner Publishers, 1999).

Swearingen, Will D., and Abdellatif Bencherifa, eds. *The North African Environment at Risk* (Boulder, CO: Westview Press, 1996).

Swidler, Arlene, ed. *Human Rights in Religious Traditions* (New York: Pilgrim Press, 1982).

Takeyh, Ray. *The Origins of the Eisenhower Doctrine: The U.S., Britain and Nasser's Egypt, 1953–1957* (New York: St. Martin's Press, 2000).

Tetreault, Mary Ann, ed. *Women and Revolution in Africa, Asia, and the New World* (Columbia, SC: University of South Carolina Press, 1994).

Thornberry, Patrick. *International Law and the Rights of Minorities* (Oxford: Clarendon Press, 1991).

Tignor, Robert L. *Modernization and British Colonial Rule in Egypt, 1882–1914* (Princeton, NJ: Princeton University Press, 1966).

Tlemcani, Rachid. *State and Revolution in Algeria* (New York: Columbia University Press, 1997).

Tolley, Howard B., Jr. *The UN Commission on Human Rights* (Boulder, CO: Westview Press, 1987).

Tomasevski, Katarina. *Women and Human Rights* (London: Zed Books, 1993).

Tomppert, Leigh, ed. *Women's Rights in the Middle East and North Africa* (Lanham, MD: Rowman & Littlefield Publishers, Inc., 2010).

Tucker, Judith E. *Women, Family and Gender in Islamic Law* (Cambridge: Cambridge University Press, 2008).

Turner, B. S. *Vulnerability and Human Rights* (Philadelphia, PA: University of Pennsylvania Press, 2006).

Udogu, E. I. "An Examination of Minority Groups and Human Rights Issues in Europe and Africa," *Journal of Political Science*, 27 (2000): 21–43.

Udogu, E. I. *Examining Human Rights Issues and the Democracy Project in Sub-Saharan Africa: A Theoretical Critique and Prospects for Progress in the Millennium* (Lanham, MD: Lexington Books, 2014).

Udogu, E. I. "Human Rights Constraints: Analysis and Potential Solutions." In E. Ike Udogu, ed. *The Developing World: Critical Issues in Politics and Society* (Lanham, MD: Scarecrow Press, 2012).

Udogu, E. I. "Human Rights and Minorities: A Theoretical Overview." In Paul T. Zeleza and Philip J. McConnaughay, eds. *Human Rights, the Rule of Law, and Development in Africa* (Philadelphia, PA: University of Pennsylvania Press, 2004).

Udogu E. I. "Human Rights and Minorities in Africa: A Theoretical and Conceptual Overview," *Journal of Third World Studies*, 28, no. 1 (2001): 87–104.

Udogu, E. I. *Leadership and the Problem of Electoral Democracy in Africa: Case Studies and Theoretical Solutions* (Newcastle upon Tyne, UK: Cambridge Scholars Publishing, 2016).

Udogu, E. I. *Liberating Namibia: The Long Diplomatic Struggle between the United Nations and South Africa* (Jefferson, NC: McFarland, 2011).

Udogu, E. I. "National Constitutions and Human Rights Issues in Africa," *African and Asian Studies*, 2, no. 2 (2003): 102–123.

Udogu, E. I., and Sambuddha Ghatak, eds. *Human Rights Dilemmas in the Developing World: The Case of Marginalized Populations at Risk* (Lanham, MD: Lexington Books, 2017).

Udogu, E. I., and Sambuddha Ghatak, eds. "Human Rights Issues of Minorities in Contemporary India: A Concise Analysis," *Journal of Third World Studies*, 29, no. 1 (2012): 203–230.

Umozurike, U. O. "The Protection of Human Rights under the Banjul (African) Charter on Human and Peoples' Rights," *African Journal of International Law*, 1 (1988): 65–83.

United Nations. *Human Rights Bibliography: United Nations Documents and Publications 1980–1990.* 5 Vols. (New York: United Nations Publication, 1993).

United States Department of State, Bureau of Democracy and Labor, *Country Reports on Human Rights Practices—Algeria* (Washington, DC: GPO, 2015)

United States Department of State, Bureau of Democracy and Labor, *Country Reports on Human Rights Practices—Egypt* (Washington, DC: GPO, 2015).

United States Department of State, Bureau of Democracy and Labor, *Country Reports on Human Rights Practices—Libya* (Washington, DC: GPO, 2015).

United States Department of State, Bureau of Democracy and Labor, *Country Reports on Human Rights Practices—Morocco* (Washington, DC: GPO, 2015).

United States Department of State, Bureau of Democracy and Labor, *Country Reports on Human Rights Practices—Tunisia* (Washington, DC: GPO, 2015).

Usborne, V. C. *The Conquest of Morocco* (London: Stanley Paul, 1936).

Valensi, Lucette. *On the Eve of Colonialism: North Africa before the French Conquest.* Translated from French by K. J. Perkins. (New York: Africana, 1977).

Van-Boven, Theo C. "The Relations between Peoples' Rights and Human Rights in the African Charter," *Human Rights Law Journal*, 7 (1986): 183–194.

Van-Boven, Theo C. "The United Nations and Human Rights: A Critical Approach," *Bulletin of Peace Proposals*, 8, no. 3 (1977): 198–208.

Vandewalle, Dirk. *A History of Modern Libya*, 2nd ed. (New York: Cambridge University Press, 2006).

Vandewalle, Dirk. *Libya since Independence: Oil and State-Building* (Ithaca, NY: Cornell University Press, 1998).

Vandewalle, Dirk, ed. *North Africa: Development and Reform in a Changing Economy* (New York: St. Martin's Press, 1996).

Vatikiotis, P. J. *The History of Modern Egypt from Muhammad Ali to Mubarak*, 4th Edition (Baltimore: Johns Hopkins University Press, 1991).

Vatin, Jean-Claude. *L'Afrique politique: Histoire et société* (Paris: Fondation Nationale des Sciences Politiques, 1974).

Viljoen, Frans. *Human Rights in Africa: National and International Protection* (Oxford: Oxford University Press, 2007).

Viljoen, Frans. *International Human Rights Law in Africa* (Oxford: Oxford University Press, 2012).

Villard, Henry Serrano. *Libya: The New Arab Kingdom of North Africa* (Ithaca, NY: Cornell University Press, 1956).

Vincent, R. J. *Human Rights and International Relations* (Cambridge: Cambridge University Press, 1986).

Waltz, Susan E. *Human Rights and Reform: Changing the Face of North African Politics* (Berkeley and Los Angeles, CA: University of California Press, 1995).

Waterfield, Gordon. *Egypt* (New York: Walker and Company, 1967).

Watterson, Barbara. *The Egyptians* (Oxford: Blackwell, 1997).

Welch, Claude E., Jr. "The African Commission on Human and Peoples' Rights: A Five-Year Report and Assessment," *Human Rights Quarterly*, 14 (1992): 43–61.

Welch, Claude E., Jr. "Human Rights and African Women: A Comparison of Protection under Two Major Treaties," *Human Rights Quarterly*, 15 (1993): 549–574.

Welch, Claude E., Jr. "The OAU and Human Rights: Towards a New Definition," *Journal of Modern African Studies*, 19, no. 3 (September 1981): 401–420.

Welch, Claude E., Jr. "The Organization of African Unity and the Promotion of Human Rights," *Journal of Modern African Studies*, 29, no. 4 (1991): 535–555.

Welch, Claude E., Jr. *Protecting Human Rights in Africa: Roles and Strategies of Non-governmental Organizations* (Philadelphia, PA: University of Pennsylvania Press, 1995).

Welchman, Lynn. *Women and Muslim Family Laws in Arab States: A Comparative Overview of Textual Development and Advocacy* (Amsterdam, Netherlands: Amsterdam University Press, 2007).

Whittaker, David J. *Counter-Terrorism and Human Rights* (Harlow, UK: Pearson Educational Limited, 2009).

Willis, Michael. *The Islamist Challenge in Algeria: A Political History* (New York: New York University Press, 1997).

Wilson, R., ed. *Human Rights, Culture and Context: Anthropological Perspectives* (London: Pluto Press, 1997).

Winston, M. "Human Rights as Moral Rebellion and Social Construction," *Journal of Human Rights*, 6 (2007): 279–305.

Winter, Michael. *Egyptian Society under Ottoman Rule, 1517–1798* (London: Routledge, 1992).

Woodhull, W. *Transfiguration of the Maghreb* (Minneapolis, MN: University of Minnesota Press, 1993).

Wright, John. *Libya: A Modern History* (Baltimore: Johns Hopkins University Press, 1981).

Young, George. *Egypt* (New York: Charles Scribner's Sons, 1927).

Zartman, William. *Morocco: Problems of New Power* (New York: Atherton, 1964).

Zartman, William, et al. *Political Elites in Arab North Africa: Morocco, Algeria, Tunisia Libya, and Egypt* (New York: Longman, 1982).

Zoubir, Y. H. "The Painful Transition from Authoritarianism in Algeria," *Arab Studies Quarterly*, 15, no. 3 (1993): 83–110.

# Index

Numbers in *bold italics* indicate pages with tables